The Culture of International Arbitration

The Culture of International Arbitration

WON L. KIDANE

OXFORD
UNIVERSITY PRESS

OXFORD
UNIVERSITY PRESS

Oxford University Press is a department of the University of Oxford. It furthers the University's objective of excellence in research, scholarship, and education by publishing worldwide. Oxford is a registered trademark of Oxford University Press in the UK and certain other countries.

Published in the United States of America by Oxford University Press
198 Madison Avenue, New York, NY 10016, United States of America.

Library of Congress Cataloging-in-Publication Data

Names: Kidane, Won, author.
Title: The culture of international arbitration / Won L. Kidane.
Description: New York : Oxford University Press, 2017. | Includes bibliographical references and index.
Identifiers: LCCN 2016037389 | ISBN 9780199973927 ((hardback) : alk. paper)
Subjects: LCSH: Arbitration (International law)
Classification: LCC KZ6115 .K53 2017 | DDC 347/.09—dc23 LC record available at https://lccn.loc.gov/2016037389

CONTENTS

PREFACE

This work offers a cultural critique of the dominant theories and common practices of international arbitration. It is not as congratulatory of international arbitration as most works in the field. At the theoretical level, the impetus for the work comes from the desire to understand the reasons behind the relentless congratulatory messaging in the face of the extraordinary lack of cultural diversity among the decision-makers, and the cultural disconnect between the decision-makers and those who must suffer the consequences of the decisions. At the practical level, the work is inspired by the author's decades of observations of cultural misunderstandings that parties coming from outside the dominant cultures routinely endure in international arbitral proceedings on top of the occasional ideological biases, veiled economic incentives affecting decisions ranging from such mundane matters as the scope of discovery to expansive rulings on jurisdiction, to the accommodation of frivolous claims shielded from ordered scrutiny and candid criticism.

The book is unique in its examination of both the theoretical underpinnings and practice of international arbitration through a cultural prism. At the most basic level, it puzzles over why more than half-a-century after the adoption of the United Nations Convention for the Recognition and Enforcement of Foreign Arbitral Awards (the New York Convention) and the International Convention for the Settlement of Investment Disputes (ICSID Convention), lack of expertise continues to justify the exclusion of everyone outside the dominate cultures when the users increasingly come from diverse backgrounds. It questions the theoretical justifications and the academic statistics, and deconstructs the mythology of technical expertise that often leads to the perception that the world's pool of arbitrators and suitable jurisdictions are limited to the usual ones. By so doing, it attempts to offer the perspectives and dilemmas of the cultural others.

Some of the opinions are expressed in strong terms that match the vigor of the expressions contained in some of the works that it critiques. Its principal objective nonetheless remains the provocation of further discussions to help improve the cultural diversity, legitimacy, efficiency, accuracy, and fairness of international arbitration.

Seattle, Washington (March 2017)

ACKNOWLEDGMENTS

Over the years, prominent jurists, colleagues, friends, and family members too many to count have influenced my thoughts and contributed to the refinement of ideas expressed in this book. I am deeply grateful to all of them. In particular, I would like to express my gratitude to Judge Abdulqawi Yusuf, vice president of the International Court of Justice, Judge Xue Hanquin of the International Court of Justice, Judge Julia Sebutinde of the International Court of justice, Mr. Thomas R. Snider of the international law firm of Greenberg Traurig, and all the other interviewees who preferred to remain anonymous but graciously agreed to meet with me and share their thoughts for this book. Their contribution has immensely advanced the clarity of the message, and for that I am deeply thankful. My thanks also extend to my colleagues Dr. Zewdineh B. Haile and Mr. Jackson Kern of the Addis Law Group LLP for their continuous dialogue that enriched this work along the way. Finally, I would also like to thank Stephanie Morrison (who at the time was a third-year law student at Cornell Law School), and Helen G. Selassie (who at the time was articling at Addis Law Group LLP) for their help in cite-checking and editing the text.

NOTE ON PREVIOUS WORKS

This book builds on some of the author's prior works in this area. In particular: (1) Kidane, Won, *The China-Africa Factor in the Contemporary ICSID Legitimacy Debate*, 35 U. Pa. J. Int'l L. 559 (2014) (parts reproduced with permission); (2) Kidane, Won, *The Inquisitorial Advantage*, 46 Akron L. Rev. 647 (2012) (parts reproduced with permission); (3) Kidane, Won, *China-Africa Dispute Settlement: The Law, Economics and Culture of Arbitration* (Kluwer, 2011).

LIST OF ABBREVIATIONS

Abbreviation	Full Name
ASIL	American Society of International Law
AALCC	Asia Africa Legal Consultative Committee
BIT	Bilateral Investment Treaty
SPP	China's Supreme People's Court
CPL	Civil Procedure Law of the People's Republic of China
COMESA	Court of Justice of the Common Market for Eastern and Southern Africa
FAA	Federal Arbitration Act
FIDIC	Fédération Internationale des Ingenieurs-Conseils
GCC	General Conditions of Contract
GAFTA	Grain and Feed Trade Association
HKIAC	Hong Kong International Arbitration Center
IBA	International Bar Association
ICSID	International Centre for Settlement of Investment Disputes
ICC	International Chamber of Commerce
ICCA	International Council for Commercial Arbitration
ICJ	International Court of Justice
LCIA	London Court of International Arbitration
PCA	Permanent Court of Arbitration
PCIJ	Permanent Court of International Justice
SIAC	Singapore International Arbitration Centre
SCC	Special Conditions of Contract
StPO	Strafprozessordnung (German Code of Criminal Procedure)
UNCTAD	United Nations Conference on Trade and Development
UNCITRAL	United Nations Commission on International Trade Law
UNESCO	United Nations Educational Scientific and Cultural Organization
VwVfG	Verwaltungsverfahrensgesetz (German Administrative Procedure Act)
ZPO	Zivilprozessordnung (German Code of Civil Procedure)

TABLE OF CASES

TABLE OF STATUTES

Germany

United States

Sweden

TABLE OF CONVENTIONS

United Nations Commission on International Trade Law, *Convention on Transparency in Treaty-Based Investor-State Arbitration (the "Mauritius Convention on Transparency")*, Dec. 10, 2014, http://www.uncitral.org/pdf/english/texts/arbitration/transparency-convention/Transparency-Convention-e.pdf. **107, 107n78**

PART ONE

Culture and the Legal Framework and Theoretical Pillars of International Arbitration

1

Introduction

Culture[1] in international arbitration[2] is an underappreciated variable. Few, if any, legal processes regularly bring together multiple legal cultures into one room as much as international arbitration does. The profound rise in recent decades of legally ordered North-South and South-South[3] economic interactions has increased the importance of appreciating the role of culture in maintaining successful relations, managing conflicts, and resolving disputes whenever and wherever they arise.

The existing legal literature curiously downplays the significance of cultural competence in ensuring accuracy, efficacy, and fairness, and in minimizing cost in international arbitration. Indeed, the treatment of this subject in the legal literature has so far been incredibly superficial. To the extent it is treated, it is in the context only of the cultural diversity or confluence and influence of the two most important Western legal traditions: the common law and the civil law; even then, in the context of the strife for dominance among arbitrators and counsel often disconnected from the cultures of the parties they serve.[4] The cultural complexities of international arbitration in today's global marketplace remain, in large measure, unexplained.

1. Defining culture is fraught with considerable difficulty. Although the book uses the term in its ordinary and broadest sense, Chapter 2 offers a comprehensive discussion of its various usages and meanings. It is important to restate from the outset, however, that the complexity of the phenomena that the term "culture" represents, as it is often said, does not lend itself to be usefully denoted by any term less complex than the term "culture" itself.

2. Although the focus of this book is on commercial and investment arbitration, the term "international arbitration" is used more broadly to include state-to-state arbitration inasmuch as the cultural issues discussed throughout the book also affect such arbitral process.

3. In development discourses, the terms "North" and "South" are typically used to signify the level of development of countries. *See, e.g.*, United Nations Conference on Trade and Development (UNCTAD), Economic Development in Africa Report 2010: South-South Cooperation: Africa and the New Forms of Development Partnership, 1, U.N. Doc. UNCTAD/ALDC/AFRICA/2010.

4. *See, e.g.*, Jan Paulsson, *Cultural Differences in Advocacy in International Arbitration*, *in* The Art of Advocacy in International Arbitration 15–21 (R. Doak Bishop & Edward G. Kehoe eds., 2d ed. 2010); Tom Ginsberg, *The Culture of Arbitration*, 36 Vand. J. Int'l L. 1335 (2003).

This book's objective is ambitious: it aims to provide a cultural critique of international arbitration. In particular, it systematically examines the role of culture in the formulation and implementation of the legal infrastructure in the actual modern-day arbitral proceeding involving parties and arbitrators from diverse cultural backgrounds whether this culture manifests itself in commercial, investment and state-to-state arbitration.

There is no shortage of literature on the fundamentals of international arbitration, that is, the process ranging from the enforcement of the arbitral agreement, to the filing of a request for arbitration, to the constitution of the arbitral tribunal, to the interpretation and enforcement of arbitral awards. However, our knowledge of what exactly goes on inside the arbitration room is essentially limited to our own sporadic anecdotes. Despite the profound curiosity about how arbitrators from different cultures interact with one another, understand diverse parties who appear before them, and manage to arrive at an acceptable result, no satisfactory and systematic studies have ever been conducted.[5] That is partly because most arbitral proceedings are held in camera and the awards are often kept confidential. Recognizing this challenge, this book includes a chapter on conversations with leading arbitrators, judges of international courts, practitioners, and academics from different legal traditions. The conversations are designed to be supplemental to the detailed analysis of the existing legal, business, sociological, and psychological literature on the epistemology of determining facts, which is one of the most culture-dependent components of any legal process.

At the most practical level, this book asks what, in reality, goes on inside the hearing room where, for example, the tribunal is composed of a French law professor, a retired English judge, and a Belgian practitioner, with the disputing parties coming from China and Angola and represented by law firms based in London and Washington D.C., respectively. Wherever the hearing takes place, the tribunal often has to select or draw up its own rules of procedure and evidence, attempt to understand the nature of the parties' relationship and the essence of the dispute, and then develop the evidentiary record through examination of the evidence (including witness testimony) and apply the law chosen by the parties or chosen for them. Ultimately the tribunal hopes to arrive at a fair and acceptable result in a cost-effective way as expeditiously as possible. How often does it get the result right? How does cultural diversity complicate the finding of facts and identification, interpretation, and application of law?

Consider the following example. Nearly 15 years ago, in an arbitral proceeding seated in a major city in Europe, the firm that this author was associated with presented a witness from rural parts of Africa before an arbitral panel composed of preeminent Western jurists. On cross-examination, the witness was asked to identify the color of his ID card. The color was an issue of material fact. This author helped prepare the witness because the author spoke the witness's language. The pleadings submitted

5. As much as recent books by practitioners such as Bernhard Berger, Michael E. Schneider, and Ugo Draetta offer some great insights based on personal experiences of the authors, they do not even begin to scratch the surface in this field. Bernhard Berger & Michael E. Schneider, Inside the Black Box: How Arbitral Tribunals Operate and Reach Their Decisions (ASA Special Series No. 42) (2014); Ugo Draetta, Behind the Scenes in International Arbitration (2011). However, these books are a sign of a new trend.

by counsel showed that the color of the ID card was orange. The witness said "yellow" in his native language, which was correctly translated as "yellow" in English. He was supposed to have said "orange." There is a word for orange in his language (used for the fruit orange), and some people in his community would probably have identified the color as orange but he did not. Almost nobody seemed to have understood why he said yellow, in the moment, when he was supposed to have said orange. This author had difficulty convincing his own colleagues about why the witness said yellow. Here is the reason: for the witness, who was not a very well educated person and who came from a rural community in Africa, a range of colors is assigned the same name—so, yellow and orange fall under the same category. It is not unusual for certain communities to identify colors this way. The author knew this was what was going on, and after the hearing, he pulled up two colors on the screen of his computer and asked the witness which one he meant to say; sure enough, he pointed to the orange color in front of his other colleagues. Although the tribunal did not specifically rule on the credibility of this particular witness, the result suggests that the tribunal did not give his testimony much credit. The argument was that a particular category of persons (identified by nationality) was issued a distinctive color identification card for purposes of easy police targeting and persecution and that the respondent state deliberately marked that group for such treatment. The tribunal ruled that a deliberate government policy was not sufficiently proven. Because there were a number of other complicating factors, it is difficult to tell if the failure of this particular witness was the only factor that influenced the outcome in that case, but it was very significant in view of the respondent state's denial that it issued that particular group a distinctive color ID card for purposes of specific identification and targeting. The state's argument was that ID card colors were assigned to various nationalities randomly. The key witness's lack of identification of the exact color by the exact name might have ended up giving credence to the respondent state's argument.[6]

As the above example demonstrates, arbitrators and counsel routinely encounter witnesses who do not make sense in particular circumstances for whatever reason, but when cultural miscommunication complicates understanding, especially when there is a power relationship, the burden of understanding is not equally shared by the witness and the tribunal. The witness fails to be understood at his side's peril because ordinarily he bears the burden of making himself understood without the

6. This is included as an example in the questions forwarded to the arbitrators and counsel whose responses are reported in Chapter 12. Similar cultural considerations could also affect the selection of expert witnesses as well. Before this hearing, this author also traveled to an African state as a junior counsel to help identify an expert witness for a particular statistical analysis. The expert was to testify before a tribunal composed exclusively of European and American arbitrators. The first potential expert witness this author and lawyers from the same firm met, said to one of the members of the counsel team: "You know what? You're the first white person I ever shook hands with." Thereafter, while driving together in a car, the candidate for expert testimony started singing Shaggy's once-popular song, "It Wasn't Me!," out of nowhere—without warning and without context. Following such observations, when this author inquired about his colleagues' impressions about this statistician, one of them said, "I think opposing counsel will chew him up and spit him out!" Everyone got a good laugh out of it, and obviously he was not hired. Nobody knows to this day what kind of statistical abilities he might have had.

tribunal's reciprocal duty to understand his. If he is unable to make himself understood, again ordinarily, one of two alternative assumptions would be made: at best he would be deemed uneducated, incompetent, and, thus, useless in resolving the dispute; at worst, he would be considered incredible and even dishonest. The worst part of it, yet again, is that he and the party who brought him before the tribunal would probably feel embarrassed by his incompetence or lack of credibility, not to mention the possibility of losing the case on the merits.

This scenario would happen less frequently in a domestic court litigation because there is often, at least in democratic societies, a presumed cultural affinity between the judge and the judged—as in the jury of peers, for example. A Cameroonian or an Ethiopian judge would know exactly why someone would say "yellow" when he meant "orange" because a range of colors is assigned the same name in certain languages and cultures. The word "*bitcha*", for instance, could encompass colors ranging from yellow to pink to orange in the Amharic language. Similar designations exist in several other languages and cultures. The problem—which is almost always framed in the context of the incompetence or incredibility of the local representatives of the parties and witnesses who come from cultures outside of the cultures that dominate international arbitration—is almost never framed in the context of the cultural competence of the tribunals to understand and serve the parties who selected them, or who make their selection possible, but rather is framed as the cultural deficiency or incompetence of the parties or their representatives who appear before such tribunals. They fail to be understood at their own peril. The tribunal rarely assumes the burden of cultural understanding. In the above example, is the problem really the African man who identified his orange ID card as "yellow" or the system of international arbitration that is not very well equipped to understand him?

As a matter of fact, more profound forces are at play behind the simple cultural miscommunications exemplified by these anecdotes. As Professor Lawrence Rosen says in a related context, "beneath assertedly neutral principles of law lurks the distribution of power,"[7] and that elaborate systems of law and their explanations have the potential to "mask the actual dynamics of power."[8]

Leaving that aside for now, there are some notable writings on the vast array of topics within the broad subject of cultural miscommunication in transnational disputes. Professors Kevin Avruch and Peter W. Black have noted that "[w]hen the parties to a conflict come from different cultures—when conflict is 'international'—one cannot presume that all crucial understandings are shared among them. Their respective ethnotheories, the notions of the root causes of conflict, and ethnopraxes, the local acceptable techniques for resolving conflicts, may differ one from another in significant ways."[9] Obviously whenever intercultural disputants desire to involve a third party for

7. Lawrence Rosen, Law as Culture: An Invitation 195 (2006) (citing to critical race theory literature.)

8. *Id.* at 195.

9. Kevin Avruch & Peter W. Black, *Conflict Resolution in Intercultural Settings: Problems and Prospects*, *in* Conflict Resolution Theory and Practice: Integration and Application 131–40 (Dennis J. Sandole & Hugo van der Merwe eds., 1993), *reprinted in* Jacqueline Nolan-Haley,

the resolution of their dispute, the third party intervener will not be remarkably successful without a deeper understanding of the cultural dimensions.[10] Indeed, the use of third party interveners in intercultural conflicts raises considerable cultural difficulty,[11] although there may not be a precise method of analyzing culture or cultural differences.

Professor Leon E. Trakman warns: "[g]iven complex public and private influences on the legal culture of international commerce, one may conclude that any serious analysis of that culture is likely to be flawed. Any effort to comprehend its nature may lead to over-simplification or even misunderstanding . . . Such misunderstanding, in turn, may lead arbitrators to over- or under-appreciate the relevance of different cultures in reaching decisions."[12] The warning is important, but despite the difficulty, the role of culture must still be taken into account because culture could affect the selection of arbitrators, the conduct of the proceedings, the determination of facts, the interpretation of law, the cost and efficiency of the process, and more important, the fairness and accuracy of the outcome of the case in many profound ways.

For example, the science of persuasion has long established that "[t]he ability to persuade is dependent on . . . the speaker's credibility and likeability, and his or her understanding of the audience . . . ."[13] Unsurprisingly,

> We also tend to like people who are similar to us. . . . Similarities lead to likability, and likability can increase the ability to persuade. This is especially true in ambiguous situations []. When information is ambiguous we are more likely to rely on the opinions and actions of those who are similar to us.[14]

Obviously "in brief exposures we tend to rely on superficial similarities, such as age, race, or the way a person dresses."[15] At least theoretically, then, all things being equal, a French arbitrator is thus more likely to be persuaded by a French counsel than an American or a Chinese one. The science simply validates what international arbitration specialists have known very well all along. Underneath the superficial criteria and battle for selection and appointment of arbitrators always lurks this very basic cultural concern, which is almost never openly recognized or acknowledged.

The new world of international arbitration has seen a remarkable rise in the diversity of the users of arbitration services. Old Eurocentric institutions are not only facing significant competition from newer and more diverse arbitral centers but also are

Harold Abramson & Pat K. Chew, International Conflict Resolution: Consensual ADR Processes 50, 51 (2005).

10. *Id.*

11. Nolan-Haley et al., *supra* note 9, at 44.

12. Leon E. Trakman, *"Legal Traditions" and International Commercial Arbitration*, 17 Am. Rev. Int'l Arb. 1, 10 (2006).

13. Brad Bradshaw, The Science of Persuasion: A Litigator's Guide to Juror Decision-Making 1 (2d ed. 2015).

14. *Id.* at 5.

15. *Id.*

confronted with the management of disputes involving parties from newly emerging economies of Asia, Eastern Europe, Africa, the Middle East, and Latin America. These new players are more likely to notice and appreciate the effects of culture in international arbitration, hence, the importance of paying more attention to cultural issues.

At the most general level, as indicated above, this book attempts to answer some very fundamental questions: What is culture in the context of international arbitration? What is the role of culture in international arbitration? Does it affect the determination of fact and interpretation of law, and hence the outcome? How can the complicating effects of cultural barriers be appreciated? Most fundamentally, are less dominant cultures inherently disadvantaged in the process by the existing status quo of cultural hierarchy? If, so, how might that be addressed?

To answer these broad questions, the book is organized into two parts and 13 chapters. Part One challenges the foundational assumptions of the theoretical pillars and legal frameworks of international commercial and investment arbitration from a cultural standpoint. To accomplish this task, it is divided into seven chapters. Chapter 2 undertakes the difficult task of defining culture. Chapter 3 provides a brief cultural and political history of international arbitration as well as the background of legal culture in the context of dispute resolution. Chapter 4 critically examines the dominant theories of international arbitration. Chapter 5 offers a cultural critique of the contemporary justifications of international arbitration. Finally, Chapters 6 and 7 provide an overview of the legal framework of commercial and investment arbitration, respectively, from a cultural perspective.

Part Two undertakes the difficult task of a cultural analysis of the actual legal process. In so doing, it critically appraises the current mythology of specialized knowledge unique to arbitration. It is comprised of Chapters 8 through 13. Chapter 8 profiles the epistemology of finding facts in the various legal traditions and offers a comparative analysis of the methods of fact-finding in the various legal traditions to show how arbitrators coming from these legal traditions come with differing conceptions and methods of discovering facts. Chapter 9 offers a detailed analysis of the complicating effects of culture in the process of the determination of fact, and the interpretation and application of law. Chapter 10 examines through a cultural prism the appointment and challenge of arbitrators in typical modern day arbitration. The chapter applies the same cultural analysis to the IBA Rules on the Taking of Evidence. Chapter 11 challenges the justifications and approval of "stranger justice" in international arbitration. Chapter 12 profiles conversations with leading arbitrators, practitioners, and academics from different legal traditions, including judges of the international court of justice who specifically offer their experience with cultural miscommunication and its possible impact on outcome in transnational legal proceedings. Chapter 13 presents a summary of the conclusions.

2

Defining Legal Culture

The definition of culture itself is culturally engrained and as such defies uniformity. The definition by the United Nations Educational Scientific and Cultural Organization (UNESCO) provides perhaps the definition closest to a consensus. It defines culture in its broadest sense as: "the whole complex of distinctive spiritual, material, intellectual and emotional features that characterize a society or social group. It includes not only the arts and letters, but also modes of life, the fundamental rights of the human being, value systems, traditions and beliefs."[1]

Although culture has many dimensions, including ideological,[2] moral, philosophical, ritual, traditional,[3] and even climate[4] and physiological,[5] the communication and behavioral aspects of it seem to have a profound impact in the area of dispute resolution. In fact, there seems to be credible scientific evidence suggesting

1. World Conference on Cultural Policies, *Mexico City Declaration on Cultural Policies*, UNESCO (Aug. 6, 1982), http://portal.unesco.org/culture/en/files/12762/11295421661mexico_en.pdf/mexico_en.pdf.

2. *See generally* Richard W. Downing, *The Continuing Power of Cultural Tradition and Socialist Ideology: Cross-Cultural Negotiations Involving Chinese, Korean and American Negotiators*, 1992 J. Disp. Resol. 105 (1992).

3. Professor Schein lists various categories and notions that are used to describe culture. Some of these descriptions include: "[o]bserved behavioral regularities when people interact: [t]he language they use, the customs and traditions that evolve, and the rituals they employ in a wide variety of situations;" or "habits of thinking, mental models, and[] linguistic paradigms: [t]he shared cognitive frames that guide the perceptions, thought, and language used by the members of a group and taught to new members in the early socialization process;" or "[s]hared meaning: the emergent understandings created by group members as they interact with each other." Edgar H. Schein, Organizational Culture and Leadership 14–15 (4th ed. 2010) (citing several authorities for each description) (citations omitted).

4. Organizational culture analysts have not reached consensus on whether "climate" is a part of an organization's culture. The more compelling argument seems to be that it is. For a comprehensive treatment of this subject, *see generally*, The Handbook of Organizational Culture and Climate (Neal M. Ashkanasy, Celeste P.M. Wilderom & Mark F. Peterson eds., 2d ed. 2011).

5. *See, e.g.*, Colin P. Silverthorne, Organizational Psychology in Cross-Cultural Perspective 235 (2005).

The Culture of International Arbitration. Won L. Kidane

that language may influence and shape one's thoughts.[6] Analyzing recent social science data, Guy Deutscher gives the following example. An English speaking person says: "I spent yesterday evening with a neighbor." This statement does not suggest anything about the gender identity of the neighbor. In other words, the language does not obligate the speaker to disclose the gender identity of the neighbor. It is, however, impossible not to disclose the gender identity in French or German as the speaker has to choose between "*voisin*" or "*voisine*," or "*Nachar*" or "*Nachbarin*."[7]

Although the English speaker does not have to specify the gender, the English language forces the speaker to provide information as to time. If, for example, dinner was involved, the speaker has to say whether they *dined, have been dining, are dining,* or *will be dining,* etc. In Chinese, for example, the same verb can be past, present, or future.[8] As such, the language in many cases may not force the speaker to think about time at all times. These kinds of examples suggest that language may play a more important cultural role than mere communication.[9]

Another interesting example Deutscher cites is the use of cardinal directions in some languages in ordinary life. Instead of saying move to the left or right, speakers would say move to the east or the west. Those communities have to constantly think in terms of cardinal direction.[10] Although the evidence seems to be clear that the language itself does not constrain or facilitate understanding any concepts, it seems that it influences or shapes thought as it contains "hidden metaphysics."[11] Thus, linguistic diversity could be a source of miscommunication. An extreme position of this suggests: "you will never understand Chinese people unless you understand Chinese language."[12]

Avruch and Black's example with respect to communication and behavior is also instructive. They describe an interesting episode of cultural miscommunication between a young American tourist and an elderly individual in a foreign country.[13] The tourist, trying to find her way around, asks the old man in English to direct her

6. *See* Guy Deutscher, *Does Your Language Shape How You Think?*, N.Y. Times, Aug. 26, 2010. http://www.nytimes.com/2010/08/29/magazine/29language-t.html.

7. *Id.* at 2.

8. *Id.*

9. *Id.* As Deutscher's article makes clear, it is important to note that the conclusions are not without controversy.

10. *See id.* (suggesting that extensive studies have been conducted analyzing this phenomenon).

11. The term "hidden metaphysics" was coined by German sociologist Edward Sapir (1884–1939). Niall Lawless, *Cultural Perspectives on China: Resolving Disputes through Mediation*, 4 Transnat'l Disp. Mgmt. 2, www.transnational-dispute-management.com/article.asp?key=1294 (last visited October 2, 2016.). In this article, as another example, Lawless suggests that there is no equivalent grammatical structure in Chinese for the following English expression: "If all the goods have arrived on time, we would have paid the invoice in full." *Id.* at 4. According to him, "[putting] aside immediate reality and entering an imaginary world of events that did not take place" might not be readily captured in Chinese. *Id.*

12. *Id.*

13. *See* Kevin Avruch & Peter W. Black, *Conflict Resolution in Intercultural Settings: Problems and Prospects, in* Conflict Resolution Theory and Practice: Integration and Application 131–40 (Dennis J. Sandole & Hugo van der Merwe eds., 1993), *reprinted in*

to a nearby train station. The old man, who does not speak English, looks at the tourist with astonishment. In trying to make herself clearer, the tourist repeats her question in a louder voice, but she gets the same kind of look from the old man. The tourist speaks yet more loudly and, looking around, tries to imitate the sound of a train, miming the pulling of an imaginary train whistle cord, singing "choo, choo." Now the quizzical look becomes open amusement, but still without comprehension. The tourist looks around again and sees a young boy approaching them. "Do you speak English?" "A little." "Do you know where the train station is?" "I do not, but I will ask this old man." He does, and the tourist makes her train. The repetition, the louder voice, and the gesture and mimicry did not help the communication. In fact, the tourist assumed that the gestures she used were more universal than the English language. Avruch and Black note:

> Alas she is wrong, for in this native's land the gesture of pulling a cord signifies a bad attack of dysentery, while the sound "choo, choo" conventionally signifies a male's appreciation of an attractive female. Not surprisingly . . . the old man is amused. Luckily, a third party comes along—a native himself—who shares enough of the tourist's linguistic code to be able to interpret and translate the question.[14]

If the old man had gotten angry for what the gestures meant to him (i.e., he had an attack of dysentery), the small boy's task as a conflict resolver would have been much more difficult because then he would have had to understand what the gestures meant to each one of them and explain why there was no reason for them to be fighting. The little English that he spoke might not have been sufficient to interpret the whole range of meanings and explain what they meant to each one of them in their respective cultures.[15] That might have been a difficult conflict to resolve for a small boy who spoke little English. Although the cultural elements are clear, this problem could essentially be resolved through effective translation. Certain cultural problems cannot, however, be resolved that way. In fact, as the authors suggest, "Shared language can fool the parties into thinking much else, or all else, is shared as well."[16]

An interesting encounter between an African American man and a Chinese man in the movie *Rush Hour* offers an excellent demonstration of Avruch and Black's statement that a shared language without shared culture could "fool the parties into thinking much else, or all else, is shared as well."[17] The African American man, played by the flamboyant Chris Tucker, is a member of the Los Angeles Police Department

Jacqueline Nolan-Haley, Harold Abramson, & Pat K. Chew, International Conflict Resolution: Consensual ADR Processes 55 (2005).

14. *Id.* at 55.

15. *Id.*

16. *Id.*

17. Rush Hour (New Line Cinema, 1998); Avruch & Black, *supra* note 13, at 57.

(LAPD). He is known for his troublemaking. The Chinese man, played by Jackie Chan, is a renowned transnational crime detective from Hong Kong. The plot of the movie revolves around the kidnapping by a Hong Kong mafia of the young daughter of the Chinese Consul General in Los Angeles. The Federal Bureau of Investigation (FBI) takes over the investigation and the LAPD is asked to provide some assistance. Because the two entities do not like each other, the leaders of the LAPD send Chris Tucker to assist the FBI. Tucker is told he is assigned to this case because of the excellent job he is known to do. In the meantime, the FBI is also told that the Chinese government has sent a detective from Hong Kong to assist with the investigation. The FBI thinks that both of these characters are useless and wants to keep them away as much as possible. Accordingly, it assigns Chris Tucker to pick up Jackie Chan from the airport and keep him entertained and away from the Consulate until the FBI solves the crime.

Tucker goes to the airport to pick up Chan and asks him: "Do you speak English?" Chan keeps silent. Tucker says it again in a louder voice: "Do you speak English?!" No reaction again. He stops his car, gets out and gets Chan out, and shouts "Dooo youuuu understand the words that are comin' out of my mouff" as the camera zooms in on his mouth. Chan looks at him with amusement. It turns out that Chan speaks English very well and was merely pretending. Eventually Chan chooses to speak to Tucker. But it gets interesting. Now the two share a common language. Tucker tells Chan that his friends in a certain neighborhood in LA may have an idea about who kidnapped the Consul General's daughter, and that he wants to ask them before he and Chan head back to the Consulate. Chan agrees and they go there. Tucker knocks on a door of what looks like a high-end neighborhood club. Someone opens the door and lets the two characters in. A few gatekeepers, all of whom are African American, stand in the front room. Tucker, who appears to have prior acquaintance with them, proceeds to greet them before he asks them to let him enter a private room where the persons whom he thought had knowledge of the identity of the kidnappers were sitting. He walks toward the gatekeepers in a loping, strutting manner and says: "Whassup, my N****?!" He then gives them fist bumps and enters the inside room. Chan, who was anxious to be immediately acculturated, tries to imitate Tucker's mannerism in approaching the huge bartender and says enthusiastically: "What's up, my N****?!" The bartender can't believe his ears and asks Chan to repeat what he said. Sure enough, not picking up on the signal, Chan repeats it more loudly. Used outside of context, "N****" being a fighting word in America, it leads to a spectacular fight that causes immense damage to property and severe injuries to persons.

The conflict here was a result not of linguistic miscommunication, but subtler cultural miscommunication. When the African American men in the nightclub met an English-speaking Chinese man accompanying another African American man, they had no reason to think that he was from anywhere other than Chinatown across the street. If he were from Chinatown, he should have known that he should not be saying what he did. Chan, whose character is from Hong Kong, sees no reason he cannot greet people the way they greet each other. If anything, he should be rewarded for trying to adapt to the culture immediately. This is a demonstration of the fact that even when there is a complete understanding between the parties about the meaning of particular terms, they may still hold different underlying conceptions. Playwright

George Bernard Shaw beautifully captures this kind of miscommunication when he says: "England and America are two countries divided by a common language."[18]

Thus, a third-party dispute resolver must necessarily begin by understanding the cultural miscommunication that caused the conflict. He or she would have to explain American history and culture to Chan, and Hong Kong history and culture to the African American men to show that the source of the conflict was a result of miscommunication, before he or she begins to resolve the issue of responsibility for whatever damage and injury might have occurred due to the physical confrontation. But then, Chan and the men would have had to select a third-party dispute resolver who would have the cultural competence to do so.

Dean Philip McConnaughay's discussion of the meaning attached to contractual terms by Western and Eastern business people moves this discussion into the legal realm. He notes that "Asian and Western parties to a commercial transaction may 'both understand clearly the terms of their agreements' but still 'hold [entirely] different conceptions of [the meaning and legal effect of their] contract."[19] In such circumstances, he says, "it is difficult to predict whether a dispute [in such a transaction] will be settled by reference to legal standards . . . or in terms of quite different conceptions."[20] One of Dean McConnaughay's examples about different legal conceptions in the West and East is the value attached to a written contract. The Western notion of the supremacy of the contract—that is, the idea that "promises must be kept though the heavens fall," is expressed in principles such as the parol evidence rule, which prohibits the consideration of any pre- and post-contractual factors—is not shared by the East.[21] He further notes that "Asian commercial relationships [are] 'relational' in the same sense that Western commercial relationship are 'legal.'[22] For Asian commercial relationships, "situational and circumstantial considerations prevail[] over contractual terms and expectations, conflict avoidance and negotiation or conciliation prevail[] over all-or-nothing adjudication, and custom and usage (along with the rest of these values) prevail[] over written law."[23] Because of such profound divergence in understanding of legal concepts in East-West relations, McConnaughay goes so far as to suggest that "the unconventional designation of general principles of equity, *amiable composition*, or *ex aequo et bono*," would be a more reliable rule of decision in East-West relations.[24]

18. The Oxford Dictionary of Quotations 638 (Angela Partington ed., 4th ed., Oxford Univ. Press 1992) (1941); *see* Silverthorne, *supra* note 5, at 220.

19. *See* Philip J. McConnaughay, *Rethinking the Role of Law and Contracts in East-West Commercial Relations*, 41 Va. J. Int'l L. 427, 440 (2001) (quoting Arthur T. von Mehren, *Some Reflections on Japanese Law*, 71 Harv. L. Rev. 1486, 1494, n.25 (1958)).

20. McConnaughay, *supra* note 19, at 437.

21. *Id.* at 437–38 (citations omitted).

22. *Id.* at 443.

23. *Id.* at 443–44 (footnotes omitted).

24. *Id.* at 470. Elaborating on the principle, he notes: "To decide *ex aequo et bono* is to seek 'a resolution . . . that is equitable, minimizes harm to either party, and enables potential adversaries to

Avruch and Black say: "If two parties who speak different languages (cultures), think they are both vying for the same *pie*, but it turns out that one is really after the bottle of *lye*, then the dispute was about their noncomprehension, and a simple translation ought to solve the problem in a positive-sum (win-win) manner."[25] However, what a simple translation cannot resolve is if both parties want the whole pie. The cultural question then becomes why and how much each party values the pie, and to what length would that party go to get the entirety of it. They conclude "these parts of the conflict, always present, are culturally constituted; they comprise ethnotheory."[26]

Nonverbal language could also be a source of profound miscommunication. Consider an example of miscommunication provided by mediators Professor Laurence Boulle and Miryana Nesic. It relates to a dispute between an Englishman, who manages a shopping center, and his lessee, a new immigrant from India living in the United Kingdom. The dispute concerned a substantial drop in the turnover of customers. When the Englishman provided a lengthy account of the reasons, arguing that it was because of factors beyond the control of the shopping center (perhaps also saying not foreseeable), the Indian man listened carefully and consistently nodded, making some affirmative noises. When he was given the opportunity, he said he disagreed with just about everything the Englishman said. The Englishman, enraged by the Indian man's utter inconsistency, asked for an explanation. The mediator explained the cultural context by saying for the Indian man, the nodding and affirmative noises meant that he was listening, not that he was agreeing.[27]

Others describe the issue of culture in terms of disciplinary bias. For example, Amir Shalakany makes a compelling argument that neither institutional nor doctrinal bias of established institutions is the cause of arguably skewed arbitral results in North-South investment arbitrations of the 1970s as much as it is the disciplinary bias of arbitrators.[28] The bias, according to him, is the "enduringly intuitive loyalty to a public/private distinction," which makes it impossible for the arbitrators to think that active state intervention in the private sphere could be healthy.[29] Hence

maintain a valuable commercial relationship; the role of such an arbitrator is said . . . to be that of an *amiable compositeur'* . . . 'The *amiable compositeur* is in fact a judge, but one who enjoys greater flexibility in adopting a solution. . . ., even though from a strict legal point of view [the solution] may not be . . . correct.'" *Id.* (quoting Louis B. Sohn, *Arbitration of International Disputes Ex Aequo et Bono, in* INTERNATIONAL ARBITRATION: *LIBER AMICORUM* FOR MARTIN DOMKE 332–33 (Pieter Sanders ed., 1967); Paul D. Carrington & Paul H. Haagen, *Contract and Jurisdiction*, 1996 SUP. CT. REV. 331, 345 (1996); RENÉ DAVID, ARBITRATION IN INTERNATIONAL TRADE 335 (1985)).

25. Avruch & Black, *supra* note 13, at 57.

26. *Id.*

27. This story was reported by Professor Laurence Boulle and Miryana Nesic in their book MEDIATOR SKILLS AND TECHNIQUES: TRIANGLE OF INFLUENCE 139–140 (Bloomsbury 2010).

28. *See* Amr A. Shalakany, *Arbitration and the Third World: A Plea for Reassessing Bias under the Specter of Neoliberalism*, 41 HARV. INT'L L.J. 419, 419–25 (2000).

29. *Id.* at 424.

the assumption that government almost always suffers from this cultural bias in arbitral proceedings.

Every person, rule, and institution has a cultural profile.[30] Culture is defined in many different ways, but the central notions almost invariably relate to behavior, beliefs, experiences, understandings, and values. For example, Nolan-Haley et al. describe culture as "a common system of knowledge and experiences that result in a set of rules or standards; these rules and standards in turn result in behavior and beliefs that the group considers acceptable."[31] Professor Lawrence M. Friedman defines legal culture as "attitudes, values and opinions held in society with regard to law, the legal system and its various parts."[32] Professors Daniel C.K. Chow and Thomas Schoenbaum define culture as: "[t]he values and norms shared by a group and the group's economic, social, political, and religious institutions."[33] After much hesitation and many disclaimers, Professor Edgar H. Schein settles on the following definition of organizational culture: "a pattern of shared basic assumptions that was learned by a group as it solved its problems of external adaptation and internal integration, that has worked well enough to be considered valid and, therefore, to be taught to new members as the correct way to perceive, think, and feel in relation to those problems."[34] Professor Tom Ginsberg endorses Freidman's broad definition of legal culture as: "those parts of general culture—customs, opinions, ways of doing and thinking that bend social forces toward or away from the law."[35] Law, some say, is "a cultural artifact."[36] That is because "it is both the product of social, cultural, economic, and political interactions and at the same time constitutes epistemological foundations that shape the very modes of engagement creating it."[37] In short, "law is in society, or laced through, between and in society's culture."[38] This book adopts the simple meaning of culture that Professor Naomi Mezey gave in her essay, "Law as Culture": "any set of shared,

30. *See* Pat K. Chew, *The Pervasiveness of Culture*, 54 J. Legal Educ. 60, 66–69 (2004), *in* Jacqueline Nolan-Haley, Harold Abramson & Pat K. Chew, International Conflict Resolution: Consensual ADR Processes 57, 57 (2005). For a comprehensive and excellent treatment of the whole notion of institutional culture, see generally Schein, *supra* note 3.

31. Chew, *supra* note 30, at 61.

32. Lawrence M. Friedman, Law and Society: An Introduction 76 (1977).

33. Daniel C.K. Chow & Thomas Schoenbaum, International Business Transactions 11 (2005).

34. Schein, *supra* note 3, at 18.

35. Tom Ginsburg, *The Culture of Arbitration*, 36 Vand. J. Int'l L. 1335, 1336 n.6 (2003) (quoting Lawrence M. Friedman, The Legal System: A Social Science Perspective 15 (1975)).

36. Eve Darian-Smith, Laws and Societies in Global Context: Contemporary Approaches 40 (2013).

37. *Id.*

38. *Id.* (quoting Carroll Seron & Susan S. Sibey, *Profession, Science, and Culture: An Emergent Cannon of Law and Society Research*, *in* The Blackwell Companion of Law and Society 31 (2004)).

signifying practices—practices by which meaning is produced, performed, contested, or transformed."[39] As she clarifies, "heterogeneous workings of culture often derive from differences of age, gender, class, race, and sexual orientation."[40]

A. A BRIEF LOOK AT CULTURE IN TRANSNATIONAL BUSINESS

In the international business realm, it is seemingly well established that a significant proportion of transnational joint ventures fail precisely because of a lack of optimal appreciation of the culture of the business counterpart.[41]

The international business literature is full of solemn warnings about the fatal consequences of ignoring cultural diversity. Dr. Yvette Essounga warns, "For companies having to operate abroad . . . culture can mean the difference between a successful strategy, and a fatal one, especially for the culturally unprepared company."[42] To substantiate this point, she notes that French cultural hostility toward American culture is partly to blame for the Disney company's loss of about $1 billion dollars in 1995.[43] Renowned cultural analyst Professor Geert Hofstede says that if one goes to a different country and makes decisions based on how one operates at home, that person is bound to make "very bad decisions."[44] This statement is exemplified by Professor Mingsheng Li's analysis of the successes and failures of Western businesses in China.[45] Professor Li cites three success stories before he cites one grave failure, which he attributes to cultural misunderstanding. He begins by saying that "[t]he degree of localization largely determines the degree to which a business succeeds or fails in China. The more the company works towards localization, the more likely it will be successful."[46] The three successful examples are KFC, McDonald's, and Volkswagen. To adapt to

39. Naomi Mezey, *Law as Culture*, 13 YALE J.L. & HUMAN. 35, 42 (2001).

40. *Id.* at 43.

41. *See, e.g.*, Silverthorne, *supra* note 5. The rate of failure as a result of cultural differences is believed to be between 37 to 70 percent, depending on the source. *Id.*

42. *See* Yvette N. Essounga, *A Review of the Effect of National Culture on Corporate Culture: An Example of the United States & France*, 9(5) REV. BUS. RES. 70, 70–74 (2009).

43. *Id.* at 70–74. Dr. Essounga notes that cultural differences can be so subtle that Americans conducting business in the Northwest can find it a daunting task to work with Americans from the Southwest. *See id.* at 70.

44. *Geert Hofstede—Cultural Dimensions*, INSYNC TRAINING & COACHING, http://www.insynctraining.nl/artikelen/hofstede_cultural_dimensions.pdf (last visited Feb. 22, 2016). Hofstede's two most recent books in this area are: GEERT HOFSTEDE, CULTURE'S CONSEQUENCES: COMPARING VALUES, BEHAVIORS, INSTITUTIONS, AND ORGANIZATIONS ACROSS NATIONS (Saga Publications 2d ed. 2001), and GEERT HOFSTEDE, GERT JAN HOFSTEDE & MICHAEL MINKOV, CULTURES AND ORGANIZATIONS: SOFTWARE OF THE MIND (McGraw-Hill 3d ed. 2010). Most interestingly, Hofstede defined culture as "the software of the mind." *See* HOFSTEDE, CULTURE AND ORGANIZATIONS, at 4–5.

45. Mingsheng Li, *When in China . . . Foreign Companies Should Devise a Localization Strategy That's Based on a Thorough Understanding of the Complex Chinese Business Culture*, 25(6) COMM. WORLD 34, 35 (Nov.–Dec. 2008).

46. *Id.* at 35.

Chinese culture, KFC and McDonald's added a wide variety of items and promoted their products through Chinese language websites, hired Chinese managers, and showed greater adaptability. Volkswagen created local managerial and manufacturing capacity, and used local designs and processes that contributed to its immense success.[47] An example of failures is the case of Peugeot of France.[48] Peugeot "directly transplanted" its corporate culture from France to China. It relied almost exclusively on expatriate staff and failed to establish good relations with local talent and officials, and its designs did not take the needs and tastes of the Chinese consumer into consideration. As a consequence, it had to sell its production facilities to Honda and exit.

B. PRELIMINARY THOUGHTS ON CULTURE IN INTERNATIONAL ARBITRATION

Under any one of the assumptions outlined above, in the context of international arbitration, it is theoretically possible that each party, lawyer, and arbitrator comes from a different cultural background. The interactions of different cultures give institutions their own cultural profiles.[49] The discussion of cultural distinctiveness in international disputes is not, however, complete without the mention of the idea that a common culture of international arbitration has emerged.[50] Professor Ginsberg makes a compelling argument that there is a convergence "to a certain degree."[51] Professor Leon E. Trakman notes that "international commercial arbitration consists of a variable amalgam of legal cultures. It is not the product of a single, determinative and pre-existing arbitral culture."[52] He recognizes that at the core of this emerging culture of international arbitration are the two dominant Western legal traditions: the common law and the civil law. He argues, however, that the "stereotypical conclusion" that international arbitration is just an amalgam of Euro-American legal traditions, although not completely untrue, is still a stereotype.[53]

47. *See id.* at 35–46. Robert House aptly summarizes it: "McDonald's serves wine and salads with its burgers in France. In India, where beef products are taboo, it created the mutton burger 'The Maharajah Mac.' Middle Easterners prefer toothpaste that tastes spicy. The Japanese like herbs in their medicine." *See* Culture, Leadership, and Organizations: The Globe Study of 62 Societies 5 (Robert J. House, Paul J. Hanges, Mansour Javidan, Peter W. Dorfman & Vipin Gupta eds., Sage Publications 2004).

48. *See* Li, *supra* note 45, at 36.

49. For example, Professor Chew says Enron had a "culture of flamboyance." *See* Chew, *supra* note 30, at 66–69.

50. *See* Ginsberg, *supra* note 35, at 1336.

51. *Id.* at 1340–42. Manifestations of the convergence include the increasing use of oral hearings, an increasing use of discovery, reliance on expert witnesses, etc. *Id.* Ginsburg concludes, however, that the causes of the convergence are economic rather than cultural. *Id.* at 1345.

52. Leon E. Trakman, *"Legal Traditions" and International Commercial Arbitration*, 17 Am. Rev. Int'l Arb. 1, 11–12 (2006).

53. *Id.* at 12–13. The stereotype is that international arbitration is "wholly rooted in either a common or civil law tradition . . . dominated by an elite cadre of lawyers who imbed a fixed American or Eurocentric conceptions into law of arbitration." *Id.* at 18.

Before he goes on to show the flaws in the stereotype, he describes its underpinnings very well as follows:

> At a formal level, international arbitration codes, laws and practices have evolved in some measure out of civil and common-law traditions that are unified in part by international organizations like the ICC. Their pervasive impact upon modern arbitration is reinforced by the realization that traditional business interests served by arbitration have converged at the leading trading cities of Europe and North America where the civil and common-law systems prevail. Consistent with this observation, premier international arbitration centers—the International Chamber of Commerce, the American Arbitration Association and the London Court of International Arbitration—are located in Paris, New York and London respectively. Further imbedding civil and common-law influences is the fact that international commercial arbitrators and counsel alike are drawn significantly from common and civil-law ranks. In addition, arbitrators from Latin America to Japan and China share codes of obligations of one form or another that trace back to civil-law roots and which form a primary source of their legal systems. The civil and common-law traditions, arguably, are even more global in their reach. Legal traditions in Africa, Asia and Americas were determined by centuries of colonialism.[54]

Despite this, however, as Trakman suggests, cultural distinctiveness is not disappearing.[55] First, he cautions that although the colonial states of Africa and Asia adopted the civil or the common law traditions of their former colonizers, it is impossible to determine how pure or impure the variations are and how much they have been influenced by pre- or postcolonial experiences.[56] Second, even if these systems are said to share some common characteristics with the common law or civil law systems, as he puts it, "modern international commercial arbitration came of age in the latter half of the Twentieth Century in the great cities of Europe and America. Neither African nor Asian countries participated much in its evolution."[57] He says, for example, that "whether common or civil law in genesis" the existing system "may be inadequate to satisfy the needs of many African environments,"[58] which are necessarily distinct. Does it mean that a shared legal culture

54. *Id.* at 14–15.

55. *Id.* at 17.

56. *Id.* at 36.

57. *Id.* at 36–37.

58. *Id.* at 36. The rest of the paragraph captures the typical characterization of Africa's situation vis-à-vis international arbitration: "With few exceptions, African countries could not then—nor indeed now—boast of having large cosmopolitan commercial cities in which international commercial disputes could be resolved. Key attributes of international commercial arbitration were not easily satisfied in African jurisdictions in which difficulties of access and procedural delays were commonplace, compared to cosmopolitan venues elsewhere, to which arbitrators, parties and witnesses had easy access. Many African cities were also considered unsuitable as arbitration venues

exists because "lawyers and business people [] travel on the same jets, []have the same habits, use the same laptops and cell phones, dress the same and speak a common language"?[59]

Judge T.O. Elias[60] presents the example of a Nigerian man, accused of the offense of riding his bike in the dark without a headlight, who was brought before a magistrate.[61] The magistrate read out the charges and asked him: "Are you guilty or not guilty?" In Judge Elias's words, "He grinned at the magistrate, shook his head, and retorted somewhat acidly: "What a question! Is that not what I have been dragged before you to find out?"[62]

Even within the Western legal tradition, the divergences can be immense. Consider Jan Paulsson's proposition:

> If you want to observe a real clash of cultures, one might be tempted to say, it is hard to find more sound and fury than what emerges when rival French lawyers appear on both sides, or rival Londoners on both sides, or Cairenes or New Yorkers! For then, it often seems, the combatants leave no prisoners.[63]

Why is such the case? Paulsson answers that it is because both sides adopt the culture of their respective clients.[64] In fact, he goes on to describe several good examples of typical clashes of legal cultures that happen in typical international arbitral proceedings. In one example, a European arbitrator who presumably

due to the perception that they were economically, socially and politically unstable. Lines of communication to and from African destinations were viewed as slow and susceptible to disruption. Some African cities still face difficulties of access, and legal practice there often is marginal when compared to practice at venues in London, New York and Paris. The African Continent in general also lacks a critical mass of established international commercial lawyers who practice as counsel or arbitrators in arbitration proceedings." *Id.* at 36–37. All of these factors, of course, don't make sense if the dispute involves an African party, do they?

59. Darian-Smith, *supra* note 36, at 12 (quoting Lawrence M. Friedman, *One World: Notes on the Emerging Legal Order, in* Transnational Legal Processes: Globalisation and Power Disparities 23, 31–32 (Michael Likosky ed., 2002) (also citing Law in Many Societies: A Reader (Lawrence M. Friedman et al. eds., 2011)).

60. T. Olawale Elias was a former president of the International Court of Justice and Nigeria's first attorney general after independence. (Queen's Counsel) *Taslim O. Elias, 76, Is Dead in Nigeria; Headed World Court,* N.Y. Times, Aug. 16, 1991, http://www.nytimes.com/1991/08/16/obituaries/taslim-o-elias-76-is-dead-in-nigeria-headed-world-court.html. He was a native of Nigeria, trained in the common law legal tradition at the University of London. *Id.*

61. T. Olawale Elias, The Nature of African Customary Law 299 (Manchester University Press, 1956).

62. *Id.*

63. Jan Paulsson, *Cultural Differences in Advocacy in International Arbitration, in* The Art of Advocacy in International Arbitration 15–21 (Doak Bishop & Edward G. Kehoe eds., Juris Publishers 2d ed. 2010).

64. *Id.*

comes from a civil law tradition walks into the hearing room only to find that the American lawyer representing one of the parties had already set the stage for "his expert witness to put on a forensic show of the kind routinely seen in U.S. courtrooms."[65] The arbitrator, who considers it one of his jobs to direct the presentation of evidence, was puzzled by such an advance show.[66] The second example is even more interesting. Again, on the first day of a hearing, an American presented a solo arbitrator from the Middle East a "draft judgment." Such practice, not uncommon in some American jurisdictions, was viewed by the arbitrator as inappropriate ex parte communication, especially because the other party was not in attendance.[67]

Although Paulsson's cultural discussion is limited to the civil law and common law realm—which will be commented upon in Chapter 11 based on the above discussion—it is fair to say that no matter how developed and convergent the systems and processes might be, each arbitrator or institution necessarily has his or her own distinctive culture.

Because of the recognition of these and similar factors, almost all professions now value the importance of cross-cultural skills. Even in the practice of domestic law, cross-cultural lawyering is deemed to require specific competence. Cultural differences could exacerbate issues of trust, credibility, and communication. Most important, as Professor Susan Bryant suggests, "Cultural differences often cause us to attribute different meanings to the same set of facts."[68] She also notes that "[i]naccurate attributions can cause lawyers to make significant errors in their representation of clients."[69] She further notes that lawyers representing clients with orientations of time different from the lawyers often have difficulty communicating with and trusting their clients, and that "[c]lients who are unable to tell a linear time-related story may also experience the same reaction from judges and juries if the client's culture is unknown to the fact finder."[70] Bryant outlines and discusses the possibility of a variety of cultures being at play in any given domestic case: lawyer-client, lawyer-legal system, and client-legal system.[71] She concludes that the influence might at times be invisible, but it can affect the outcome of the case in some fundamental ways.[72]

65. *Id.* at 17.

66. *Id.* at 16–17.

67. *Id.* at 17–18. For an interesting response to some of Paulsson's observations, *see* Dieter Flader, *Comment on Jan Paulsson's Essay: Cultural Differences in Advocacy in International Arbitration*, TRANSNAT'L. DISP. MGMT 1 (2011), http://www.transnational-dispute-management.com.

68. Susan Bryant, *The Five Habits: Building Cross-Cultural Competence in Lawyers*, 8 CLINICAL L. REV. 33, 42 (2001).

69. *Id.* at 42.

70. *Id.* at 45.

71. *Id.* at 68.

72. *Id.*

C. CONCLUSION

Regardless of the precision of the figures of the lost money, or the percentages of successes and failures, or even the accuracy of the claims,[73] the reality is that any analysis that does not take culture into account is incomplete.[74] As indicated above, however, analyzing culture is not an easy task. For example, Professor Stanley B. Lubman goes so far as saying that Chinese and Western legal institutions sometimes appear so disparate that comparing them "seems hardly appropriate."[75] If they do business, however, they must attempt to understand each other. It is said that "law is an element in the perpetual remaking of the language and the culture that determines" the identity of people and institutions.[76] Glendon asks: "What stories are told in a given body of law at a given time?" [77] Isn't it "social data" that is "imaginatively reconstructed as legal fact and concepts[?]"[78]

Shouldn't arbitrators understand the culture of their co-arbitrators, the parties, and the representatives of the parties that appear before them as a condition of appropriate resolution of the controversy? In these times of remarkable cultural diversity, do they attempt to understand the parties and their counsel that hired them, or insist on being understood instead?

Before exploring these issues in great detail, it is necessary to examine the cultural and political history of international arbitration in various legal traditions to see what it is supposed to accomplish and how the justifications and theories evolved and continue to evolve. The following chapters will address these issues.

73. Although questions are always raised about the sufficiency of evidence and accuracy of studies, the organizational culture literature overwhelmingly suggests that organizational culture is a significant component of success. *See, e.g.*, Celeste P.M. Wilderom, Ursula Glunk & Ralf Maslowski, *Organizational Culture as a Predictor of Organizational Performance, in* THE HANDBOOK OF ORGANIZATIONAL CULTURE AND CLIMATE 193–209 (Neal M. Ashkanasy, Celeste P. M. Wilderom & Mark F. Peterson eds., 2d ed. 2011) (reciting some extensive studies linking performance with organizational culture, but questioning the sufficiency); John L. Graham, *Culture and Human Resources Management, in* ALAN M. RUGMAN & THOMAS L. BREWER, THE OXFORD HANDBOOK OF INTERNATIONAL BUSINESS 504–36 (Oxford Univ. Press 2001) (noting that studies conducted for seven years involving 250 Southern California firms confirmed that the most serious challenge of doing international business is cultural differences. One of the reasons, he notes, is that cultural differences are hidden and are difficult to quantify). It is important to note that this writing is not at all concerned with organizational culture in the sense that it is considered in the business literature. The business literature is cited to help in understanding the meaning of culture, and identifies some benchmarking factors.

74. As Robert House puts it: "Globalization opens many opportunities for businesses, but it also creates major challenges. One of the most important challenges is acknowledging and appreciating cultural values, practices and subtleties in different parts of the world." *See* House et al., *supra* note 47, at 5.

75. STANLEY B. LUBMAN, BIRD IN A CAGE: LEGAL REFORM IN CHINA AFTER MAO 12 (Stanford Univ. Press 1999).

76. MARY ANN GLENDON, PAOLO G. CAROZZA & COLIN B. PICKER, COMPARATIVE LEGAL TRADITIONS: TEXT, MATERIALS AND CASES ON WESTERN LAW 22 (3d ed. 2007).

77. *Id.*

78. *Id.*

3

The Political and Cultural History of International Arbitration in Various Legal Traditions

From uncertain historical origin[1] to more accurately determinable roots in the eighteenth and nineteenth centuries[2] grew a mechanism of state-to-state dispute settlement called arbitration primarily because states did not have a common and standing court to go to. Efforts in the early twentieth century resulted in the establishment of the Permanent Court of Arbitration (PCA) by the Hague Convention of 1899 as amended in 1907.[3] As Gary Born puts it, "[t]he 1899 and 1907 Hague Conventions provided the foundation for more formal inter-state adjudication, the Permanent Court of International Justice (PCIJ) and International Court of Justice (ICJ)."[4]

The origins of international commercial arbitration appear equally uncertain although "[a]rbitration was no less common in ancient Greece for the resolution of commercial and other 'private' disputes than for 'state-to-state disputes.'[5] At every stage of its development, arbitration, as an alternative method of dispute settlement, required some justification. Roebuck, writing in the context of Ancient Greek arbitration, says that arbitration was perhaps the most natural means of dispute

1. *See generally* 1 Gary Born, International Commercial Arbitration 6–12 (Kluwer Law International 2014). ("The origins of international arbitration are sometimes traced, if uncertainly, to ancient mythology."). *Id.* at 7.

2. There are several examples of eighteenth and nineteenth century international treaties containing arbitration clauses. Some examples include the 1794 Jay's Treaty between the United States and Great Britain, and the 1848 Treaty of Guadalupe Hidalgo between the United States and Mexico. *See id.* at 12–13.

3. *See id.* at 15–19.

4. *Id.* at 17.

5. *Id.* at 25 (citing D. Roebuck, Ancient Greek Arbitration 45–46, 348–49, 358 (2001)).

The Culture of International Arbitration. Won L. Kidane

settlement as opposed to court litigation or even self-help.[6] Even then, Roebuck claims "[a]rbitration was the natural and regular process of choice for those who could not afford litigation, were afraid of its outcome, preferred privacy, or were manipulating the alternatives."[7] Along the same lines, "[i]n the post-Classical period, arbitration became increasingly popular in many parts of the Roman Empire because of the deficiencies in the state court systems, which were characterized as unreliable, cumbersome and costly, and faced particular difficulties in international and other cross-border matters."[8]

Similar considerations seem to have underpinned the development of international arbitration in the European middle ages. Born states that international arbitration was preferred in the middle ages "for reasons of expedition and commercial expertise, as well as, increasingly, the inadequacy of the local courts or other decision-makers to deal with the special jurisdictional and enforcement obstacles presented by foreign or 'international' litigation."[9] From the restoration of harmony *ex aequo et bono* to the application of formal rules in different parts of Europe in the middle ages, the arbitrators were supposed to be "honest men" who could put an end to legal controversies.[10]

Arbitration did not, however, enjoy smooth and unopposed development in early common law and civil law traditions.[11] The historical vacillation in the common law of England between favoring the enforcement of arbitral agreements on the basis of party autonomy on the one hand and the opposition to the system on concerns of ouster of the court's jurisdiction on the other hand got a compromised and formal expression in the Common Law Procedure Act of 1854, which provided for the irrevocability of the arbitral agreement.[12] The 1889 English Arbitration Act, extensively adopted by the Commonwealth nations, maintained the court's review power on at least some questions of law.[13] Subsequently, the English Arbitration Act

6. *Id.* at 25 n.158 ("Everywhere in the Ancient Greek world, including Ptolemaic Egypt, and all times within our period, disputing parties considered arbitration to be a natural, perhaps the most natural, method of resolving the differences they could not settle themselves, even though they sometimes resorted to litigation (or in earlier times self-help) when they could not get their way.").

7. *See id.* at 26.

8. *Id.* at 29.

9. *Id.* at 31 (citing 3 W. BLACKSTONE, III, COMMENTARIES ON THE LAWS OF ENGLAND *33 (1768) (quoted in Earl S. Wolaver, *The Historical Background of Commercial Arbitration*, 83 U. PA. L. REV. 132, 136 (1934)) ("The reason of their original institution seems to have been, to do justice expeditiously among the variety of persons that resort from distant places to a fair or market; since it is probable that no inferior court might be able to serve its process, or execute its judgment, on both or perhaps either of the parties.").

10. *Id.* at 32 (quoting G. MALYNES, *LEX MERCATORIA*, OR THE ANCIENT LAW MERCHANT; DIVIDED INTO THREE PARTS: ACCORDING TO THE ESSENTIAL PARTS OF TRAFFICKE: NECESSARIE FOR ALL STATESMEN, JUDGES, MAGISTRATES, TEMPORAL AND CIVIL LAWYERS, MINTMEN, MERCHANTS, MARINERS, AND ALL OTHERS NEGOTIATING IN ALL PLACES OF THE WORLD ch. XV (1685 ed.)).

11. *See id.* at 35–41.

12. *Id.* at 38–39.

13. *Id.*

of 1952 and 1996 progressively lessened the courts' involvement while still maintaining some level of oversight.[14]

The dilemmas were equally felt in the civil law tradition as well. France offers a good example. As Born puts it: "[t]he Edict of 1560 and merchant practice led to widespread use of arbitration for resolving commercial disputes in the 16th, 17th and 18th centuries [but] the French Revolution changed this like much else."[15] In fact, the right to arbitrate had once acquired a constitutional stature: "[t]he right of citizens to have their disputes settled by arbitrators of their choice shall not be violated in any way whatsoever."[16] The revolutionaries opposed arbitration essentially because they believed "parties should be protected against the advance and abstract waiver of access to judicial protection and guarantees."[17] In other words, the assumption is that "[o]ne does not find with an arbitrator the same qualities that it is assured to find with a magistrate: the probity, the impartiality, the skillfulness, [and] the sensitivity of feelings necessary to render a decision."[18]

Significantly, the Napoleonic Code of Civil Procedure of 1806 excluded the enforceability of agreements to arbitrate future disputes. Along the same lines, in 1884, in the *Prunier* case, the French Court of Cassation held that agreements to arbitrate future disputes are not enforceable inasmuch as they fail to identify the exact controversy and the exact persons who were supposed to sit in judgment.[19] This was, of course, meant to protect citizens from their own ignorance or indiscretions at the time of signing of the agreement without being assured of what kind of arbitrator they will get for what kind of issue.[20]

Arbitration seems to have undergone an equally uncertain path in the Middle East, Asia, and Africa. In the Middle East, as Born notes based on commentary, "[e]nforcement of awards generally depended on the moral authority of the arbitrators . . . ."[21] Indeed an instance where the Prophet Himself was chosen as an arbitrator to help clans settle disputes has also been noted.[22]

14. The 1996 UK Arbitration Act is the most recent enactment. Arbitration Act 1996, c. 23 (Eng.), http://www.legislation.gov.uk/ukpga/1996/23/contents.

15. Born, *supra* note 1, at 39.

16. *Id.* at 40 (citing French Constitution of Year I, 1793, Art. 86; French Constitution of Year III, 1795, Art. 210).

17. *Id.* at 41.

18. *Id.* (citing J.-L. Delvolvé, J. Rouche & G.H. Pointon, French Arbitration Law and Practice: A Dynamic Civil Law Approach to International Arbitration ¶ 8 (2d ed. 2009)).

19. *Id.* (quoting *Judgment of 10 July 1843*, Cie, L'Alliance v. Prunier, 1843 Dalloz 561 (French Cour de cassation civ.), reprinted in 1992 Rev. arb. 399.).

20. *See id.* at 41 n.272 and accompanying text.

21. *Id.* at 54 (citing A. El-Ahdab & El-Ahdab, Arbitration with the Arab Countries 5 (3d ed. 2011)).

22. *Id.* (citing M. Abu-Nimer, Non-violence and Peacebuilding in Islam, Theory & Practice 63 (2003)).

Similarly, in China and Japan, arbitration, which resembled mediation, often recognized the authorities of elders and relatives.[23] In India, "local luminaries, often village elders or others of high social stature" settled disputes within communities.[24]

In Africa, customary judges essentially acted like arbitrators, as Arthur Philips notes:

> The native method would tend to adjust disturbances of the social equilibrium to restore peace and goodwill, and to bind or rebind the two disputing groups together in a give-and-take reciprocity. The European method would tend to widen the gulf between the two groups by granting all the rights to one of them to the exclusion of the other, because it would in general concern itself with acts and legal principles and take no cognizance of social implications.[25]

In relation to this, Judge T.O. Elias says that "[t]he judge or judges must apply the law to the facts as found and do so in such a way as to command the respect and approval of the overwhelming majority of the people."[26] To support this conclusion, Elias quotes Aristotle as saying:

> It is equity to pardon human failings, to look to the lawgiver and not to the law . . . to wish to settle a matter by words rather than by deeds; lastly, to prefer arbitration to judgment, for the arbitrator sees what is equitable, but the judge only the law, and for the this an arbitrator was first appointed, in order that equity might flourish.[27]

How then did arbitration get from a mechanism of dispute settlement by village elders or luminaries or honest men known to the parties for their high moral authority to international dealmakers with "symbolic capital,"[28] or—as the chief justice of Singapore, Sundaresh Menon says—"businessmen looking for business

23. *See id.* at 58–59 (relying on Law and Legal Institutions of Asia: Traditions, Adaptations, and Innovations 28 (E. Black & G. Bell eds., 2011) and P. Huang, Chinese Civil Justice, Past and Present 4, 29 (2010)).

24. *Id.* at 59 (citing R. Josh & G. Narvani, Panchayat Raj in India: Emerging Trends Across the States 13 (2002)).

25. Won Kidane, China-Africa Dispute Settlement: The Law, Economics and Culture of Arbitration 191 (2011) (quoting Arthur Phillips, Report on Native Tribunals in Kenya, ch IV, ¶¶ 188–192 (1945)).

26. *Id.* at 191 (quoting T. Olawale Elias, The Nature of African Customary Law 272 (Manchester University Press, 1956)).

27. *Id.* at 191 n.180 (citing Elias, *supra* note 26, at 272).

28. In their 1996 groundbreaking work, *Dealing in Virtue*, Yves Dezalay and Bryant Garth coined the term "symbolic capital" to describe the accumulation of reputation to qualify as an arbitrator in the increasingly complicated world of transnational commerce. This concept is explored further in this chapter. *See* Yves Dezalay & Bryant Garth, Dealing in Virtue: International Commercial Arbitration and the Construction of a Transnational Legal Order 8 (1996) ("Only a very select and elite group of individuals is able to serve as international arbitrators. They are purportedly selected for their 'virtue'—judgment, neutrality, expertise—yet rewarded as if

opportunities,"[29] or even more interestingly to the "entrepreneurial arbitrator" who may "rule expansively on his own jurisdiction"?[30]

A. THE POLITICAL AND CULTURAL HISTORY OF CONTEMPORARY INTERNATIONAL ARBITRATION

In the not too ancient past, the Northern powers regularly resorted to self-help to protect the private economic interests of their own persons.[31] International arbitration appears to be a part of the broader and "gradual legalization" of North-South relations.[32] Professor Jeswald W. Salacuse writes: "[A]t the end of World War II—what one might call the 'ancien[t] regime'—failed to adequately protect the foreign investment of their [capital-exporting] nationals from injurious actions by host country governments .... The need for such protection was heightened by the prospect of post-War economic expansion and the decolonization of territories that had previously been under the control of capital-exporting states."[33]

Along the same lines, Professor Andreas Lowenfeld says:

> By the early 1960s, following the wave of decolonization in Africa and parts of Asia, and a wave of take-overs of foreign investments throughout the Third World, it had become apparent that it would be very difficult to achieve consensus on the obligations of host countries toward alien investment (read multinational corporations). The leading international aid institution, the World Bank, began to consider how, on the one hand, it could avoid being embroiled in controversies between home and host states concerning

they are participants in international deal-making. In more sociological terms, the symbolic capital acquired through a career of public service or scholarship is translated into a substantial cash value in international arbitration.").

29. *See* Jan Paulsson, The Idea of Arbitration 148 (2013) (citing Sundaresh Menon, Keynote Address at the Congress of the International Counsel for Commercial Arbitration (May 2012), *in* ICCA Congress Series No. 17: International Arbitration: The Coming of a New Age for Asia (and Elsewhere) 6 (2013).

30. *Id.* at 148.

31. *See, e.g.*, Louis Wells, *Preface* to Jose E. Alvarez et al., The Evolving International Investment Regime, at xvi (2011) ("In the rather distant past, the United States and other rich countries would occasionally act militarily or insist on state-state arbitrations when their investors claimed mistreatment abroad. Later, the United States would threaten (and occasionally act) to cut off aid, vote against loans by multilateral financial institutions to offending countries, and cancel trade preferences . . .").

32. The term "gradual 'legalization'" is coined by Dezalay and Garth in *Dealing in Virtue*. *See* Dezalay & Garth, *supra* note 28, at 64. However, they do caution that "[i]t is [] not sufficient to conclude with the observation that the result was the economic relations of north and south were gradually 'legalized.' While it is true that the dispute came to be handled through the domain of law, law does not exist as a distinctive thing. It is necessary therefore to explore the set of power relationships implicated by the particular constructions of law that come to be applied within the transnational legal field." *Id.*

33. Jeswald W. Salacuse, *The Emerging Global Regime for Investment*, 51 Harv. Int'l L.J. 427, 436 (2010).

> expropriations, and on the other hand, how it could assist the resolution of such controversies . . . .[34]

The growth of North-South arbitration of all types is clearly a part of what Yves Dezalay and Bryant Garth hesitatingly call "the gradual 'legalization" of the economic relations. The history and practice of ICISD[35] provides a good example. Its creation in 1966 is directly linked to perceived necessity of having legal protection of foreign investment in newly decolonized states of Africa and other parts of the world.[36]

The International Centre for Settlement of Investment Disputes (ICSID) Convention came into effect on October 14, 1966.[37] It required 20 ratifications. The first 15 to ratify were African states.[38] Without Africa, there would have been no ICSID because Latin American countries were completely opposed to it at the time on strongly held and solid ideological grounds.[39] There was only one reason for the African countries' acceptance of a World Bank-affiliated dispute settlement body: they believed that without it nobody would invest in Africa, because the legal

34. *See* Andreas Lowenfeld, International Economic Law (International Economic Law Series) 536–37 (2008).

35. ICSID was created by the Convention on the Settlement of Investment Disputes Between States and Nationals of Other States (hereinafter ICSID Convention) in 1966. Convention on the Settlement of Investment Disputes Between States and Nationals of Other States (as amended), Oct. 14, 1966, 17 U.S.T. 1270, 575 U.N.T.S. 159, https://icsid.worldbank.org/apps/ICSIDWEB/icsiddocs/Pages/ICSID-Convention.aspx. For a comprehensive commentary of the Convention, *see* Christoph H. Schreuer, The ICSID Convention: A Commentary (2d ed. 2009).

36. *See* Lowenfeld, *supra* note 34, at 536–37.

37. Comprehensive information on the history, structure, and operations of ICSID is available on the official website at www.worldbank.org/icsid.

38. The 15 original African contracting states were: Benin, Burkina Faso, Central African Republic, Chad, Congo (Republic of), Côte d'Ivoire, Gabon, Ghana, Madagascar, Malawi, Mauritania, Nigeria, Sierra Leone, Tunisia, and Uganda. A total of 21 instruments of ratification were deposited that day. The remaining six were: Iceland, Jamaica, Malaysia, Netherlands, Norway, and the United States. ICSID, *List of Contracting States and Other Signatories of the Convention*, ICSID/3 (Nov. 17, 2015), https://icsid.worldbank.org/apps/ICSIDWEB/icsiddocs/Documents/List%20of%20Contracting%20States%20and%20Other%20Signatories%20of%20the%20Convention%20%20Latest.pdf.

39. The Calvo doctrine provided the philosophical background for the unanimous rejection of the idea of a World Bank-affiliated dispute settlement body by Latin American countries. *See* Lowenfeld, *supra* note 34, at 540. Indeed, when the ICSID proposal was presented at the annual meeting of the Bank in Tokyo in 1964, all South American states voted no. The Latin press famously touted "El No de Tokyo!" *Id.* A World Bank affiliated commentator aptly called it the "Calvoesque rejection of foreign intervention." *See* Paul C. Szasz, *The Investment Disputes Convention and Latin America*, 11 Va. J. Int'l L. 256, 259 (1971). Although there are other related reasons for the Latin American countries' rejection of the idea, it is clear that the dominant reason was one derived from the Calvo doctrine, "that the Convention, which of course can be used only in relation to an alien investor, offends against the rule that foreigners must be treated equally with citizens." Szasz, *supra*, at 261 (citing Jose R. Chiriboga, *International Arbitration*, 4 Int'l Law 801, 804 (1970)).

systems were not acceptably constituted as to win the comfort of foreign investors who mainly come from former colonial powers.[40] The history is very clear that ICISD is supposed to make up for the perceived inadequacies and lack of neutrality of the domestic courts in the former colonies.

The history of other types of arbitration, such as commercial arbitration, is largely linked to the history of political movements and changes that affected the old world economic order of direct or indirect rule. Focusing on "north-south conflicts, which made up most of the celebrated arbitrations of the period [1970s and 1980s]," Dezalay and Garth posit "[t]he main question is how political and economic conflicts between north and south became translated into general business conflicts that could be managed by a transnational legal order, and in particular by institutions of international commercial arbitration."[41] What they ask afterward is highly instructive: "How was the law—or more precisely, the law that developed along with the field of international commercial arbitration—able to extend authority over countries that had no developed legal traditions, no trust in Western-dominated institutions, and in particular no faith in some new form of international law?"[42] They continue writing: "Without this achievement, the boom in international commercial arbitration would not have taken place."[43]

In answering the main question of why the nations of the South accepted such legal order, they caution that "[i]t is too easy—and vastly oversimplified—to say that the power of the developed capitalist countries of the north was sufficient to impose their institutions on the countries of the third world."[44] They offer a nuanced answer to the main questions, which they summarize in part as follows:

> An escalation of conflict took the form of law, requiring both sides to invest in the law and legal practice, especially U.S.-style adversarial legal practice, thus

40. *See* ICSID Publication, II-1 History of the ICSID Convention 239 (1968, *reprinted* 2009) (summarizing the statement by the executive secretary of the Economic Commission for Africa made during the ICSID consultation meeting in Addis Ababa in 1963 on the need for a legal regime to protect foreign capital). The statements of the representative of Sierra Leone during the ICSID African legal consultative meeting offers a good example of how the Africans felt at the time: "It would be easier for the developing countries to obtain the investments they needed if all agreements contained a clause to the effect that disputes could be referred to the Center [ICSID]." *Id.* at 255. For a discussion of the expectations at that time, *see generally* Won Kidane, *The China-Africa Factor in the Contemporary ICSID Legitimacy Debate*, 35 U. Pa. J. Int'l L. 559, 560ff (2014). Studies have since questioned the proposition that there is a direct link between treaties that purport to attract foreign investment and results thereof. *See, e.g.*, J. Salacuse & N.P. Sullivan, *Do BITs Really Work? An Evaluation of Bilateral Investment Treaties and Their Grand Bargain*, 46 Harv. Int'l L.J. 67 (2005); Karl P. Sauvant & Lisa E. Sachs, The Effect of Treaties on Foreign Direct Investment: Bilateral Investment Treaties, Double Taxation Treaties, and Investment Flows (2009).

41. Dezalay & Garth, *supra* note 28, at 63–64.

42. *Id.* at 64.

43. *Id.*

44. *Id.*

> building comparable sides in an adversarial proceeding that, in turn, served to provide the independence, neutrality, and legitimacy that enabled the law and lawyers to prosper.[45]

Further on the issue of where the legitimacy comes from, here is what they say:

> The legitimacy of the transnational legal order rests on the way representation is structured. In simple terms, one side defends the established interests, others speak for the dominated interests, and this opposition serves collectively to produce the universality of law and make prosperity for the intermediaries. That, in short, is the story of the setting of the legal scene for north-south conflicts.[46]

They exemplify this by using the phenomenon of what they call the third-world countries effort to "increase their sovereignty and share of the wealth from natural resources."[47] They further note that "[w]hen multinational businesses found their mineral concessions undermined or nationalized, they turned loose lawyers who had until then been kept in a relatively secondary, even marginal, role."[48]

The Libyan Oil Cases of the 1970s are considered the "'founding acts' for the international arbitration community, serving to build reputations and beliefs in the law that went well beyond the importance of those arbitrations in the particular disputes that generated them."[49] This leads to the conclusion that captures the dominant theory as follows:

> In . . . north-south conflicts, the lawyers unleashed on behalf of one side quite often found colleagues from similar law firms and legal practices on the other side. This tactic of a legal escalation, however, initially placed the young governments of the third world at a handicap, since they were uniformly under-equipped in matters of legal competence.[50]

45. *Id.* Dezalay and Garth continue writing: "[I]n the construction of this adversarial arrangement, part of the success of the U.S. style of advocacy came from the situation in which a certain group of lawyers found themselves. It was not just that the U.S. adversary system made it relatively easy to legitimize aggressive advocacy on behalf of countries with radically divergent interests. It was also important that developments inside the United States generated a group of lawyers eager to seek out just such opportunity and, therefore, to play the double role of promoting third-world perspectives and extending the power of U.S. legal practice—indeed, giving it roots in third-world countries that were politically opposed to the United States." *Id.* at 64–65.

46. *Id.* at 65.

47. *Id.*

48. *Id.*

49. *Id.*

50. *Id.* at 66 (citations omitted). Dezalay and Garth give the supposed lack of competence a political explanation in the following terms: "For some countries, including those of the Persian Gulf, non-religious legal traditions were more or less nonexistent. Other new regimes distrusted their lawyers,

But Dezalay and Garth also make a more important point when they say: "Even if there were competent national jurists in whom the third-world leaders had confidence, that would not have helped very much in ensuing legal battles, since they typically took place on the terrain of their adversaries."[51]

The multinationals that faced the various government measures sought a "legal" way of enforcing what they thought to be their rights by filing legal actions in multiple fora. An example Dezalay and Garth cite is the 35 cases that lawyers for British Petroleum filed when Libya nationalized its interests in 1971.[52] They note further that "The third-world countries were then obligated to defend themselves in some fashion or another. They turned to 'legal mercenaries' from Europe or the United States."[53] The big American firm made sense both in terms of its ability to administer many cases in multiple fora at the same time as well as the quality and zeal of advocacy that its members provided. It made perfect sense.[54] Dezaley and Garth cite a British lawyer they interviewed as saying "they [third world governments] had to participate in a 'process which they think they did not understand . . . And in order to do so they had to deliver themselves into the hands of Western European lawyers—not just Western European arbitrators—but Western European lawyers."[55]

Most enduringly, however, the three "founding" Libyan Oil Cases set the ideological tone that generations of students of international arbitration were incubated with. The resulting stereotype identified all of the newly independent African states as cousins of Muammar Gaddafi, a presumption they needed to overcome every time they appeared before arbitral tribunals sited in Europe or North America. Indeed in all three Libyan Oil Cases,[56] the expropriating state lost and was required to pay compensation, although the legal standards on the quantum of damages proved elusive.[57]

since they were seen as part of the comprador bourgeoisie closer to the interest and the culture of the West than the groups who led the nationalist movement. The army of Nasser's Egypt exemplified this fairly widespread hostility to the local legal profession." *Id.*

51. *Id.* at 66–67.

52. *Id.* at 67.

53. *Id.* ("As a prominent Arab lawyer pointed out, they thought they had to pick 'the best lawyers,' and they assumed them to be Western.").

54. *Id.* Moreover, "the young nationalist leaders who had recourse to their services could avoid returning to the colonial powers against whom they had recently been contending for independence." *Id.*

55. *Id.* at 67 n.8.

56. The three cases are: British Petroleum Exploration Co. (Libya) v. Libyan Arab Republic, 53 Int'l L. Rep. 297 (Lagergren, sole arb., 1973); Texaco Overseas Petroleum Co. v. Libyan Arab Republic, 55 Int'l L. Rep. 354 (consolidated with the case of California Asiatic Oil Company (CALASIATIC) (René-Jean Dupuy, sole arb., 1975); Libya American Oil Co. (LIAMCO) v. Libyan Arab Republic, 62 Int'l L. Rep., 140; 20 ILM 1 (1981) (Mahamassani, sole arb., 1977). For a summary of these cases, *see* Kidane, *supra* note 25, at 126–29. For a fuller discussion, *see* Robert Von Mehren & Nicholas P. Kourides, *International Arbitration between States and Private Parties: The Libyan Nationalization Cases*, 75 Am. J. Int'l L. 476 (1981).

57. *See* Kidane, *supra* note 25, at 126–29.

As Dezalay and Garth put it, international arbitration is largely a legal order unwittingly created by the petroleum industry.[58] Unfortunately, the facts of the founding Libyan Oil Cases and the much publicized confiscatory measures did not help the image of the newly independent African states, prompting the occasional indictment of the system for ideological bias in favor of private investors.[59]

B. THE EVOLUTION OF THE COURTS' TOLERANCE OF INTERNATIONAL ARBITRATION IN VARIOUS LEGAL TRADITIONS

Courts of various traditions tolerate arbitration for various reasons, and place varying degrees of control on its operation. As Alan Redfern and Martin Hunter aptly put it: "The relationship between national courts and arbitral tribunals swings between forced cohabitation and true partnership."[60] This section briefly contextualizes the nature of this cohabitation in the different legal traditions to show why the courts cede their jurisdiction to businessmen.

1. Common Law Legal Tradition

Courts in the United States and the United Kingdom have struggled in understanding the purpose and setting the limits of arbitral decision-making down through the ages. A few seminal cases by the highest courts demonstrate the dilemma.

In the United States, as in many other jurisdictions, the debate about the uncomfortable sharing of competence between the courts and privately constituted arbitral tribunals occurred both in the context of domestic arbitration as well as international arbitration, with the courts first showing more willingness vis-à-vis the latter.

Prior to the enactment of the Federal Arbitration Act (FAA),[61] the courts in the United States adopted the English courts' traditional resistance to arbitration, concerned about the ouster of their jurisdiction. Elaborating on this point, the Second Circuit Court of Appeals, in *Kulukundis Shipping Co. v. Amtorg Trading Corp.*,[62] noted that:

> Some centuries ago, because of the jealousy of the English courts for their own jurisdiction, they refused to enforce specific agreements to arbitrate upon the ground that the courts were thereby ousted from their jurisdiction. This jealousy

58. Dezalay & Garth, *supra* note 28, at 75 ("The petroleum industry may therefore have produced the legal order, but it did so merely by accident and without self-awareness.").

59. *See generally* Amr A. Shalakany, *Arbitration and the Third World: A Plea for Reassessing Bias under the Specter of Neoliberalism*, 41 Harv. Int'l L.J. 419 (2000).

60. Nigel Blackaby et al., Redfern and Hunter on International Arbitration 439 (5th ed. 2009).

61. Federal Arbitration Act, 9 U.S.C. § 1 *et seq.* (enacted February 12, 1925).

62. Kulukundis Shipping Co. v. Amtorg Trading Corp., 126 F.2d 978, 985 (2d Cir. 1942).

> survived for so long a period that the principle became firmly embedded in the English common law and was adopted with it by the American courts. The courts have felt that the precedent was too strongly fixed to be overturned without legislative enactment, although they have frequently criticized the rule and recognized its illogical nature and the injustice which results from it. The bill declares simply that such agreements for arbitration shall be enforced, and provides a procedure in the Federal courts for their enforcement. [] It is particularly appropriate that the action should be taken at this time when there is so much agitation against the *costliness and delays of litigation*. These matters can be largely eliminated by agreements for arbitration, if arbitration agreements are made valid and enforceable."[63]

The English courts' hostility, according to the *Kulukundis* court, was mainly because of the concern of the ouster of their jurisdiction,[64] which the court suggests had an element of economic competition.[65] The virtues on the other hand were minimization of cost and ensuring expediency. As the court further noted, the English courts traditionally tolerated arbitration agreements to have arbitrators determine some questions of fact that were perceived to be important for the court's determination of the legal issue.[66] Even with the assistance of the FAA, however, the court failed to enforce the arbitration agreement on the grounds that the FAA does not cover arbitration agreements that are broad enough to include a contention about the very existence of the underlying contract within which they are found.[67]

Ages of hostility was irreversibly put to rest by *Mitsubishi v. Soler Chrysler-Plymouth*,[68] in which the U.S. Supreme Court held that:

> [t]he first task of a court asked to compel arbitration of a dispute is to determine whether the parties agreed to arbitrate that dispute. The court is to make this

63. *Id.* at 985 (emphasis added).

64. The famous relevant case is Kill v. Hollister, 19 Geo. II 1746, 1 Wils. K.B. 129.

65. *Kulukundis*, 126 F.2d at 983–84 ("Lord Campbell explained the English attitude as due to the desire of the judges, at a time when their salaries came largely from fees, to avoid loss of income. Indignation has been voiced at this suggestion; perhaps it is unjustified. Perhaps the true explanation is the hypnotic power of the phrase, 'oust the jurisdiction.' Give a bad dogma a good name and its bite may become as bad as its bark.").

66. *Id.* at 984 ("That English attitude was largely taken over in the 19th century by most courts in this country. Indeed, in general, they would not go as far as Scott v. Avery, supra, and continued to use the 'ouster of jurisdiction' concept: An executory agreement to arbitrate would not be given specific performance or furnish the basis of a stay of proceedings on the original cause of action. Nor would it be given effect as a plea in bar, except in limited instances, i.e., *in the case of an agreement expressly or impliedly making it a condition precedent to litigation that there be an award determining some preliminary question of subsidiary fact upon which any liability was to be contingent.* In the case of broader executory agreements, no more than nominal damages would be given for a breach.") (emphasis added) (footnote omitted) (citing Hamilton v. Liverpool, 1890, etc., Ins. Co., 136 U.S. 242, 255).

67. *Kulukundis*, 126 F.2d at 986–88.

68. Mitsubishi v. Soler Chrysler-Plymouth, 473 U.S. 614 (1985).

determination by applying the "federal substantive law of arbitrability, applicable to any arbitration agreement within the coverage of the Act."[69]

And that body of law counsels:

> [t]hat questions of arbitrability must be addressed with a healthy regard for the federal policy favoring arbitration . . . . The Arbitration Act establishes that, as a matter of federal law, any doubts concerning the scope of arbitrable issues should be resolved in favor of arbitration, whether the problem at hand is the construction of the contract language itself or an allegation of waiver, delay, or a like defense to arbitrability.[70]

The ultimate triumph of arbitration in *Mitsubishi* set the stage for its worldwide preeminence.[71] At the most general level, the Supreme Court's endorsement of the notion of "shak[ing] off the old hostility"[72] was essentially predicated on

69. *Id.* at 626.

70. *Id.* (quoting Moses H. Cone Memorial Hospital v. Mercury Constr. Co., 460 U.S. 1, 24 (1983)) (citing Prima Paint Corp. v. Flood & Conklin Mfg. Co., 388 U.S. 395, 400–04 (1967); Southland Corp. v. Keating, 465 U.S. 1, 12 (1984)). Mitsubishi was the culmination of the line of cases that included such seminal ones as Wilko v. Swan, 346 U.S. 427 (1953) and Scherk v. Alberto-Culver Co., 417 U.S. 506 (1974) that advanced the process of eroding the old hostility. In each one of these cases, the Court struggled to set the limits of party autonomy and arbitral power in various contexts.

71. *Mitsubishi* was but a culmination of the Supreme Court's steady expansive interpretation of the FAA. For a discussion of the proposition that the Court interpreted the FAA expansively by pronouncing a federal policy in favor of arbitration, *see generally* Margaret L. Moses, *Privatized "Justice,"* 36 Loy. U. Chi. L.J. 535 (2005). She argues rather convincingly that the Court's expansive interpretation of the FAA results in loss of certain benefits of judicial decision-making. She notes:

> At particular risk of being disadvantaged is the consumer, who may be unaware that by agreeing to an arbitration clause she has given up her right to a jury trial, and she will pay higher fees for the arbitral process than she would have to pay as court fees in litigation. Moreover, she will have no right to an appeal on the merits of the case, and may be prohibited from bringing her action as a class action.

Id. at 535. Moses also notes in particular that the "[l]egislative history suggests that the drafters of the FAA envisioned arbitration between merchants of roughly equal bargaining power, and specifically did not believe the Act provided for imposition of arbitration through adhesion contracts." *Id.* at 536 (quoting Prima Paint Corp. v. Flood & Conklin Mfg. Co., 388 U.S. 395, 414 (1967) (Black, J., dissenting)).

72. *Mitsubishi*, 473 U.S. at 638 ("As international trade has expanded in recent decades, so too has the use of international arbitration to resolve disputes arising in the course of that trade. The controversies that international arbitral institutions are called upon to resolve have increased in diversity as well as in complexity. Yet the potential of these tribunals for efficient disposition of legal disagreements arising from commercial relations has not yet been tested. If they are to take a central place in the international legal order, national courts will need to 'shake off the old judicial hostility to arbitration' . . . ." (citing Kulukundis Shipping Co. v. Amtorg Trading Corp., 126 F.2d 978, 985 (2d Cir. 1942)).

the assumption that international arbitration would be conducted by "*competent, conscientious, and impartial arbitrators*."[73]

In the United Kingdom, from Lord Coke's 1609 dictum in Vynior's case[74] that "hardened into solid precedent" that arbitration agreements are "revocable" at will,[75] to the 1698 Arbitration Act allowing merchants and traders to make their agreement "a rule of any of His Majesty's Courts of Record,"[76] to the 1854 Common Law Procedure Act prescribing the irrevocability of all arbitration agreements subject to extensive judicial review,[77] the history of the development of arbitration has had profound transformation that continues to instruct current debate. For example, the well-known Lord Campbell opinion in *Scott v. Avery* holds:

> Is there anything contrary to public policy in saying that the Company shall not be harassed by actions, the costs of which might be ruinous, but that any dispute that arises shall be referred to a domestic tribunal, which may speedily and economically determine the dispute? . . . I can see not the slightest ill consequences that can flow from such an agreement, and I see great advantages that may arise from it . . . . Public policy, therefore, seems to me to require that effect be given to the contract.[78]

The public policy is again cost and speed. Indeed, the English Common Law Procedure Act required arbitrators to issue their awards within three months.[79] The Act permitted judicial review of points of law by each party as of right.[80] In 1889, England

73. *Mitsubishi*, 473 U.S. at 634 ("For similar reasons, we also reject the proposition that an arbitration panel will pose too great a danger of innate hostility to the constraints on business conduct that antitrust law imposes. International arbitrators frequently are drawn from the legal as well as the business community; where the dispute has an important legal component, the parties and the arbitral body with whose assistance they have agreed to settle their dispute can be expected to select arbitrators accordingly. We decline to indulge the presumption that the parties and arbitral body conducting a proceeding will be unable or unwilling to retain competent, conscientious, and impartial arbitrators."). The Supreme Court's sustained promotion of arbitration in general has been a subject of criticism. *See, e.g.*, Imre Stephen Szalai, Outsourcing Justice: The Rise of Modern Arbitration Laws in America (2013) (arguing that "the U.S. Supreme Court has grossly misconstrued [the arbitration] laws and unjustifiably created an expansive, informal, private system of justice touching almost every aspect of American society and impacting the lives of millions." *Id.* at back cover.

74. Gary Born, International Arbitration: Cases and Materials (2011) (citing Vynior v. Wilde (1609) 77 Eng. Rep. 595 (K.B.)).

75. *Id.* at 16.

76. *Id.* (citing English Civil Procedure Act 1698, 9 & 10 Will. III c. 15).

77. *Id.* at 17 (citing English Common Law Procedure Act 1854, 17 & 18 Vict. c. 125).

78. *Id.* (citing Scott v. Avery (1856) 5 H.L. Cas. 809, 853 (House of Lords)).

79. *Id.* at 18 n.129 (citing English Common Law Procedure Act 1854, 17 & 18 Vict. § 15).

80. *Id.* at 18.

enacted what could be considered the first modern arbitration act in the common law tradition.[81] This English Arbitration Act of 1889 confirmed the enforceability of arbitration agreements and awards subject to limited judicial review on questions of law.[82]

More than a century later, the English Arbitration Act of 1996[83] consolidated the salient features of many legislative[84] and common law rules that emerged over that period into a more modern and detailed instrument inspired largely by the 1985 UNCITRAL Model Law.[85] As remarkable of a development as it might have been, the Act breaks from worldwide trend by embedding a default rule of allowing the English courts to review certain questions of law under limited circumstances.[86]

81. *Id.* (citing Adam Samuel, *Arbitration Statutes in England and the USA*, 8 ARB. & DISP. RES. L.J. 2, 6 (1999) ("The 1889 Arbitration Act can be regarded as the first modern arbitration statute in the common law world.").

82. *Id.* (citing English Arbitration Act 1889, 52 & 53 Vict. c. 49).

83. Arbitration Act 1996 (Eng.).

84. Preexisting legislative rules include the Arbitration Acts 1950, 1975, and 1979. For a discussion of the development, *see* SANDRA SYNKOVÁ, COURTS' INQUIRY INTO ARBITRAL JURISDICTION AT THE PRE-AWARD STAGE: A COMPARATIVE ANALYSIS OF THE ENGLISH, GERMAN AND SWISS LEGAL ORDER 133–48 (2013).

85. *See* BORN, *supra* note 74, at 59 (quoting Roy Goode, *The Role of* Lex Loci Arbitri *in International Arbitration*, 17 ARB. INT'L 19, 19 (2001) ("The Arbitration Act 1996, unlike early versions of the draft Arbitration Bill prepared for the Departmental Advisory Committee on Arbitration, bears the strong impress of the Model Law.").

86. Section 69 of the 1996 English Arbitration Act is exceptional in its permission of court review. The scope is difficult to describe. The text reads as follows:

> Appeal on point of law.
>
> (1) Unless otherwise agreed by the parties, a party to arbitral proceedings may (upon notice to the other parties and to the tribunal) appeal to the court on a question of law arising out of an award made in the proceedings.
>
> An agreement to dispense with reasons for the tribunal's award shall be considered an agreement to exclude the court's jurisdiction under this section.
>
> (2) An appeal shall not be brought under this section except—
> (a) with the agreement of all the other parties to the proceedings, or
> (b) with the leave of the court.
>
> The right to appeal is also subject to the restrictions in section 70(2) and (3).
>
> (3) Leave to appeal shall be given only if the court is satisfied—
> (a) that the determination of the question will substantially affect the rights of one or more of the parties,
> (b) that the question is one which the tribunal was asked to determine,
> (c) that, on the basis of the findings of fact in the award—
> (i) the decision of the tribunal on the question is obviously wrong, or
> (ii) the question is one of general public importance and the decision of the tribunal is at least open to serious doubt, and
> (d) that, despite the agreement of the parties to resolve the matter by arbitration, it is just and proper in all the circumstances for the court to determine the question.
>
> (4) An application for leave to appeal under this section shall identify the question of law to be determined and state the grounds on which it is alleged that leave to appeal should be granted.

Section 1 of the Act sets forth the principal objectives as follows:

(a) The object of the arbitration is to obtain the fair resolution of disputes by an impartial tribunal without unnecessary delay or expense;
(b) The parties should be free to agree how their disputes are resolved, subject only to such safeguards as are necessary in the public interest;
(c) In matters governed by this the court should not intervene except as provided by this Part.[87]

Economy of time and resources being the main objectives, the Act, just like any other source of arbitration rules, takes impartiality as a baseline, and naturally assumes competence without mentioning it. Be that as it may, the English courts continue to struggle with the age-old dilemma on the allocation of competence between the courts and arbitral tribunals.[88]

2. Civil Law Legal Tradition

In the civil law tradition, historically, for the most part, there appears to have prevailed no less suspicion of privatized justice than in the common law legal tradition. As Jean-Louis Delvolvé, Jean Rouche, and Gerald H. Pointon write, in France, during the revolution, initially, the "*Assemblée Constituanté* believed arbitration to be the usual and natural way of settling disputes and rendering justice . . . within a short time the process of arbitration began to be abused, and manifest injustice was done."[89] It was a result of this perception of injustice that the Napoleonic *Code de Procédure Civile* of

(5) The court shall determine an application for leave to appeal under this section without a hearing unless it appears to the court that a hearing is required.
(6) The leave of the court is required for any appeal from a decision of the court under this section to grant or refuse leave to appeal.
(7) On an appeal under this section the court may by order—
    (a) confirm the award,
    (b) vary the award,
    (c) remit the award to the tribunal, in whole or in part, for reconsideration in the light of the court's determination, or
    (d) set aside the award in whole or in part.
    The court shall not exercise its power to set aside an award, in whole or in part, unless it is satisfied that it would be inappropriate to remit the matters in question to the tribunal for reconsideration.
(8) The decision of the court on an appeal under this section shall be treated as a judgment of the court for the purposes of a further appeal.

But no such appeal lies without the leave of the court which shall not be given unless the court considers that the question is one of general importance or is one which for some other special reason should be considered by the Court of Appeal.

87. English Arbitration Act 1996 § 1. For a discussion, *see* SYNKOVÁ, *supra* note 84, at 133–39.

88. *See generally* SYNKOVÁ, *supra* note 84.

89. JEAN-LOUIS DELVOLVÉ, JEAN ROUCHE & GERALD H. POINTON, FRENCH ARBITRATION LAW AND PRACTICE 3 (2003).

1806 imposed severe restrictions on arbitration.[90] In 1843, the *Cour de cassation* disallowed the enforceability of agreements to arbitrate future disputes that did not name the arbitrators.[91]

Such decision essentially arrested the growth of arbitration in France until the French Law of December 31, 1925, lifted the restriction and allowed the enforceability of arbitration agreements dealing with future disputes inasmuch as they pertained to commercial matters and did not involve the state, local authorities, and public institutions.[92] In subsequent decades, French courts relaxed the restrictions, especially relating to international arbitration, even upholding the validity of arbitration agreements involving the state and local authorities.[93] However, as Delvolvé, Rouche, and Pointon put it, "France retained part of its ambivalent attitude towards arbitration" even after it ratified such treaties as the New York Convention of 1958 and the ICSID Convention of 1965, as well as the European Geneva Convention on International Commercial Arbitration of 1961.[94] By the end of the 1970s, their conclusion is that "French arbitration law appeared, on the whole, to be relatively liberal and supportive of arbitration as a means of dispute resolution, especially in international arbitration,"[95] although the rules lacked clarity.[96] Subsequent legislative and judicial efforts have given the law a degree of clarity.[97]

The reasons for French law's increasing acceptance of international arbitration are similar to those accepted elsewhere. Delvolvé, Rouche, and Pointon summarize the reasons as follows:

> Among other reasons are: flexibility of the procedure, including organization and management of the procedure and hearings to take account of the nature of the case; court procedures may not always be suited to the resolution of the dispute; a judge is not trained to handle technical matters, whereas an arbitrator

90. Among these restrictions are the restrictions on the state, local authorities, and public institutions to submit to arbitration. *See id.* at 3–4.

91. *Id.* (citing Cass. civ. 10 July 1843, S. 1843.1. p. 561 and D. 1843.1 p. 343; *republished in* Rev. Arb. 1992, 399 with the opinion of Advocate General Hello to the contrary.).

92. *Id.* at 4–5.

93. *Id.*at 5–6 (citing Civ. I. 2 May 1966, the *Galakis* case, J.D.I., 1966, p. 648, note P. Level; Rev. Crit. 1967. P. 553, note b. Goldman; D. 1966, p. 575; note J. Robert).

94. *Id.* at 6.

95. *Id.* at 6–7.

96. *Id.* at 7. As to the state of the law they remark that "[t]he relevant rules were not easy to understand, since the statutory provisions were incomplete, and reference had to be made to decisions in countless cases, which were not always consistent with each other, and did not show any clear train of evolution; even learned writers found the decided cases confusing." *Id.*

97. *Id.* at 7–8. The main current source of arbitration law in France is articles 2059–2061 of Code Civile and articles 1442–1507 of the New Code of Civil Procedure as well as many judicial decisions interpreting these provisions of the law. *Id.* at 9. France has not adopted the 1985 UNCITRAL Model Law and there does not appear to be a "likelihood" of it doing so. *Id.* at 10.

> may well be a person skilled in the subject-matter of the dispute or have a background which means that he is familiar with the relevant customs and usages; the confidentiality of the arbitral process; the greater likelihood of reaching an agreed settlement between the parties during private proceedings rather than during a formal and public combat before a judge; the greater possibility of granting an arbitrator, rather than a court, the power of an *amiable compositeur*; in case of international arbitration, the desire for a neutral forum instead of the national courts of one party, which the other party may, rightly or wrongly, fear will not be impartial, coupled with the advantage that under the relevant Conventions on the recognition and enforcement of foreign awards, the award will be more readily enforceable than a judgment of a national court.[98]

This is a fairly accurate statement of all the standard reasons. Just like other systems, the French system also makes the assumption that arbitration will be more economical, expedient, skilled, and impartial. As discussed at length in Chapter 5, most of these justifications are not necessarily true.

3. Chinese Legal Tradition

As Stanley B. Lubman says, "attempting to capture the imprint of history on China can be a truly dismaying enterprise. The history is long; the languages are different; the cultural distances between Westerners and Chinese are vast and their perspectives on each other complex."[99] Hence, no such attempt is made here. There are, however, a few historical facts that need to be highlighted. The first one is that Chinese indigenous conceptions of law and legal institutions are as old, sophisticated, and important as the two major legal traditions of the West: common law and civil law.[100] "China's true legal history, as the precedents upon which Confucius based his philosophy of proper behavior and proper governance were set during the Western Zhou period, which dates from 1100 BCE to around 771 BCE."[101] The Confucian Code was the ideological foundation of Chinese societies for millennia,[102] and continues to impact laws and institutions even after China came in contact with the Western world.[103]

98. *Id.* at 15.

99. Stanley B. Lubman, Bird in a Cage: Legal Reform in China after Mao 3–4 (1999).

100. *See* John W. Head & Yanping Wang, Law Codes in Dynastic China: A Synopsis of Chinese Legal History in the Thirty Centuries from Zhou to Qing 3–4 (2005).

101. *Id.* at 9.

102. *See* James M. Zimmerman, China Law Deskbook: A Legal Guide to Foreign-Invested Enterprises 36–38 (3d ed. 2010).

103. *See* James A.R. Nafziger & Ruan Jiafang, *Chinese Methods of Resolving International Trade, Investment, and Maritime Disputes*, 23 Willamette L. Rev. 619, 624 (1987) ("Today, the Chinese continue to be concerned about the propriety and attitudinal change just as they are intent on rapidly developing formal law.").

The existing Chinese law is, however, a product of both internal and external influences. The external influences including extraterritorial privileges that Western powers imposed through unequal treaties after the so called "Opium War" of 1839–1842, Marxism-Leninism, and post-1978 investment related modern legal reforms.[104]

Traditionally mediation and conciliation[105] played a prominent role in Chinese society.[106] The existing legal apparatus is highly influenced by the long-standing cultural preference for the dissolution of disputes rather than resolution of them after they arise.[107] The modern Civil Procedure Code's emphasis on conciliation seems unusual. For example, the trial court is authorized to offer conciliation right before it renders its final judgment.[108] In fact, even the appellate courts may offer conciliation.[109] Similarly, under the existing PRC Arbitration Law,[110] arbitral tribunals are authorized to conduct mediation or conciliation even after they have heard all the evidence and are ready to render an award.[111]

104. *See* ZIMMERMAN, *supra* note 102, at 41 *et seq.*

105. Under Chinese law mediation and conciliation seem to refer to the same process, and the terms are used interchangeably. *See* Jingzhou Tao, *Arbitration in China, in* INTERNATIONAL COMMERCIAL ARBITRATION IN ASIA 40 n.54 (Philip McConnaughay & Thomas B. Ginsburg eds., 2d ed. 2006).

106. A regularly invoked Chinese saying is that "it is better to be vexed to death than to bring a law suit." The English version of this saying is quoted in Urs Martin Lauchli, *Cross-Cultural Negotiations, With a Special Focus on ADR with the Chinese,* 26 WM. MITCHELL L. REV. 1045, 1062 (2000). It is also quoted in Carlos de Vera, *Arbitrating Harmony: "Med-Arb" and the Confluence of Culture and Rule of Law in the Resolution of International Commercial Disputes in China,* 18 COLUM. J. ASIAN L. 149 (2004); also quoted in Robert F. Utter, *Dispute Resolution in China,* 62 WASH. L. REV. 283, 384–85 (1987). By 1987, China had created the world's largest mediation system with 6 million certified mediators mediating cases ranging from family affairs in the villages to modern business disputes. *See* Jun Ge, *Mediation, Arbitration and Litigation: Dispute Resolution in the People's Republic of China,* 15 UCLA PAC. BASIN L.J. 122, 123–24 (1996).

107. Stanley B. Lubman and Gregory Wajnowski say that "[a] striking feature of Chinese commercial behavior is the desire . . . to avoid acknowledging that a serious dispute exists at all, not only due to the cultural patterns, and the Chinese bureaucratic habits but due also to a genuine desire to make disputes 'disappear.'" Stanley B. Lubman & Gregory Wajnowski, *International Commercial Dispute Resolution in China: A Practical Assessment,* 4 AM. REV. INT'L ARB. 107, 115 (1993).

108. "At the end of the court debate, a judgment shall be made according to law. Where conciliation is possible prior to rendering the judgment, conciliation efforts may be made; if conciliation fails, a judgment shall be made without delay." Civil Procedure Law of the People's Republic of China (promulgated by Order No. 44 of the President of the People's Republic of China, Apr. 9, 1991), art. 128 (hereinafter PRC Civil Procedure Law).

109. PRC Civil Procedure Law, art. 155 ("In dealing with a case on appeal, a people's court of second instance may conduct conciliation.").

110. For the history of the development of the Chinese arbitration law, *see* generally, JINGZHOU TAO, ARBITRATION LAW AND PRACTICE IN CHINA 2–22 (3d ed. 2012).

111. Arbitration Law of 1995 of the People's Republic of China (promulgated by Order No. 31 of the President of the People's Republic of China, Aug. 31, 1994), art. 51 (hereinafter the "Arbitration Law of 1995") (". . . [A]n arbitration tribunal may first attempt to conciliate. If the parties apply for

A notable Chinese scholar comments on another distinguishing feature of Chinese arbitration law as follows:

> [W]here Chinese law applies, equitable principles will, of necessity, be followed by operation of law. In that respect, many fundamental Chinese statutes expressly provide for the application of equitable principles . . . It can therefore be said that by virtue of the principles of equity embodied in numerous fundamental Chinese statues, arbitrators apply not merely the relevant provisions of Chinese law but also operate to a certain extent as *amiable compositeurs* . . . whilst in many countries the determination of arbitral disputes may, with the authorization of the parties, be effected purely on a basis of *ex aequo et bono,* it must be effected in Chinese arbitration in accordance with the law, which through its embodiment of equitable principles, permit arbitrators to act as *amiable compositeurs* without the authorization of the parties."[112]

China has made a deliberate effort to modernize its laws by acceding to the relevant international conventions and adopting a piece of modern arbitration legislation.[113] The Supreme People's Court supported the development by issuing numerous arbitration-friendly interpretations.[114] Most notably, the SPC requires lower courts to report to the higher courts including ultimately to the SPC whenever they deny recognition of enforcement of a foreign award.[115] China's acceptance of international arbitration as a means of resolving disputes with its foreign economic partners is a part of its opening up and a condition of doing business across regions.[116] The SPC support for arbitration must be understood in that context.

4. African Legal Tradition

The dominant narrative about the historical development of international arbitration in Africa is neatly presented by Jan Paulsson as follows:

> As most African States awoke to independence in the 1960s, it became clear that the colonial epoch had not done much good for arbitration. "Alternative dispute resolution" in colonial Africa means customary law, and the issue was

conciliation voluntarily, the tribunal shall conciliate. If conciliation is unsuccessful, an award shall be made promptly. When a settlement agreement is reached by conciliation, the arbitration tribunal shall prepare the conciliation statement or the award on the basis of the results of the settlement agreement. A conciliation statement shall have the same legal force as that of an award.

112. Tao, *supra* note 110, at 115–16.

113. *See id.* at 8–18.

114. *Id.* at 18–22.

115. *See id.* at 18–19. For the same proposition and a brief description of the hierarchy and function of Chinese courts, *see* Kidane, *supra* note 25, at 176–77, 248–60.

116. *See* Kidane, *supra* note 25, at 72–73, 165–88.

> how the institutions of the metropolitan power might tolerate or even accommodate such form of traditional law in the interstices of a Western superstructure which remained utterly alien to most Africans. To the extent that the metropolitan system exported its ideas of arbitration under the colonial law, it was retrograde. The great jurisprudential and legislative developments in France were yet to come, and the English law of arbitration was complex in its heterogeneous sources and cumbersome in practice; a constant to-and-fro between arbitrators and courts. As for Portugal and Spain, the less said the better; the Salazar and Franco dictatorships, averse to any notion of sharing authority with unfettered "pirate justice", had no time for arbitration at home—and even less so in the subjugated colonies.
>
> As they confronted the challenges of nation-building, the new African States had other priorities. The Anglophones kept antiquated colonial statues on their books. The Francophones were not necessarily attuned to the path-breaking cases that were being decided in Paris—and to the extent they did, may well have resisted them on political grounds. After all, the prominent doctrine of the day had more to do with Marxism than with globalizing free markets.[117]

Paulsson's perspective in these remarks appears to be limited to the development of modern arbitration laws in Africa and does not capture the imprint of complex historical circumstances that contributed to the development or lack thereof. As Professor René David writes: "The colonial powers did declare, as a matter of principle, their intention to respect customary law, but the actual measure implemented with a view to guaranteeing its application resulted in its complete deformation."[118] What happened in Africa is, thus, more than a lack of interest in graceful copying.

Historically, as Dr. Amazu A. Asouzu notes in his seminal work, *International Commercial Arbitration and African States*, "Negotiation, arbitration and other extra-judicial institutions for the settlement of disputes are not entirely an innovation of the European imperial powers. Arbitration and conciliation proceedings were and are of frequent occurrence and importance in African society."[119] Eugene Amissah and Austin N.E. Cotran, in their work, *Arbitration in Africa*, also say: "[A]rbitration and alternative dispute-settlement processes were not introduced to Africa by the colonial administrations that largely governed the continent in the 19th and early 20th Centuries. African societies knew and made use of them in their customary machinery of government and judicial processes."[120]

117. Jan Paulsson, *Forward* to ARBITRATION IN AFRICA: A PRACTITIONER'S GUIDE, at xlv (Lise Bosman ed. 2013).

118. RENÉ DAVID & JOHN E.C. BRIERLEY, MAJOR LEGAL SYSTEMS OF THE WORLD TODAY: AN INTRODUCTION TO THE COMPARATIVE STUDY OF LAW 561 (3d ed. 1985).

119. AMAZU A. ASOUZU, INTERNATIONAL COMMERCIAL ARBITRATION AND AFRICAN STATES: PRACTICE, PARTICIPATION AND INSTITUTIONAL DEVELOPMENT 116–17 (2001).

120. Eugene Cotran & Austin N.E. Amissah, *Preface* to ARBITRATION IN AFRICA, at xx (Eugene Cotran & Austin N.E. Amissah eds., 1996).

But this does not complete the story. African states have been active players in the international arbitration world since the 1970s Libyan old cases, which are rightfully called the "founding cases."[121] Indeed at least 20 percent of all ICSID cases to date have involved African states.[122] However, the participation of the Africans in decision-making was limited to nominating their arbitrator in a process that they often dreaded.[123]

To the extent courts anywhere in Africa confronted modern international arbitration matters, although it is difficult to make any generalizations about them, it has been less than enthusiastic, to say the least. Most arbitral decisions are not published, making an accurate assessment difficult; however, *Salini v. Ethiopia*[124] offers an excellent example of almost every aspect of Africa's complex contemporary relationship with international arbitration. This section presents a detailed discussion of every aspect of this decision as it also advances the central claim of this book.

a. Case Study 1

i. The Parties, the Tribunal, and the Dispute

The award discussed in great detail hereunder captions the parties as *Salini Construttori S.p.A. (Claimant) v. The Federal Democratic Republic of Ethiopia, Addis Ababa Water and Sewerage Authority (Ethiopia) (Respondent)*. The award itself is captioned as "Award Regarding Suspension of the Proceedings and Jurisdiction." It was rendered on December 7, 2001.[125] The claimant is an Italian company based in Rome. Although the identity of the respondent was contested, the award lists it as the Federal Democratic Republic of Ethiopia, Addis Ababa Water and Sewerage Authority. The claimant was represented by Professor Antonio Crivellaro of Bonelli Erede Pappalardo, and the respondent was represented by Eric A. Schwartz of the Paris office of Freshfields.[126]

The claimant, Salini, commenced the arbitral proceeding on August 12, 1999, by filing a request for arbitration with the International Chamber of Commerce International Court of Arbitration (the "ICC Court")[127] pursuant to Article 4 of the ICC Rules then in force.[128] With the Partial Award under discussion rendered on

121. Dezalay & Garth, *supra* note 28, at 65.

122. *See* Kidane, *The China-Africa Factor in the ICSID Legitimacy Debate, supra* note 40, at 562 (citing *The ICSID Caseload—Statistics (Issue 2012-1)*, 11 (2012), https://icsid.worldbank.org/apps/ICSIDWEB/resources/Documents/2012-1%20%20-%20English.pdf).

123. See Kidane, *supra* note 40, at 602–03.

124. Salini Construttori S.p.A. v. The Federal Democratic Republic of Ethiopia, Addis Ababa Water & Sewerage Authority, ICC Arbitration No. 10623/AER/ACS (ICC Int'l Ct. Arb.), http://www.italaw.com/documents/Salini_v._Ethiopia_Award.pdf (last visited October 2, 1016) [hereinafter Partial Award, Salini v. Ethiopia].

125. *Id.* at cover.

126. *Id.* ¶¶ 1–2.

127. *Id.* at 3.

128. This was under the ICC Rules that came into effect on January 1, 1998. ICC—International Chamber of Commerce Arbitration Rules 1998, art. 4, Lex Mercatoria, at http://www.jus.uio.

December 7, 2001, the jurisdictional issues, that will be discussed later, effectively took nearly two-and-a-half years to resolve.

The dispute arose out of an August 1996 FIDIC[129] contract between the contractor, Salini, and the employer, the Addis Ababa municipality, for the construction of an emergency raw water sewerage reservoir for the city of Addis Ababa together with a 10 km transmission pipe to an existing water treatment facility for a total of US$ 30,627,266.41 to be completed within 22 months as of September 14, 1996.[130]

A commencement order made according to the contract required the contractor to commence work on September 14, 1996. The 22-month period having passed without work completion, the contactor initiated the arbitral tribunal on August 12, 1999, under Clause 67 of the General Conditions of Contract, which purported to incorporate the ICC Rules by reference.[131] The pertinent part reads: "amicable settlement has not been reached within the period stated in Sub-Clause 67.2 . . . shall be finally settled, unless otherwise specified in the Contract, under the Rules of Conciliation and Arbitration of the International Chamber of Commerce by one or more arbitrators appointed under such Rule."[132]

The Special Conditions of Contract on the other hand contained the following dispute settlement provision under Clause 67:

> Settlement of Dispute—Arbitration
>
> Add the following new sub clause to 67.3 of Part I.
>
> 67.3.1 The place of arbitration shall be Addis Ababa, Ethiopia
>
> 67.3.2 The language of arbitration shall be English
>
> 67.3.3 The substantive law(s) applicable shall be the Ethiopian law
>
> 67.3.3 The rules for arbitration shall be the Civil Code of Ethiopia under Article 3325 et. seq.[133]

no/lm/icc.arbitration.rules.1998/. The ICC Rules were amended in January 2012. ICC Rules of Arbitration, (in force as from January 1, 2012), http://www.iccwbo.org/products-and-services/arbitration-and-adr/arbitration/icc-rules-of-arbitration/. The new rules made no changes that would have affected this case.

129. The General Conditions and Special Conditions of Contract that the parties signed were taken from the Fourth Edition (1987) of the Conditions of Contract for Works of Civil Engineering Construction published by the Fédération Internationale des Ingenieurs-Conseils (FIDIC). *See* Partial Award, Salini v. Ethiopia, ¶ 9.

130. Partial Award, Salini v. Ethiopia, ¶ 7. It must be noted again that the exact identity of the respondent is disputed. *See id.* at n.1. What is not disputed is that the Addis Ababa municipality, namely the Water and Sewerage Authority, is the employer. The dispute pertains to the question of whether its conduct could be attributed to the Ethiopian state, thereby making the Ethiopian state a party to the proceeding, which the tribunal interestingly answered in the affirmative. *See* Sec. (a)(ii)(1) infra.

131. Partial Award, Salini v. Ethiopia, ¶ 11.

132. *Id.* (quoting Sec. 67.3(b) of the General Conditions of Contract).

133. Reproduced in *id.* ¶ 12.

In the Request for arbitration, the claimant sought a total of US$ 26,700,000 in damages for breach of contract plus costs and interest. Opting for a three-arbitrator panel, the claimant nominated Professor Piero Bernardini as arbitrator.[134] The respondent objected to the ICC arbitration, arguing that the parties' agreement under Section 67 of the Special Conditions of Contract called for ad hoc arbitration under the selected Ethiopian Civil Code provisions.[135] The respondent's objection to the ICC arbitration was based on the argument that the Special Conditions of

134. *Id.* ¶ 14.

135. *Id.* ¶ 16. These are provisions of the Civil Code of the Empire of Ethiopia 1960, which is still in effect. Civil Code of the Empire of Ethiopia, art. 3329–3336 (Eth.) (hereinafter the Ethiopian Civil Code). The most pertinent provisions are reproduced here for convenient reference. It is important to note that the tribunal does not reproduce or even cite to these provisions in the entire award.

Art. 3329.—Interpretation.
The provisions of the arbitral submission relating to the jurisdiction of the arbitrators shall be interpreted restrictively.

Art. 3330.—*Scope of jurisdiction.*
(1) The arbitral submission may authorize the arbitrator to decide difficulties arising out of the interpretation of the submission itself.
(2) It may in particular authorize the arbitrator to decide disputes relating to his own jurisdiction.
(3) The arbitrator may in no case be required to decide whether the arbitral submission is or is not valid.

Art. 3331.—*Appointment of arbitrator—1. By the parties.*
(1) The arbitrator may be appointed either in the arbitral submission or subsequently.
(2) The submission may provide that there shall be one arbitrator or several arbitrators.
(3) Where the submission fails to specify the number of arbitrators or the manner in which they shall be appointed, each party shall appoint one arbitrator.

Art. 3332.—2. *By the arbitrators or by the court.*
(1) Unless otherwise provided, where there is an even number of arbitrators they shall, before assuming their functions, appoint another arbitrator who shall as of right preside the arbitration tribunal.
(2) Where their number is odd, the arbitrators shall appoint the president of the arbitration tribunal from among themselves.
(3) Failing agreement between the arbitrators, the appointments provided in sub-art. (1) and (2) shall be made by the court at the request of one of the parties.

Art. 3333.—3. *Procedure for appointment.*
(1) Where necessary, the party availing himself of the arbitral submission shall specify the dispute he wishes to raise and appoint an arbitrator.
(2) Notice thereof shall be given to the other party and, where appropriate, to the person entrusted with the appointment of an arbitrator under the arbitral submission.

Art. 3334.—4. *Time-limit.*
(1) Where the other party or the person required to appoint an arbitrator fails to do so within thirty days, the court shall appoint such arbitrator.
(2) The time-limit shall run from the day when the notice provided in Art. 3333 (2) reached its destination.
(3) Modifications to these rules may be provided in the arbitral submission.

Contract (SCC), which ranks higher in the order of contractual instruments over the General Conditions of Contract (GCC), had replaced the model provision contained in the GCC, which selects ICC arbitration by selecting ad hoc arbitration under the Ethiopian Civil Code.[136] Despite the respondent's objection, the ICC Court took on the matter by application of the claimant and decided that the tribunal should be constituted and deal with the jurisdictional dispute itself.[137]

After the ICC Court decided to move the ICC arbitration forward by confirming the claimant's nominee, the respondent nominated Dr. Nael Bunni. Subsequently, Dr. Bunni of Ireland, the respondent's appointee, and Professor Berbardini of Italy, the claimant's appointee, elected Professor Emmanuel Gaillard of France as chairman.[138]

The tribunal then quickly moved to establish the Terms of Reference. The Terms of Reference had an unusual importance because the tribunal later used it to justify an unwise decision. The critical problem that led to the complication of the whole issue of jurisdiction was the tribunal's insistence on conducting the hearing in Paris rather than in Addis Ababa. Although Addis Ababa was selected as the seat of the arbitration, the *draft* Terms of Reference provided:

> 38. In accordance with Sub-Clause 67.3.1 of the Contract, added by the Conditions of the Particular Application, Addis Ababa (Ethiopia) is the place of arbitration.
>
> 39. However, the Arbitral Tribunal may decide to conduct hearings or meetings at any other appropriate place. Neither such decision nor the participation of the parties in any such hearing shall be construed as a departure from the choice of Addis Ababa as the place of arbitration.
>
> 40. Irrespective of the place of signing the award(s) shall be deemed to have been made in Addis Ababa (Ethiopia).[139]

Art. 3335.—5. *Equality of Parties.*
The arbitral submission shall not be valid where it places one of the parties in a privileged position in regards to the appointment of the arbitrator.

Art. 3336.—*Default of arbitrator.*—1. *Replacement.*
(1) Where an arbitrator refuses his appointment, dies, becomes incapable or resigns, he shall be replaced by the procedure prescribed for his appointment, in accordance with the provisions of the preceding Articles.
(2) Where an arbitrator is disqualified or removed, the new arbitrator shall be appointed by the court.
(3) The provisions of this Article may be modified by agreement between the parties.

136. Partial Award, Salini v. Ethiopia, ¶ 16. Clause 67.3 of the GCC says "unless specified in the contact." The Respondent argued that the SCC specified the Ethiopia Civil Code provisions, which meant ad hoc arbitration.

137. *Id.* ¶ 18.

138. *Id.* ¶¶ 20–21.

139. *Id.* ¶ 26.

The representatives of the parties signed the Terms of Reference on February 17, 2000, having made certain modifications to the draft.[140] The Terms of Reference also summarized the parties' arguments and the issues to be determined by the tribunal. The claimant's allegations of breach of contract included lack of provision of appropriate design and materials, delay in payment for works done, and other miscellaneous matters. The respondent focused its arguments on the lack of jurisdiction. It argued that it never agreed to arbitrate under the ICC Rules.[141] On the basis of the parties' submission, the Terms of Reference listed the issues as follows:

> (i) Whether the Arbitral Tribunal has jurisdiction in respect of this arbitration.
> (ii) If the Arbitral Tribunal does have jurisdiction, whether the Claimant is entitled to any relief in respect of its claim and, if so, in what amount.
> (iii) Whether interest is payable on any amount awarded by the Arbitral Tribunal and, if so, in what amount.
> (iv) The extent to which each Party should bear the costs of this arbitration.[142]

With respect to location of the hearing, as the tribunal quoted in the Partial Award, the signed Terms of Reference say:

> 44. In accordance with Sub-Clause 67.3.1 of the Contact, added by the Conditions of Particular Application, Addis Ababa (Ethiopia) is the place of arbitration.
>
> 45. However, the *Arbitral Tribunal may, after the consultation of the parties, decide* to conduct hearings or meetings at any other appropriate place. Neither such decision nor the participation of the parties in any such hearing shall be construed as a departure from the choice of Addis Ababa as the place of this arbitration.
>
> 46. Irrespective of the place of signing, the award(s) shall be deemed to have been made in Addis Ababa (Ethiopia).[143]

After the Terms of Reference were duly signed, the respondent asked the tribunal to decide the jurisdictional issue first; however, "[t]he Tribunal decided, after hearing the parties at the procedural meeting on February 17, 2000, immediately following the agreement and signature of the Terms of Reference, that the jurisdiction issue would not be considered as a preliminary issue but would be decided with the merits."[144] It then set up the procedural timetable asking the parties to submit

140. *Id.* ¶ 29.

141. *Id.* ¶¶ 30–32.

142. *Id.* ¶ 33 (citation omitted).

143. *Id.* ¶ 34 (emphasis added).

144. *Id.* ¶ 38.

memorials on both the jurisdictional issues and the merits.[145] This unexplained merger of the jurisdictional issue with the merits clearly upset the respondent for reasons that will be further explained later. Despite that upset, the respondent continued to follow all the procedural rules and submitted all the required memorials and evidence over a period of time that extended to about a year.[146]

Once the date of the evidentiary hearing had been agreed to, the respondent asked the tribunal to hold the hearing in Addis Ababa, arguing that "the choice of Addis Ababa as the place of arbitration created a presumption in favor of Addis Ababa as the venue for the hearing and there were no compelling considerations of convenience to overcome that presumption. To the contrary, there were good reasons to hold the hearing in Addis Ababa: (i) it would allow the Arbitral Tribunal to make a visit to the site of the project; and (ii) there were no obvious alternative venues to Addis Ababa."[147] The claimant objected to this and proposed Paris to be the venue of the hearing because "the majority of the participants in the hearing were based in Europe."[148] After so many exchanges of letters, despite the respondent's very strong objection,[149] the tribunal decided that Paris should be the venue of the hearing. In its own words:

> 15. Under Articles 44–46 of the Terms of Reference, the Tribunal is empowered to decide to hold hearings or meetings at appropriate places other than Addis Ababa, without prejudice to Addis Ababa remaining the place of the arbitration.
>
> 16. The Tribunal has carefully considered the parties' submissions regarding the appropriate venue for the hearings. The Tribunal has decided that it is more appropriate to hold the hearings, including the hearing on jurisdiction, in Paris.
>
> 17. In reaching this decision, the Tribunal has taken particular account of the fact that the majority of the participants in the hearing are based on Europe. Given the significant travel time to Addis Ababa, and the relative difficulty of coordinating travel arrangements for the non-Ethiopian party, counsel, the arbitrators, and particularly the non-Ethiopian witnesses, it will greatly simplify matters if the hearings take place in Paris. This is especially the case given the Respondent's estimation that the hearing might take up to 10 days.[150]

The respondent, already enraged by the tribunal's decision to delay the jurisdictional decision by two years until it had the opportunity to hear the merits, did

145. *Id.* ¶ 39.

146. *Id.* ¶¶ 40–49.

147. *Id.* ¶ 48(c).

148. *Id.* ¶ 49(c).

149. *Id.* ¶ 54 ("In a letter dated January 12, 2001, the Respondent expressed its strong objections to holding the hearing anywhere other than in Addis Ababa.").

150. *Id.* ¶ 60.

not appreciate the tribunal's decision to conduct the evidentiary hearing in Paris because of the stated reason of the convenience of the members of the tribunal and the claimant's counsel and witnesses. The tribunal summarized the respondent's outrage in the following mild terms:

> The same day, February 7, 2001, the Respondent sent a letter to the Arbitral Tribunal that strongly criticized the Tribunal's decision to hold the upcoming hearing in Paris. The Respondent asserted that the decision was evidence of a lack of impartiality on the part of the decision-makers, that the Tribunal was insensitive to the legitimate concerns and expectations of the Respondent, and that the Tribunal had accorded greater weight to the Claimant's and the Tribunal's own convenience over that of the Respondent. The Respondent also complained about the Tribunal's decision not to hear jurisdiction as a preliminary issue and suggested that this indicated a lack of fair-mindedness or impartiality on the Tribunal's part.[151]

The tribunal defended its decision by relying on the Terms of Reference in which the parties agreed that the tribunal may decide the place of hearing, after consultation with the parties.[152]

The respondent's frustration having grown, it challenged all three arbitrators before the ICC Court on grounds of failure to act "fairly and impartiality" contrary to Article 12 of the ICC Rules, as well as abuse of discretion.[153] The ICC Court rejected the challenge outright.[154]

Frustrated even more, the respondent resorted to domestic court remedies. It petitioned the Addis Ababa Court of Appeal to review the ICC Court's decision of March 30, 2001, and also petitioned the Ethiopian Supreme Court to issue an injunction against the arbitral tribunal to temporarily suspend the proceedings until the appeal was determined.[155] The respondent also commenced a separate proceeding before the Federal First Instance Court of the Federal Democratic Republic of Ethiopia challenging the tribunal's jurisdiction in the matter.[156] Having reviewed the petition for injunction, the Supreme Court issued an injunction "suspending the arbitration and temporarily enjoining the Arbitral Tribunal from proceeding with the case."[157]

Because one of the issues for the injunction was the allegation that the tribunal "arbitrarily delayed" the decision on jurisdiction, the claimant asked the tribunal

151. *Id.* ¶ 62.

152. *Id.* ¶¶ 63–64.

153. *Id.* ¶ 68.

154. *Id.* ¶ 74.

155. *Id.* ¶¶ 75–76.

156. *Id.* ¶ 77.

157. *Id.* ¶ 78.

to decide the jurisdictional issue before the hearing on the merits on the written pleadings alone[158]—a position that had always been advocated by the respondent from the very beginning.

On the basis of the foregoing, the tribunal addressed the suspension and the jurisdictional issue in the Partial Award presently under discussion. Although the tribunal discussed the suspension issue first, the following discussion reverses the order and describes and comments on the jurisdictional decision before addressing the suspension decision.

ii. Competence-Competence

Professor Gaillard and his co-arbitrators Professor Bernardini and Dr. Bunni unleashed their theoretical and intellectual power to defend a set of indefensible principles and decisions. This section will address the tribunal's opinion on the question of jurisdiction as well as the priority of the Ethiopian Supreme Court's interference.

(1) Jurisdiction

As indicated above, the tribunal decided to defer the question of whether it was duly constituted according to the parties' agreement; in other words, whether or not it had jurisdiction, until the parties briefed the substantive merits of the case. That process took about two years. The tribunal never gave a valid reason for not deciding the jurisdictional issue first instead of asking the parties to incur all the expenses over a period of two years. Indeed, once the Ethiopian Supreme Court issued an injunction to suspend the arbitral proceedings, the claimant asked the tribunal to rule on its jurisdiction on the record as developed by then.[159] When asked about this suggestion, the respondent answered:

> In the circumstances, the Arbitral Tribunal obviously has no choice but to respect the Orders of the Ethiopian Supreme Court and, accordingly, to suspend the arbitration proceedings. The Claimant's proposed alternative of an early award on jurisdiction obviously is no longer feasible as it could not be effected without violating the Ethiopian Court's Order.[160]

The tribunal invited both parties for an oral hearing but in view of the Ethiopian Court's injunction, the respondent refused to attend the hearing and warned that the tribunal as well as the claimant would be held in contempt if they proceeded in disregard of the injunction. However, the tribunal decided to proceed with the hearing in the absence of the respondent and ruled on jurisdiction on the basis of the written submissions without hearing witnesses.[161] This made one of two alternative matters clear: either

158. *Id.* ¶ 80.

159. *Id.* ¶ 80.

160. *Id.* ¶ 82.

161. *Id.* ¶¶ 91–92 & 99 ("The Claimant had confirmed during its submissions on the suspension issue that the jurisdictional issue could be decided without hearing any witnesses. The Claimant had

the tribunal did not need to wait until it heard the merits of the case to decide on its own jurisdiction, or its ultimate jurisdictional decision without hearing witnesses was uninformed. In any case, the tribunal went on deciding the jurisdictional issue.

The core of the jurisdictional objection was based on the contractual instruments that the parties had signed. Whereas the SCC refers to arbitration under the Ethiopian Civil Code Articles 3325 et seq.,[162] which envisions ad hoc arbitration, the GCC refers to the ICC Rules with a notation "unless otherwise specified in the Contract." As it was otherwise specified in the Contract, the provisions of the GCC stood overridden. Furthermore, in the case of ambiguity, the provisions of the SCC prevail as a matter of the Contract itself.[163] The claimant basically argued that the ICC Rules expressly chosen must be given precedent. Had the parties chosen to eliminate them, they should have deleted them. Moreover, the two rules are not necessarily inconsistent.[164]

The tribunal quickly rejected the priorities argument by saying "the fact that the reference to the arbitration rules of the Civil Code of Ethiopia is contained in the Special Conditions of Particular Application, while the reference to the ICC Rules is contained in the General Conditions, is not, in itself, determinative. According to Clauses 2 and 3 of the Contract Agreement of August 7, 1996, the Special Conditions of Particular Application only takes priority over the General Conditions in the event that there are 'ambiguities or discrepancies.'"[165] Having said that there are no ambiguities, "[t]he Tribunal concludes that these two provisions must be read in a complementary way, so that the reference to the arbitration rules of the Civil Code of Ethiopia as local procedural rules supplements the choice of the ICC arbitration in Sub-Clause 67.3."[166]

This argument completely and perhaps deliberately ignores the main reason the parties argued about jurisdiction, which is the power of appointment of arbitrators and jurisdiction to supervise. Indeed, the tribunal failed to cite to the important provisions of the applicable Ethiopian law while maintaining the position on lack of ambiguity. It is unclear how the tribunal thought the Civil Code provisions and the ICC Rules could supplement rather than displace each other on the vital issues of contention. Consider, for example, the following provisions of the Ethiopian Civil Code:

> Art. 3329.—*Interpretation.*
> The provisions of the arbitral submission relating to the jurisdiction of the arbitrators shall be interpreted restrictively.

also confirmed that it did not need to make any oral submissions to supplement its written submission on this point.").

162. Ethiopian Civil Code, art. 3325–3346 (Eth.).

163. Partial Award, Salini v. Ethiopia, at ¶¶ 185–190.

164. *Id.* ¶¶ 191–202.

165. *Id.* ¶ 206; *see also* ¶ 214 (listing the priority of contractual instruments and showing SCC higher than GCC).

166. *Id.* ¶ 218.

Art. 3332.—2. *By the arbitrators or by the court.*

(1) Unless otherwise provided, where there is an even number of arbitrators they shall, before assuming their functions, appoint another arbitrator who shall as of right preside the arbitration tribunal.

(2) Where their number is odd, the arbitrators shall appoint the president of the arbitration tribunal from among themselves.

(3) Failing agreement between the arbitrators, the appointments provided in sub-art. (1) and (2) shall be made by the court at the request of one of the parties.

Art. 3342.—3. *Procedure.*

(1) An application for disqualification shall be made to the arbitration tribunal by a party before the giving of the award and as soon as such party knew of the grounds for disqualification.

(2) The parties may stipulate that the application for—disqualification be made to another authority.

(3) Where the application for disqualification is dismissed, this decision may be appealed against in court within ten days.

Art. 3343.—*Removal of arbitrator.*

Where an arbitrator, having accepted his appointment, unduly delays the discharge of his duty, the authority agreed upon by the parties, or in the absence of such agreement, the court, may remove the arbitrator on the application of either party.

If the above Ethiopian Civil Code provisions apply, the Ethiopian courts retain complete authority for default appointment and removal of arbitrators, which is the most important power. If the ICC Rules were to apply at all, which is to say even if they are not entirely displaced by the express selection of the Ethiopian Civil Code within the Special Conditions of Contract, the ICC Rules are institutional rules subordinated to the *lex arbitri loci*.

The ICC Rules have their own mechanism for the appointment and challenge of arbitrators. In regards to a challenge of arbitrator, the ICC Rules then in effect provide as follows:

Article 11—Challenge of Arbitrators

1. A challenge of an arbitrator, whether for an alleged lack of independence or otherwise, shall be made by the submission to the Secretariat of a written statement specifying the facts and circumstances on which the challenge is based.
2. For a challenge to be admissible, it must be sent by a party either within 30 days from receipt by that party of the notification of the appointment or confirmation of the arbitrator, or within 30 days from the date when the party making the challenge was informed of the facts and circumstances on which the challenge is based if such date is subsequent to the receipt of such notification.

3. The Court shall decide on the admissibility, and, at the same time, if necessary, on the merits of a challenge after the Secretariat has afforded an opportunity for the arbitrator concerned, the other party or parties and any other members of the Arbitral Tribunal to comment in writing within a suitable period of time. Such comments shall be communicated to the parties and to the arbitrators.[167]

These rules patently cannot *supplement* the Ethiopian Civil Code provisions that grant this power to the Ethiopian courts. The parties disputed jurisdiction precisely because the two sets of rules would have differing results. They are not complementary, but competing. Regardless, without citing to the appropriate provision of Ethiopian law and without hearing any witnesses, the tribunal concluded that the parties did indeed choose ICC arbitration, which meant it had jurisdiction.[168] Most notably, the tribunal disregarded the factual contentions because it said that it couldn't determine the facts in the face of conflicting witness statements.[169] Whereas the respondent's witness stated that the respondent expressly warned the claimant that it would not be awarded the contact if it insisted on an ICC arbitration, the claimant's witness said that it insisted on an ICC arbitration and the respondent accepted that.[170] The tribunal gave up on the facts and decided on the basis of the text itself, further calling into question its motives for delaying its jurisdictional decision until it had heard the evidence on the merits.

The jurisdictional decision came two years late without genuine justification. The tribunal's initial justification for delaying a ruling on jurisdiction was the development of the factual record, but it showed its capacity to rule on its own jurisdiction without the facts.[171] It could have done so at the very beginning. In any case, its decision on the law and the contract was also fundamentally wrong. It ignored the rules of priority on the grounds that it did not see ambiguities when the jurisdictional dispute itself was because of the ambiguity. It tried to reconcile rules the irreconcilability of which was the core of the dispute, as in the authority to appoint or disqualify. Eventually, it showed that it could have decided the jurisdictional issue without facts.[172] A close examination of the chosen Ethiopian Civil Code provisions reproduced above, the relevant ICC Rules, and the tribunal's decision suggest that the tribunal delayed the ruling on jurisdiction probably because it knew from the very beginning that it lacked jurisdiction, but did not want to give up jurisdiction for whatever reason. Indeed, by doing so, it ignored the applicable provision of the

167. ICC—International Chamber of Commerce Arbitration Rules 1998, *supra* note 128, at art. 11.

168. Partial Award, Salini v. Ethiopia, ¶ 263.

169. *Id.* ¶ 245.

170. *Id.* ¶¶ 241–262.

171. *Id.* ¶¶ 263–264.

172. *Id.* ¶¶ 263–264.

law that says: "The provisions of the arbitral submission relating to the jurisdiction of the arbitrators shall be interpreted restrictively."[173]

The tribunal reached this conclusion after devoting significant energy and time to justify its refusal to comply with the Ethiopian Supreme Court's order to suspend the proceedings.[174] The tribunal's analysis on the suspension issue is considered below.

(2) Court Interference

In the jurisdictional decision, the tribunal did not see any conflict between the Ethiopian Civil Code provisions that grant the Ethiopian courts the jurisdiction to decide on a challenge of arbitrators and those of the ICC Rules. It did, however, go on to disregard the injunction issued by the Supreme Court for the purpose of reviewing the ICC Court's decision on the challenge of all three arbitrators on grounds of bias, lack of impartiality, and abuse of discretion. It advanced many theories to justify this result.

(3) The Theories

The first theory was that the tribunal's primary duty was owed to the parties. It began by saying that "[t]his Tribunal is an ICC arbitral tribunal, constituted under the ICC Rules" by referring to its own decision on jurisdiction.[175] As an ICC Tribunal, it "has a discretion as to whether or not it should comply with [the Supreme Court's] order."[176] That is because "[a]n international arbitral tribunal is not an organ of the state in which it has the seat in the same way that a court of the seat would be. The primary source of the Tribunal's powers is the parties' agreement to arbitrate. An important consequence of this is that the Tribunal has a duty vis-à-vis the parties to ensure that their arbitration agreement is not frustrated. In certain circumstances, it may be necessary to decline to comply with an order issued by a court of the seat, in the fulfillment of the Tribunal's larger duty to the parties."[177] It said this although one of the parties did not invite or welcome the tribunal's own existence, let alone ask it to be duty-bound.

Recognizing that the notion of duty to the parties without any sovereign will is theoretically flawed, it went on writing: "Of course, this is not to say that a contract, including an arbitration agreement, has a validity that is independent of any legal order. Indeed, a contract derives its binding force from its recognition by one or more legal orders. However, an agreement to submit disputes to international arbitration is not anchored exclusively in the legal order of the seat of arbitration. Such agreements are validated by a range of international sources and norms extending beyond the domestic seat itself."[178] To justify this assertion, the tribunal cited to

173. Ethiopian Civil Code, art. 3329.

174. Partial Award, Salini v. Ethiopia, ¶¶ 121–124.

175. *Id.* ¶ 125.

176. *Id.* ¶ 127.

177. *Id.* ¶ 128.

178. *Id.* ¶ 129.

Article II of the New York Convention, which requires the recognition and enforcement of an arbitral agreement although Ethiopia was not a party to it.[179] The tribunal began by saying that its power came from some international sources, mainly the New York Convention but not the Ethiopian legal order, although the tribunal was sited there by agreement. It had to then address the Ethiopian legal order's existence outside of the New York Convention regime. It said:

> It should be noted that, although Ethiopia has not yet ratified or acceded to the New York Convention, it does recognize the validity of arbitration agreement under the provisions of the Civil Code of Ethiopia, which is a notable example of a modern statute of international arbitration. This renders moot, in many respects, the issue of Ethiopia's non-ratification of the New York Convention.[180]

It then concluded that "Given that all of these countries are prepared to recognize the validity of arbitration agreements that meet certain basic conditions, it is clear that the Arbitral Tribunal's duty in respect of the parties' arbitration agreement is not founded exclusively in the Ethiopian legal order."[181]

All of a sudden, a tribunal supposed to be supervised by the courts of the arbitral seat claimed superior authority that came from some international legal order originating out of the New York Convention, when it is not even applicable on account of the similarity of the principles contained in the domestic legal order that it disavows. This theory, apart from not answering the actual question of whether the Ethiopian courts have the jurisdiction under Ethiopian law to review the ICC Court's decision on the challenge of arbitrators, invented some sort of customary international law giving tribunals the power to ignore the authority of the courts of the seat of the tribunal.

The second theory that it relied upon was its own duty to render an award that is likely to be enforceable. The basic gist of this argument is that the tribunal should not be concerned about the possible refusal of enforcement by the Ethiopian courts of the tribunal's awards as long as there might be other countries that might be willing to enforce an award annulled in Ethiopia. For this, the tribunal relies on some old scholarly writings.[182] It also seems that the tribunal, although it does not cite it, was relying on the *Chromalloy* line of cases holding that an award annulled at the

179. *Id.* ¶¶ 130–131 (citing Article II(1) of the United Nations Convention on the Recognition and Enforcement of Foreign Arbitral Awards (June 10, 1958), http://www.newyorkconvention.org/) ("Each Contracting Party shall recognize an agreement in writing under which the parties undertake to submit to arbitration all or any differences which have arisen or which may arise between them in respect of a defined legal relationship, whether contractual or not, concerning a subject matter capable of settlement by arbitration.").

180. *Id.* ¶ 132.

181. *Id.* ¶ 134.

182. *Id.* ¶ 141.

seat of the arbitration may be enforced elsewhere under Article V of the New York Convention, which makes refusal to enforce optional when it says "may" rather than "shall."[183] This line of argument has since been largely revisited in such cases as *Termorio S.A.E.S.P. v. Electranta S.P.*[184] In this case, the D.C Circuit held:

> Furthermore, appellants are simply mistaken in suggesting that the Convention policy in favor of enforcement of arbitration awards effectively swallows the command of Article V(1)(e). A judgment whether to recognize or enforce an award that has not been set aside in the State in which it was made is quite different from a judgment whether to disregard the action of a court of competent authority in another State. "The Convention specifically contemplates that the state in which, or under the law of which, the award is made, will be free to set aside or modify an award in accordance with its domestic arbitral law and its full panoply of express and implied grounds for relief." Yusuf Ahmed Alghanim & Sons, 126 F.3d at 23; see also Karaha Bodas II, 364 F.3d at 287–88. This means that a primary State necessarily may set aside an award on grounds that are not consistent with the laws and policies of a secondary Contracting State. The Convention does not endorse a regime in which secondary States (in determining whether to enforce an award) *routinely second-guess the judgment of a court in a primary State, when the court in the primary State has lawfully acted pursuant to "competent authority" to "set aside" an arbitration award made in its country*. Appellants go much too far in suggesting that a court in a secondary State is free as it sees fit to ignore the judgment of a court of competent authority in a primary State vacating an arbitration award. *It takes much more than a mere assertion that the judgment of the primary State "offends the public policy" of the secondary State to overcome a defense raised under Article V(1)(e).*[185]

The tribunal did not have the opportunity to review this because this was decided after the award. In any case, it may not even have cared. But the theory that there exists some supranational system of international arbitration rooted in the New York Convention that binds even nonmembers is an indefensible academic theory ill-suited for the resolution of real disputes affecting real people.

Significantly, part of the tribunal's decision was not about the parties before it; it was academic in nature, and was mainly about the general well-being of international arbitration that the members of the tribunal felt the duty to preserve and defend. Consider the following paragraph.

> To conclude otherwise [to accept the court order to suspend would] entail a denial of justice and fairness to the parties and conflict the legitimate

183. *See generally*, Chromalloy Aeroservices Inc. v. Ministry of Def. of Republic of Egypt, 939 F. Supp. 907 (D.D.C.1996).

184. Termorio S.A.E.S.P. v. Electranta S.P., 487 F.3d 928 (D.C. Cir. 2007).

185. *Id.* at 937 (emphasis added).

> expectations they created by entering into an arbitration agreement. It would allow the courts of the seat to convert an international arbitration agreement into the dead letter with intolerable consequences for the practice of international arbitration more generally.[186]

Along the same lines, answering a question that it was never asked to determine, the tribunal added:

> More generally, if Respondents were able to stay the proceedings in this way, through applications made to the courts of the seat during the course of the proceedings, it would have disastrous consequences for international arbitration in general. It would create an intolerable precedent inviting parties to arbitration agreements to attempt to frustrate those agreements.[187]

The tribunal does not say why the Addis Ababa Water and Sewerage Authority should care about the impact of its case on international arbitration generally. The members of the tribunal considered themselves the guardians of the international arbitral order while at the same time claiming that their authority came from the parties' agreement and that they owed an obligation to the parties. The focus on the precedential impact is both disingenuous and irrelevant. It is disingenuous because it purports to be concerned about the parties when the parties could not agree on whether they agreed to arbitrate before the same tribunal unless, of course, by parties it is meant one of the parties. The consequences to the practice of international arbitration are totally irrelevant to the parties. Its only relevance is to the arbitrators, who considered themselves as the guardians of the system, not the parties.

The tribunal's use of authority was equally disingenuous and irrelevant. Instead of relying on the party-chosen applicable Ethiopian law, the tribunal went on relying on arbitral case law that the parties have never even mentioned or contemplated.[188]

The third theory ranks higher than the previous two by its irrelevance. It concerns a misidentification, misrepresentation, and misapplication of principles of public international law to a simple question of the allocation of competence between the courts of the seat and the arbitral tribunal. The theory is titled: "A State or State Entity Cannot Resort to the State's Courts to Frustrate an Arbitration Agreement." In the old days, the debate in international arbitration was whether state entities could be subject to arbitral decision-making. This was partly inspired by the French law's traditional resistance to subjecting local and state entities to arbitration.[189] To date, some jurisdictions prohibit the arbitrability of administrative contracts. For example, Egyptian law, before courts relaxed the prohibition in 1997, inspired by

186. Partial Award, Salini v. Ethiopia, ¶ 143.

187. *Id.* ¶ 154.

188. *See, e.g., id.* ¶ 145 (relying on a Brazilian case); *see also id.* at 57 n.68 (citing to a procedural order in some other case that the claimant supplied a copy of to the arbitral tribunal and the respondent).

189. *See, e.g.,* Delvolvé et al., *supra* note 89, at 4–5.

the French Civil Code, had imposed a prohibition on the arbitrability of administrative contracts. Even today, an administrative agency, such as a city municipality in charge of water and sewerage, must get approval from the ministry in charge of that department to subject the department to arbitration.[190] Subjecting an administrative agency to private decision-making was traditionally considered an affront to the sovereignty of state. Indeed, the Ethiopian Civil Code, drafted by the renowned comparatist René David, again inspired by the French Civil Code, seems to disallow the arbitrability of administrative contacts.[191] In fact, one of the reasons the claimant in this case insisted on an ICC arbitration might have been because it suspected that the Ethiopian courts would uphold that notion if asked to enforce the arbitration agreement. It is not clear from the Partial Awards whether the agency had waived the possible immunity by contract—which is very common.[192] In any case, consider the tribunal's extreme departure from this principle to the opposite direction. Simply put the tribunal's argument is that the Addis Ababa Water and Sewerage Authority is the Ethiopian state under public international law.[193]

By going to court to suspend the ICC arbitration, the respondent is impermissibly using its own courts to disavow an international obligation of sorts. Leaving alone the issue of attribution for now, consider further the tribunal's line of argument. First, it said, "by agreeing to the ICC Rules, the Respondent agreed that any challenge of the arbitrators would be decided by the ICC Court under Article 11(3) of the ICC Rules."[194] But when the question itself was who should decide whether the parties agreed to an ICC arbitration in the first place, the tribunal's reliance on its own jurisdictional decision that completely disregarded the domestic legal order, as well as the applicable law, boggles the mind, especially when it is advanced by respected members of the international arbitral community such as Gaillard.

In line with the same concept, the tribunal further said that "by entering into an ICC arbitration agreement, the Respondent equally agreed that the Arbitral Tribunal would have the power to determine whether it has jurisdiction."[195] However, the question was rather the role of the courts of the seat in deciding a challenge of arbitrators under the selected *lex loci arbitri.*

190. For a discussion of the state of Egyptian law and the condition of administrative contracts, *see* Kidane, *supra* note 25, at 373–74.

191. Article 315(2) of the Ethiopian Civil Code reads: "No arbitration may take place in relation to administrative contracts as defined in article 3132 of the civil code or in other case where it is prohibited by law in the civil procedure code." *See* Ethiopian Civil Code, art. 3132.

192. It is important to note that the status of the provision of the Ethiopian Civil Code that seems to exempt administrative contracts from arbitration is not without uncertainty in view of other provisions of the Ethiopian Civil Code, and is not regularly enforced by the courts. However, its genesis is very clear: it is rooted in the French Civil Code, René David being the principal drafter.

193. *See* Partial Award, Salini v. Ethiopia, ¶ 156 "([t]he Respondent as a state entity must be equated with the state itself for purposes of this analysis.").

194. *Id.* ¶ 159.

195. *Id.* ¶ 160.

To avoid answering that question, the tribunal regressed the analysis into the public international law domain by saying: "There is a substantial body of law establishing that a state cannot rely on its own law to renege on an arbitration agreement."[196] Ironically, all of a sudden, having sourced its power from the parties' agreement and some detached and disinterested international legal order, the tribunal renders the selected seat, its courts, and its laws not only irrelevant but also turns them into instruments of oppression. The respondent was turned from a municipality trying to build a city sewer system to a state that is using its laws and courts to oppress the innocent contractor. To show a pattern of behavior, the tribunal relies on arbitral case law involving the same parties, in which another tribunal said:

> International public policy would be strongly opposed to the idea that a public entity, when dealing with foreign parties, could openly, knowingly, and willingly, enter into an arbitration agreement, on which its contractor would rely, only to claim subsequently, whether during the arbitral proceedings or on enforcement of the award, that its own undertaking was void.[197]

The problem is that this passage is cited to support the proposition that a state may not use its laws to renege on an arbitration agreement. The passage clearly refers to an argument that relies on the Civil Code provision that restricts the arbitrability of administrative contracts to get out of an arbitration agreement altogether. It is unclear how that would support the conclusion that an arbitral tribunal may disregard a set of domestic laws selected by the parties and how appealing a decision on the basis of those laws amounts to using a state's law to renege on an arbitration agreement.

Continuing to engage in some more arbitral rule-making,[198] the tribunal finally stated its justification as follows:

> For the avoidance of doubt, we do not mean to suggest that any application by a state party to its own courts, in their capacity as the courts of the seat in arbitral proceedings, would be objectionable. The courts of the seat retain

196. *Id.* ¶ 161.

197. *Id.* ¶ 161 (citing the English translation of a French text).

198. *Id.* ¶¶ 165–167. Those paragraphs read as follows:

> 165. The question of whether a state can resort to its own courts, as opposed to its own law, to renege on an arbitration agreement that it has freely entered into, has not given rise to a similarly well-established body of case law. Nevertheless, the question is really in the same terms.
>
> 166. In effect, there is no difference between a state unilaterally repudiating an international arbitration agreement or changing its internal laws in an attempt to free itself from such an agreement, on the one hand, and a state going before its own courts to have the arbitral proceedings suspended or terminated (whether on the basis of alleged nullity of the arbitration agreement, alleged bias on the part of the arbitral tribunal, or some other ground), on the other hand. Both amount to the state reneging on its own agreement to submit disputes to international arbitration.

> their usual valid role in supervising arbitral proceedings. The problem arises in this particular case from the fact that a state entity is resorting to the state's own courts in an illegitimate effort to renege upon the arbitration agreement. It is unacceptable for a state party to invoke its own law in an effort to avoid the effect of an arbitration agreement that it has freely entered into. For similar reasons, it is unacceptable for a state party to resort to its own courts for the same purpose.
>
> [] These arbitral proceedings will not be suspended, notwithstanding the injunctions issued by the Federal Supreme Court and the Federal First Instance Court. Faced with the present situation, the Arbitral Tribunal will continue to prosecute these arbitral proceedings in accordance with its duty to the parties, in a manner consistent with their arbitration agreement.[199]

Although the tribunal relies on the New York Convention in a very interesting way, it never even cites, let alone explains away Article II(3) of the same Convention, which states:

> 3. The court of a Contracting State, when seized of an action in a matter in respect of which the parties have made an agreement within the meaning of this article, shall, at the request of one of the parties, refer the parties to arbitration, unless it finds that the said agreement is null and void, inoperative or incapable of being performed.[200]

This, of course, must have been the guiding principle in the allocation of competence. As discussed in Chapter 4, the chair of the tribunal belongs to the school of thought that limits the court's powers to a prima facie review, which is a respectable position, but he does not even accord that chance to the Ethiopian courts in the face of the well-founded submission that another arbitral tribunal, not the courts, may have jurisdiction in this case. As Eric Schwartz, the lawyer who represented the Ethiopian party later wrote:

> [T]he arbitral tribunal also failed in its Award to refer to any provision of Ethiopian law that precluded the Ethiopian party from submitting the question of the arbitral tribunal's jurisdiction to the Ethiopian courts in the manner that it did. Rather, the arbitral tribunal found that it was improper for the Ethiopian party to apply to the Ethiopian court because Article 6(2) of the ICC Rules of Arbitration authorizes the arbitral tribunal to decide upon

> 167. This principle does not depend in any way on a suggestion that the courts of a state would be unduly influenced by the executive power, would misapply the law in the interest of the state, or would otherwise act improperly. To the contrary, we naturally assume, both in general and specifically in this case, that the courts would strictly observe their duties and act in good faith.

199. *Id.* ¶¶ 176–178.

200. New York Convention, art. II(3).

> the matter of its own jurisdiction. However, given that the very issue to be decided was whether the parties had a right to apply to the court before, as in this case, the arbitral tribunal had made any such determination (which it had refused to do as a preliminary matter) depended upon Ethiopian law and not the ICC Rules.[201]

Put simply, "it is in principle not for the arbitrators to judge the judges, but rather the other way round."[202]

B. Africa's Dilemma in Summary

The *Salini* case is an excellent demonstration of Africa's worst nightmare. At the most basic level, for the ordinary observer who can read a case, a panel of three European arbitrators effectively rebuffed and insulted the Supreme Court of a sovereign state on the basis of an international power that they said emanated from the state's own consent expressed in an agreement one of its municipalities signed with a private contractor for the construction of a sewer system. The story does not end there: the three European arbitrators not only refused to be bound by the laws of the African state that the parties had chosen for them and refused to be supervised by the courts, but also accused the municipality of using its own courts to frustrate the arbitration agreement when all it did was go to court on a point of contract interpretation. Furthermore, the three European members of the tribunal not only refused to be supervised by this African court, but also refused to go to Africa for a hearing. Moreover, two more points demand emphasis. The first is the inappropriate and costly delaying of the jurisdictional decision, and the second is the overall justification of the arbitrators' conduct.

A close reading of the Partial Award clearly suggests that the respondent did not want to have an ICC arbitration. In a way, the Partial Award is a validation of its fear. An ICC arbitration meant three European arbitrators, possibly operating under all sorts of preconceptions about African states and African cities, possibly with the skill to justify any outcome, and possibly with the economic incentive to retain jurisdiction, possibly with the ideological bias in favor of the private party, possibly

201. Eric A. Schwartz, *Do International Arbitrators Have a Duty to Obey the Orders of the Courts of the Place of the Arbitration? Reflections on the Role of the* Lex Loci Arbiti *in the Light of a Recent ICC Award*, *in* Global Reflections on International Law, Commerce and Dispute Resolution 805 (Gerald Aksen et al. eds., 2005). The text continues:

> As the chairman of the arbitral tribunal has himself explained in his international arbitration treatise:
>
> > [H]ow can an arbitrator, solely on the basis of an arbitration agreement, declare that agreement to be void or even hear a claim to that effect? The answer is simple: the basis of the competence-competence principle lies not in the arbitration agreement, but in the arbitration laws of the country where the arbitration is held . . . .

Id.

202. *Id.* at 805 (quoting M. Scherer, *The Place or "Seat" of Arbitration*, ASA Bul. 112, 113–14 (2003)).

without the interest to learn the chosen African law and without having the cultural competence to understand the facts. These concerns keep African states up at night, and the *Salini* case validates their concerns.

Consider the jurisdictional issue further. There was no legitimate reason to delay it for two years until the merits were litigated. The only justification raised by the tribunal was that witnesses needed to be heard, and that the same witnesses might testify on both questions of jurisdiction and the merits. As it turned out, the tribunal's decision on jurisdiction did not need witnesses after all. The tribunal did indeed improperly merge the jurisdictional issue with the merits when it knew that there was a serious argument against its jurisdiction. This meant years of work and expense for the parties. Indeed, this also meant significant financial gains for all the players, including the institution, the arbitrators, and law firms on each side. There is no doubt that there was a legitimate jurisdictional objection to the ICC tribunal. The honorable course of action would have been to decide that issue as expeditiously as possible and allow whatever legitimate appeals process permissible under the law that the parties had chosen to take its course. The tribunal effectively sabotaged that.

The level of disregard for the African party was such that the tribunal refused to go to the seat of the arbitration, instead choosing to write a 82-page justification from Paris on how the parties granted it the discretion to stay in Paris in the Terms of Reference that they all signed.

A reasonable observer could relate to the outrage that the respondent felt when everything that it resented is justified in the name of its own consent. It went to court to see if it indeed consented to all of what the tribunal was saying, but the tribunal would not allow that. The tribunal found a way to justify the unjustifiable. When the profound 82-page Partial Award is reduced into ordinarily language, what it says to African states is to be careful of ICC arbitration in Paris. The arbitrators think *your courts do not work, your cities are inconvenient, you want to use your laws and courts to get out of your obligations*. Was the respondent justified in thinking that the arbitrators were not fair for delaying the jurisdictional decision and refusing to get out of Europe for a hearing? Was the respondent justified in thinking that there was some kind of incentivized bias? Such has been the nature of Africa's relationship with the world of international arbitration. Indeed, as the vice president of the International Court of Justice, Abdulqawi Ahmed Yusuf said in a keynote speech at a London seminar, held at Wilmer Hale in his honor, "judicial settlement is working with respect to African states. Arbitration—not so much."[203] Citing to indefensible ICSID statistics of appointment of African arbitrators, he surmises: "Imagine cases concerning the European Union countries, in which most of the arbitrators are Africans or Latin Americans? What would Europeans feel like?"[204] The next chapter will look at the theories and theoreticians of international arbitration.

203. Lacey Yong & Alison Ross, *Africa Must Have More Representation on Tribunals, Says Somali Judge*, 10 Global Arb. Rev. 2 (Oct. 15, 2015), http://globalarbitrationreview.com/news/article/34232/tribunals-need-africans-says-somali-judge/.

204. *Id.* at 2.

4

The Theories and Theoreticians of International Arbitration

As a supranational legal framework[1] that, when it works, commands the obedience of courts of sovereign states, international arbitration requires a credible theoretical justification. While a scant body of scholarly work by practitioners attempts to provide such theoretical justification,[2] courts of law of various legal traditions continue

1. The preponderance of the literature considers international arbitration "a system" rather than "a framework," and even expresses disappointment for lack of coherence in the substantive jurisprudence, especially as it relates to investment arbitration. *See, e.g.*, JAN PAULSSON, DENIAL OF JUSTICE IN INTERNATIONAL LAW 241 (2005) ("[T]he idea is not consistency at any cost, but respectable consistency."); Charles N. Brower & Stephan W. Schill, *Is Arbitration a Threat or a Boon to the Legitimacy of International Investment Law?*, 9 CHI. J. INT'L L. 471, 473–74 (2009) (suggesting that although inconsistency is currently a problem, the passage of time will lead to more uniform results); Susan D. Franck, *The Legitimacy Crisis in Investment Treaty Arbitration: Privatizing Public International Law through Inconsistent Decisions*, 73 FORDHAM L. REV. 1521, 1524 (2005) (proposing the creation of a permanent appellate body, enhanced transparency, and increased academic scrutiny in order to combat inconsistency); Jacques Werner, *Making Investment Arbitration More Certain: A Modest Proposal*, 4 J. WORLD INV. 767, 782–85 (2003) (endorsing an appellate level of review for investment arbitration decisions, and arguing that arbitrators should play an active role in consolidating proceedings or staying decisions where other arbitral panels have already issued an award). For more arguments along the same lines, *see* THE BACKLASH AGAINST INVESTMENT ARBITRATION: PERCEPTIONS AND REALITY (Michael Waibel et al. eds., 2010) and GUS VAN HARTEN, INVESTMENT TREATY ARBITRATION AND PUBLIC LAW (2007). However, Professor David Caron very instructively says that international investment arbitration (let alone commercial arbitration) is not a "system," it is a "framework," and to the extent there is some coherence in the jurisprudence, it is incidental. In his own words: "[International investment arbitration] is a framework in the same sense that municipal contract law provides a frame within which discrete and possibly unknown private arrangements are concluded." David D. Caron, *Investor State Arbitration: Strategic and Tactical Perspectives on Legitimacy*, 32 SUFFOLK TRANSNAT'L L. REV. 513, 513–16 (2009). The various theories are evaluated further in subsequent sections.

2. The academic literature on the theories of international arbitration is generally scant. For example, Gary Born's three-volume-4000-page treatise relies on just a handful of classical and contemporary authorities advancing various recognizable theories. Some English writings are

to puzzle over the boundaries of their authority vis-à-vis these privately constituted supranational determiners of fact and interpreters of their laws with legal effect within their domains.[3]

It took courts of law everywhere a while to begin to appreciate the justifications and develop the tolerance.[4] To be sure, defining the foundational parameters of this uncomfortable sharing of powers still remains a work in progress.

This chapter puts the theoretical justifications in cultural context and critically examines the dominant contemporary legal theories of international arbitration and their practical implications in the resolution of day-to-day transnational disputes.

A. THE THEORIES AND THEORETICIANS

International arbitration is essentially theorized and justified by practitioner-academics who are members of a prosperous epistemic community that stands to

added to a few French language works on the subject. The most prominent one is EMMANUEL GAILLARD, LEGAL THEORY OF INTERNATIONAL ARBITRATION (2010). Another one is ADAM SAMUEL, JURISDICTIONAL PROBLEMS IN INTERNATIONAL COMMERCIAL ARBITRATION (1989), and yet another one is an older work by Kenneth S. Carlston, *Theory of the Arbitration Process*, 17 L. & CONTEMP. PROBS. 631 (1952). *See* text accompanying 1 GARY BORN, INTERNATIONAL COMMERCIAL ARBITRATION (2014), 214–15 n.1527–1540. Another notable contribution, published after Gaillard's 2010 book and not cited in Born's treatise, is JAN PAULSSON, THE IDEA OF ARBITRATION (2013). Collectively, these works provide a sketch of the basic theories.

3. This broad area of the allocation of competence between the courts and arbitral tribunals is often discussed in the literature under the domain of competence-competence in connection with the notion of the severability of the arbitration agreement from the underlying agreement out of which a particular dispute might arise. The most serious theoretical question is: Who has the authority to decide jurisdictional disputes: the national courts or the arbitrators? The choice is often made by some form of hard law such as statutes and even treaties, but the most important question is what justifies such choice, which is one of the most important theoretical questions that this chapter explores. For a good technical analysis and references on the broad topic of competence-competence, *see* GARY B. BORN, INTERNATIONAL ARBITRATION: CASES AND MATERIALS 201–34 (2011). Two of the leading cases in this regard are the U.K. House of Lords case of Fiona Trust & Holding Co. v. Privalov [2007] UKHL 40 (HL) and the U.S. Supreme Court case, Buckeye Check Cashing, Inc. v. Cardegna, 546 U.S. 440 (2006). An equally important, but older one is the U.S. Supreme Court case, First Options of Chicago, Inc. v. Kaplan, 514 U.S. 938 (1995). Other notable cases include the Indian Supreme Court case, Shin-Etsu Chemical Co. v. Aksh Optifibre Ltd., [2005] 7 SCC 234, XXXI 2006 Y.B. COM. ARB. 747, and the *French Cour de cassation* case of (Cass.) Judgment of 7 December 1994, V 2000 (Formerly Jaguar France v. Project XJ 220 Ltd), 1997 Rev. arb. 537 (Fr.). Excerpts of all of these cases are reproduced in BORN, *supra*, at 201–34. The theoretical foundations of the cases are discussed in some detail in this chapter.

4. A notable example is the U.S. Supreme Court opinion in Mitsubishi Motors Corp. v. Soler Chrysler-Plymouth Inc., 473 U.S. 614 (1985), which is also discussed in some detail in this chapter.

profit from its widespread acceptance. This section critically examines some of the foremost theories by leading protagonists.

1. Emmanuel Gaillard's Theory

Professor Emmanuel Gaillard's *Legal Theory of International Arbitration* is perhaps one of the leading scholarly attempts at charting the legal theories of international arbitration.[5] In this book, Gaillard explores three possibilities before endorsing the last one: (1) International Arbitration Relegated to a Component of a Single National Legal Order, (2) International Arbitration Anchored in a Plurality of National Legal Orders, and (3) International Arbitration as an Autonomous Legal Order: The Arbitral Legal Order. Each one of his theories is examined below followed by a critique of his chosen theory.

a. International Arbitration Relegated to a Component of a Single National Legal Order

As a component of a single national order, the arbitrator's authority emanates from the national laws of the seat of the arbitration, and as such, "the seat is understood as a forum: the award's legal force stems exclusively from the law of the State where the arbitration took place. An award is not so much 'international' as it is 'Colombian' or 'English' because the arbitral proceedings were held in Colombia or in England."[6]

The philosophical postulate, as Gaillard describes, essentially rests on state positivism, which is predicated on the assumption that "[a]ny right stems from a given rule which in turn derives from another rule, in a perfect structure of which only the cornerstone remains a mystery."[7] He offers a good quote from Jean Francois Poudret and Sebastien Besson to illustrate the core idea:

> Without entering into a philosophical debate, we consider that the parties' will is necessarily based on a legal system from which it derives its validity. The *lex arbitrii* builds the foundation (*Grundnorm*) for the effectiveness of the arbitration agreement. Together with public international law, it constitutes one of the two potential bases for arbitration.[8]

5. Emmanuel Gaillard, Legal Theory of International Arbitration (2010).

6. *Id.* at 15.

7. *Id.* at 21.

8. *Id.* (quoting Jean Francois Poudret & Sebastien Besson, Comparative Law of International Arbitration 83 (2007)). He also relies on F.A. Mann for the same proposition: "Every right or power a private person enjoys is inexorably conferred by or derived from a system of municipal law which may conveniently and in accordance with tradition be called the *lex fori*, though it would be more exact (but also less familiar) to speak of the *lex arbitri* or, in French, *la loi de l'arbitrage*." *Id.* at 21–22 (quoting F.A. Mann, Lex Facit Arbitrum, *in* International Arbitration: *Liber Amicorum* for Martin Domke 160 (Pieter Sanders ed. 1967)).

Gaillard argues that this theory favors order over justice.[9] He considers it a matter of choice not of legal mandate. The following passage summarizes his position on this theory very well:

> In the current context of differing laws and diverging ways in which domestic courts apply those laws, the only valid question is whether a single law, irrespective of its degree of conservatism and the manner in which domestic courts decide to apply it, is entitled to govern an arbitration for the sole reason that it happens to be that of the country where the arbitration is taking or has taken place. In terms of order, the benefit is tangible. In terms of justice, hardly so. One simply has to consider the numerous situations in which the courts of the seat have developed idiosyncratic theories with a view to helping one of the parties to the arbitration, often a national of that country. Anti-suit injunctions will be addressed below. At this juncture, it suffices to observe that the centralizing conception of the source of the arbitrator's power to adjudicate belongs to a philosophical tradition that readily favors injustice over chaos.[10]

He adds an interesting footnote to this by saying: "This tradition, which is characteristic of the positive doctrine, is not entirely lacking in the natural law school of thought. On the notion that one may tolerate the application of an unfair rule to avoid a scandal or chaos."[11]

Admittedly, the fundamental impetus for rejecting the territorial or the national legal order approach is the perceived injustice that might befall the foreign party. To demonstrate the types of injustice that adherence to this theory might bring about, he discusses three cases all involving state entities or state-owned enterprises resorting to judicial remedy. He states his underlying assumption as:

> It is indeed tempting for a State, or a State-Owned entity, to renege on an arbitration agreement to which it freely consented by resorting to its own courts to have the other contracting party enjoined from initiating an arbitration against it, or if arbitration proceedings have already been initiated, from pursuing them.[12]

Not surprisingly the examples he gives involve state entities of developing countries such as Bangladesh, Indonesia, and Ethiopia.[13] The Bangladesh case involved an Italian contractor, Saipem SpA and a Bangladeshi state-owned company, Petrobangla. It was an ICC arbitration sited in Dhaka. The tribunal was composed

9. *Id.* at 24.

10. *Id.* (footnotes omitted).

11. *Id.* at 24, n. 73. (citation omitted).

12. *Id.* at 71.

13. *See id.* at 71–86.

of Werner Melis, chair, Riccardo Luzzatto, and Ian Brownlie.[14] Dissatisfied with the tribunal's procedural decision, Petrobangla obtained an injunction from the Supreme Court against the tribunal and the other party, but the tribunal disregarded and continued to make an award.[15] Because the Bangladesh courts refused to enforce the award, holding it invalid, the Italian company initiated a treaty claim before ICSID.[16] An ICSID tribunal composed of Gabrielle Kaufmann-Kohler, chair, Christophe Schreuer, and Philip Otton agreed with the ICC tribunal faulting the Bangladesh Supreme Court.[17] Without going into the details of these cases, it is sufficient to note the political dynamics: two tribunals, composed largely of prominent European jurists, rejecting the jurisdiction of the Supreme Court of a developing county on the theoretical grounds—at least in the manner Gaillard uses in this case—that the power of the arbitrators does not emanate from the national legal order but from some international legal order, which will be described later. But again, the foundational principle that overrides the positivist domestic legal order is justice to the foreign party.

Continuing the same conversation, consider the political reality of the Indonesian case that Gaillard relies on. The dispute arose out of a contract for the exploitation and development of geothermal resources between Himpurna California Energy Ltd, a Bermuda company, and the Republic of Indonesia.[18] The tribunal set up under the UNCITRAL Rules and seated in Jakarta was composed of Jan Paulsson, appointed chair by the ICSID secretary general, presumably because the two party-nominated arbitrators could not agree;[19] Antonino de Fina, the claimant's appointee; and Priyatna Abdurrasyid, an Indonesian national, the Indonesian government's appointee.[20] The tribunal decided to hear the case in The Hague, without officially moving the seat under Article 16 of the UNCITRAL Rules. The main point this case is cited for is that the majority of the tribunal refused to abide by the Indonesian court's order to suspend the proceedings.[21] Because the tribunal had moved the venue to The Hague, Indonesia petitioned The Hague Court of First Instance, which rejected the petition.[22] Two of the three arbitrators then went on

14. *Id.* at 79.

15. *Id.* at 79–80.

16. *Id.* at 80.

17. *Id.* at 79 (citing to ICC Case No. 7934, unpublished, described in the Decision on jurisdiction and provisional measures rendered on March 21, 2007 in ICSID Case No. ARB/05/07, Saipem SpA v. Bangladesh, International Arbitration Report, April 2007, p. B-1, and Award rendered on June 30, 2009 in ICSID Case No. ARB/05/7, Saipem SpA v. Bangladesh).

18. *Id.* at 81.

19. *Id.* at 81–82.

20. *Id.*

21. *Id.*

22. *Id.* at 81.

rendering an award in favor of the claimant "[a]fter recalling that States are responsible for the actions of their courts under international law."[23] The basis of the tribunal's decision was the principle of pacta sunt servanda and denial of justice.[24] The lawyer for the Indonesian government is reported to have expressed his frustration in the following terms:

> As to the content of the purported order, we are outraged that a tribunal sitting in a dispute governed by the law of Indonesia has deemed it unnecessary to give any consideration to such laws, and has deemed it appropriate not only to disregard an order of, but to issue official insults to, the courts of such jurisdiction.[25]

Furthermore, in an unsuccessful challenge submitted to the Secretary General of ICSID, which was the appointing authority in this case, lawyers for the Indonesian party said:

> [The President of the Tribunal][Jan Paulsson] is well known throughout the arbitration community to be in a constant crusade to elevate international arbitration, and thus the power of international arbitrators such as himself, to a level above and beyond the jurisdiction of any court in the world.[26]

Gaillard's third illustration is the *Salini v. Ethiopia*[27] case for which he served as the presiding arbitrator appointed by the ICC Court. His legal theory about the allocation of competence between the courts of the selected seat and the arbitral tribunal or tribunals is not dissimilar to Jan Paulsson's legal theory in the Indonesia case. As discussed at length in Chapter 3, the allocation of competence issue in the *Salini v. Ethiopia* case was not even who decided whether there was a valid arbitration

23. *Id.* (citing 2000 Y.B. Com. Arb. 469; also citing Jan Paulsson, Denial of Justice in International Law 150–53 (2005)).

24. *Id.* at 81–82. The tribunal said in particular:

> [C]onsidering that the purported injunction violates the Republic of Indonesia's undertakings in the Terms of Appointment by which the present international Arbitration Tribunal was established, whereas the sanctity of agreements is a fundamental rule of international law;
>
> Considering that to prevent an arbitral tribunal from fulfilling its mandate in accordance with procedures formally agreed by the Republic of Indonesia is a denial of justice.

Id. (citing *Award of September 26, 2009*, 2000 Y.B. Com. Arb. 109, 144 (quoting *Order of September 7, 1999*).

25. *Id.* at 82.

26. *Id.*

27. Salini Costruttori S.P.A. v. The Federal Democratic Republic of Ethiopia, Addis Ababa Water Sewerage Authority, ICC Arbitration No. 10623/AER/ACS (ICC Int'l Ct. Arb.), http://www.italaw.com/documents/Salini_v._Ethiopia_Award.pdf (last visited October 2, 2016) [hereinafter Partial Award, Salini v. Ethiopia].

agreement or not—that was conceded; the question was a more interesting one, namely, *who decides, who decides* [note that the repetition is not an error]—the court or the already instituted ICC arbitral tribunal—whether the ICC tribunal or a yet to be constituted ad hoc tribunal because of the ambiguity that existed as a result of reference to both in the agreement. The ICC tribunal, which was formed first, refused to defer that question to the court, and effectively usurped the power.[28] But consider how Gaillard, the tribunal's president, characterizes this case in his book written almost a decade later:

> ICC Case No. 10623 between the Italian company Salini Construttori SpA and the Federal Democratic Republic of Ethiopia provides a further example of an international tribunal considering itself not bound by an anti-suit injunction issued at the place of arbitration. The dispute concerned a FIDIC contract for the construction of a raw water sewerage reservoir for the city of Addis Ababa. The contract contained an arbitration clause providing for ICC arbitration in Addis Ababa. The Italian company, which had various claims, brought the dispute before an Arbitral Tribunal composed of Emmanuel Gaillard, President, Piero Bernardini and Nael Bunni.
>
> In accordance with the provisions of the Terms of Reference—already present in the applicable ICC Arbitration Rules—which expressly provided the possibility of conducting hearings at any location it considered appropriate, the Tribunal decided that the hearing in which certain witnesses would be heard would take place in Paris, while Addis Ababa was maintained as the seat of the arbitration. The Respondent, deeming that this constituted an illegitimate procedural decision, unsuccessfully challenged the arbitrators before the ICC International Court of Arbitration. The Respondent subsequently requested—and obtained—an anti-suit injunction from the Federal Supreme Court of Ethiopia which ordered the Arbitral Tribunal to immediately stay the proceedings until such time as the Court had rendered a decision relative to the ICC's dismissal of the challenge of the arbitrators.[29]

First, this description, perhaps deliberately, not only fails to provide context, but also misstates or omits important details. The most important one is the nature of the jurisdiction indicated above, that is, the jurisdictional conflict that prompted the court's interference is not between the court and the arbitral tribunal—which may be reconciled by applying the principle of competence-competence with a prima facie review of the absence of nullity, inoperability, or incapability of performance—but is about the allocation of competence between two possible arbitral tribunals.[30] That was the most important question. Gaillard's tribunal usurped competence not only from the court to decide on this issue of the allocation of competence not as

28. *See supra* Chapter 3.

29. GAILLARD, *supra* note 5, at 83-84.

30. Partial Award, Salini v. Ethiopia, ¶ 16.

between the court and the arbitral tribunal, but as between two possible international tribunals.[31] For greater clarity, the jurisdictional question was not whether the court or the already set-up arbitral tribunal should decide the arbitral tribunal's jurisdiction, but rather who decides as between the court or the arbitral tribunal which one of the two (already set-up ICC or yet-to-be-set-up ad hoc) tribunal would have jurisdiction over the matter.[32] Gaillard, of course, does not talk about this in his book and, as a matter of fact, even in the *Salini* decision.[33]

Second, the reason the Ethiopian Supreme Court issued an injunction was not because it was told that the ICC Court's rejection of the challenge was based on the tribunal's decision to hear "certain witnesses in Paris,"[34] but that it was told the whole story—which Gaillard's book does not tell. As discussed in Chapter 3, one of the most serious accusations against the members of the tribunal was their delaying of the decision on their own jurisdiction until they had had heard the merits.[35] Any moderately informed person would understand the possible inappropriate economic and ideological considerations that might have shaped this decision. The tribunal offered no remotely plausible justification for this delay in jurisdictional decision when the jurisdictional challenge was very serious. To this already sour taste was added the arrogance of effectively moving the hearing (the only hearing by the parties' agreement and not the hearing of only certain witnesses, as Gaillard says) from Addis Ababa, the seat of the arbitration, to Paris, where the president of the tribunal, Gaillard, resided.

The tribunal's decision was based on the Terms of Reference in which the parties agreed that the tribunal may, after consultation with the parties, decide on a hearing location.[36] In agreeing to these terms, the respondent must have had some confidence in the tribunal's ability to make decisions with some minimum courtesy to the needs and sensitivities of both parties, not just one of the parties.

Third, the injunction was a temporary one until the Supreme Court decided the challenge issue vis-à-vis the ICC's own jurisdiction. Gaillard's theory denies the court any involvement whatsoever, even the chance to conduct *a* prima facie review[37] of the arbitration agreement to determine whether the agreement itself

31. *Id.* ¶¶ 17–18.

32. *Id.* ¶ 16.

33. *Id.* ¶ 19; GAILLARD, *supra* note 5, at 84.

34. GAILLARD, *supra* note 5, at 84.

35. Partial Award, Salini v. Ethiopia, ¶¶ 263–264; *see* Chapter 3.

36. Partial Award, Salini v. Ethiopia, ¶¶ 26–29.

37. Gaillard accepts that the courts have jurisdiction to conduct at least a prima facie review of the existence and validity of arbitration agreements. *See* GAILLARD, *supra* note 5, at 87. This standard of review is by no means universal. In the United States for example, courts apply a "clear and unmistakable evidence" standard to determine that parties' intend to relinquish judicial remedy by agreement. *See, e.g.*, First Options of Chicago, Inc. v. Kaplan, 514 U.S. 938, 945 (1995), stating:

> This Court, however, has (as we just said) added an important qualification, applicable when courts decide whether a party has agreed that arbitrators should decide arbitrability: Courts

exists, whether it is on its face valid, and, if so, which tribunal should decide the jurisdictional questions.

Celebrating the tribunal's refusal to be bound by the Ethiopian Supreme Court's injunction, Gaillard continues quoting his opinion in the *Salini* case as follows:

> An international arbitral tribunal is not an organ of the state in which it has the seat in the same way that a court of the seat would be. The primary source of the Tribunal's powers is the parties' agreement to arbitrate. An important consequence of this is that the Tribunal has a duty vis-à-vis the parties to ensure that their arbitration agreement is not frustrated. In certain circumstances, it

> should not assume that the parties agreed to arbitrate arbitrability unless there is "clea[r] and unmistakabl[e]" evidence that they did so. In this manner the law treats silence or ambiguity about the question "who (primarily) should decide arbitrability" differently from the way it treats silence or ambiguity about the question "whether a particular merits-related dispute is arbitrable because it is within the scope of a valid arbitration agreement"—for in respect to this latter question the law reverses the presumption. ("[A]ny doubts concerning the scope of arbitrable issues should be resolved in favor of arbitration")
>
> But, this difference in treatment is understandable. The latter question arises when the parties have a contract that provides for arbitration of some issues. In such circumstances, the parties likely gave at least some thought to the scope of arbitration. And, given the law's permissive policies in respect to arbitration, one can understand why the law would insist upon clarity before concluding that the parties did not want to arbitrate a related matter (issues will be deemed arbitrable unless "it is clear that the arbitration clause has not included" them). On the other hand, the former question—the "who (primarily) should decide arbitrability" question—is rather arcane. A party often might not focus upon that question or upon the significance of having arbitrators decide the scope of their own powers. And, given the principle that a party can be forced to arbitrate only those issues it specifically has agreed to submit to arbitration, one can understand why courts might hesitate to interpret silence or ambiguity on the "who should decide arbitrability" point as giving the arbitrators that power, for doing so might too often force unwilling parties to arbitrate a matter they reasonably would have thought a judge, not an arbitrator, would decide. (Arbitration Act's basic purpose is to "ensure judicial enforcement of privately made agreements to arbitrate").

(citations omitted). On the opposite end of the spectrum, courts would defer jurisdiction unless they found that the arbitration agreement is "manifestly null." *See, e.g.*, (Cass.) Judgment of 7 December 1994, V 2000 (Formerly Jaguar France) v. Project XJ 220 LTD, 1997 Rev. arb. 537 (excerpted in Born, *supra* note 3, at 205–07). The standard is contained in the French Code of Civil Procedure Articles 1458, 1466 & 1502. *See* Born, *supra* note 3, at 202. Article 1458 states: "Whenever a dispute submitted to an arbitral tribunal by virtue of an arbitration agreement is brought before a court of the [French Republic], such court shall decline jurisdiction. If the arbitral tribunal has not yet been seized of the matter, the court should also decline jurisdiction unless the arbitration agreement is manifestly null. In neither case may the court determine its lack of jurisdiction on its own motion." Excerpted in Born, *supra*, at 202. The Swedish Arbitration Act on the other hand under Sections 2 and 34(1) provides that: "The arbitrators may rule on their own jurisdiction to decide the dispute. The aforesaid shall not prevent a court from determining such a question at the request of a party. The arbitrators may continue the arbitral proceedings pending the determination by the court. Notwithstanding that the arbitrators have, in a decision during the proceedings, determined that they possess jurisdiction to resolve the dispute, such decision is not binding." Excerpted in Born, *supra*, at 202. For more discussion of the various standards adopted by various laws and courts, *see id.* at 201–15.

> may be necessary to decline to comply with an order issued by a court of the seat, in the fulfillment of the Tribunal's larger duty to the parties.
>
> Of course, this is not to say that a contract, including an arbitration agreement, has a validity that is independent of any legal order. Indeed, a contract derives its binding force from its recognition by one or more legal orders. However, an agreement to submit disputes to international arbitration is not anchored exclusively in the legal order of the seat of the arbitration. Such agreements are validated by a range of international sources and norms extending beyond the domestic seat itself.[38]

The ideological point being that "a State or a State-owned entity cannot avail itself of its own law in order to renege on an arbitration agreement to which it freely consented."[39] In *Salini*, the opinion as well as the book by Gaillard converted the Addis Ababa Water and Sewerage Authority to a state enterprise that was attempting to use its own courts to renege on its arbitral obligation, as opposed to a simple contracting party who goes to court to challenge the jurisdiction of one of two possible arbitral tribunals. This case is one of many cited to support the theory that there exists a supranational legal order that allows international arbitrators such as Gaillard to disregard the courts of the place where the arbitration is seated. In Gaillard's own words:

> The three above-mentioned cases demonstrate that when faced with actions that aim to frustrate an arbitration agreement to which the parties have freely consented, arbitrators do not hesitate to make their own determination on the merits of the respective positions of the parties without considering themselves bound by the decisions rendered by the courts of the seat of the arbitration. This shows that, as far as arbitrators are concerned, the source of the juridicity of international arbitration is not to be found, at least exclusively, in the legal order of the seat of the arbitration. This is the very premise on which is based the representation of international arbitration that recognizes the existence of an arbitral legal order.[40]

Unfortunately, this theory was made up by arbitrators, and it is not soundly justified and defended. As discussed below, even Paulsson considers it an exorbitant theory. The evidence that Gaillard offers paints the political picture of well-known and well-connected arbitrators ignoring the courts of developing countries under the pretext of denial of justice to the private party, claiming that the arbitrators' authority came from the parties' agreement, detached from the laws that gave that agreement the force of law in the first place. The laws and courts of the seat are superseded by necessities of justice to the foreign party. This theory defines the core of arbitration

38. Gaillard, *supra* note 5, at 85 (quoting Partial Award, Salini v. Ethiopia, ¶¶ 128–129).

39. Gaillard, *supra* note 5, at 86.

40. *Id.*

as an alternative means of dispute settlement in general. As the U.S. Supreme Court aptly describes it in the domestic context: The Arbitration Act's basic purpose is to "ensure judicial enforcement of privately made agreements to arbitrate."[41] There is no such thing as an arbitral legal order without the laws of sovereign states giving it effect.

The next section discusses Gaillard's take on plurality of national orders giving effect to international arbitration.

b. International Arbitration Anchored in a Plurality of National Legal Orders

Gaillard puts the philosophical postulate of the plurality theory in the middle of his continuum as follows:

> The representation of international arbitration that anchors the arbitral process in a plurality of national legal orders shares with the former the fact that it is based on strict State positivism. They differ only in that it conceives relationships among States following a Westphalian model of sovereignty.[42]

His resentment of this theory is diluted by the possibility that the validity of the arbitration agreement, the sanctity of which he cherishes, would have a second or third or fourth chance of being upheld under the regime of recognition of "foreign arbitral awards" set up by the New York Convention. Discussing the approach taken by the New York Convention, he states:

> As the ICC had suggested, the law of the seat becomes secondary and can be trumped by an agreement between the parties with respect to the composition of the arbitral tribunal or the conduct of the arbitral proceedings (Article V(1)(d)). On these important matters, compliance with the prescriptions of the law of the seat is no longer subject to sanctions in other countries. The same logic applies to the arbitration agreement: party autonomy prevails over the law of the seat (Article V(1)(a). Moreover, the arbitrability of the dispute and the award's compliance with the requirements of public policy are assessed in light of the conceptions of the State in which enforcement is sought (Article V(2)).[43]

Having accurately described the regime set up by the New York Convention on the compromises that states have made in defining the parameters of their respective authorities, Gaillard misstates the effect to enable him to move into his preferred theory of autonomous legal order. The misstatement goes: "In the Westphalian

41. Dean Witter Reynolds Inc. v. Byrd, 470 U.S. 213, 219 (1985); *see also* First Option of Chicago v. Kaplan, 514 U.S. 938, 945 (1995).

42. Gaillard, *supra* note 5, at 26.

43. *Id.* at 29–30.

representation of arbitration, each State has a title to impose its conception of what constitutes an arbitration worthy of legal protection only within the confines of its own legal order."[44] This, of course, ignores the limits upon such title set by the New York Convention, for at least the states party.

c. International Arbitration as an Autonomous Legal Order: The Arbitral Legal Order

The Arbitral Legal Order, for Gaillard, is located at the right end of the spectrum both literally and figuratively. Here is how he presents the continuum:

> The monolocal representation of international arbitration, centered around the notion of the seat, has brought about a multilocal (or Westphalian) representation, which, in turn, has led to a transnational representation which no longer considers each State individually but rather focuses on the trends arising from the normative activity of the community of States. The main difference between the latter two representations is that the multilocal approach considers the plurality of States, while the transnational approach contemplates the collectivity of States.[45]

The conclusion does not syllogistically flow from the two premises in the continuum (the monolocal gave rise to the multilocal and the multilocal gave rise to the transnational) because both the monolocal and multilocal derive their power from sovereign sources, whereas the transnational seems to be an accidental byproduct without a concrete source of normative power.

Gaillard elevates the "arbitrator" to a sovereign status and considers him as a source of law. To show the strength of the arbitral legal order over the Westphalian conception of plurality of legal orders, he posits: "As compared to the previous model of international arbitration [Westphalian], this representation [the Arbitral Legal Order] essentially factors in *the arbitrators' perspective*."[46] The "arbitrator" appears to have the power to have a perspective of legal significance outside of the monolocal or even multilocal. And that power comes from the transnational legal order, which is in turn based on the "arbitrator's perspective." Further along the same line, he states:

> From the States' viewpoint, this consideration may be sufficient. It may indeed suffice to consider that each State is free to regulate, pursuant to its own views, arbitrations that come into contact with its legal order, be it because the dispute is brought before its courts despite the existence of an arbitration agreement, because its courts are called upon to grant certain measures in support of the arbitration, or because its courts are required to enforce an award. *Yet,*

44. *Id.* at 35.

45. *Id.* at 37.

46. *Id.* at 35 (emphasis added).

> *from the arbitrators' point of view*, these considerations seem insufficient, which accounts for the instability of the Westphalian model.[47]

Again "the arbitrator's point of view" appears to have an independent existence, although Gaillard does not say why anyone should care about "the arbitrator's point of view" while he exemplifies how the arbitrator might be subject to conflicting commands. His solution to these conflicting commands is his ultimate legal theory of international arbitration. Here is how he presents it:

> Where confronted with conflicting views of several legal orders in relation to a given arbitration—one holds the arbitration agreement to be valid, the other considers it void; one claims that the arbitrators lack the required impartiality while the other allows the procedure to continue—the arbitrators cannot simply take account of this plurality of positions. They must make their own determination, either by choosing among the conflicting positions pursuant to a choice of law methodology—with the correlating disadvantage of reducing an inherently international situation into a domestic one, as the choice of law method does—or by resorting to the direct application of substantive rules, which are more likely to take into account the international nature of the situation and the plurality of legal orders that have expressed their views on what they consider to constitute an arbitration worthy of legal protection. In situations where arbitrators, confronted with this plurality of views, endeavor to identify rules that are generally endorsed at a given time by the international community and determine that they should prevail over those reflecting a State's isolated position, the question arises as to the transnational source of the arbitrators' power to adjudicate and that of the existence of an arbitral legal order.[48]

His theory of international arbitral legal order is as lacking grounding in principle as it is dangerous. It is unclear what he refers to by "rules that are generally endorsed at a given time by the international community." Unless he is referring to customary

47. *Id.* at 36 (emphasis added).

48. *Id.* at 36–37. In his widely circulated 2015 article on sociology of international article, Gaillard adds a philosophical point more fitting to his theory of international arbitration than to his sociological analysis. That point is the following:

> When the French Court of cassation affirmed in *Putrabali* that an international award is a "decision of international justice", it expressed values as to what arbitration is, or should be, to a broader audience than the parties concerned or the French legal circles. Similarly, when the House of Lords recognized the severability of the arbitration agreement in *Fiona Trust*, it set forth an international standard in addition to providing a solution for the case at hand.

Emmanuel Gaillard, *Sociology of International Arbitration at Arbitration International*, 31 Arb. Int'l 1, 7 (2015) (footnotes omitted). It is unclear whether he would give the same level of value-setting status to other courts around the world—such as the Indian Supreme Court, or the Supreme Peoples' Court of the PRC, or even the Kenyan Supreme Court or the Ethiopian Court of Cassation.

international law, which does not appear to be the case, those terms could be a source of more serious confusion of conflicting sovereign commands. Moreover, such supranational legal order administered by "arbitrators' point of view" cannot by any means avoid jurisdictional complications. In fact, the injection of any purported inherently indeterminate rules that are neither national nor international not only adds considerable complication but also call the legitimacy of the entire system into question. Laws made by business persons always on the lookout for business opportunities do not always inspire confidence. The notion of arbitrator-made-arbitrator-administered transnational legal order is a dangerous travesty. The problem with Gaillard's preferred theory is, thus, its movement from a descriptive framework of pluralism to a normative endorsement of a hierarchy of substantive norms and values in a legal vacuum.[49]

2. Jan Paulsson's Theory

Gaillard is by no means alone in advocating for a supranational status for arbitration and arbitrators. Indeed, Paulsson does not even have Gaillard's modesty in expressing his opinion about the supermen who should make, interpret, and apply their own transnational rules of arbitration, although he gets there through a fancier path than that of Gaillard's transnational legal order.

Paulsson's most recent work, *The Idea of Arbitration*, begins by offering a very useful definition of the idea of arbitration as a "binding resolution of disputes accepted with serenity by those who bear its consequences because of their special trust in chosen decision-makers."[50] The emphasis is on "trust" of the "chosen decision-maker." The question that it begs is: Who should be trusted and why? Paulsson answers that question without hesitation, but the starting point is what he posits as "[w]e wish to be judged by someone wise and familiar, perhaps an idealized version of ourselves—not someone clever and strange."[51] The idea of arbitration therefore is "[t]he vision of serene closure, without loss of dignity, [which] is at the heart of the idea of arbitration."[52] The entire book is thus an attempt to show how the existing regime of international arbitration achieves idealized self-justice with dignity.

He puts the fundamental dilemma very well when he states: "The great paradox of arbitration is that it seeks the cooperation of the very public authorities from which it wants to free itself."[53] He expounds four legal theories before he endorses

49. *See, e.g.*, Paul Schiff Berman, *Global Legal Pluralism*, 80 S. Cal. L. Rev. 1155, 1166 (2007) ("[P]luralism recognizes the inevitability (if not always the desirability) of hybridity. Pluralism is thus principally a descriptive, not a normative framework. It observes that various actors pursue norms and it studies the interplay, but does not propose a hierarchy of substantive norms and values.").

50. Jan Paulsson, The Idea of Arbitration 1 (2013).

51. *Id.* at 5.

52. *Id.* at 7.

53. *Id.* at 30.

a combination of two. The first theory is the same as Gaillard's *monolocal theory,* which Paulsson calls the *territorial thesis;* it states that "any arbitration is necessarily national; it lives or dies according to the law of the place of arbitration."[54] The second is what Gaillard calls *"multilocal"*; Paulsson calls it the *pluralistic thesis,* which states that "arbitration may be given effect by more than one legal order, none of them inevitably essential."[55] Paulsson does not give the third theory a name, but it is substantially similar to Gaillard's "transnational arbitral order," which states—in Paulsson's words—"arbitration is the product of *an autonomous legal order accepted as such by arbitrators and judges."*[56] Gaillard would probably omit "judges" from this proposition. The fourth theory, Paulsson's own addition, states that "arbitration may be effective under *arrangements that do not depend on national law or judge at all."*[57] He ultimately fashions a pluralistic legal theory that is liberated from national laws or judges.[58]

Consider his analysis in more detail. What he does for the first theory is merely a description of the obvious.[59] He traces the articulation of the theory to Francis

54. *Id.*

55. *Id.*

56. *Id.*

57. *Id.*

58. *Id.*

59. Paulsson begins by introducing the paradox requiring theoretical explanation by example. One of the two examples is relevant here. It concerns Professor René-Jean Dupuy's puzzlement over his own authority in the Texaco Overseas Petroleum Co. and California Asiatic Oil Co. v. Libya case. *Id.* Dupuy, appointed by the then-president of the International Court of Justice, Manfred Lachs of Poland, had to identify and justify the legal sources of his own authority in the face of Libya's objection and failure to participate on the grounds that the arbitration agreement was extinguished by the expropriation decree. *See id.* at 30–31 (citing Preliminary Award 27 November 1975; Award on the Merits, 19 January 1977; 17 ILM 1 (1978)). Dupuy ultimately decided that the source of his authority was international law not because the parties chose "general principles of law" as the applicable law but because the agreement itself is evidence of an internationalization of the parties' relationship. *Id.* at 31. Paulsson presents Dupuy's line of argumentation in the following terms:

> In his award, Dupuy sought to understand the legal basis on which he was being asked to act. The concession agreements contained an unusual stipulation of applicable law: the principles of Libyan law insofar as they were common to the principle of international law, and, in the absence of such common principles, "general principles of law". Dupuy perceived that the deeds were to be construed in accordance with this concentration of norms, but also that he first needed to determine something else: the legal foundation of his authority. By what right could he organize the proceedings; summon the parties to present evidence and arguments; decide, as he did, that the place of arbitration would be Geneva; rule on the continued validity of the arbitration agreement; and in the end render a final award on the merits? This legal foundation, he concluded, was international law. The stipulation of applicable law was a relevant *indication* of this foundation since it was evidence of an internationalization of the parties' relationship, but did not in and of itself constitute that foundation. The distinction to be made, he wrote . . . was between "law which governs the contract and the legal order from which the binding nature of the contract stems".

Id. at 31.

Mann's 1967 article "*Lex Facit Arbitrum*."[60] Mann's central claim is that "[n]o act of the parties have any legal effect except as the result of the sanction given to it by a legal system . . . it is unavoidable to ascertain such system before the act of the parties can be upheld."[61] But Paulsson faults Mann's work for its brevity[62] and presumed conflation of the law to be applied with the legal foundation of arbitration, as well as for being a "sustained attack on those who argued for the freedom of arbitrators to base their decisions on perceptions of equity or of supranational norms."[63] Mann's main concern was that "[a]ny other [other than territorial] solution would involve the conclusion that it is open to the arbitrator to disregard the law."[64] Mann's concern is real. A good example is Gaillard's opinion in *Salini v. Ethiopia*, discussed at length in the previous section.[65] However, Paulsson provides a more credible substantive critique of the territorial approach on the basis of the New York Convention, which appears to tolerate the possibility of a different outcome in the state where enforcement is sought.[66] This could be the possibility of refusal to enforce an award considered perfectly valid by the state where it is made or vice versa on some of the grounds set forth under Article V of the Convention.[67] Indeed, the possibility of more than two different, but equally legitimate outcomes cannot be ruled out under the New York Convention. Hence, as Paulsson credibly asserts, "[i]f the courts of

60. *Id.* at 33.

61. *Id.* (quoting Lex Facit Arbitrum, *in* INTERNATIONAL ARBITRATION: *LIBER AMICORUM* FOR MARTIN DOMKE 161 (Pieter Sanders ed. 1967)). The whole quote reads:

> Just as, notwithstanding its notoriously misleading name, every system of private international law is a system of national law, every arbitration is a national arbitration, that is to say, subject to a specific system of national law. The *lex arbitri* cannot be the law of any country other than that of the arbitration tribunal's seat. No act of the parties can have any legal effect except as the result of the sanction given to it by a legal system. Hence, it is unavoidable to ascertain such system before the act of the parties can be upheld. When we say in the conflict of laws: "contracts are governed by the law chosen by the parties," we do so, and can do so, by reason of the fact that the rule is part of the law of a specific legal system.

62. Incidentally, Francis A. Mann wrote a revised version of his 1967 essay in 1985. F.A. Mann, *The Doctrine of International Jurisdiction Revised after Twenty Years*, *in* 3 *RECUEIL DES COURS*: COLLECTED COURSES OF THE HAGUE ACADEMY OF INTERNATIONAL LAW (1984). He still maintained that "laws extend so far as, but not further than the sovereignty of the State which puts them in force." *Id.* at 20.

63. PAULSSON, *supra* note 50, at 33.

64. *Id.*

65. *See* Section A.1 above.

66. PAULSSON, *supra* note 50, at 35.

67. *Id.* He gives the following example: "[O]ne must doubt that anyone would seriously argue that an award set aside in Country X because it was rendered by a female or irreligious arbitrator should be rejected by the courts of Country Y, making the judge of the latter complicit in a violation of international public policy." *Id.* It is unclear what he considers international public policy, but this might be an example of a national public policy that would dictate a differing legal consequence to the extent that it is conceivable that such policies are embedded in international commerce anywhere.

another country examine the award and find it eligible for enforcement, it cannot possibly be said that this is so because the award finds its foundation in Swiss law, given the explicit exclusion of any possible Swiss judicial stance with respect to it."[68]

That leads to the pluralistic theory, which, in fact, Paulsson accurately characterizes as "not a theory, but a simple observation of fact."[69] The animating predicate is, again, the New York Convention's formulation that allows for differing legal effect in different states of the same arbitral agreement or award. As he puts it: "More generally, it is undeniable that Article V(2) of the New York Convention leaves it to any of a multitude of enforcement fora to evaluate the conformity of an award with their particular conceptions of arbitrability or public policy. It is impossible to deny the plurality of legal orders that may give effect—or not—to arbitration agreements and awards."[70]

By far the most interesting aspect of Paulsson's narrative is its criticism of Gaillard's endorsement of the transnational autonomous arbitral order. To build his new theory, Paulsson had to first take a detour to demolish Gaillard's theory of transnational legal order, and does so remarkably well. Paulsson takes Gaillard's theory so seriously that he offers a systematic rebuttal starting with its premise by noting that "Gaillard's demonstration falls into the same trap as that of Mann's 1967 article, namely looking at substantive rules for deciding a dispute as though they were reflections of a legal order giving effect to the process itself."[71] It is indeed in search of a legitimizing legal order that he ends up endorsing a proposition that Paulsson calls an "extravagant" and "hallow" claim that "may do more harm than the resistance of non-believers and scoffers."[72] Significantly, Paulsson states: "The proposition that an effective legal order may be built upon diaphanous abstractions like *positive perspectives* or *transnational dynamics* are more likely to impede than to facilitate respect for the arbitral process."[73] Substantively, the refutation is centered on the idea that:

> [s]tates have never accepted that the norms of the international community are derived from "progressive tendencies" embraced by other states; they insist on their own individual adhesion. They are even less likely to embrace such amorphous norms as limitations on their national laws, in their national space, when dealing with a private-law feature like arbitration.[74]

Indeed he rightfully points out that "[s]uch pronouncements are unlikely to go down well with judges who would be violating their oath of office if they showed

68. *Id.*

69. *Id.* at 39.

70. *Id.*

71. *Id.* at 41.

72. *Id.* at 42–44.

73. *Id.* at 44.

74. *Id.* at 41.

fealty to a 'transnational' order rather than that of the state to which they have sworn allegiance."[75]

Although Paulsson is concerned about the effect that this kind of overzealous extravagancy on the arbitral process in general, he does not mention the possibility, indeed the reality, of how many real cases this "extravagant" claim might have poisoned. The *Salini v. Ethiopia* case discussed in Chapter 3 and above is again an excellent example of the dangers of Gaillard's theory of an autonomous arbitral order administered by arbitrators without review of any kind. A better name for it might be arbitrator-absolutism. Paulsson disagrees with Gaillard, but does not go as far as calling all his decisions that rested on this theory *void ab initio*.

Quite remarkably, however, having accused Gaillard of making an extravagant claim, Paulsson goes on to make his own extravagant claim. The expectations that are elevated by the effectiveness of the demolishment work are soon disappointed by the amorphousness and unhelpfulness of Paulsson's preferred theory. The argument itself loses its lucidity as it regresses from the normative to the descriptive. To ensure the accuracy of the assessment here, it is important to consider his own words: "Reality is more consistent with the pluralistic concept, but, as we shall see, tends to transcend it without hesitation . . . . Even the pluralistic model, however, is too restrictive and therefore unsatisfactory. It leaves out too much of the picture."[76]

Paulsson's vision is "arbitration which functions routinely without judicial assistance."[77] This is a utopian notion of self-governance and self-sanction not unlike many constituent groups that he mentions, such as the grain and feed trade.[78] In fact, he says that "[t]hey may be the hallmark of a fluid legal universe, with significant elements of self-governance, as the arbitrants themselves, replacing the legislative and executive arms of the state, create norms, and ensure their sanctions."[79] In defense of pluralism run amok, he even suggests that the period between 1648, the year of the Treaty of Westphalia, to the present was "an interruption" to pluralism.[80] The important message is the necessity "to understand the capacity of a variety of social institutions for authoritative decision-making."[81]

Paulsson's chosen theory would not help resolve real-life controversies. He recognizes that much when he discusses *kompetenz-kompetenz*.[82] But even within the examples of the self-sanctioning variety of social institutions, contestations that require some form of coercive resolution are inevitable. If such inevitability is admitted, the theory is not useful. If the inevitability is not admitted, it is still not

75. *Id.*

76. *Id.* at 45.

77. *Id.*

78. *See, e.g., id.* at n.30.

79. *Id.* at 48.

80. *Id.* at 50.

81. *Id.*

82. *Id.* at 54–58.

useful, because there is no need for a binding arbitration as the elders' decisions are complied with anyway. And, in fact, in such kinds of harmonious communities, less formal mechanisms of dispute settlement would work. In any case, Paulsson's revised pluralistic take is consistent with the growing pluralistic movement, which "refuse[s] to focus solely on who has the formal authority to articulate norms or the coercive power to enforce them. Instead, [pluralists] aim to study empirically which statements of authority tend to be treated as binding in actual practice and by whom."[83] This academic work is in its infancy—it is in the process of being transformed from the merely descriptive to the normative. A pluralistic framework for managing legal conflicts is being debated in the academy.[84] No one seems to know the answer to how pluralism might be managed outside of the formal and the familiar although its existence and its inevitability is acknowledged. Paulsson's pluralistic analysis may be interesting as a scholarly piece of work, much like Susan Silbey's *Invocations of Law on Snowy Streets,* in which she puzzles over the legal implications of the practice of putting physical items in the streets of Boston or Chicago on snowy days as evidence of one's entitlement to go back to for clearing the snow, and the respect that the community accords that claim outside of the judicial process.[85] This is an important debate to have, but in a situation where transnational business disputes threaten the success of a power plant or a city's sewer system, injecting indeterminable sources of law into actual disputes does not facilitate the solution as much as it could cause confusion and delay. Paulsson is as guilty of undermining the credibility of the system as Gaillard—whom he accuses of doing so.

It is not difficult to imagine what Gaillard might do with Paulsson's modified pluralist theory in the *Salini* case, but consider the "disciplined self-governing and self-sanctioning" societies such as the grain and free trade. The Grain and Feed Trade Association (GAFTA) based in London has its own arbitration rules.[86] The Secretariat operates more or less like the other nonspecialized arbitral institutions.[87] It has a closed list of arbitrators many of them non-lawyers.[88] A simple review of the number of cases that get appealed to the High Court of London, Commercial Branch—be it through a Section 69 review process of the 1996 UK Arbitration Act or otherwise—shows the limits of harmonious communal coexistence. Indeed, the author of this book has encountered a level of irregularity and court appeals with GAFTA not seen in regular arbitrations.

To suggest that some of the authoritative decision-making social institutions can thrive unassisted by courts and hard law not only oversimplifies the challenges

83. *See* Berman, *supra* note 49, at 1178 (emphasis omitted).

84. *See id.* at 1179–89.

85. Susan S Silbey, *J. Locke, Op. Cit.: Invocations of Law on Snowy Streets, in* Using Legal Culture 120–52 (David Nelken ed., 2012).

86. Information about GAFTA is available on its website. GAFTA, http://www.gafta.com/ (last visited Mar. 11, 2016).

87. *See id.*

88. *See id.*

of arbitration, but encourages arbitrators already inclined to look for ways to liberate themselves from the party-chosen laws and forums and to engage in creative maneuvers such as what Gaillard did in the *Salini* case. To paraphrase James Madison,[89] if arbitrators were angels, Paulsson's modified pluralism would have worked.

To be fair, he is not totally silent on the practical problems of the allocation of competence between the courts and arbitral tribunals, but the solution he proposes is not all that different from Gaillard's, because they begin from the same premise, that is, whoever wants to go to court is presumably intent on improperly disrupting the arbitral process. In fact, Paulsson is very explicit in assuming that "[i]n jurisdictions that embrace arbitration, it is expected that arbitrators will not overreach, and accepted that if they do so it suffices that the courts may correct them in due course."[90] This is a totally unwarranted assumption, especially in light of the obvious and undeniable wrong economic incentives that pervade the whole system, and anecdotal evidence offered by cases such as *Salini*. With such assumption, Paulsson states when he might tolerate court interference in the following terms: "In the event of legitimate apprehension of irreparable harm."[91] The example that he gives is "in truly exceptional cases of bogus arbitrations."[92] Whether Paulsson might consider *Salini* one such case is hard to say. The standards he outlines will however continue to influence other arbitrators and make other *Salini* cases more—not less—probable.

3. Catherine Rogers's Theory

Catherine Rogers's seminal work, *Ethics in International Arbitration*,[93] is also a part of the contemporary theoretical debate. She confronts with admirable courage an issue that everybody wishes to avoid: ethics.

Professor Rogers's sense of urgency in regulating the behaviors of arbitrators and counsel in international arbitration is animated by the increasing diversity of the players.[94] In her own words:

> Predictably, in response to local needs and concomitant with the rise of regional centers, parties are appointing arbitrators and counsel who are from outside the traditionally European pool of participants. These trends mean not only participants who are new to international arbitration, but also an increase in participation by lawyers who are not part of the global network

89. The Federalist No. 51, at 264 (James Madison) (Ian Shapiro ed., 2009) ("If men were angels, no government would be necessary.").

90. Paulsson, *supra* note 50, at 58.

91. *Id.* at 60.

92. *Id.*

93. Catherine A. Rogers, Ethics in International Arbitration (2014).

94. *Id.* at 28.

> of mega-firms. Ultimately, diversification of participants has contributed to a breakdown in the insular, once-shared professional norms. Those shared norms had operated as a basis for informal self-regulation, but as they have broken down, nothing has come to take their place.[95]

Implicit in this analysis is a recognition perhaps of Gaillard's autonomous arbitral order operated by a close-knit epistemic community of largely European arbitrators with common standards and aspirations.[96] She considers international arbitration a global legal order founded by scholars and practitioners who shared a common intellectual enterprise.[97] It is something that is purposefully created or made up. In fact, the founders "also shared a professional ethos that was preoccupied with transcendent principles of justice" that is quickly degenerating into an "ethical no-man's land" as the pool diversifies.[98] In her words:

> A "no-man's land" is a space between the formally occupied territories of two warring sovereigns. In the absence of a governing sovereign . . . [a]ttacks from both sides are constant. Most importantly, the uncertain political status of a no-man's land means that it is unclear what rules or laws apply because the warring sovereigns each claim legal dominion. Perhaps this feature best captures [what] makes professional conduct in international arbitration an ethical no-man's land.[99]

For example, Rogers says, "no one seems to know what, if any, ethical rules apply to attorneys in international arbitral proceedings."[100] To exemplify the problem, she asks what ethical rules might govern the conduct of a German lawyer with a New York bar license representing a Japanese client against an Austrian counterparty for a dispute governed by French substantive law before a tribunal seated in Switzerland.[101] There is more than an element of confusion about what rules apply, as Rogers indicates; a survey conducted by the International Bar Association (IBA) Task Force on Counsel Conduct in Arbitration showed that uncertainty when

95. *Id.* (citation omitted) For a similar suggestion, *see* Sundaresh Menon, *The Transnational Protection of Private Rights: Issues, Challenges, and Possible Solutions*, *in* Practicing Virtue: Inside International Arbitration 27 (David D. Caron & Stephen W. Schill eds., 2015). ("But the internationalization of arbitration has resulted in an exponential increase in the number of arbitral institutions, cases, and practitioners. It is impossible for the industry to continue to depend on implied norms, understandings, peer standards, and shared values when these might no longer exist.")

96. *See* Gaillard, *supra* note 5, at 36–37; *see also* Section A.1 above.

97. Rogers, *supra* note 93, at 28.

98. *Id.* at 17–18.

99. *Id.* at 18 (citation omitted).

100. *Id.*

101. *Id.*

63 percent of respondents said that they believed they were subject to the rules of professional conduct of their home bar, and 27 percent more follow their bar rules although they don't know if it applies.[102]

Her working assumption, in terms of the legal theory of international arbitration, is that "international arbitration operates largely on assumptions of its ability and need to self-regulate. Its processes exist largely independent of national legal systems, unregimented by national procedural rules."[103] But, "[t]he new generation of arbitrators does not have the professional nobility or stature to invoke 'grand principles of law' or vague notions of equity with the same innate sense of legitimacy on which the earlier generation relied"[104]—hence the need for regulation.

Rogers, therefore, seems to belong to the school of thought that sees the existence of a legal order of its own that is capable of self-regulating.[105] She does not doubt the existence of the "*self*" in "self-regulation." Although she devotes many pages to defining "*regulation*,"[106] she does not define who the "*self*" that needs regulation might be. She offers no more evidence of the existence of the so-called arbitral legal order than echoing Gaillard's philosophical postulate, although not directly.

Admittedly, the final recommendations for substantive standards cannot be anything more than best practices subject to "mandatory national ethical rules or the role of national regulatory authorities."[107] Embodied in this great work is the ultimate and pragmatic solution: "An internationally harmonized choice-of-law rules."[108] A real counter-conceptual to the notion of self-regulation. Self-regulation without a definable "*self*" is the irony of international arbitration as "a transnational legal order" that is founded by the "Invisible College of International Lawyers."[109] Whether there is a "*self*" in "self-regulation" or not, whether there is a supranational legal order or not, whether "the invisible college" was more righteous or not, whether diversity's effects on the righteousness is making regulation more necessary or not, Professor Rogers very helpfully makes a fundamental matter very clear: wherever its domain might be, international arbitration is indeed an "ethical no-man's land."[110]

102. *Id.*

103. *Id.* at 19.

104. Catherine A. Rogers, *Transparency in International Commercial Arbitration*, 54 Kan. L. Rev. 1301, 1316 (2006) (citation omitted).

105. Rogers, *supra* note 93, at 19.

106. *Id.* at 221–73.

107. *Id.* at 370.

108. *Id.*

109. *Id.* at 17.

110. *Id.* at 18. ("The result is that today, instead of being constituted of an Invisible College, those participating in international arbitration dwell in an ethical no-man's land.").

4. Gary Born's Theory

Gary Born focusing on practice, gives limited coverage to theory. He devotes only four pages on it in his three-volume 4100-page leading treatise.[111] He does, however, outline three theoretical possibilities before he endorses one. The first is the contractual theory that regards arbitration as a function of party autonomy:

> It is the arbitration agreement that gives [the arbitral award] its existence; it is from the arbitration agreement that it derives all its substance; it has, then, like the arbitration agreement, the character of a contract; and the precise truth is that it is only the performance of the mandate that the parties have entrusted to the arbitrators; it is even, to put it precisely, only an agreement to which the parties have bound themselves by the hands of the latter (the arbitrators).[112]

As Born suggests, the emphasis of this school of thought is on the arbitrators' role as private actors, not as public officials, and unlike judges. In other words, they live and die by the party contract.[113] What they do is what the parties ask them to do.[114]

The second is the jurisdictional theory. It holds that "arbitration is essentially adjudicative, involving the exercise of independent, impartial decision-making by the arbitrators."[115] In a way, arbitrators are "private judges" with "judicial function."[116]

The third theory is a hybrid of both contractual and jurisdictional theories. Because the judicial function is recognized by law as a result of party agreement, arbitration is in essence contractual as well as jurisdictional in character.[117]

Born concludes the theoretical discussion by offering the following thought of his own:

> Thus, it is true that the field of international arbitration draws essential doctrine and rules from contract law and from the law of civil procedure and judgments. But in many cases, particularly in international matters, these disciples are at most analogies, providing the starting point, not the end result, of analysis. In all cases, it remains essential to categorize and treat arbitration as a distinctive and autonomous discipline, specially designed to achieve a particular set of objectives, which other branches of private international law fail to satisfactorily resolve.[118]

111. Born, *supra* note 2, at 214–18.

112. *Id.* at 214 (quoting P. Merlin, 9 Recueil alphabétique des questions de droit 139, 145 (1829), quoted in Adam Samuel, Jurisdictional Problems in International Commercial Arbitration 34 (1989)).

113. *Id.* at 214.

114. *Id.* at 214.

115. *Id.* at 214–15.

116. *Id.* at 215.

117. *Id.* at 215–16.

118. *Id.* at 217.

In such manner, he resolves the theoretical dilemma by resorting to objectives. The trivial logical fallacy notwithstanding, his statement of the objective is very instructive because resolving a private international law problem is the main objective and justification of international arbitration. As discussed in Chapter 5, in great detail, every other justification is mainly promotional.

5. Sundaresh Menon's Theory

The chief justice of Singapore, Sundaresh Menon, has also weighed in on the debate about the legal theory of international arbitration. Having considered a range of options from the strict territorialist approach to the supranational approach, interestingly, he comes down on the side of territorialism on theoretical and pragmatic grounds.[119]

On the theoretical side, his theory is largely predicated on the assumption articulated by the Singapore Court of Appeal that "the *erga omnes* effect of a successful application to set aside an award would generally lead to the conclusion that there is simply no award to enforce."[120] He argues that the permissive language employed in Article V(1)(*e*) of the New York Convention is not meant to accord discretion to the enforcing court as much as it is a function of inartful drafting.[121] He seeks support for this proposition from none other than one of the drafters of the New York Convention, Piet Sanders, as well as Albert Jan van den Berg,[122] and M.B. Holmes.[123]

At the more practical level, he argues that "the territorial approach does the most to safeguard the international character of arbitration [by preventing] vaguely defined domestic normative values of the enforcement court from intruding into the realm of international arbitration."[124] Second, he argues that

119. *See* Speech by Sundaresh Menon, Chief Justice, Singapore, Keynote Address, Standards in Need of Bearers: Encouraging Reform from Within, at Chartered Institute of Arbitrators: Singapore Centenary Conference 23–31 (Sept. 3, 2015), http://www.ciarb.org.sg/wp-content/uploads/2015/09/Keynote-Speech-Standards-in-need-of-Bearers-Encouraging-Reform-from-.pdf.

120. *Id.* at 23 (citing PT First Media TBK (formerly known as PT Broadband Multimedia TBK) v. Astro Nusantara International BV and others and another appeal [2014] 1 SLR 372 at [77]) (Sing.)).

121. *Id.* at 27–28.

122. *Id.* As van den Berg reports, Sanders, one of the drafters, said that "as there no longer exists an arbitral award and enforcing a non-existing arbitral award would be an impossibility or even go against the public policy of the country of enforcement," courts will "refuse the enforcement of an award set aside in the country of origin." *Id.* at 28 (quoting Albert Jan van den Berg, *Enforcement of Arbitral Awards Annulled in Russia: Case Comment on Court of Appeal of Amsterdam, April 29, 2009*, 27 J. Int'l Arb. 179, 187 (2010).

123. *Id.* at 28 (citing M.B. Holmes, *Enforcement of Annulled Arbitral Awards: Logical Fallacies and Fictional Systems*, 79 Arb. 244, 246 (2013)). Menon's proposition, supported by Holmes, is that "it is possible that Art. V(1)(*e*) of the New York Convention was inartfully drafted. Conceivably, the drafters had only hoped to give the enforcement court the discretion to enforce an award notwithstanding the fact that it had not yet become binding on the parties or when it had been suspended in the seat." *Id.*

124. *Id.* at 26.

the territorial approach "upholds party choice [because] [w]here there is an enforceable bargain . . . there is also an equally enforceable bargain to submit to the supervision of the courts at the seat of arbitration."[125] His third point is perhaps the most convincing both in terms of theory and practicality; he argues that:

> [T]he territorial approach, if widely accepted, would tend to discourage forum shopping. When the award is set aside in the seat, the game would by and large be over. Thus a party would not be incentivized to shop around the world in order to find a court somewhere which is willing to enforce the award.[126]

Having endorsed the idea that the court of the chosen seat "specifies the conduct of the arbitration and gives the award its nationality,"[127] he casually addresses the subtext of the entire debate, which is that courts of the developed world would want to review the decisions of the developing world often presented in terms of strong and weak rule of law.[128] To the extent such concerns exist, Menon's point is well taken when he says "it can easily work the other way where an award that really should be and is set aside is subsequently upheld in another jurisdiction perceived as having a weaker rule of law framework."[129]

One of his other points worth highlighting is the impact that open-ended and almost infinite enforcement possibilities would have on the finality of arbitral awards as one of the oft-cited justifications for international arbitration.[130]

6. David Caron's Theory

Professor David Caron does not waste time and energy inventing theory to justify a preconceived outcome. He calls it as it is. International arbitration—be it investment

125. *Id.* He continues arguing that "parties should be taken to have expressly or implicitly embraced the laws and judicial system of the seat of arbitration, 'warts and all'. Allowing enforcement courts to appeal to vaguely defined domestic normative values in deciding whether to enforce an annulled award materially alters the bargain between the parties and also introduces a significant unstable variable into the arbitral process. It would significantly increase transaction costs if parties had to take into account the laws and judicial system of not just the seat, but all the places where enforcement may possibly be sought subsequently when deciding whether to include an arbitration agreement." *Id.* (citing M.B. Holmes, *Enforcement of Annulled Arbitral Awards: Logical Fallacies and Fictional Systems*, 79 Arb. 244, 251, 253–54 (2013)).

126. *Id.* at 27.

127. *Id.* at 25.

128. *Id.* at 27.

129. *Id.*

130. *Id.*

or commercial—is not a system; it is a framework.[131] His framework theory is highly instructive. In his own words:

> Any discussion of coherency in the ICSID system must begin by noting that the root of the problem is embedded very deeply in the structure of arbitration itself. Arbitration generally, and international commercial arbitration in particular, is not in fact a system, but rather is a framework within which discrete and possibly unknown private actions are taken. It is a framework in the same sense that municipal contract law provides a frame within which discrete and possibly unknown private arrangements are concluded. The quandary for ICSID is that it basically, *but not entirely,* adopts arbitration as the method it utilizes for dispute resolution, and thus the present effort to build a system on top of ICSID's use of a framework inherently poses great challenges.
>
> An illustrative example of this quandary is found in the role of the arbitrators in international commercial arbitration. In such arbitration, the focus of the arbitrators is on the dispute before them. For such arbitrators, there is no system with which they should endeavor to be consistent and—to the degree there is such a known body of relevant jurisprudence—it is not clear why the arbitral panel constituted by the parties has the duty to devote their time to ensure that a consistent body of a jurisprudence, arguably a public good, is developed. The duty of arbitrators, sometimes expressed in an oath or in an institutional rule, focuses on the mandate received from the parties which ordinarily focuses on the particular dispute. In short, much of the debate on consistency is tied to uncertainty as to whether the panel's focus should be on particular disputes or instead, on the "system" that emerges from these disputes. ICSID can be schizophrenic in this way—on the one hand, imagining ICSID as a framework calls for a concentrated focus on the particular dispute, while at the same time, imagining ICSID as a system represents an attempt to rearrange all of the free standing arbitrations as though they were part of a court system. This situation can lead to great surprise and frustration when the realization hits home that patterns sometimes present are more coincidental than planned. The question of whether there is a system present depends on whether the questions shared by the various tribunals are identical, or perhaps nearly so. Certainly ICSID tribunals share the procedural and jurisdictional limitations of the ICSID convention, but they do not necessarily address the same identical substantive questions since usually different concessions or BITs are involved. However, in the case of NAFTA Chapter 11 arbitration, for example, the tribunals are all part of a de facto system in that they all share the substantive text.[132]

131. David D. Caron, *Investor State Arbitration: Strategic and Tactical Perspectives on Legitimacy*, 32 Suffolk Transnat'l L. Rev. 513, 516 (2009).

132. *Id.* at 516–17.

The other legal theories assume the existence of a system just because there is a common treaty—whether it is the New York Convention or the ICSID Convention—for the enforcement of awards when in reality all these treaties do is essentially require courts of signatory states to respect awards made in other signatory states.

As Professor Caron rather convincingly notes, neither the New York Convention nor the ICSID Convention created a system of arbitration.[133] The other theoreticians are looking for a system where it does not in fact exist.

That said, Caron's theory appears to lean toward the territorialist approach, although he does not explicitly say so. That is because he emphasizes the fragmented territorial contractual relations everywhere seeking remedy within a framework.[134] As he puts it: "It is a framework in the same sense that municipal contract law provides a frame within which discrete and possibly unknown private arrangements are concluded."[135]

B. CONCLUSION

International arbitration is not a system. As Professor Caron suggests, it is a framework under which a wide range of matters across the world are individually resolved.[136] The inconvenient truth is that a privilege left behind by the world's power and economic hierarchy and the resulting concentration of most of the world's high-value arbitration cases of all types in Europe have created the illusion that there is a supranational autonomous arbitral order seated in Europe. Manifestations of power relations as they were, the theories that consider international arbitration anything other than merely a framework "like mist on eye glasses obscure fact."[137]

133. *Id.*

134. *Id.* at 516.

135. *Id.*

136. *Id.*

137. Charlie Chan in Egypt (20th Century Fox 1935).

5

The Evolving Justifications of International Arbitration

Through the ages, the justifications for international arbitration ranged from the promotional promises of low cost, speed, flexibility, confidentiality, expertise, and neutrality[1] to the more foundational premise of "[w]e cannot have trade and commerce in world markets and international waters exclusively on our terms, governed by our laws, and resolved in our courts."[2] This chapter outlines the evolving justifications and critically assesses the contemporary justifications. The leading texts on international arbitration demonstrate a unity of vantage points on the advantages and disadvantages of international arbitration. This chapter contends that the dominant narrative on the advantages of international arbitration is that of the archetypal multinational business that wants to stay out of what it considers inhospitable, biased and ignorant local courts and take its opponent to a more familiar, presumably enlightened, and culturally acceptable forum. The local party's story in the new forum is hard to profitably tell. This chapter tells that story.

A. INITIAL JUSTIFICATIONS

As indicated in Chapter 3, during the French Revolution, initially, the "*Assemblée Constituante* believed arbitration to be the usual and natural way of settling disputes

1. Every contemporary textbook lists these factors. The leading ones are extensively referenced throughout this chapter.

2. Bremen v. Zapata Off-Shore Co., 407 U.S. 1, 9 (1972). ("The expansion of American business and industry will hardly be encouraged if, notwithstanding solemn contracts, we insist on a parochial concept that all disputes must be resolved under our laws and in our courts . . . . We cannot have trade and commerce in world markets and international waters exclusively on our terms, governed by our laws, and resolved in our courts."). *Id.; see also* Mitsubishi Motors Corp. v. Soler Chrysler-Plymouth, 473 U.S. 614, 629 (1985). Although, in *Bremen,* the Supreme Court said this in the context of a forum selection clause, in *Mitsubishi* it incorporated the basic principle into the arbitration domain. *Bremen,* 407 U.S. at 9–12; *Mitsubishi,* 473 U.S. at 629. It said in particular: "[a]n agreement to arbitrate before a specified tribunal [is], in effect, a specialized kind of forum-selection clause that posits not only the situs of suit but also the procedure to be used in resolving the dispute." *Mitsubishi,* 473 U.S. at 630.

The Culture of International Arbitration. Won L. Kidane

and rendering justice" before the system quickly fell out of favor because of allegations of abuse and rendition of "manifest injustice."[3] As a result of this perception of injustice, the *Napoleonic Code de Procédure Civile* of 1806 imposed severe restrictions on arbitration.[4] Indeed, in 1843, the *Cour de cassation* disallowed the enforceability of agreements to arbitrate future disputes that failed to name the specific arbitrators.[5]

Almost half a century later, on November 23, 1892, the London Chamber of Arbitration was founded on the premise that:

> [The] Chamber is to have all the virtues which the law lacks. It is to be expeditious where the law is slow, cheap where the law is costly, simple where the law is technical, a peace-maker instead of a stirrer up of strife.[6]

During the same era, a similar sentiment prevailed in America. In a famous 1906 speech delivered at the annual meeting of the American Bar Association, Roscoe Pound, who later became dean of Harvard Law School, said:

> Uncertainty, delay and expense, and above all, the injustice of deciding upon points of practice, which are the mere etiquette of justice, direct results of the organization of our courts and the backwardness of our procedure, have created a deep-seated desire to keep out of court, right or wrong, on the art of every sensible businessman in the community.[7]

In the time since the early 1900s, none of these justifications seemed to have particularly inspired confidence. In the meantime, however, many other contemporary justifications have emerged. The "gradual legalization"[8] of the North-South relations and increased transnational commerce and associated jurisdictional and court judgment enforcement problems led to the adoption of the New York Convention.[9]

3. Jean-Louis Delvolvé, Jean Rouche & Gerald H. Pointon, French Arbitration Law and Practice 3 (2003) [hereinafter Delvolvé et al.].

4. Among these restrictions are those on the state, local authorities, and public institutions to submit to arbitration. *See id.* at 3–4.

5. *Id.* at 4 (citing Cass. civ. 10 July 1843, S. 1843.1. p. 561 and D. 1843.1 p. 343; *republished in* Rev. Arb. 1992, 399 with the opinion of Advocate General Hello to the contrary).

6. Blackaby et al., Redfern and Hunter on International Arbitration 61 (5th ed. 2009) (citing V.V. Veeder & Brian Dye, *Lord Bramwell's Arbitration Code*, 8 Arb. Int'l 330 (1992) (quoting Manson (1983) IX LQR)).

7. Roscoe Pound, *The Causes of Popular Dissatisfaction with the Administration of Justice*, 29 A.B.A. Rep. pt. I, 395, 404 (1906).

8. *See* Yves Dezalay & Bryant Garth, Dealing in Virtue 64 (1996).

9. U.N. Convention on the Recognition and Enforcement of Foreign Arbitral Awards (New York), 330 U.N.T.S., 21 U.S.T. 2517, 7 I.L.M. 1046 (June 10, 1958), http://www.uncitral.org/pdf/english/texts/arbitration/NY-conv/New-York-Convention-E.pdf [hereinafter New York Convention]. Comprehensive information on the New York Convention, including the *travaux préparatoires*, is available at New York Convention, http://www.newyorkconvention.org/ (last visited October 2, 2016).

Similar factors in the investment arena led to the adoption of the ICSID Convention[10] and the proliferation of regional and bilateral investment agreements.[11] The purposes and justifications of international arbitration cannot be understood detached from the purposes and justifications of the legal instruments that enabled their existence. Nonetheless, contemporary justifications do not necessarily mirror the main purposes of these instruments. The following sections critically examine the contemporary justifications.

B. CONTEMPORARY JUSTIFICATIONS

Textbooks, journal articles, other forms of academic and trade publications, and speakers in conferences as well as courts of different jurisdictions have advanced various justifications for the increased use of international arbitration that include cost, expediency, procedural flexibility, control over the decision-making process through appointment of arbitrators, confidentiality, neutrality, and enforceability of the agreements, as well as the awards. However, decades of experience with international arbitration have shown that most of these justifications are promotional or uncertain at best.

The justifications could be bifurcated into principal justifications and subsidiary justifications. The leading treatises have now settled on two principal justifications and some uncertain subsidiary justifications. The principal ones are: neutrality and enforceability.[12] Neutrality refers to the neutrality of both the forum and the selected arbitrators. Enforceability refers to the availability of the legal frameworks that enable the enforcement of foreign arbitral awards, such as the New York Convention.[13] The subsidiary and uncertain advantages include flexibility, expertise, confidentiality, and the special roles of arbitrators.[14]

10. Convention on the Settlement of Investment Disputes Between States and Nationals of Other States (as amended), Oct. 14, 1966, 17 U.S.T. 1270, 575 U.N.T.S. 159, https://icsid.worldbank.org/apps/ICSIDWEB/icsiddocs/Pages/ICSID-Convention.aspx [hereinafter ICSID Conference]. Comprehensive information on the ICSID Convention including information on cases is available on the official website at International Centre for Settlement of Investment Disputes, https://icsid.worldbank.org (last visited October 2, 2016.).

11. The United Nations Conference on Trade and Development (UNCTAD) maintains a database of most of the world's Bilateral Investment Treaties (BITs). The texts and additional information of thousands of BITs are available on the official website of UNCTAD at UNCTAD, IIA Databases, http://unctad.org/en/pages/DIAE/International%20Investment%20Agreements%20(IIA)/IIA-Tools.aspx (last visited October 2, 2016).

12. *See* Blackaby et al., *supra* note 6, at 31–32. *See* also Margaret L. Mosses, The Principles and Practice of International Commercial Arbitration 3–4 (2d ed. 2012). Gary Born's textbook offers more nuanced discussions on the subject. *See* Gary Born, International Arbitration: Cases and Materials 87–102 (2011). Margaret Mosses writes matter-of-factly: "The benefits of international commercial arbitration are substantial . . . the two most significant reasons were (1) the neutrality of the forum (that is, being able to stay out of the other party's court) and (2) the likelihood of obtaining enforcement." Mosses, *supra*, at 3. The other advantages she mentions are confidentiality, less discovery, and speed. Mosses, *supra*, at 3–4.

13. Blackaby et al., *supra* note 6, at 31.

14. *Id.* at 33–34.

Each justification is described before a critical examination is offered in the next subsection. Neutrality is one of the two principal justifications. Alan Redfern presents its virtues as follows:

> Parties to an international contract usually come from different countries. The national court of one party will be a foreign court to the other party. It will be "foreign" in almost every sense. It will have its own formalities and its own rules and procedures, which may (quite naturally) have been developed to deal with domestic matters and not for international commercial or investment disputes. It will also be "foreign" in the sense that it will have its own language—which may or may not be the language of the contract—and its own bench of judges and lawyers.[15]

The supposed strictly neutral tribunal makes perfect sense only if certain improbable assumptions are made, that is, that the other party would not face the same obstacles when the case is moved to some far-off cosmopolitan location. This goes to the question of the balance of neutrality, and will be discussed in more detail in the next section. But the second justification is the greater enforceability of the award under the existing legal infrastructure set up by the New York Convention, the ICSID Convention, and other regional and bilateral arrangements.[16] Evidently, because of these instruments, the odds of enforcing arbitral awards are now better than the odds of enforcing court judgments in many parts of the world.[17] Within the

15. *Id.* at 32. The passage continues:

> This means that a party to an international contract which does *not* contain an agreement to arbitrate may find, when a dispute arises, that it is obliged to commence proceedings in a foreign court, to employ lawyers other than those who are accustomed to its business and to embark upon the time-consuming and expensive task of translating the contract, the correspondence between the parties, and other relevant documents into the language of the foreign court. Such a party will also run the risk, if the case proceeds to a hearing, of understanding very little of what is said about its own case.

Id.; see also text accompanying n.69.

16. *Id.* at 31–33.

17. *Id.* at 33. There is no universal court judgment recognition convention to date. HCCH's attempts have not been remarkably successful in this regard. Comprehensive information including drafts are available at Convention of 1 February 1971 on the Recognition and Enforcement of Foreign Judgments in Civil and Commercial Matters, HCCH, Feb. 1, 1971, https://www.hcch.net/en/instruments/conventions/full-text/?cid=78. The European Union, however, has a binding treaty, that is, European Council Regulation No. 44/2001. Council Regulation (EC) No 44/2001 on jurisdiction and the recognition and enforcement of judgments in civil and commercial matters, The Council of the European Union, Dec. 22, 2000, http://eur-lex.europa.eu/LexUriServ/LexUriServ.do?uri=OJ:L:2001:012:0001:0023:en:PDF. In the United States, there is the Uniform Foreign Money Judgment Recognition Act of 1962. The Uniform Act has no legal effect but is a recommendation for the states. *See* NATIONAL CONFERENCE OF COMMISSIONERS ON UNIFORM STATE LAWS, UNIFORM FOREIGN MONEY-JUDGMENTS RECOGNITION ACT (1962), https://lettersblogatory.com/wp-content/uploads/2011/01/UFMJRA.pdf. Apparently, the community of nations has found it easier to agree on recognition of arbitral awards than their respective courts' judgments.

enforceability advantage, Redfern incudes finality of the award.[18] This is essentially the absence of an appellate process.[19] Others consider this a disadvantage.

Within the subsidiary but uncertain justifications fall two perceived advantages: (1) the flexibility of the rules that might be adjusted to fit certain cases and industries,[20] and (2) the ability to choose one's own arbitrators who, "should be able to grasp quickly the salient issues of fact or law in dispute. This will save the parties both time and money, as well as offering them the prospect of a sensible award."[21] However, these perceived advantages are based on several unwarranted assumptions, such as the system's superior ability to select arbitrators who would always quickly grasp facts and law and dispense fair justice. The merits of these justifications will also be assessed in the next section.

Confidentiality[22] is another justification. It is supposed to protect parties that are dragged into arbitration against their will, or that are compelled to resort to arbitration against their wish.[23] It protects trade secrets or competitive advantages, or even shields their own "bad-decision-making."[24] What else it shields from scrutiny is not a part of the narrative frequently told.

The leading textbooks also contain discussions on disadvantages of international arbitration. The disadvantages-list often contains cost, delay, and some jurisdictional complications.[25]

It appears more specifically that the leading developed nations considered arbitral awards, which were then expected to be seated and made in the developed countries by jurists from the developed world, to be more acceptable to the courts of the developed world than court judgments of the developing world.

18. Blackaby et al., *supra* note 6, at 32.

19. Although ordinarily, in most modern systems, the merits of final awards are not subject to judicial review, other possible post-award processes such as annulment proceedings and permissible resistance to enforcement action often deprive arbitral awards of finality.

20. Blackaby et al., *supra* note 6, at 32–33.

21. *Id.* at 33.

22. A related concept is privacy, which is limited to the privacy of the proceedings. Confidentiality agreements often restrict access to information of all types, including the pleadings and awards.

23. Blackaby et al., *supra* note 6, at 33–34.

24. *Id.* at 33.

25. *Id.* at 34–36. Redfern highlights the limitations of arbitral power as a disadvantage in the following terms:

> In general, the power accorded to arbitrators, whilst adequate for the purpose of resolving the matter in dispute, fall short of those conferred upon a court of law. For example, the power to require the attendance of witnesses under penalty of fine or imprisonment, or to enforce awards by the attachment of a bank account or the sequestration of assets, are powers which form part of the prerogative of the State. They are not powers that any State is likely to delegate to a private arbitral tribunal, however eminent or well-intentioned that arbitral tribunal may be. In practice, if it becomes necessary for an arbitral tribunal to take a coercive action in order to deal properly with the case before it, such action must usually be taken indirectly though the machinery of the local courts, rather than directly as a judge himself can do." *Id.* at 36.

Most recent surveys by stakeholders do not necessarily illuminate the textbook renditions when examined carefully. A 2015 survey of 763 questionnaire responses and 105 interviews by White & Case LLP and the School of International Arbitration of Queen Mary University of London[26] is one of the most recent ones. The White & Case Survey found that 90 percent of respondents surveyed prefer international arbitration to resolve cross-border commercial disputes over litigation,[27] and that the most preferred venues are in London and Paris, with Hong Kong and Singapore standing third and fourth, respectively.[28]

The survey generally shows that the advantages of arbitration are enforceability of the awards, avoidance of specific legal systems, flexibility, and selection of arbitrators in descending order.[29] Cost and lack of speed have been cited as disadvantages.[30] Consider the perspective again: ability to stay out of a particular court, and enforce foreign awards. Consider also the five most preferred seats: London, Paris, Hong Kong, Singapore, and Geneva, with Singapore and Hong King selected as the most improved.[31] The preferred arbitral institutions are: ICC, LCIA, HKIAC, and SIAC.[32]

One of the most important questions that the survey asked was: "What are the three most valuable characteristics of international arbitration?"[33] The results were interesting: 65 percent of the respondents chose enforceability, 64 percent chose avoiding specific legal systems/national courts, 38 percent chose flexibility, 38 percent chose selection of arbitrators, 33 percent chose confidentiality and privacy, 25 percent chose neutrality, 18 percent chose finality, 10 percent chose speed, 2 percent chose cost, and 2 percent chose other things.[34] The results are evaluated below, but consider the breakdown of the respondents of the survey. The survey asked where the respondents are based; the result was the following: 53 percent in Europe, 26 percent in Asia, 18 percent in the Americas, 2 percent in Africa, and 1 percent in Oceania.[35] In terms of the representation of legal systems: 39 percent civil law, 36 percent common law, 22 percent both civil and common law, and 3 percent others.[36]

26. White & Case LLP & Queen Mary University of London, 2015 International Arbitration Survey: Improvements and Innovations in International Arbitration (2015), http://www.whitecase.com/publications/insight/2015-international-arbitration-survey-improvements-and-innovations [hereinafter White & Case Survey].

27. *Id.* at 2.

28. *Id.* at 12 chart 7.

29. *Id.* at 17 chart 13.

30. *Id.* at 2.

31. *Id.*

32. *Id.*

33. *Id.* at 6 chart 2.

34. *Id.*

35. *Id.* at 52 chart 47.

36. *Id.* at 52.

This, in fact, appears to be a relatively good demonstration of the current realization of the contemporary reasons for international arbitration. For example, regarding the survey question on the most valuable characteristics of international arbitration, the scores of neutrality and arbitrator selection, 18 percent and 38 percent respectively, are both interesting because they mean that of all the respondents, only 18 percent and 38 percent considered neutrality and arbitrator selection to be the most valuable characteristics of arbitration.[37] As indicated in the survey results, one interviewee put it nicely when he paraphrased what Winston Churchill said about democracy: "Arbitration is the worst form of international dispute resolution, except for all those other forms that have been tried from time to time."[38]

This would suggest that the most legitimate reason for arbitration is the ability to stay out of the other party's court and a better chance of enforcing the award.

During about the same period as the White & Case Survey, the International Bar Association Arb 40 Subcommittee also issued what it called "The Current State and Future of International Arbitration: Regional Perspectives."[39] The IBA Report noted that although growth is anticipated in all regions, in Africa, Latin America, and some parts of Asia, national court litigation remained the predominant means of dispute settlement.[40]

More substantively, the factors for growth that the IBA Report cites include: legislative reform (enactment of more supportive legislation), party autonomy (the ability to choose arbitrators and flexible procedures), enforcement regime (the New York Convention), speed and cost (better than court litigation), expertise (better decision- makers than court judges), neutrality (of forum), and confidentiality.[41] The IBA Report does not attempt to empirically prove the propositions, but it is a rehash of the mythology of efficiency, expertise, speed, flexibility, neutrality, confidentiality, and enforceability as universal advantages and justifications.

Among the hurdles that the Report cites are the lack of court support (in the enforcement of the agreements or awards, or even during proceedings) in some jurisdictions—such as in Africa[42]—increasing costs, a limited pool of arbitrators, problems with enforcement, and the demand for transparency.[43] On an important and related note, the Report says in particular that the limited pool of arbitrators "was of particular concern to practitioners in Europe, North America and Asia-Pacific.

37. *Id.* at 7 chart 3.

38. *Id.* at 10.

39. International Bar Association Arb 40 Subcommittee, The Current State and Future of International Arbitration: Regional Perspectives (2015), http://www.ibanet.org/LPD/Dispute_Resolution_Section/Arbitration/Publications.aspx [hereinafter IBA Report].

40. *Id.* at 9.

41. *Id.*

42. The Report notes in particular that: "In Africa, it was observed in many jurisdictions that there is often a lack of support generally from the courts, if not hostility on occasions." *Id.* at 10.

43. *Id.*

Primarily, the concern expressed was that a limited pool of arbitrators is leading to delays in the proceedings and awards being rendered."[44] The Report also indicated other concerns that arise out of the limited size of the pool without saying why the pool had to be limited. It states that: "arbitrators were not being proactive enough by identifying preliminary issues, were not prepared for hearings, were too biased in favor of the appointing party and were not producing quality arbitral awards."[45] The mythology of the need for an elite group of arbitrators, by IBA's own admission, has led to this kind of unprepared, unresponsive, and biased justice that ultimately the system appears to consider a minor glitch.[46] This particular matter is central to this study and will be explored in greater detail in subsequent chapters.

As far as Africa is concerned, the IBA Report says that "while much of the demand for international arbitration is driven by international companies investing in Africa, local entrepreneurs are beginning to embrace international arbitration."[47] In terms of the preference of seat, "most [African] contributors consider their home jurisdictions to be safe seats for the settlement of small commercial disputes, while some referenced the United Kingdom, France and Switzerland as safe seats when dealing with large and sensitive commercial disputes."[48] The IBA Report does not, however, say why the African respondents made that distinction.[49] To the extent that such a statistical entry represents a school of thought, it would appear that the school equates the accuracy of the legal process and the quality of justice that emerges out of it to technological and material advancement.

C. ASSESSING THE CREDIBILITY OF THE CONTEMPORARY JUSTIFICATIONS

Contrary to what is consistently and repeatedly stated in the leading texts, there is no universal set of justifications applicable in all circumstances for all parties. In transnational contacts, as far as how disputes should be settled, the parties' interests and preferences are almost always divergent.[50] Arbitration is mostly an option preferred by the party that wants to stay out of the other party's home courts. In cases of foreign investment or projects carried out by foreign companies in a particular country, it is typically the foreign company that insists on moving the dispute out of the country in which the project is supposed to be implemented.[51] As such, the justifications

44. *Id.*

45. *Id.*

46. *Id.*

47. *Id.* at 20.

48. *Id.*

49. *See generally id.*

50. *See generally* 1 Gary B. Born, International Commercial Arbitration 70–71 (2d ed. 2014).

51. *See generally, id.* at 74–76.

for arbitration are often provided from the point of view of the foreign party. There are a number of complex historical, political, and ideological reasons for that, but those are beyond the scope here. For purposes of this critical analysis, the contemporary justifications could be classified into two broad categories: jurisdictional and promotional. The jurisdictional justifications (which include front-end and back-end enforcement issues) are real, but the promotional justifications (which include cost, speed, efficiency, flexibility, expertise, confidentiality, etc.) are situational and mainly economic. This section assesses both sets of justifications in turn.

1. Jurisdictional Justification

Every textbook, every study, and report rightfully mentions the superiority of the legal infrastructure for the enforcement of arbitral awards as opposed to court judgments as one of the justifications and advantages of international arbitration.[52]

Gary Born endorses many of the standard and promotional answers on the benefits of arbitration, including neutrality, cost, speed, confidentiality, flexibility, competence, and enforceability,[53] but unlike most writers, he also provides a more serious and nuanced scholarly note on the purpose and objective of international arbitration and the real jurisdictional justifications thereof.

International arbitration alleviates some of the serious front-end and back-end jurisdictional problems, while of course, creating its own jurisdictional complications along the way.[54] Born's description of the problem is instructive:

> In today's global economy, business enterprises of every description can find themselves parties to contracts with foreign companies (and states) from around the world, as well as parties to litigation before courts in equally distant locales. The Consequence of these proceedings—and of losing them—are often enormous. A contract means no more than what it is interpreted to say, and how it is enforced; corrupt, incompetent, or arbitrary decisions can rewrite a party's agreements or impose staggering liabilities and responsibilities.[55]

Born properly describes the challenges of decision-making. Indeed "corrupt, incompetent, or arbitrary decisions can rewrite a party's agreements or impose staggering liabilities and responsibilities,"[56] but how is arbitration immune from this? In an attempt to answer this question, Born continues writing: "There are many reasons why the same dispute can have materially different outcomes in different forums.

52. *See, e.g., id.* at 77–80.

53. *See id.* at 73–93.

54. Granted that international arbitration also brings its own jurisdictional complexities that would not have existed, on balance, it would appear that it eliminates more jurisdictional problems than it creates.

55. Born, *supra* note 50, at 70.

56. *Id.* at 70.

Procedural choice-of-law and substantive legal rules differ dramatically from one country to another."[57] So far arbitration does not seem to enjoy any particular advantage, but consider more of his statements:

> Other considerations, such as inconvenience, local bias and language, may make a particular forum much more favorable for one party than another. More pointedly, the competence and integrity of judicial officers also vary substantially among different forums; annual corruption indices and other studies leave little doubt as to the uneven levels of integrity in some national judiciaries. Those indices are, regrettably, confirmed by contemporary anecdotal experience as to the corruption endemic in civil litigation in some jurisdictions.[58]

Hence, local courts are biased, corrupt, and lack integrity. All of these might be true of judiciaries around the world, but what superior mechanism does the arbitral system have to avoid all of the above, that is, bias and lack of integrity? Born does not say much about this but continues writing: "Precisely because national legal systems differ profoundly, parties inevitably seek to ensure that, if international disputes arise, those disputes are resolved in the forum that is most favorable to their interests."[59] If by "parties" we always mean parties who agree that the local courts are biased and corrupt, it makes perfect sense for them to be looking for some disinterested and pure dispenser of justice, but if one of the parties disagrees, removal of the case to a forum more favorable to the other party only shifts the risk—it does not eliminate it.

In any case, the more genuine problem is jurisdictional. Born describes it well in the following terms:

> In turn, that can mean protracted litigation over jurisdiction, forum selection and recognition of foreign judgments. These disputes can result in lengthy and complex litigation—often in parallel or multiple proceedings—which produce more in legal costs and uncertainty than anything else. In this regard, contemporary international litigation bears unfortunate, but close, resemblances to the difficulties reported by Medieval commentators regarding transnational litigation in early eras.[60]

The dispute resolution provision in contracts would indeed help these jurisdictional difficulties. Born assumes the achievability of a reliable forum that would resolve these problems, and further assumes that international arbitration would offer such reliability.[61]

57. *Id.*

58. *Id.* at 70–71 (citations omitted).

59. *Id.* at 71.

60. *Id.*

61. *Id.* "Because of the importance of forum selection in the international context, parties to cross-border commercial transactions very often include dispute resolution provisions in their agreements, selecting a contractual forum in which to resolve their differences. By selecting a forum in

Leaving aside the assumptions that Born makes about the universal reliability of international arbitration, which could be as biased as litigation—if not more—this passage describes the serious jurisdictional uncertainties and possible multiplicity of litigations that international arbitration, if legitimately organized, could potentially avoid. To be sure, although international arbitration might mitigate such possibilities, it cannot eradicate the problem of parallel and other types of litigation complications. The recent Yukos debacle of multiple judicial proceedings offers a good example.[62]

Arbitration agreements could avoid the front-end jurisdictional problems as they function like a forum selection clause enforceable as a matter of international obligation, whether through the New York Convention, the ICSID Convention, or some other regional or bilateral treaties. When the contracts are done well, the front-end jurisdictional problems—including personal jurisdiction, subject matter jurisdiction, venue, etc.—could be avoided. Arbitration agreements could also avoid back-end problems as the awards, if done properly, would be enforced by courts of law under the same legal infrastructure. Although arbitration could sometimes give rise to its own jurisdictional complications, leading to complex litigation both relating to the enforcement of the agreement and to the award, it does, more frequently than not, help avoid jurisdictional problems.

Although international arbitration sometimes introduces its own jurisdictional complications, the minimization of front-end and back-end jurisdictional and associated choice-of-law problems is perhaps the legitimate and peculiar advantage of international arbitration.[63] Almost every other justification, as stated earlier, is either incorrect, situation dependent, or merely promotional.

advance, parties are able to mitigate these costs and uncertainties of international dispute resolution, through the centralization of their dispute in a single, reliable forum." *Id.* (citations omitted).

62. In what is considered to be the largest arbitral award to date, an arbitral tribunal siting in The Hague found the respondent state, Russia, liable for damages in the amount of $50 billion. Russia, in addition to filing an annulment action in The Hague, continues to challenge enforcement on various legal grounds, including in the United States. The result is yet to be seen. Information about the various aspects of this case is available at Dmytro Galagan & Patricia Živković, *The Challenge of the Yukos Award: An Award Written by Someone Else—a Violation of the Tribunal's Mandate?*, Kluwer Arb. Blog (Feb. 27, 2015), http://kluwerarbitrationblog.com/2015/02/27/the-challenge-of-the-yukos-award-an-award-written-by-someone-else-a-violation-of-the-tribunals-mandate/. *See also* Neil Buckley & Courtney Weaver, *France and Belgium Freeze Russian State Assets over Yukos Case*, Fin. Times (June 18, 2015), http://www.ft.com/cms/s/0/3ab475a6-15da-11e5-a58d-00144feabdc0.html#axzz3tLfF1VF1; Jake Rudnitsky & Anton Doroshev, *Russia Set for Global Asset Fight over Yukos after Seizures*, Bloomberg Bus. (June 18, 2015), http://www.bloomberg.com/news/articles/2015-06-18/russia-braces-for-global-asset-fight-over-yukos-after-seizures-ib2boyg9.

63. The theoretical foundations of this jurisdictional advantage are very well summarized by the U.S. Supreme Court in Scherk v. Alberto-Culver Co., 417 U.S. 506, 516–17 (1974) (citing The Bremen v. Zapata Offshore Co., 407 U.S. 1, 7–15 (1972)) as follows:

> [U]ncertainty will almost inevitably exist with respect to any contract touching two or more countries, each with its own substantive laws and conflict-of-laws rules. A contractual provision specifying in advance the forum in which disputes shall be litigated and the law to be applied is, therefore, an almost indispensable precondition to achievement of the orderliness and predictability essential to any international business transaction. Furthermore,

2. Promotional Justifications

Among the textbook justifications claiming universal appeal are neutrality, expertise, flexibility, and confidentiality. The meaningfulness of all of these justifications assumes the invariable validity of the following proposition: integrity of arbitrators of the highest order despite the absence of meaningful review and checks and balances. A critical review of each follows.

A. Neutrality

Consider the assumptions that Born as well as the other writers make. First, neutrality of the arbitral forum as a justification is often cited together with the incapacity, bias, or simple inconvenience of domestic courts. Corruption is also frequently added to the mix of what ails judiciaries around the world.[64] In situations where the contracting parties do not come from comparably developed countries the neutrality justification is often expressed with greater emphasis.[65] But when the disputing

such a provision obviates the danger that a dispute under the agreement might be submitted to a forum hostile to the interests of one of the parties or unfamiliar with the problem area involved.

A parochial refusal by the courts of one country to enforce an international arbitration agreement would not only frustrate these purposes, but would invite unseemly and mutually destructive jockeying by the parties to secure tactical litigation advantages. In the present case, for example, it is not inconceivable that if Scherk had anticipated that Alberto-Culver would be able in this country to enjoin resort to arbitration he might have sought an order in France or some other country enjoining Alberto-Culver from proceeding with its litigation in the United States. Whatever recognition the courts of this country might ultimately have granted to the order of the foreign court, the dicey atmosphere of such a legal no-man's-land would surely damage the fabric of international commerce and trade, and imperil the willingness and ability of businessmen to enter into international commercial agreements . . . .

Two Terms ago in *The Bremen v. Zapata Off-Shore Co.*, we rejected the doctrine that a forum-selection clause of a contract, although voluntarily adopted by the parties, will not be respected in a suit brought in the United States "unless the selected state would provide a more convenient forum than the state in which suit is brought." Rather, we concluded that a "forum clause should control absent a strong showing that it should be set aside." We noted that "much uncertainty and possibly great inconvenience to both parties could arise if a suit could be maintained in any jurisdiction in which an accident might occur or if jurisdiction were left to any place [where personal or *in rem* jurisdiction might be established]. The elimination of all such uncertainties by agreeing in advance on a forum acceptable to both parties is an indispensable element in international trade, commerce, and contracting."

An agreement to arbitrate before a specified tribunal is, in effect, a specialized kind of forum-selection clause that posits not only the situs of suit but also the procedure to be used in resolving the dispute. The invalidation of such an agreement in the case before us would not only allow the respondent to repudiate its solemn promise but would, as well, reflect a "parochial concept that all disputes must be resolved under our laws and in our courts. . . . We cannot have trade and commerce in world markets and international waters exclusively on our terms, governed by our laws, and resolved in our courts."

64. *See* Born, *supra* note 50, at 71 (citing *Corruption Perception Index 2011*, Transparency Int'l, http://www.transparency.org/cpi2011/ (last visited Mar. 16, 2016)).

65. *See generally id.* at 80–81.

parties are from the same level of development—say between the United States and Japan—neutrality as a reason for arbitration is often not accompanied by the same level of zeal, especially if the alternative is litigation in U.S. courts. In fact, it is not inconceivable that the Japanese party might want to litigate in the United States depending on what is at stake, and vice versa.[66] Indeed, in these times of a complex multination corporate world, it might even be impossible to know exactly what nationality the corporation has for purposes of assigning local bias. A Toyota plant hiring hundreds of thousands of Americans in southern parts of the United States may not want to go to Japan for a dispute affecting the economic interests of the American workers. As such, Gary Born's example that a dispute between a U.S. company and a Japanese company are better off arbitrating in Switzerland or England[67] is an outdated concept. It all depends on so many factors in each individual case.

The conventional thinking described above assumes that choices are unencumbered and unlimited, that neutrality is always achievable, that courts everywhere are not neutral, and that the neutrality that could be obtained through party choice is superior to the courts. It looks at the advantages from one particular vantage point. It suggests the universality of the advantages and disadvantages. It ignores the possibility that for every winner, there are losers, and losers would look at everything from a different perspective. Redfern expands on his discussion of the virtues of neutrality as follows:

> [A] party to an international contract which does *not* contain an agreement to arbitrate may find, when a dispute arises, that it is obliged to commence proceedings in a foreign court, to employ lawyers other than those who are accustomed to its business and to embark upon the time-consuming and expensive task of translating the contract, the correspondence between the parties, and other relevant documents into the language of the foreign court. Such a party will also run the risk, if the case proceeds to a hearing, of understanding very little of what is said about its own case.[68]

The above passage focuses—in very broad terms—on the cultural barrier and uncertainties that the foreign party would face. Beyond shifting the cultural barrier to the other party, "neutrality" has some more advantages.

> By contrast, a reference to arbitration means that the dispute is likely to be determined in a neutral forum (or place of arbitration) rather than on the home ground of one party or the other. Each party will also be given an opportunity to participate in the selection of the tribunal. If this tribunal is to consist of a single arbitrator, he or she will be chosen by agreement of the parties, or by some outside institution to which the parties have agreed; and he or she will be

66. *See generally id.*

67. *See id.* at 75.

68. Blackaby et al., *supra* note 6, at 32; see also text accompanying n.15.

> required to be independent and impartial. If the tribunal is to consist of three arbitrators, two of them may be chosen by the parties themselves, but nevertheless each of them will be required to be independent and impartial (and may be dismissed if this proves not to be the case). In this sense, whether the tribunal consists of one arbitrator or of three, it will be a strictly "neutral" tribunal.[69]

This is obviously excellent advice to a company that does business in some far-off foreign land. But consider, for example, this "strictly neutral" proposition from the perspective of an African state involved in a dispute with a European multinational. This advice would take the dispute out of Africa to Europe. The private investor would be satisfied because—according to the proposition—the removal of the proceeding from an unfamiliar environment to a familiar environment would save it from stranger justice where she had to hire unfamiliar lawyers, translate documents, and navigate unfamiliar rules. But then if one considers it from the African party's perspective, it would be subjected to exactly the types of stranger justice that the private party wishes to avoid in the name of neutrality: hire unfamiliar lawyers, translate documents, go to some far-off forum, etc. Neutrality in this sense is not neutral. Neutrality in the true sense of the term is difficult to achieve, at least in the current state of North-South economic hierarchy. If a true neutral forum were to be devised in the above scenario, the disputants would take their case to Seoul or Beijing where they have to hire Korean lawyers and translate documents into Korean or Chinese. Therefore, even in the context of the dominant thinking of neutrality, it cannot justify international arbitration as a means of dispute resolution in the existing world economic order, at least when developing countries are involved. It is a concept that mainly shifts the risk.

Even then, the value that the users and practitioners assign to it does not seem very high. The White & Case Survey shows that only 25 percent of the respondents chose neutrality as one of the most valuable characteristics of arbitration.[70] Even when the regional imbalance is taken out of the equation, as the White & Case Survey indicates, neutrality as a justification ranks very low. Part of this is explained by the lack of confidence in the neutrality of party-appointed arbitrators. The IBA Report puts this as concerns over arbitrators being "*too biased in favour of the appointing party* and were not producing quality arbitral award."[71] This properly expresses the reality of the current marketplace of arbitration.[72] Neutrality as a justification for international arbitration in general is, thus, principally promotional. The textbooks and treatises need updating.

69. *Id.* at 32.

70. White & Case Survey, *supra* note 26, at 6 chart 2.

71. IBA Report, *supra* note 39, at 10 (emphasis added).

72. A somewhat extreme position would even suggest a more serious and fundamental flaw:

> To put it simply, if a doctor is sponsored by a pharmaceutical company, we might question whether the medicine prescribed is the best for our health; if a public servant receives money from a lobbyist, we might question whether the policies they promote are in the public

B. Confidentiality

At the most basic level, recognizing that some cultures would legitimately value confidentiality for its own sake, in modern commercial dealings confidentiality often presupposes that at least one party wants to hide something from public scrutiny. Although at times legitimate interests might need protection, confidentiality cannot be a universal virtue. If anything it requires its own independent justification because a system of justice that shields itself from public scrutiny cannot escape suspicion. Confidentiality as an objective of international arbitration is sometimes cited as a reason to avoid aggravation of the parties' dispute, or as Born puts it, avoidance of "trial by press release" while acknowledging that "commercial parties sometimes affirmatively desire certain disputes and their outcomes be made public."[73]

What is often not told is what else confidentiality hides about the system of justice. In international arbitration, apart from the occasional legitimate party request for protection from disclosure of certain parts of the commercial relations and the dispute thereof, confidentiality appears to be structurally promoted by arbitral institutions,[74] arbitrators, counsel, and the arbitration literature in general. But inasmuch as it protects information that the parties do not want disclosed, it also shields from scrutiny the nature and quality of the justice that emerges out of the process. Most important, it shields bad decisions and bad players; obviously it also deprives credit to good decisions and good actors.

A system of justice that thrives behind closed doors cannot escape suspicion. In many cases, it is fair to assume that the party that is making unsubstantiated claims or wishes to manipulate procedure for lack of confidence in the merits of the claim

> interest. In the same vein, if an arbitrator's main source of income and career opportunities depends on the decision of companies to sue, we should wonder how impartial their decisions are.
>
> And concerns not only arise from the financial benefits arbitrators gain. Arbitrators frequently combine their role with several other hats: working as practitioners, academics, policy advisers or as media commentators. With these various roles, this small group of investment lawyers can influence the direction of the investment arbitration system in a way that they can continue benefiting from it.
>
> A close examination of the arbitration world soon reveals why arbitrators, far from being neutral, have become powerful players who have shaped the pro-corporate investment arbitration system that we see today.

Corporate Europe Observatory, *Chapter 4: Who Guards the Guardians? The Conflicting Interests of Investment Arbitrators* (Nov. 27, 2012), http://corporateeurope.org/trade/2012/11/chapter-4-who-guards-guardians-conflicting-interests-investment-arbitrators.

73. Born, *supra* note 50, at 89.

74. The ICC Court, for example, states on its website that: "The Court respects your privacy. In contrast with ordinary courtroom proceedings under public and media gaze, ICC does not divulge details of an arbitration case and keeps the identities of the parties completely confidential. So your business remains nobody else's business. Sometimes, of course, parties will publicize an award—but ICC's lips are always sealed. If you wish, you may also enter into a confidentiality agreement with the opposing party as an additional safeguard." *Frequently Asked Questions on ICC Arbitration*, http://www.iccwbo.org/faqs/frequently-asked-questions-on-icc-arbitration/#Q4 (last visited Mar. 16, 2016).

may be more inclined to seek confidentiality. Unfortunately, the default thinking being confidentiality, arbitrators are quick in embracing confidentiality where there is room for discretion.

The recent backlash against investment arbitration[75] is partly fueled by suspicions about confidentiality. Its public manifestation is captured very well by a passage from a *New York Times* report: "Their meetings are secret. Their members are generally unknown. The decisions they reach need not be fully disclosed. Yet the way a small number of international tribunals handles disputes between investors and foreign governments has led to national laws being revoked, justice systems questioned and environmental regulations challenged."[76]

Indeed, recent trends are toward more public accountability and transparency. For example, the investment dispute settlement section of the Trans-Pacific Partnership Agreement contains the following transparency requirement:

> Article 9.24: Transparency of Arbitral Proceedings
> 1. Subject to paragraphs 2 and 4, the respondent shall, after receiving the following documents, promptly transmit them to the non-disputing Parties and make them available to the public:
>   (a) the notice of intent;
>   (b) the notice of arbitration;
>   (c) pleadings, memorials and briefs submitted to the tribunal by a disputing party and any written submissions submitted pursuant to

The LCIA Rules are even more explicit. Article 30 on Confidentiality states:

> 30.1 The parties undertake as a general principle to keep confidential all awards in the arbitration, together with all materials in the arbitration created for the purpose of the arbitration and all other documents produced by another party in the proceedings not otherwise in the public domain, save and to the extent that disclosure may be required of a party by legal duty, to protect or pursue a legal right, or to enforce or challenge an award in legal proceedings before a state court or other legal authority.
>
> 30.2 The deliberations of the Arbitral Tribunal shall remain confidential to its members, save as required by any applicable law and to the extent that disclosure of an arbitrator's refusal to participate in the arbitration is required of the other members of the Arbitral Tribunal under Articles 10, 12, 26 and 27.
>
> 30.3 The LCIA does not publish any award or any part of an award without the prior written consent of all parties and the Arbitral Tribunal.

LCIA Arbitration Rules (2014), LCIA, http://www.lcia.org/Dispute_Resolution_Services/lcia-arbitration-rules-2014.aspx#Article 30.

75. *See, e.g.*, The Backlash against Investment Arbitration: Perceptions and Reality (Michael Waibel et al. eds., 2010); Gus Van Harten, Investment Treaty Arbitration and Public Law (2007).

76. Anthony DePalma, *NAFTA's Powerful Little Secret; Obscure Tribunals Settle Disputes, but Go Too Far, Critics Say*, N.Y. Times (Mar. 11, 2001), http://www.nytimes.com/2001/03/11/business/nafta-s-powerful-little-secret-obscure-tribunals-settle-disputes-but-go-too-far.html?pagewanted=all&src=pm.

Article 9.23.2 (Conduct of the Arbitration) and Article 9.23.3 and Article 9.28 (Consolidation);

(d) minutes or transcripts of hearings of the tribunal, if available; and

(e) orders, awards and decisions of the tribunal.[77]

The United Nations Convention on Transparency in Treaty-based Investor-State Arbitration, called the "Mauritius Convention on Transparency,"[78] is another example of the most contemporary trend.[79] This is also reinforced by the White & Case Survey, which found that only 33 percent of the respondents chose confidentiality and privacy as the most valuable characteristic of international arbitration.[80] The White & Case Survey also indicates that lack of transparency regarding arbitrator performance was one of the negative factors.[81] With the exception of some specific and legally protected information in various industries, confidentiality as a virtue in all sorts of arbitral proceedings and as a general justification for international arbitration is thus an outdated concept. In practice, arbitrators and some counsel seem to

77. Text of the Trans-Pacific Partnership was released on November 5, 2015. It is available at *Chapter 9: Investment*, http://www.mfat.govt.nz/downloads/trade-agreement/transpacific/TPP-text/9.%20Investment%20Chapter.pdf (last visited Mar. 16, 2016).

78. Text of the Convention is available at UNCITRAL, *Convention on Transparency in Treaty-based Investor-State Arbitration (the "Mauritius Convention on Transparency")* (2014), http://www.uncitral.org/pdf/english/texts/arbitration/transparency-convention/Transparency-Convention-e.pdf.

79. The Convention incorporates the UNCITRAL Rules on Transparency in Treaty-based Investor State Arbitration. UNCITRAL, *Rules on Transparency in Treaty-based Investor-State Arbitration*, http://www.uncitral.org/uncitral/en/uncitral_texts/arbitration/2014Transparency.html (last visited October 2, 2016) These Rules require the publication of documents as follows:

> Article 3. Publication of documents
> 1. Subject to article 7, the following documents shall be made available to the public: the notice of arbitration, the response to the notice of arbitration, the statement of claim, the statement of defense and any further written statements or written submissions by any disputing party; a table listing all exhibits to the aforesaid documents and to expert reports and witness statements, if such table has been prepared for the proceedings, but not the exhibits themselves; any written submissions by the non-disputing Party (or Parties) to the treaty and by third persons, transcripts of hearings, where available; and orders, decisions and awards of the arbitral tribunal.
> 2. Subject to article 7, expert reports and witness statements, exclusive of the exhibits thereto, shall be made available to the public, upon request by any person to the arbitral tribunal.
> 3. Subject to article 7, the arbitral tribunal may decide, on its own initiative or upon request from any person, and after consultation with the disputing parties, whether and how to make available exhibits and any other documents provided to, or issued by, the arbitral tribunal not falling within paragraphs 1or 2 above. This may include, for example, making such documents available at a specified site.

80. *See* White & Case Survey, *supra* note 26, at 6 chart 2. Confidentiality signifies the prohibition imposed on the parties not to disclose information whereas privacy simply restricts access to third parties. See Born, *supra* note 50, at 89 n.614 and accompanying text.

81. *See* White & Case Survey, *supra* note 26, at 7.

be more interested in confidentiality than the parties they represent. Even in commercial arbitration, however, the default position of confidentiality seems to be gradually receding. And again, the textbooks need updating both figuratively and literally.

c. Flexibility

Daniel Fisher of Forbes wrote on February 8, 2015, that "[t]he FAA reflected mayhem in the federal court system, where until the Federal Rules of Civil Procedure were passed in 1938, each judge picked whatever procedural rules he wanted and courts were overwhelmed with Prohibition-related cases anyway."[82] This passage suggests that the lack of defined rules of procedure gave too much discretion to judges, which led to mayhem in the court system. Congress attempted to address this problem by allowing a private means of dispute resolution. But then, the Federal Rules of Civil Procedure brought order to the civil justice system. That means in enacting the FAA, the suggestion is that Congress felt that lack of procedural regularity in the court system required the assistance of a more structured private justice system. However, once the Federal Rules of Civil Procedure came into being, court proceedings improved. The conclusion that logically flows from this is that defined rules of procedure reduce mayhem in any system. In other words, discretionary procedural flexibility has its own perils.

In arbitration, procedural flexibility is a function of party autonomy, which allows the parties to grant the arbitrators discretion on many procedural issues. As Born suggests "parties are typically free to agree upon the existence and scope of discovery or disclosure, the modes for presentation of fact and expert evidence, the length of the hearing, the timetable of the arbitration and other matters. The parties' ability to adopt (or, failing agreement, the tribunal's power to prescribe) flexible procedures is a central attraction of international arbitration—again as evidenced by empirical research and commentary."[83]

The White & Case Survey shows that 38 percent of the respondents chose international arbitration for its flexibility.[84] Theoretically, flexibility of procedures is perfectly appealing, however, in practice, what flexibility means is essentially trusting and empowering arbitrators with almost unreviewable power to decide on vital issues of procedure. This might include burden and standard of proof, the extent of disclosure, the nature and presentation of evidence, time limits, decisions on weight and admissibility of evidence, etc. These procedural powers would allow tribunals to effectively shape the outcome of the case regardless of the merits, not to mention their control over the costs of the proceedings.

82. Daniel Fisher, *Arbitration vs. Litigation: It Is Not an Either-Or Proposition*, Forbes (Nov. 8, 2015), http://www.forbes.com/sites/danielfisher/2015/11/08/arbitration-vs-litigation-its-not-an-either-or-proposition/.

83. Born, *supra* note 50, at 85. One of the empirical studies cited is 2013 International Arbitration Survey: Corporate Choices in International Arbitration: Industry Perspectives, Queen Mary University of London 8 (2013), finding that flexibility is the second most important benefit of arbitration.

84. *See* White & Case Survey, *supra* note 26, at 6.

Fundamentally, flexibility often assumes that arbitral tribunals are always manned by persons of the highest integrity who would not abuse their power in any case. The political economy of modern day investment and commercial arbitration between parties of uneven access and power is such that the above cannot always be assumed.

In an ideal world of selfless and unbiased justice, flexibility would be beneficial, but in the real world of unreviewable discretionary power, it could be a fertile source of abuse. Granted that a serious due process vitiation might result in annulment or refusal of enforcement, abuse of process often comes clothed in neutral and subtle packaging. There is a reason courts of law everywhere (including in democratic societies where judges are elected or carefully chosen) have procedural powers restricted by law. Flexibility, just like confidentiality, has the potential to legitimize arbitrary and even corrupt outcomes. Procedural flexibility often gives too much unchecked power to arbitrators.

As everyone who practices international arbitration would recognize, for the party that benefits from the balance on the tribunal because of ideology, incentives, or otherwise, it is always good, but for the party that is in the minority (i.e., one of three arbitrators), procedural flexibility is not her friend. Flexibility as an advantage assumes too much. One would get a good perspective by appearing as counsel for a party that is ideologically disfavored by at least two of the three arbitrators and see how procedural flexibility could be used to disadvantage one party and shape the outcome.[85]

D. Expertise

The dominant narrative of international arbitration is that arbitrators are persons of the highest expertise, wisdom, and integrity who could be trusted with flexible procedures. To paraphrase James Madison, if arbitrators were angels, there would be no need for concern. But nonetheless before considering the concerns, note Gary Born's delivery of the conventional line:

> Another essential objective of international arbitration is providing a maximally competent, expert dispute resolution process. It is a harsh, but undeniable, fact that some national courts are distressingly inappropriate choices for resolving international commercial disputes. In some states, local courts have little experience or training in resolving international transactions or disputes and can face serious difficulties in fully apprehending the business context and terms of the parties' dispute.[86]

85. Consider, for example, a hypothetical tribunal in a construction dispute ruling by a majority vote to order the production of every single minutes of meetings for six years amounting to tens of thousands of pages of documentation to allow the contractor to see if it could find anything of interest, and effectively delay the proceedings after other evidence made it clear that the contractor would lose. This is possible because of flexible rules on discovery, which effectively means whatever two members of the tribunal want.

86. Born, *supra* note 50, at 80.

He adds an interesting footnote to this: "Even where such experience exists, the need to translate evidentiary materials or legal authorities into the language of the forum will often create practical problems and jeopardize a tribunal's comprehension of the case."[87] It appears that Born is writing from the perspective of the English- or French-speaking business that would like to avoid the "distressingly inappropriate" local courts because the judges lack expertise and probably don't even speak English or French. But if one looks at it from the perspective of the local party—say a government-owned local power company in a developing country—the deficiencies of the local courts may not seem all that distressing because that is all they have got when not dealing with foreign parties. What might be distressing would be appearing before a tribunal with technical knowledge of the power industry, but with no idea about the cultural context of the facts as well as the subtleties of the differences between the local laws and their mixed colonial and customary origin. Perhaps the transnational problem that the English-speaking company fears would befall the local company because the arbitrators do not understand the local language; perhaps—as Born fears of the local courts—the arbitrators' "comprehension would be jeopardized" if they are required to arbitrate in the local language. Adjudicating in the local language seems unthinkable only because everyone is accustomed to thinking in terms of a Northern victim of injustice in the South, not necessarily because of principles of impartial justice for all.

To support the expertise rationale, Born makes an even bigger claim: "Even more troubling, in some states, basic standards of judicial integrity and independence are lacking."[88] His examples are Nigeria and China.[89] He exempts "courts in New York, England, Switzerland, Japan, and Singapore and a few other jurisdictions."[90] Even these are not as good as arbitration because "even in these jurisdictions, local idiosyncrasies can interfere with the objectives of competence and objectivity in resolving commercial disputes."[91] His examples of negative idiosyncrasies are the civil jury trial in the United States and the divided legal profession in England.[92]

The argument is that arbitration could remedy all of these perceived shortcomings of local judiciaries ranging from Nigeria to the United States. It is uncorrupt, competent, and unencumbered with local idiosyncrasies. Such proposition, apart from being decidedly elitist and perhaps mildly uninformed, forgets so many encumbrances that plague international arbitration, ranging from pervasive conflicts, wrong financial

87. *Id.* at 80 n.556.

88. *Id.*

89. *Id.* at 80 n.557 (citing Okechukwu Oko, *Seeking Justice in Transitional Societies: An Analysis of the Problems of Failure of the Judiciary in Nigeria*, 31 Brook. J. Int'l L. 9 (2005); Eric W. Orts, *The Rule of Law in China*, 34 Vand. J. Transnat'l L. 43 (2001)). Born also relies on Transparency International, Global Corruption Report 2007: Corruption in Judicial Systems (2007); U.S. State Department, Country Reports on Human Rights Practices (2013)).

90. Born, *supra* note 50, at 81.

91. *Id.*

92. *Id.* at 81 n.560.

incentives, and absence of ethical rules and meaningful means of checks and balances, to confidentiality's shield of impropriety and sloppy work, elitism, and cultural incompetence to name just a few.

The empirical evidence is not so supportive of the claim that arbitration is chosen because of perceived expertise. In the White & Case Survey, only 38 percent of the respondents said they selected international arbitration because of the ability to choose arbitrators.[93] That means a significant proportion did not do so because they thought arbitrators brought the level of expertise and integrity that courts lacked. The result is not surprising. The pool of "qualified" arbitrators is unacceptably low. It is a market phenomenon with no resemblance to what arbitrators are supposed to do in the real world: determine local facts and apply local law. Some arbitrators claim involvement in 600[94] or even 700[95] arbitrations in every conceivable industry and area of law whether as arbitrators or as counsel, whereas others who have the time and do not lack the skills would be lucky to get three appointments a year.

The 2015 Arbitration Scorecard offers a remarkable insight into the small world of international arbitration.[96] The report captured 69 contracts disputes and 59 treaty disputes over the $1 billion mark active during the two-year period preceding the reporting in July 2015.[97]

First, it empirically confirms what everybody already knows that "the same small group of arbitrators are routinely deciding the world's biggest disputes."[98] The numbers are staggering. The report puts it in the following terms: "Indeed, our roster of leading arbitrators has shown remarkable stability in the past decade. The top 18 arbitrators in this contest include all the top 10 from 2013, 2011 and 2009, nine off the top 10 from 2007, and seven of the top 10 arbitrators from 2005."[99] Who are they? They are called "the mafia" but they call themselves "a large family."[100] The family is described in *Profiting from Injustice*: "Pro-business,

93. *See* White & Case Survey, *supra* note 26, at 6.

94. *See, e.g.*, Gary Born's bio at Gary Born, Wilmer Hale, https://www.wilmerhale.com/gary_born/ (last visited Mar. 19, 2016) ("Mr. Born. Has participated in more than 600 arbitrations").

95. *See* Jan Paulsson's bio at Jan Paulsson, U. Miami School of L., http://www.law.miami.edu/faculty/jan-paulsson (last visited October 2, 2016).

96. Michael D. Goldhaber, *2015 Arbitration Scorecard: Deciding the World's Biggest Disputes*, TAL Asian Lawyer (July 1, 2015), http://www.international.law.com/id=1202731078679/2015-Arbitration-Scorecard-Deciding-the-Worlds-Biggest-Disputes [hereinafter *2015 Arbitrator Scorecard*].

97. *See id.*

98. *Id.*

99. *Id.*

100. *Id.* The "mafia" reference comes from Dealing in Virtue, in which Dezalay and Garth report a young arbitrator as having said: "It's a mafia because people appoint one another. You always appoint your friends—people you know." *Id.* The "big family" reference comes from what Brigitte Stern, who usually tops the chart, said to the authors of the *2015 Arbitrator Scorecard* in

males and from the rich North."[101] Indeed, it appears that only 15 of the "rich northerners" have decided 55 percent of the world's investment arbitration ever.[102] The percentage of arbitrators from developing countries is perhaps too small for a statistical entry to be made but the percentage of women has for

particular: "Some people call it a mafia. A nicer way to put it would be a large family, or even an unorganized non-governmental organization of arbitrators! They are mostly very good lawyers and interest people. It's a large family I am proud of to be a part of." *Id.* Corporate Europe Observatory adds this anecdote: "This small group of lawyers, referred to by some as an 'inner mafia', sit on the same arbitration panels, act as both arbitrators and counsels and even call on each other as witnesses in arbitration cases. This has led to growing concerns, including within the broader legal community, over conflicts of interest." PIA EBERHARDT ET AL., PROFITING FROM INJUSTICE: HOW LAW FIRMS, ARBITRATORS, AND FINANCIERS ARE FUELING AN INVESTMENT ARBITRATION BOOM 8 (Helen Burley ed., 2012), http://corporateeurope.org/sites/default/files/publications/profiting-from-injustice.pdf [hereinafter PROFITING FROM INJUSTICE].

101. *2015 Arbitrator Scorecard, supra* note 96 (quoting PROFITING FROM INJUSTICE). The text under the subtitle, "Pro-business, males and from the rich North" in PROFITING FROM INJUSTICE adds the following note:

> Most of the members of this club are men from a small group of developed countries:
>
> - *Proportion of arbitrators from Western Europe and North America:* 69% for all cases held at the World Bank's International Centre for Settlement of Investment Disputes (ICSID) and 83% if taking into account arbitrators who have sat in more than 10 cases.
> - *Proportion of arbitrators who are women*: 4%. Two women (Brigitte Stern and Gabrielle Kaufmann-Kohler) dominate this list, accounting for three quarters of the cases taken by women.
>
> Even more important for the cohesion of the arbitration industry is their shared outlook of the world. "Arbitrators have to make choices to resolve the disputes, which are of course informed by their political standpoint", Brigitte Stern has noted. Evidence shows that many of the arbitrators enjoy close links with the corporate world and share businesses' viewpoint in relation to the importance of protecting investors' profits. Given the one-sided nature of the system, where only investors can sue and only states are sued, a pro-business outlook could be interpreted as a strategic choice for an ambitious investment lawyer keen to make a lucrative living.

PROFITING FROM INJUSTICE, *supra* note 100, at 36 (citations omitted). It is also indicated incidentally that the most frequent hosts of these proceedings are Washington (24), Paris (20), London (18), and Switzerland (13) "with a smattering of disputes outside the U.S. and Europe." 2015 Arbitrator Scorecard, *supra* note 96, at 2.

102. *See* PROFITING FROM INJUSTICE, *supra* note 100, at 38–39 tbl. 2 ("Together they have decided on: 55% (247 cases) out of 450 investment-treaty disputes known today; 64% (79 cases) out of 123 treaty disputes of at least $100 million; 75% (12 cases) out of 16 treaty dispute of at least $4 billion.") The table shows the following breakdown: Brigitte Stern (France) 39 of 450 cases, 8.7% of all known treaty cases; Charles Brower (U.S.), 33 cases, 7.3% of all cases; Marc Lalonde (Canada), 30 cases, 6.7% of all cases; L. Yves Fortier (Canada), 28 cases, 6.2% of all cases; Gabrielle Kaufmann-Kohler (Switzerland), 28 cases, 6.2% of all cases; Albert Jan van den Berg (Netherlands), 27 cases, 6.0% of all cases; Karl-Heinz Böckstiegel (Germany), 21 cases, 4.7% of all cases; Bernard Hanotiau (Belgium), 17 cases, 3.8% of all cases; Jan Paulsson (France), 17 cases, 3.8% of all cases; Stephen M. Schwebel (U.S.), 15 cases, 3.3% of all cases; Henri Alvarez (Canada), 14 cases, 3.1% of all cases; Emmanuel Gaillard (France), 14 cases, 3.1% of all cases; William W. Park (US), 9 cases, 2.0% of all cases; and Daniel Price (U.S.), 9 cases, 2.0% of all cases. The diagram that PROFITING

long stayed at a depressing 4 percent, with two women consistently topping the chart.[103] Some dispute the accuracy of the statistics but nobody denies the diversity challenge and the legitimacy problem.[104]

The generalist judge would probably adjudicate thousands of cases in her lifetime involving many different types of subject matter. If that is a disadvantage to her in developing expertise in a particular subject matter, how is the number of cases one is involved in a proxy for specialized expertise? In many cases, appointments are made on the basis of how many cases one had handled before—often regardless of the particular sector.

The reason for such levels of repeat appointments is a subject of profound curiosity and debate. Opinions range from "it's a mafia because people appoint one another. You always appoint your friends—people you know"[105] to "[i]t's the parties that close the circle" because they don't trust outsiders.[106]

The responses on one end of the spectrum are well presented in the Corporate Europe Observatory's *Profiting from Injustice*, which essentially concludes that international arbitration is "a lucrative industry built by illusions of neutrality" by powerful

FROM INJUSTICE drew to show the web of interconnectedness of these arbitrators sitting together on panels or serving as counsel when others are arbitrating is described by Michael D. Goldhaber, the author of 2015 Arbitration Scorecard, as "a diagram on an FBI blackboard."). *2015 Arbitrator Scorecard, supra* note 96.

103. *The 2015 Arbitration Scorecard, supra* note 96. They are Brigitte Stern and Gabrielle Kaufmann-Kohler. *Id.*

104. *See, e.g.*, Susan D. Franck et al., *The Diversity Challenge: Exploring the "Invisible College" of International Arbitration*, 53 COLUM. J. TRANSNAT'L L. 429, 430 (2015) empirically showing that "[t]he median international arbitrator was a fifty-three year old man who was a national of a developed state reporting ten arbitral appointments; and the median counsel was a forty-six year old man who was a national of a developed state and had served as counsel in fifteen arbitration." The analysis also shows that 17.6 percent of arbitrators were women and up to as many as 20 percent of arbitrators are from the developing world. *Id.* This study further notes that: "Recognizing the data revealed diversity in international arbitration is a complex phenomenon, the data nevertheless supported, rather than disproved, claims that international arbitration is a relatively homogenous group." *Id.* The results are summarized in the abstract.

105. This is attributed to Dezalay and Garth's interview of a young arbitrator. *See 2015 Arbitration Scorecard, supra* note 96, at 3.

106. This is attributed to Brigitte Stern in *id.* at 3. Gaillard's statement is more forceful. He faults the diagram that Corporate Europe Observatory created to show the frequency of 15 arbitrators who sat side by side by saying:

> First, it fails to capture the hundreds of occasional or less frequent appointments which should be featured around the activity of the perceived core players. Second, and more importantly, it misses the reason why repeat players are nominated by the parties. In most cases, the appointments are made by the parties themselves, not by the institutions. So it is the conservatism of the parties, both on the State side and the investor side, which explains the chart. Anecdotal evidence shows that institutions actively seek to appoint newcomers and promote diversity. It is the parties who resist change.

Emmanuel Gaillard, *Sociology of International Arbitration* 31 ARB. INT'L 1, 15–16 (2015).

economic and political beneficiaries that discourage change.[107] The responses on the other end of the spectrum are equally forceful; they appear to unite the "family" across ideological lines. As the 2015 Arbitrator Scorecard reports: "Though Gaillard and Stern differ on legal issues [Stern being governments' favorite and Gaillard being businesses' favorite], Stern shares his view of the process. 'I agree we need more diversity,' she says. 'But the fault is not in the family. The fault is in the parties. I've been trying very hard to propose women, public international lawyers, and newcomers from outside Europe and the U.S. The parties say, "Ah, we don't trust these people because we don't know how they think." It's the parties that close the circle.'"[108]

In October 2015, 20 years after *Dealing in Virtue* was published, one of the authors, Bryant Garth, gave a keynote speech at Dutch Arbitration Day in Amsterdam on October 15, 2015. The Global Arbitration Review reported the keynote under the title: "*Dealing with Defensiveness: Garth Shares Views Two Decades after Seminal Book.*" The report indicated that Garth said that "the core players remained largely the same—'just older'—and that they are now on the defensive."[109] Interestingly, he said that Gaillard and other members of the elite "have an agenda, which can be seen as a defense of the field."[110]

The response was offered by none other than Jan Paulsson, who is reported to have said: "If arbitrators are on the defensive 'so be it'" because the survival of the system depends not on their defense, but "on the adequacy and fairness of the process. If viewed as incapable of cost efficiency and deficiency in ethics, arbitration will 'perish'"[111]

Such extreme positions appear to obscure the fundamental issues. The first gives arbitrators and law firms and their academic friends more power that they could possibly wield in the world economic and political order. The "family's" position is also either naïve or deliberately less than forthcoming. The "rich-male-northerners" are merely beneficiaries of what Dezalay and Garth call the "gradual legalization" of North-South relations[112] who were at the right place at the right time. It is a complex world economic and political order they neither created nor could they ever destroy, but the most serious puzzlement is: Why then do parties nominate or appoint out of the same "family"?

The answer is not because of a combination of a campaign of misinformation and threat by the family as those in the left-end of the spectrum would suggest,

107. *See* Profiting from Injustice, *supra* note 100, at 5, 70.

108. *2015 Arbitration Scorecard, supra* note 96.

109. Alison Ross, *Dealing with Defensiveness: Garth Shares Views Two Decades after Seminal Book*, Global Arb. Rev. (Nov. 18, 2015), http://globalarbitrationreview.com/news/article/34351/dealing-defensiveness-garth-shares-views-two-decades-seminal-book/.

110. Id. at 4.

111. *Id.* He is also reported to have said that "while they might defend the current system to the hilt, Paulsson suggested that, if it were suddenly changed so that arbitration counsel were assigned to cases by tombola and arbitrators randomly allocated by UNCITRAL computer, Gaillard and he would adapt to the evolving system 'with all the skill that they could muster." *Id.*

112. *See* Yves Dezalay & Bryant Garth, Dealing in Virtue 64 (1996).

or because they don't trust anyone outside of the "family" as the right-end would suggest. The real reason is what one might call the prisoner's dilemma. The parties are constantly striving to match the weapons in the duel. It is not a new phenomenon. Irish Code Duello, the version that became popular in America, had a basic rule: "Typical weapons were cased dueling pistols which were tuned for identical appearance, reliability and accuracy."[113] What determined Aaron Burr's choice of weapon and position was Alexander Hamilton's choice because under the duel rules, the challenged would have the choice of weapon and position.

Unlike the real duel, however, in investor-state or private-public disputes, the party initiating the dispute, that is, the private party, always has the choice of weapon by nominating from among the "family." The challenged party, who needs to tune the weapon "for identical appearance, reliability and accuracy" would have to look for someone within the "family" who is likely to be respected by its members. If the private investor brings a tank, the respondent also brings a tank, although the dispute could have been settled better by two matching pistols. What limits the choice and brings the extravagance is the initial appointment. In selecting the chair, the two members of the "family" obviously appoint another member of the "family"—someone who both members will likely respect as chair. If these two members are unable to agree, the institution in the exercise of prudence will fill the void by appointing a chair from the same "family." The whole selection process is dictated by the right of first choice of weapons, which in investment cases, is always held by the private party. It sets the stage in all investment arbitration cases and spills over to commercial arbitration, reinforcing the mythology of competence and integrity.

The more profound problem is the frequent mismatch between the expertise held by the arbitrators and the expertise the job requires. The expertise the "family" brings is not the kind of expertise that many disputes demand. The selection criteria are skewed by the political economy. Most cases require the simple ability and integrity to determine local facts and apply local law. Expertise in the kinds of skills needed to accurately understand the facts and the law in any given dispute is necessary; however, the promotional justification of "expertise" in the sense of the volume of cases, publications, and public speeches does not have a directly proportional correlation with an accurate and acceptable outcome. If anything it may even have a negative correlation because of the problem of availability and lack of attention. As this book suggests throughout, the politics, economics, and promotions aside, a sufficient degree of familiarity with the cultural origin of the facts and the specific applicable laws, lack of conflict, availability, and proven record of integrity are the only necessary preconditions for appointment. It is only in that sense that expertise of the arbitrators could be promoted as an advantage of international arbitration over litigation. There is no legitimate expertise-related reason that limits the pool of arbitrators. It is a self-perpetuating myth.

113. Adopted "at the Clonmel Summer Assizes, 1777, for the government of duellists, by the gentlemen of Tipperary, Galway, Mayo, Sligo and Roscommon, and prescribed for general adoption throughout Ireland." *See Code Duello*, Fact Index, http://www.fact-index.com/c/co/code_duello.html (last visited Mar. 20, 2016).

D. CONCLUSION

International arbitration is a "system" or a "framework"[114] whose advantages are limited to bridging the gap between courts of different nations. It is a gap filler—nothing else—but market forces of its own have supplied and grown theories and promotional justifications that have become true because of repetition.

Initially it was cost. Nobody now thinks that international arbitration is less costly in an era of discovery broader than even the Federal Rules of Civil Procedure in the United States would tolerate and—in certain cases—with thousands of pages of post- hearing briefs.[115] Low cost can no longer be used for promotional purposes. In fact, the most common criticism of international arbitration (both commercial and investment) within the community itself has now become rising costs and delay.[116]

The system's self-diagnosis has also identified three factors that contributed to increased costs and delay. The first one is the use of disputes rather "as a weapon than a means of overcoming disagreement."[117] This is said to have exacerbated the fight into a "total war."[118]

The second factor is the caveat emptor one that Augustus Hand warned about nearly a century ago:

> Arbitration sometimes involves perils that even surpass the "perils of the sea". Whether in any particular instance it is a desirable risk is not for us to say. It is a mode of procedure fostered by statute and in the present case invoked under the agreement of the parties. If they consent to submit their rights to a tribunal with extensive powers and subject to a most restricted review, they cannot expect the courts to relieve them from the effect of their deliberate choice.[119]

Menon brings up this issue in the sense of the misinformation of courts and parties about the perils of agreeing to arbitrate and regretting the choice. Here is how

114. On whether it is a "system" or a "framework," *see generally*, Chapter 4 *supra*.

115. *See* Sundaresh Menon, Singapore Chief Justice, Address at the Chartered Institute of Arbitrators London Centenary Conference 23 (July 2, 2015), https://www.ciarb.org/docs/default-source/centenarydocs/london/ciarb-centenary-conference-patron-39-s-address-(for-publication).pdf?sfvrsn=0 (citing Bernard Hanotiau who said that he received a 4,000-page post-hearing brief).

116. *See, e.g.*, Sundaresh Menon, Singapore Chief Justice, Standards in Need of Bearers: Encouraging Reform within at the Chartered Institute of Arbitrators: Singapore Centenary Conference 12–13 (Sept. 3, 2015), http://www.ciarb.org.sg/wp-content/uploads/2015/09/Keynote-Speech-Standards-in-need-of-Bearers-Encouraging-Reform-from-.pdf (citing 2006 and 2013 studies by the School of International Arbitration at Queen Mary University of London, the results of which show that the concerns over costs and delays have remained unaddressed over the seven-year period between the two studies). The studies from 2006 until 2015 are available at School of International Arbitration, Queen Mary University of London, http://www.arbitration.qmul.ac.uk/research/2015/index.html (last visited October 2, 2016). All show the concern over cost and delay. *Id.*

117. *See* Menon, *supra* note 116, at 14. Menon also mentions the decline in voluntary compliance. *Id.* at 15.

118. *Id.* at 14.

119. *In re* Canadian Gulf Line, 98 F. 2d 711, 714 (2d Cir. 1938).

he presents the perils that might force parties to seek judicial remedy: "Given the sheer volume of materials that are placed before arbitrators, the chances of arbitrators committing errors of fact and law are not negligible."[120]

Other factors add to the reality of error of fact and law "because of the one-tier feature of arbitration, issues will often not have been distilled and become crystallized by the time the award is presented to the court, as they ordinarily would be where a case progresses through the appellate structure in commercial litigation. This also increases the chances of errors." He concludes that "such errors can often give rise to a justifiable sense of grievance."[121] Grievance obviously raises concerns of legitimacy and leads to problems of enforcement.

The third factor that Menon cites is the formalization of the arbitral process itself in a desire to make it challenge-proof on obvious due process and related grounds.[122] The fourth factor is the elephant in the room, but Menon does not give it more than an honorable mention in the following terms:

> The fourth broad factor I wish to touch upon relates to causes of discontent which are arbitrator-specific. Parties look to appoint arbitrators who have an established reputation in the international arbitration community and a depth of experience in a particular industry and/or area of law. The pool of arbitrators who satisfy these criteria is not very deep. This means that the arbitrators that the parties often look to tend to be busier and sometimes may tend to over commit themselves and this inevitably results in delays in the arbitral process. Additionally, arbitrators may not have the time to adequately prepare for hearings and the consequent lack of familiarity will often contribute to the hearing being unwieldy because critical issues have not been identified beforehand.[123]

The source of the problem is the marketplace. It is the monopoly of trade in services, not by explicit conspiracy, but by an old and outdated custom that considers the number of cases handled a proxy for expertise, availability, temperament, and even integrity. The solution to all is not complicated. It is the recognition that in most cases arbitration should be a simple exercise of finding local facts and applying local law—just like any judicial proceedings. Its glorification, mystification, exclusion, and promotion is a function of economics, not of justice. The reality is more

120. *See* Menon, *supra* note 116, at 17.

121. *Id.* He adds that this "in turn results in the aggrieved party resorting to various legal manoeuvres to have them rectified. A judge who accedes to an invitation for him to intervene and correct errors of fact and law, will often be promoting an outcome which runs completely contrary to the expectations of finality with which the parties agreed to arbitration in the first place. The point I make here is that judges may well be persuaded to do so and parties must be advised of this possibility upfront so that they can either choose a different seat court or adjust their expectations from the start. Some of the dissatisfaction parties have with arbitration may be a result of their not having been so advised." *Id.*

122. *Id.* at 18 (citing Blackaby et al., *supra* note 6, 40 ¶ 1.115)

123. *Id.* at 18–19 (citing PricewaterhouseCoopers LLP & Queen Mary University of London, International Arbitration: Corporate Attitudes and Practices 2006, at 16–17, http://www.arbitration.qmul.ac.uk/docs/123295.pdf.

like what Lord Mustill said: "[Arbitration has] all the elephantine laboriousness of an action in court, without the saving grace of the exacerbated judge's power to bang together the heads of recalcitrant parties."[124] And without—one might add—the checks and balances of laws that produce accountable and disinterested judges in democratic societies.[125]

The promotional justifications must be understood for what they are. As serious questions continue to be asked and measures taken,[126] identifying the outdated justifications and focusing on the real jurisdictional advantages of international arbitration and attempting to remedy the serious problems of legitimacy, accuracy, and fairness would only help promote it for the right reasons.

124. *Id.* at 18 (quoting Michael John Mustill, *Arbitration: History and Background*, 6 J. Int'l Arb. 43, 56 (1989)).

125. The deleterious effects of the absence of checks and balances are not unique to international arbitration. Domestic arbitration also suffers from the same type of accountability problems. The *New York Times* documented serious concerns about the system of arbitration in a series of articles titled "Beware the Fine Print" in October and November 2015. Susan Lehman, *Podcast: Beware the Fine Print*, N.Y. Times, Nov. 11, 2015, http://www.nytimes.com/2015/11/11/insider/podcast-beware-the-fine-print.html?_r=0. In one of these reports published on November 1, 2015, it is stated that: "Over the last 10 years, thousands of businesses across the country—from big corporation to storefront shops—have used arbitration to create an alternate system of justice. There, rules tend to favor businesses, and judges and juries have been replaced by arbitrators who commonly consider the companies their clients, The Times found." Jessica Silver-Greenberg & Michael Corkery, *In Arbitration, a "Privatization of the Justice System"*, N.Y. Times, Nov. 1, 2015, http://www.nytimes.com/2015/11/02/business/dealbook/in-arbitration-a-privatization-of-the-justice-system.html?_r=0. The *Times* study makes interesting findings and offers interesting observations about the system. First it states that "[t]he secretive nature of the process makes it difficult to ascertain how fairly the proceedings are conducted." *Id.* As a result, "[b]ehind closed doors, proceedings can devolve into legal free-for-alls. Companies have paid employees to testify in their favor. A hearing that lasted six hours cost the plaintiff $150,000. Arbitrations have been conducted in the conference rooms of lawyers representing the companies accused for wrongdoing." *Id.* Second, the *Times* investigation has found that "[t]o deliver favorable outcomes to companies, some arbitrators have twisted or outright disregarded the law, interviews and records show." *Id.* Third, "records obtained by The Times showed that 41 arbitrators each handled 10 or more cases for one company between 2010 and 2014." *Id.* The *Times* quotes a California appeals court judge, Anthony Kline, as saying, "Private judging is an oxymoron. This is a business and arbitrators have an economic reason to decide in favor of the repeat players." *Id.* Having documented several real cases that resulted in deplorable outcomes because of bias and conflicts in areas ranging from employment to eldercare, the *Times* reported that the more than three dozen arbitrators that the *Times* interviewed said that they "felt beholden to the companies. *Beneath every decision, the arbitrators said, was the threat of losing business.*" *Id.* (emphasis added).

126. *See, e.g.*, The Hague Convention on Choice of Court Agreement is now being hailed as a game changer. The Hague Conference on Private International Law, *Convention on Choice of Court Agreements* (June 30, 2005), http://www.hcch.net/index_en.php?act=conventions.text&cid=98 (came into effect Oct. 1, 2005). The European Commission's recent proposal for a standing investment court is also gaining traction. *See, e.g.*, Press Release, European Commission, Commission proposes new Investment Court System for TTIP and other EU trade and investment negotiations (Sept. 16, 2015), http://europa.eu/rapid/press-release_IP-15-5651_en.htm. Singapore has also recently set up a new International Commercial Court (SICC). Information about this new court is available at *Establishment of the SICC*, Singapore International Commercial Court, http://www.sicc.gov.sg/About.aspx?id=21 (last visited Mar. 20, 2016).

6

Culture and the Legal Infrastructure of Commercial Arbitration

A culture of its own has developed around the legal framework that sets up the current structure of international commercial arbitration, although whether that culture is representative of all users of international arbitration remains a subject of curiosity and speculation. The principal legal instruments that lay the foundation for commercial arbitration is the New York Convention. With membership exceeding 150 states, a great majority of them are developing countries. Evidently, however, the jurisprudence continues to be disproportionately influenced by a handful of jurisdictions. Cultural rituals such as conferences, workshops, and trade publications are also disproportionately hosted by a handful of institutions. This chapter conducts a cultural analysis of the legal framework for commercial arbitration. Chapter 7 does the same for investment arbitration.

A. A CULTURAL ANALYSIS OF THE LEGAL FRAMEWORK

This section takes a brief look at the objectives of the New York Convention from a historical and cultural standpoint.

1. The New York Convention

The New York Convention,[1] acclaimed as "a universal constitutional charter for the international arbitral process,"[2] is by dominant accounts a success story "whose sweeping terms have enabled both national courts and arbitral tribunals to develop durable, effective means for enforcing international arbitration agreements and

1. U.N. Convention on the Recognition and Enforcement of Foreign Arbitral Awards (New York), 330 U.N.T.S., 21 U.S.T. 2517, 21 U.S.T. 2517, 7 I.L.M. 1046 (June 10, 1958), http://www.uncitral.org/pdf/english/texts/arbitration/NY-conv/New-York-Convention-E.pdf [hereinafter the New York Convention].

2. I. Gary Born, International Commercial Arbitration 99 (Kluwer Law International, 2d ed. 2014).

The Culture of International Arbitration. Won L. Kidane

arbitral awards."[3] It sets up an advanced and intricate mechanism to lawfully take jurisdiction away from national courts without concerning itself much about what happens to the case where it is going. Although it sets forth clear provisions on when and how courts must defer jurisdiction to arbitral tribunals, and obligates them to recognize and enforce the end results, it leaves the question of who the tribunal must consist of and how it must operate to the parties and national laws. It assumes that the case goes away to a better place and comes back with a superior result that requires deference.

A. History

Like all treaties of the 1950s, the New York Convention is a product of its time. It was conceived and realized through the efforts of the relatively advanced economies of the era with minor or no contributions from the newly independent countries.[4] The Travaux Préparatoires is full of documents showing the challenges of the moment for the meaningful participation of less advanced countries—many of which were former colonial states. For example, a May 1957 Note by the then-United Nations secretary general contains the following expression of concern:

> 13. The need for creating conditions more conducive to the use of arbitration in the settlement of international commercial disputes arises in particular in economically less developed countries. Many such countries lack not only the appropriate institutional facilities but also the adequate laws necessary for a successful reliance on arbitration. On the other hand, the existence of such laws and facilities may remove the obstacles to economic development created by misgivings which—rightly or wrongly— arise when foreign traders or investors are faced with the need to submit to jurisdictions of other countries.[5]

3. *Id.* at 99.

4. The draft was presented in 1953 by the International Chamber of Commerce. *Id.* at 100. The initial draft, according to Born, "would have provided for a 'denationalized' form of international arbitration, with both the international arbitral process and arbitral awards contemplated to be largely detached from national laws." *Id.* (citing A. van den Berg, The New York Arbitration Convention of 1958, at 6–10, 29–40 (1981)). Former president of the ICC, and a delegate at the 1958 Conference, Ottoarndt Glossner's "veteran's diary" presented on the occasion of the fortieth anniversary of the New York Convention pays tribute to the following key contributors to the successful adoption of the Convention: Ambassador Willem Schurmann, Lord Tangley, Frederic Eisemann, Pieter Sanders, Mario Matteucci, Eugenio Minoli, Benjamin Worltey, Niel Pearson, Georges Holleaux, Rene Arnaud, Arthur Biilow, Martin Domke, Monsignor James Griffith, and Lazare Kopelmanas. Ottoarndt Glossner, *From New York (1958) to Geneva (1961)—A Veteran's Diary*, *in* U.N., Enforcing Arbitral Awards under the New York Convention: Experience and Prospects, at 5–7, U.N. Sales No. E. 99. V. 2 (1999), http://www.newyorkconvention.org/travaux+preparatoires.

5. U.N. Secretary-General, Note on Consideration of Other Measures for Increasing the Effectiveness of Arbitration in the Settlement of Private Law Disputes (Item 5 on the Agenda) United Nations Conference on International Commercial Arbitration, U.N. Doc. E/CONF.26/6, at 6 (May 1, 1957), *available at* http://www.arbitration-icca.org/media/0/12734521657370/4281_001.pdf.

The secretary-general expressed his view at the time that building arbitral institutions, encouraging changes in the laws of developing countries, and offering training was necessary, and that it could be achieved through the provision of technical assistance within a short period of time.[6] And, of course, why he thought that the expertise gap could be filled relatively easily and why it took more than 50 years to do so remains unclear.

A related subject of importance was what the secretary-general's Note, titled "[a]ssistance in establishing impartial machinery for designation of neutral arbitrators and places of arbitration," presented. He presented this concern in the following terms:

> 22. The parties to a dispute, or the arbitration institutions to which they respectively wish to entrust its settlement, frequently do not agree on the choice of the place of arbitration and of the applicable law and rules by which the arbitral proceedings should be governed. The ECE Working Group on Arbitration foresaw that in such instances independent machinery may be useful in assisting the parties to resolve their difficulties. The need for such independent and impartial machinery may in particular be felt in the settlement of disputes arising out of commercial transactions between areas of free and of planned economies, or between less developed areas and highly industrialized countries. The Conference might wish to give further thought to the need for creating such a machinery which could assist the parties in the choice of an impartial arbitrator and a neutral place of arbitration, and to the role that could be played in that regard by organs of the United Nations.[7]

The above passages suggest three assumptions: (1) the Convention would help economic development by promising a neutral and more acceptable dispute settlement process to foreign traders or investors, (2) a mechanism would be designed for the selection of impartial arbitrators and neutral forums acceptable to both sides, and (3) developing countries would modernize their laws, develop the competence, and have their own arbitral institutions within a very short period of time.

Although the Convention establishes an effective mechanism of pushing cases from courts to arbitral tribunals, it does not contain a robust system of ensuring that the cases get a superior treatment by arbitral tribunals or that arbitral processes would be acceptable to both sides. To be sure, the provisions pertaining to

6. *Id.* at 7. Interestingly though, the Secretary-General believed that the technical assistance would resolve the problem within a short time. In his own words: "The technical assistance that may be required for the improvement of arbitration facilities in some countries could take the form of furnishing to or through the Government concerned experts competent to advise on the drafting of appropriate arbitration legislation and familiar with the problems relating to the setting up of arbitration institutions capable of providing adequate facilities for the requirements of international commerce. It would probably not be necessary to make available the services of such experts on a long term basis; *their presence in the country concerned for a few weeks or months might be sufficient in most cases.*" *Id.* (emphasis added).

7. *Id.* at 9.

annulment and refusal of enforcement are designed to ensure the integrity of the arbitral process itself, but fall short of offering a mechanism of ensuring impartiality and fairness to all parties. It appears that there was no United Nations follow-up on the mechanism of establishing impartial machinery for designating neutral arbitrators and places of arbitration suggested by the secretary general in 1957. Indeed, once adopted, the Convention itself stopped being a United Nations project. The tasks of ensuring impartiality of the arbitrators and neutrality of the fora were left entirely to private arrangements and leading arbitral institutions such as the ICC. The United Nations did not take an active role in ensuring that less-developed countries got the required technical assistance in developing their own institutions of arbitral settlement of disputes. The result has been a great concentration of cases in developed countries of Europe, which in turn made international arbitration a developed-country trade.

On the occasion of the fortieth anniversary of the adoption of the Convention, the then-chairman of the International Court of Arbitration of the International Chamber of Commerce, Robert Briner, looking back on the 40 years of performance, and looking forward on the challenges ahead, said the following:

> Globalization and privatization have produced an ever-growing number of parties to international transactions, with all the disputes and litigious phenomena this entails. The new actors on the international scene lack experience. The reservoir of arbitrators in many parts of the world is small and they are often not properly equipped and educated. In 1997, less than 60 percent of the parties to the ICC arbitration came from Western Europe and North America, but more than 85 percent of the arbitrators nominated were domiciled in these regions and in almost 90 percent of the cases the seat of the arbitration was chosen in the western part of the world.[8]

The myth of lack of competence as a justification for lack of developing countries' representation aside, this fortieth anniversary assessment is evidence of the United Nations' failure in following through on its promise of making international arbitration accessible and fair to all parties. Whether it is because of lack of meaningful technical assistance or other forms of neglect, the result has been an unacceptable marginalization of developing countries from the actual decision-making process. The negative consequences of such marginalization is difficult to measure, but recent ICSID statistics[9] also show a continued concentration of international arbitration cases in the developed world manned by jurists from the developed world.

8. Robert Briner, *Philosophy and Objectives of the Convention*, *in* U.N., Enforcing Arbitral Awards under the New York Convention: Experience and Prospects 10, U.N. Sales No. E. 99. V. 2 (1999), http://www.newyorkconvention.org/travaux+preparatoires.

9. Won Kidane, *The China-Africa Factor in the Contemporary ICSID Legitimacy Debate*, 35 U. Pa. J. Int'l L. 559, 572–73 (2014); *see also* ICSID, The ICSID Caseload-Statistics (2016-1), https://icsid.worldbank.org/apps/ICSIDWEB/resources/Documents/ICSID%20Web%20Stats%202016-1%20(English)%20final.pdf.

B. Operations

At the most basic level, the New York Convention operates to enable the enforcement of arbitral agreements as well as arbitral awards. The initial and principal purpose was to create a mechanism for the enforceability of foreign arbitral awards. For that reason, the first provision states:

> 1. This Convention shall apply to the recognition and enforcement of arbitral awards made in the territory of a State other than the State where the recognition and enforcement of such awards are sought, and arising out of differences between persons, whether physical or legal. It shall also apply to arbitral awards not considered as domestic awards in the State where their recognition and enforcement are sought.[10]

As Ottoarndt Glossner writes, the concept of a "denationalized" international award was advocated at the time, but was not accepted. What was accepted was "the concept of *a foreign arbitral award*."[11] And the text is also very clear on that point. It authorizes the enforceability of foreign arbitral awards, and that is all it does. This is, of course, another reason to dismiss the notion that the Convention supports an autonomous legal order as discussed in Chapter 4.

Remarkably, one of the drafters, Pieter Sanders, notes the enforceability of arbitral agreements was a last-minute addition. In his own words:

> My review of the Convention's history will deal in particular with what, during the Conference, was called the "Dutch proposal". It was conceived during the first weekend of the Conference. I spent that weekend at the house of my father-in-law in a suburb of New York. I can still see myself sitting in the garden with my small portable typewriter on my knees. It was there, sitting in the sun, that the "Dutch proposal" was conceived . . . at a very late stage of the Conference, a provision on the arbitration agreement was inserted in the Convention, the present article II.[12]

10. New York Convention, *supra* note 1, art. I(1).

11. Glossner, *supra* note 4, at 6 (emphasis added). In his own words:

> In the aftermath of the war, Frederic Eisemann had recognized early on that the League of Nations' Protocol on Arbitration Clauses and the Convention on the Execution of Foreign Arbitral Awards, both of Geneva of the 1020s, did not sufficiently free international arbitration of the legal strings. As a man of vision he requested a denationalized, international arbitral award, but finally accepted with grace that the world was not ready to go beyond the concept of a foreign arbitration award.

Id.

12. Pieter Sanders, *The Making of the Convention*, *in* U.N., Enforcing Arbitral Awards under the New York Convention: Experience and Prospects, at 3–4, U.N. Sales No. E. 99. V. 2 (1999), http://www.newyorkconvention.org/travaux+preparatoires.

Article II of the Convention, which is the main instrument that effectively outsources the decision-making process to arbitral tribunals was artfully drafted. It reads:

> 1. Each Contracting State shall recognize an agreement in writing under which the parties undertake to submit to arbitration all or any differences which have arisen or which may arise between them in respect of a defined legal relationship, whether contractual or not, concerning a subject matter capable of settlement by arbitration.[13]

It makes it a state responsibility to enforce both an agreement to submit disputes that have already arisen or a future agreement to arbitration, effectively putting an end to the traditional resistance of some jurisdictions to enforce arbitral agreements to submit future disputes to arbitration. The one area that this provision leaves for state discretion is the definition of subject matters that are capable of settlement by arbitration.

Several pro-arbitration legal doctrines quickly developed, helping the widespread use of arbitration in many parts of the world. Subject matters once deemed unsuitable for arbitration—ranging from securities laws[14] to antitrust law matters[15] to administrative contracts[16]—gradually shrank.

The Convention's emphasis on sending cases away from the courts without caring much about where they are going also created a conducive environment for the development of more legal doctrines that push more cases out of the courts. Some of these doctrines include the separability or severability doctrine, and the prima facie review of validity of the agreement.

The doctrine that considers the arbitration agreement embedded in the underlying contract as an independent and autonomous contract[17] coupled with the doctrine of competence-competence[18] immeasurably maximized the number of cases that go to arbitration. These doctrines are not exactly organic to ordinary contact law. Consider, for example, the U.S. Second Circuit Court of Appeals 1942 opinion

13. New York Convention, *supra* note 1, art. II(1).

14. Scherk v. Alberto-Culver Co., 417 U.S. 506 (1974) (permitting the arbitrability of causes of action arising under U.S. securities laws).

15. *See, e.g.*, Mitsubishi v. Soler Chrysler-Plymouth, 473 U.S. 614, 629 (1985) (allowing the arbitrability of causes of action arising out of U.S. antitrust laws).

16. *See, e.g.*, Jean-Louis Delvolvé, Jean Rouche & Gerald H. Pointon, French Arbitration Law and Practice 3–5 (2003) (discussing the French dilemma in this regard).

17. Authorities often cited for this proposition include Prima Paint Corp. v. Flood & Conklin Mfg. Co., 388 U.S. 395 (1967); and Fiona Trust & Holding Co. v. Privalov [2007] UKHL 40 (HL).

18. The same authorities cited for separability almost invariably deal with the issue of competence-competence because the pro-arbitration approach to extract the arbitration agreement from a possibly invalid underlying contract and granting arbitral tribunals the jurisdiction to decide the validity of the arbitration agreement only without the need to determine the validity of the underlying agreement out of which the dispute arose.

in *Kulukundis Shipping Co. v. Amtorg Trading Corp.*, "The Arbitration Act does not cover an arbitration agreement sufficiently broad to include a controversy as to the existence of the very contract which embodies the arbitration agreement."[19] It also added: "As the arbitration clause here is an integral part of the charter party, the court, in determining that the parties agreed to that clause, must necessarily first have found that the charter party exists."[20]

It further added the following famous statement about its understanding of the concept of competence-competence as it relates to the severability doctrine:

> If the issue of the existence of the charter party were left to the arbitrators and they found that it was never made, they would, unavoidably (unless they were

19. Kulukundis Shipping Co. v. Amtorg Trading Corp., 126 F.2d 978, 985 (2d Cir. 1942). The court opined further that Section 2 of the Arbitration Act describes only three types of agreements covered by the Act:

> One type is "an agreement * * * to submit to arbitration an existing controversy arising out of * * * a contract, transaction," etc.; thus the parties here, after a dispute had arisen as to the existence of the charter party, might have made an agreement to submit to arbitration that "existing" controversy. But that is not this case. Section 2 also includes a "provision in * * * a contract evidencing a transaction * * * to settle by arbitration a controversy thereafter arising out of such contract or transaction * * *." Plainly such a provision does not include a provision in a contract to arbitrate the issue whether the minds of the parties ever met so as to bring about the very contract of which that arbitration clause is a part; a controversy relating to the denial that the parties ever made a contract is not a controversy arising out of that contract. Nor is it a controversy "arising out of a transaction evidenced by a contract," for if no contract existed then there was no such transaction evidenced by a contract and, therefore, no controversy arising out of that transaction. The third type of arbitration agreement described in Section 2 of the Act is a provision in a contract to settle by arbitration "a controversy thereafter arising out of * * * the refusal to perform the whole or any part thereof." This is familiar language; it refers to a controversy, which parties to a contract may easily contemplate, arising when a party to the contract, without denying that he made it, refuses performance; it does not mean a controversy arising out of the denial by one of the parties that he ever made any contract whatsoever.
>
> It is clear then that, even assuming, arguendo, that a contract could be drawn containing an arbitration clause sufficiently broad to include a controversy as to whether the minds of the parties had ever met concerning the making of the very contract which embodies the arbitration clause, such a clause would not be within the Arbitration Act. Accordingly, it perhaps would not be immunized from the pre-statutory rules inimical to arbitration, i.e., would not serve as the basis of a stay of the suit on the contract, leaving the parties to the arbitration called for by their agreement. Were the arbitration clause here sufficiently broad to call for arbitration of the dispute as to the existence of the charter party, it would, therefore, perhaps be arguable that it was entirely outside of the Act and, accordingly, irrelevant in the case before us; we need not consider that question, as we hold that the breadth of the arbitration clause is not so great and it is within the terms of Section 2 of the Act.
>
> We conclude that it would be improper to submit to the arbitrators the issue of the making of the charter party.

Id. at 986 (citations omitted).

20. *Id.* at 985.

> insane), be obliged to conclude that the arbitration agreement had never been made. Such a conclusion would (1) negate the court's prior contrary decision on a subject which, admittedly, the Act commits to the court, and (2) would destroy the arbitrators' authority to decide anything and thus make their decision a nullity.[21]

Subsequent pro-arbitration developments considered this approach unwise and took the conceptions of severability and competence-competence to the extreme. A few cases now chart the dominant approach. One of the principal contemporary cases is the 2007 UK House of Lords case of *Fiona Trust & Holding Co. v. Privalov*.[22] In this case, the House of Lords opined that:

> Ever since Heyman v Darwins Ltd. (1942) the English common law has been evolving towards a recognition that an arbitration clause is a separate contract which survives the destruction (or other termination) of the main contract . . . A major evolutionary step was taken in Harbour v Kansa (1993) in which it was decided that the arbitration clause applied to a dispute regardless of whether the agreement in which it was embedded was void for initial illegality.[23]

Fiona Trust is now commonly cited for the proposition that unless the alleged invalidity directly pertains to the arbitration agreement, the arbitral tribunal retains jurisdiction to arbitrate the validity of the arbitration agreement. The principle of severability working in tandem with the principle of competence-competence now effectively outsources the determination of the very existence or validity of the underlying contract itself to arbitral tribunals. Although these might now seem very natural and entrenched notions, the development of these notions and their apparent contemporary solidification is a relatively recent phenomenon.

In any case, these creative legal doctrines do not operate without significant technical difficulties. The foundational principle of the New York Convention is contained in Article II(3) of the Convention. It reads: "The court of a Contracting State, when seized of an action in a matter in respect of which the parties have made an agreement within the meaning of this article, shall, at the request of one of the parties, refer the parties to arbitration, unless it finds that the said agreement is null and void, inoperative or incapable of being performed."[24]

21. *Id.* at 986 (citing Philip G. Phillips, *The Paradox in Arbitration Law*, 46 Harv. L. Rev. 1258, 1270–72 (1933); Phillip G. Philips, *A Lawyer's Approach to Commercial Arbitration*, 41 Yale L.J. 31 (1934); 6 Williston on Contracts § 1920 (rev. ed. 1938).

22. Fiona Trust, [2007] UKHL 40 (HL).

23. *Id.* ¶ 22 (relying on Section 7 of the 1996 English Arbitration Act: "Unless otherwise agreed by the parties, an arbitration agreement which forms or was intended to form part of another agreement (whether or not in writing) shall not be regarded as invalid, non-existent or ineffective because that other agreement is invalid, or did not come into existence or has become ineffective, and it shall for that purpose be treated as a distinct agreement.").

24. New York Convention, *supra* note 1, art. II(3).

That the court has the initial power to see if the arbitration agreement is "null and void, inoperative or incapable of being performed" is not doubtful; however, the principle of competence-competence would have the tribunal decide whether it has the jurisdiction to decide on the validity of the arbitration agreement itself. For example, the UNCITRAL Model Law provides in Article 23 that:

> Article 23(1). The arbitral tribunal shall have the power to rule on its own jurisdiction, including any objections with respect to the existence or validity of the arbitration agreement. For that purpose, an arbitration clause that forms part of a contract shall be treated as an agreement independent of the other terms of the contract. A decision by the arbitral tribunal that the contract is null shall not entail automatically the invalidity of the arbitration clause.[25]

An application of the *Kulukundis* rule would consider any suggestion that the tribunal could potentially arrive at a different conclusion than the court on the question of the validity of the arbitration agreement "insane," but a technical answer seems to have emerged for the resolution of this classic dilemma. For example, the French Code of Civil Procedure states in Article 1458:

> Wherever a dispute submitted to an arbitral tribunal by virtue of an arbitration agreement is brought before a court of the [French Republic], such court shall decline jurisdiction. If the arbitral tribunal has not yet been seized of the matter, the court should also decline jurisdiction unless the arbitration agreement is manifestly null. In neither case the court may determine its lack of jurisdiction on its own motion.[26]

25. The UNCITRAL Model Law is available at G.A. Res. 65/22 (Dec. 6, 2010), UNCITRAL Arbitration Rules (as revised in 2010), https://www.uncitral.org/pdf/english/texts/arbitration/arb-rules-revised/arb-rules-revised-2010-e.pdf.

26. C. Civ. art. 1458 (Fr.) *reprinted in* Gary Born, International Arbitration: Cases and Materials 202 (2011). The English Arbitration Act of 1996 takes a more nuanced approach: Section 32 reads:

> Determination of preliminary point of jurisdiction.
> (1) The court may, on the application of a party to arbitral proceedings (upon notice to the other parties), determine any question as to the substantive jurisdiction of the tribunal.
> A party may lose the right to object (see section 73).
> (2) An application under this section shall not be considered unless—
> (a) it is made with the agreement in writing of all the other parties to the proceedings, or
> (b) it is made with the permission of the tribunal and the court is satisfied—
> (i) that the determination of the question is likely to produce substantial savings in costs,
> (ii) that the application was made without delay, and
> (iii) that there is good reason why the matter should be decided by the court.
> (3) An application under this section, unless made with the agreement of all the other parties to the proceedings, shall state the grounds on which it is said that the matter should be decided by the court.

A categorical push of all matters including the tribunal's jurisdiction in all circumstances save manifest nullity necessarily errs on the side of arbitrability. It is a policy choice, but not one required by the New York Convention.

The U.S. Supreme Court in the *First Options of Chicago, Inc. v. Kaplan*[27] case offered perhaps the most logical and instructive guidance with respect to the problem of the allocation of competence. The Court first properly identified the issue of who should decide—the court or the arbitral tribunal—and held that whether or not there is a valid arbitration agreement depends on whether or not the parties agreed that the tribunal should decide that issue.[28] It also articulated a standard: "Courts should not assume that the parties agreed to arbitrate arbitrability unless there is 'clea[r] and unmistakabl[e]' evidence that they did so."[29] The Court was interpreting the FAA on the issue of competence-competence,[30] but its articulation of the issue is far reaching as a guidance for the resolution of this uncomfortable strife between courts and arbitral tribunals for occupation of the same space at the same time. Consider the Court's opinion on the "who" question:

> We believe the answer to the "who" question (*i.e.*, the standard-of-review question) is fairly simple. Just as the arbitrability of the merits of a dispute depends upon whether the parties agreed to arbitrate that dispute . . . so the question "who has the primary power to decide arbitrability" turns upon what the parties agreed about *that* matter. Did the parties agree to submit the arbitrability question itself to arbitration? If so, then the court's standard for reviewing

> (4) Unless otherwise agreed by the parties, the arbitral tribunal may continue the arbitral proceedings and make an award while an application to the court under this section is pending.
> (5) Unless the court gives leave, no appeal lies from a decision of the court whether the conditions specified in subsection (2) are met.
> (6) The decision of the court on the question of jurisdiction shall be treated as a judgment of the court for the purposes of an appeal.
>
> But no appeal lies without the leave of the court which shall not be given unless the court considers that the question involves a point of law which is one of general importance or is one which for some other special reason should be considered by the Court of Appeal.

Arbitration Act 1996, c. 23, § 32 (Eng.).

27. First Options of Chicago, Inc. v. Kaplan, 514 U.S. 938 (1995).

28. *Id.* at 942–43.

29. *Id.* at 944 (citing AT&T Technologies, Inc. v. Commc'ns Workers, 475 U.S. 643, 649 (1986)).

30. All the FAA provides in this regard is what is contained in 9 U.S.C. § 2 (February 1925):

> A written provision in any maritime transaction or a contract evidencing a transaction involving commerce to settle by arbitration a controversy thereafter arising out of such contract or transaction, or the refusal to perform the whole or any part thereof, or an agreement in writing to submit to arbitration an existing controversy arising out of such a contract, transaction, or refusal, shall be valid, irrevocable, and enforceable, save upon such grounds as exist at law or in equity for the revocation of any contract.

> the arbitrator's decision about *that* matter should not differ from the standard courts apply when they review any other matter that parties have agreed to arbitrate.[31]

Any approach other than looking for the parties' agreement on this particular issue misses the main point. As to the specific issue of who decides a challenge on the validity of the arbitration agreement as opposed to a blanket challenge to the entire contract, the U.S. Supreme Court's solution in *Buckeye Check Cashing, Inc. v. Cardegna*[32] is similar to the *Fiona Trust* solution discussed above. The Court said: "[w]e reaffirm today that, regardless of whether the challenge is brought in federal or state court, a challenge to the validity of the contract as a whole, and not specifically to the arbitration clause, must go to the arbitrator."[33]

The Convention's last minute inclusion of what is called the "Dutch proposal" in Article II on the enforcement of arbitral agreements, although praised as an innovative positive addition, injected enormous technical challenges that are not often discussed. Although it authorizes and even requires the outsourcing of cases to arbitral tribunals, it leaves a conspicuous gap between the enforcement of the agreement and the enforcement of the award addressed in Article III. It conspicuously keeps silent about what happens between the enforcement of the arbitral agreement and the enforcement of the arbitral award. It fails to set minimum standards to ensure the fairness and acceptability to all sides of the arbitral process itself. The Convention assumes that arbitral tribunals, as institutions of justice, would be at least comparable, if not better, than the courts that are required to defer jurisdiction. The huge gap between Article II and III has been the greatest source of trouble because it enabled a least constrained justice system.

At the most basic level, Article III requires the enforcement of arbitral awards with few eroding exceptions contained in Article V. The text of Article III itself is straightforward:

> Each Contracting State shall recognize arbitral awards as binding and enforce them in accordance with the rules of procedure of the territory where the award is relied upon, under the conditions laid down in the following articles. There shall not be imposed substantially more onerous conditions or higher fees or charges on the recognition or enforcement of arbitral awards to which this Convention applies than are imposed on the recognition or enforcement of domestic arbitral awards.[34]

Arbitral awards are thus presumptively enforceable no matter who renders them and however they are obtained unless they fall under narrow grounds of refusal

31. *First Options*, 514 U.S. at 943.

32. Buckeye Check Cashing, Inc. v. Cardegna, 546 U.S. 440 (2006).

33. *Id.* at 449.

34. New York Convention, *supra* note 1, art. III.

set forth in Article V.[35] These grounds focus on the validity and scope of the arbitral agreement and compliance to its terms on the composition of arbitrators, the finality of the award, and glaring denial of due process. Even then, the use of the term "may" has created a split of opinions with some courts and jurists suggesting that even awards vitiated by these defects may still be enforced.[36] This shows that the Convention is unconcerned about the process between the enforcement of the arbitral agreement and the enforcement of the arbitral award. It is left for the parties' agreement and any rules of national law that they have subjected it to. The Convention requires courts of law to recognize and enforce awards rendered by institutions of justice that no one meaningfully controls. The Convention was drafted by the ICC and, of course, the ICC and other leading institutions came to fill in the void. Their growth and performance since the adoption of the Convention in 1958 has been phenomenal.

35. *Id.* art. V.

1. Recognition and enforcement of the award may be refused, at the request of the party against whom it is invoked, only if that party furnishes to the competent authority where the recognition and enforcement is sought, proof that:
   (a) The parties to the agreement referred to in article II were, under the law applicable to them, under some incapacity, or the said agreement is not valid under the law to which the parties have subjected it or, failing any indication thereon, under the law of the country where the award was made; or
   (b) The party against whom the award is invoked was not given proper notice of the appointment of the arbitrator or of the arbitration proceedings or was otherwise unable to present his case; or
   (c) The award deals with a difference not contemplated by or not falling within the terms of the submission to arbitration, or it contains decisions on matters beyond the scope of the submission to arbitration, provided that, if the decisions on matters submitted to arbitration can be separated from those not so submitted, that part of the award which contains decisions on matters submitted to arbitration may be recognized and enforced; or
   (d) The composition of the arbitral authority or the arbitral procedure was not in accordance with the agreement of the parties, or, failing such agreement, was not in accordance with the law of the country where the arbitration took place; or
   (e) The award has not yet become binding on the parties, or has been set aside or suspended by a competent authority of the country in which, or under the law of which, that award was made.
2. Recognition and enforcement of an arbitral award may also be refused if the competent authority in the country where recognition and enforcement is sought finds that:
   (a) The subject matter of the difference is not capable of settlement by arbitration under the law of that country; or
   (b) The recognition or enforcement of the award would be contrary to the public policy of that country.

36. *See, e.g.*, Chromalloy Aeroservices Inc. v. Arab Republic of Egypt, 939 F. Supp. 907 (D.D.C.1996) (allowing enforcement of an award set aside at the seat); *but see* Termorio S.A. E.S.P. v. Electranta S.P., 487 F.3d 928 (D.D.C. 2007) (disallowing the enforcement of an award annulled at the seat, and offering a more nuanced reasoning second-guessing courts of other sovereign states).

B. CONCLUSION

The community of nations gave priority to the recognition and enforcement of "foreign arbitral" awards over "foreign court judgments" and built a superior legal infrastructure around it. Part of the reason for the reluctance to recognize and enforce foreign court judgments served as a justification for the promotion of the recognition and enforcement of foreign arbitral awards. The unequal levels of development of judiciaries around the world coupled with the exaggerated view of their deficiencies as well as the unavoidable procedural complexities of transnational litigation helped the development of international arbitration as the preferred means of transnational dispute settlement in commerce and investment.

The legal infrastructure discussed in this chapter focuses on the ways and means of outsourcing the resolution of disputes to arbitral tribunals. It assumes that the chronic and inherent problems that plague courts of law around the world, such as incompetence, conflict, ethical violations, prejudice, bias, negligence, greed, fear, and even outright corruption, is less likely to afflict arbitral tribunals. There is no obvious reason that arbitral tribunals are immune from all of these obstacles that courts of law face, when theoretically the tribunals are less constrained by checks and balances. Indeed, every judiciary in modern times attempts to place checks and balances and controls whether through the enforcement of professional rules of ethics or through appellate mechanisms. Some succeed in minimizing the obstacles to unencumbered justice, but some continue to struggle. Without checks and balances abuse is almost certain to occur.

The arbitral legal infrastructure, focused on pushing cases out of the court system and requiring them to enforce the awards, does not play a robust role in ensuring the integrity of the arbitral process itself. It leaves the regulation of the arbitral process and the conduct of the players to administering institutions, or almost no one when it is ad hoc. It is left to operate in what Professor Rogers calls an "ethical no-man's land." There is a reason courts of law struggle around the world because of abuse despite all sorts of checks and balances, mandatory rules of law, and sanctions. Assuming that arbitrators would be immune from issues that plague judiciaries around the world is not without perils.

Even assuming that the lack of accountability, absence of appellate review, lack of binding rules of professional conduct, and secrecy would have no negative consequences on the delivery of arbitral justice, international arbitration is yet again confronted with unique technical problems of its own to get the results right. As indicated throughout this book, cultural diversity among members of the tribunal, counsel, and the parties is a source of miscommunication and misunderstanding, and even an additional invisible source of conflict that might impact the accuracy and fairness of the arbitral process and outcome. The following chapter will take the discussion to the realm of international investment arbitration.

7

Culture and the Legal Infrastructure of Investment Arbitration

Investment arbitration faces a more pronounced version of the challenges of commercial arbitration. This chapter discusses these challenges by focusing on the most prominent mechanism, which is that set up by the International Convention for the Settlement of Investment Disputes (ICSID).[1] The Convention, which established the International Centre for Settlement of Investment Dispute (the "Centre"), came into force on October 14, 1966, when the twentieth instrument of ratification was deposited with the Secretariat of the United Nations.[2] Interestingly, 15 of the original deposits of the ratification instruments came from African states.[3] Naturally, the very first respondent state in ICSID proceedings was also an African state.[4]

Examination of the history of the ICSID Convention suggests that many developing countries accepted ICSID because of the perception that doing so would increase the flow of badly needed foreign direct investment (FDI) from the

1. Convention on the Settlement of Investment Disputes Between States and Nationals of Other States, 17 U.S.T. 1270, 575 U.N.T.S. 159 (Oct. 14, 1966), www.worldbank.org/icsid [hereinafter ICSID Convention]. For a comprehensive article-by-article commentary of the Convention, see Christoph H. Schreuer, The ICSID Convention: A Commentary (2d ed. 2009).

2. *See List of Contracting States and Other Signatories of the Convention (as of November 1, 2013)*, Int'l Ctr. for Settlement of Inv. Disp. (Nov. 1, 2013), http://icsid.worldbank.org/ICSID/FrontServlet?requestType=ICSIDDocRH&actionVal=ShowDocument&language=English (listing 158 States that have signed the Convention and 150 states that have deposited their instruments of ratification) (hereinafter ICSID, *List of Contracting States*).

3. *Id.* The 15 original African contracting states were: Benin, Burkina Faso, Central African Republic, Chad, Republic of Congo, Côte d'Ivoire, Gabon, Ghana, Madagascar, Malawi, Mauritania, Nigeria, Sierra Leone, Tunisia, and Uganda. A total of 20 instruments of ratification were deposited that day. The remaining six came from Iceland, Jamaica, Malaysia, Netherlands, and the United States. *Id.*

4. Holiday Inns S.A. & Others v. Morocco, ICSID Case No. ARB/72/1 (1972). For a list of all concluded ICSID cases, see *List of Concluded Cases*, Int'l Ctr. for Settlement Inv. Disp. [ICSID], https://icsid.worldbank.org/apps/ICSIDWEB/cases/pages/concludedcases.aspx?status=c (last visited Mar. 26, 2016).

The Culture of International Arbitration. Won L. Kidane

developed world,[5] although the Convention itself makes no such express promise.[6] Structurally, however, ICSID's close affiliations with the World Bank never sat very comfortably with the Africans, for example, from the very beginning. The history is full of examples of expressions of misgivings about the establishment of a dispute settlement mechanism under the auspices of Africa's principal financier.[7]

Although the history of Africa's relations with the Bank itself has been a troubled one,[8] it is remarkable that over the last half-century, many African states voluntarily submitted to the jurisdiction of ICSID tribunals and answered charges of expropriation and other alleged violations of the rights of private investors in Washington, DC, and various European fora. Indeed, since its inception, more than 20 percent of all ICSID cases involved African states as respondents, with 16 percent involving Sub-Saharan states.[9] Interestingly, however, so far, only 2 percent of the arbitrators

5. The statements of the representative of Sierra Leone during the African legal consultative meeting that occurred in Addis Ababa in 1963 (which is discussed more fully *infra* Section B(2) summarizes the general understanding very well: "[i]t would be easier for the developing countries to obtain the investments they needed if all agreements contained a clause to the effect that disputes could be referred to the Center [ICSID]." *Settlement of Investment Disputes, Consultative Meeting of Legal Experts, in* ICSID, 2-1 HISTORY OF THE CONVENTION: DOCUMENTS CONCERNING THE ORIGIN AND FORMULATION OF THE CONVENTION 236, 255 (1968) [hereinafter History of ICSID]. For a discussion of this history, see *infra* Section B(2). Studies have since questioned this proposition. *See, e.g.*, THE EFFECT OF TREATIES ON FOREIGN DIRECT INVESTMENT: BILATERAL INVESTMENT TREATIES, DOUBLE TAXATION TREATIES, AND INVESTMENT FLOWS (Karl P. Sauvant & Lisa E. Sachs eds., 2009) (questioning the impact of BITs on foreign direct investment flows); Jeswald W. Salacuse & Nicholas P. Sullivan, *Do BITs Really Work?: An Evaluation of Bilateral Investment Treaties and Their Grand Bargain*, 46 HARV. INT'L L.J. 67, 90 (2005) ("[I]nvestors . . . that are covered by a BIT certainly enjoy a higher degree of protection from the political risks of governmental intervention . . . .").

6. ICSID Convention, *supra* note 1, at pmbl. It appears to have been carefully drafted to avoid exactly that implication. It reads in relevant part: "Considering the need for international cooperation for economic development, and the role of private international investment therein; Bearing in mind the possibility that from time to time disputes may arise in connection with such investment between Contracting States and nationals of other Contracting States." *Id.*

7. AMAZU A. ASOUZU, INTERNATIONAL COMMERCIAL ARBITRATION AND AFRICAN STATES: PRACTICE, PARTICIPATION AND INSTITUTIONAL DEVELOPMENT 224–25 (2001) (summarizing the discussions indicating the African states' concerns about the affiliation of the Centre with the World Bank, including concerns about the merger of the positions of the Bank's presidency with the chair of the Administrative Council of the Centre).

8. *See, e.g.*, Celia W. Dugger, *World Bank Neglects African Farming, Study Says*, N.Y. TIMES (Oct. 15, 2007), http://www.nytimes.com/2007/10/15/world/africa/15worldbank.html ("Professor Sachs called the evaluation 'a blistering, devastating critique.' Professor Easterly, a research economist at the bank for more than a decade, likened the evaluation to saying Coca-Cola is bad at making its signature soft drink. 'Here's your most important client, Africa, with its most important sector, agriculture, relevant to the most important goal—people feeding their families—and the bank has been caught with two decades of neglect,' he said.").

9. *The ICSID Caseload—Statistics*, ICSID 11 (2012), https://icsid.worldbank.org/apps/icsidweb/resources/pages/icsid-caseload-statistics.aspx [hereinafter ICSID 2012 STATISTICS]. These latest ICSID statistics show that 16 percent of all ICSID cases were from Sub-Saharan Africa whereas 10 percent were from the Middle East and North Africa. ICSID follows the World Bank's regional

and conciliators have been from Sub-Saharan Africa.[10] Approximately 70 percent of all the arbitrators, conciliators, and ad hoc committee members have been Western Europeans or North Americans.[11] Significantly, 47 percent of all arbitrators and conciliators have been Western Europeans,[12] whereas the number of Western European states that were ever called upon to answer charges before ICSID tribunals in Washington or elsewhere is limited to a mere 1 percent.[13] Even more remarkably, less than 5 percent of all arbitrators, conciliators, and ad hoc committee members have been women.[14]

In light of this background, this chapter offers a cultural analysis of ICSID's half-century of experimentation involving developing countries, especially African countries.

A. THE ICSID LEGITIMACY DEBATE

The fact that ICSID tribunals have always suffered from a serious shortage of cultural diversity is not a subject of dispute, as it can clearly be seen from ICSID's publicly available arbitrator-nationality pie chart.[15] Interestingly, however, the scholarly discourses have largely downplayed the possibility that this deficit may impact arbitration outcomes; instead, scholars frame the issue, at a more general level, as contributing to coherency of the jurisprudence produced and procedural regularity.[16] Remarkably, there is little discussion about the sources of the imbalance and the justifications that sustain it.

At the most general level, the dominant narrative is that "[i]nvestment arbitration is a success story"[17] and, of course, ICSID is a major part of it—with NAFTA Chapter 11 arbitrations exemplifying the alleged success.[18] Measured

classification and merges North African states with the Middle East. Because many of the North African states have had cases before ICSID, the percentage of African states is clearly more than 20 percent. *Id.*

10. *Id.* 16.

11. *Id.*

12. *Id.*

13. *Id.* at 11.

14. Michael Waibel & Yanhui Wu, Are Arbitrators Political? 27 & tbl.2 (Nov. 5, 2011) (unpublished manuscript) (on file with author) [hereinafter Waibel & Wu Study] (conducting an empirical study based on ICSID database review).

15. ICSID 2012 Statistics, *supra* note 9, at 16 chart 13.

16. *See infra* notes 24–53 and accompanying text (discussing the mainstream scholarly discourse surrounding the coherence and consistency of ICSID tribunal decisions).

17. August Reinisch, *The Future of Investment Arbitration*, *in* International Investment Law for the 21st Century: Essays in Honour of Christoph Schreuer 894, 894 (Christina Binder, Ursula Kriebaum, August Reinisch & Stephan Wittich eds., 2009).

18. The public attention to the *Methanex* case supports this notion. Methanex Corp. v. United States, Final Award of the Tribunal on Jurisdiction and Merits, 44 I.L.M. 1345 (NAFTA Ch. 11 Arb.

by caseload growth and enforcement track record, ICSID has indeed been a "success story." Having stayed almost dormant for decades—averaging one to four cases a year—the caseload began an upward trajectory in 1997, then receiving 10 cases and steadily increasing to reach 38 by the end of 2011.[19] This "success" is attributed to several factors, including the phenomenal growth of BITs, most of which provide for free access to investor-state arbitration.[20]

As the foundational assumption that BITs improve the developing world's ability to attract foreign investment has increasingly come under scrutiny,[21] and a critical mass of investment treaty arbitration decisions and awards became publicly available for review, critical inquiries about the legitimacy of the system as a whole began to emerge. Bolivia's public renunciation of the Convention in 2007,[22] and Ecuador's similar action in 2009,[23] fueled the curiosity of the scholarly community, resulting in the production of a corpus of instructive commentary on the legitimacy of the international investment arbitration system in general and ICSID in particular.[24]

Trib. 2005), http://www.state.gov/documents/organization/51052.pdf. *See* Anthony DePalma, *NAFTA'S Powerful Little Secret; Obscure Tribunals Settle Disputes, but Go Too Far, Critics Say*, N.Y. Times (Mar. 11, 2001), http://www.nytimes.com/2001/03/11/business/nafta-s-powerful-little-secret-obscure-tribunals-settle-disputes-but-go-too-far.html?pagewanted=all (highlighting the ICSID arbitration case *Methanex v. United States* and discussing the use of investment arbitration due to the vast reach of multinational corporations).

19. ICSID 2012 Statistics, *supra* note 9, at 7. The total cases as of that date are 369. This figure includes the ICSID Additional Facilities cases.

20. *See* Reinisch, *supra* note 17, at 895. Currently, there are approximately 3,000 BITs in effect.

21. *See, e.g.*, Salacuse & Sullivan, *supra* note 5 (arguing that BITs do help countries promote foreign direct investment, though the benefits are slow to appear).

22. Press Release, ICSID, Bolivia Submits a Notice under Article 71 of the ICSID Convention (May 16, 2007), https://icsid.worldbank.org/ICSID/StaticFiles/Announcement3.html ("On May 2, 2007, the World Bank received a written notice of denunciation of the Convention on the Settlement of Investment Disputes between States and Nationals of Other States (the ICSID Convention) from the Republic of Bolivia. In accordance with Article 71 of the ICSID Convention, the denunciation will take effect six months after the receipt of Bolivia's notice, i.e., on November 3, 2007. In its capacity as the depository of the ICSID Convention, and as required by Article 75 of the ICSID Convention, the World Bank has notified all ICSID signatory States of the Republic of Bolivia's denunciation of the ICSID Convention.").

23. Press Release, ICSID, Ecuador Submits a Notice under Article 71 of the ICSID Convention (July 9, 2009), https://icsid.worldbank.org/ICSID/StaticFiles/Announcement20.html ("On July 6, 2009, the World Bank received a written notice of denunciation of the Convention on the Settlement of Investment Disputes between States and Nationals of Other States (the ICSID Convention) from the Republic of Ecuador. In accordance with Article 71 of the ICSID Convention, the denunciation will take effect six months after the receipt of Ecuador's notice, i.e., on January 7, 2010. In its capacity as the depository of the ICSID Convention, and as required by Article 75 of the ICSID Convention, the World Bank has notified all ICSID signatory States of the Republic of Ecuador's denunciation of the ICSID Convention.").

24. Chief among them is International Investment Law for the 21st Century, *supra* note 17. Another example is the *Harvard International Law Journal*, which largely dedicated the second

The most serious indictment of the system, of course, goes to the very essence of the investor-state arbitration system and the arbitrator accountability issue. Gus Van Harten describes these concerns very well: "arbitrators autonomously resolve core questions of public law: whether legislation is discriminatory, whether regulation is expropriation, whether a court decision is unfair or inequitable. . . . Th[e] lack of judicial supervision renders the arbitrator's interpretation of public law—itself a fundamentally sovereign act—unaccountable in the conventional sense."[25]

Professor David Caron analyzes the dominant narrative about ICSID legitimacy concerns under four headings: "(1) the coherency of the system, (2) the integrity of decision-makers, (3) the representation of the public and (4) the curtailment of state public choice."[26]

The concern that is often framed in the context of coherency essentially pertains to the consistency of the substantive jurisprudence that the tribunals have generated over the last half-century.[27] Professor Caron does not believe that the

issue of its fiftieth volume, published in the summer of 2009, to this topic. 50 HARV. INT'L L.J. (2009), *available at* http://www.harvardilj.org/2009/06/issue_50-2. Around the same time period, the *Chicago Journal of International Law* (Vol. 9, Winter 2009) and the *Suffolk Transnational Law Review* also dedicated symposium issues to this issue. 9 CHI. J. INT'L L. (2009); 32 SUFFOLK TRANSNAT'L L. REV. (2009). Summarizing the objectives and proceedings of the Suffolk symposium, Professor David Caron noted: "In this Symposium's discussion of investor state arbitration, there may at first blush appear to be two very different points of perspective. On the one hand, a number of the articles view investor state arbitration as a system from afar: The view from '20,000 feet'. On the other hand, a number of articles are from the perspective of having been involved in individual arbitrations: The view from 'in the trenches'. At the level of individual arbitrations, questions often focus on how to win, or how to survive, the arbitration. From the perspective of the system, questions often focus on how the system of investment arbitration might better meet its objectives which in part often involve assessments about the legitimacy of the system as a whole." David D. Caron, *Investor State Arbitration: Strategic and Tactical Perspectives on Legitimacy*, 32 SUFFOLK TRANSNAT'L L. REV. 513, 513 (2009). Other notable parts of this corpus include a collection of essays in THE BACKLASH AGAINST INVESTMENT ARBITRATION: PERCEPTIONS AND REALITY (Michael Waibel et al. eds., 2010) and GUS VAN HARTEN, INVESTMENT TREATY ARBITRATION AND PUBLIC LAW (2007).

25. VAN HARTEN, *supra* note 24, at 156.

26. Caron, *supra* note 24, at 516.

27. This is one of the main factors that attracted the most commentary. *See, e.g.*, JAN PAULSSON, DENIAL OF JUSTICE IN INTERNATIONAL LAW 241 (2005) ("[T]he idea is not consistency at any cost, but respectable consistency."); Charles N. Brower & Stephan W. Schill, *Is Arbitration a Threat or a Boon to the Legitimacy of International Investment Law?*, 9 CHI. J. INT'L L. 471 (2009) (positing that, although inconsistency is currently a problem, the passage of time will lead to more uniform results); Susan D. Franck, *The Legitimacy Crisis in Investment Treaty Arbitration: Privatizing Public International Law through Inconsistent Decisions*, 73 FORDHAM L. REV. 1521 (2005) (proposing the creation of a permanent appellate body, enhanced transparency, and increased academic scrutiny in order to combat inconsistency); Jacques Werner, *Making Investment Arbitration More Certain: A Modest Proposal*, 4 J. WORLD INV. 767 (2003) (endorsing an appellate level of review for investment arbitration decisions, and arguing that arbitrators should play an active role in consolidating proceedings or staying decisions where other arbitral panels have already issued an award).

jurisprudence is so incoherent as to deprive "the system" of legitimacy.[28] Indeed, he argues, rather convincingly, that "the root of the problem is embedded very deeply in the structure of arbitration itself" because, in essence, it is not "a system" but "a framework" within which investment claims are resolved under very diverse legal regimes, much like commercial arbitration.[29] For him, the challenge of coherency is inherent.[30] In fact, to the extent there is coherency, it is more "coincidental than planned."[31] Moreover, coherency is more of an academic concern than a practical one because the users of the investment dispute settlement framework seem to tolerate a significant level of irregularity that academics might consider erroneous.[32] Caron similarly rejects the academic call for appellate discipline because, according to him, there is "little evident desire thus far on behalf of parties and states to build appeal structures which might yield greater consistency."[33]

Other critics give the issue of jurisprudential coherence more weight than Professor Caron because, unlike a purely private commercial arbitration, ICSID tribunals often sit in judgment of a sovereign act, with profound public implications. For example, following the rendering of conflicting awards against the Czech Republic in *CME v. Czech Republic*[34] and *Lauder v. Czech Republic*,[35] Blackaby of Freshfields is quoted as saying: "Any system where diametrically opposed decisions can legally coexist cannot last long. It shocks the sense of rule of law or fairness."[36] These two cases, along with the expressions of frustration by lawyers, are profound demonstrations of the jurisprudential incoherency that characterizes investment arbitration today. Both cases were predicated on the same BIT provision and

28. Caron, *supra* note 24, at 516.

29. *Id.* Caron rejects the idea that commercial and investment arbitrations are recognizably distinct. *Id.* at 513–14.

30. *Id.* at 516.

31. *Id.* at 517 ("ICSID can be schizophrenic in this way—on the one hand, imagining ICSID as a framework calls for a concentrated focus on the particular dispute, while at the same time, imagining ICSID as a system represents an attempt to rearrange all of the free standing arbitrations as though they were part of a court system. This situation can lead to great surprise and frustration when the realization hits home that the patterns that sometimes present are more coincidental than planned. The question of whether there is a system present depends on whether the questions shared by the various tribunals are identical, or perhaps nearly so. Certainly ICSID tribunals share the procedural and jurisdictional limitations of the ICSID convention, but they do not necessarily address the same identical substantive questions since usually different concessions or BITs are involved.").

32. *Id.*

33. *Id.*

34. Reinisch, *supra* note 17, at 907 (citing CME Czech Republic B.V. v. Czech Republic, UNCITRAL, Partial Award (Sept. 13, 2001), 9 ICSID Rep. 121 (2006); 14 World Trade & Arb. Mat'ls 109 (2002)).

35. Lauder v. Czech Republic, UNCITRAL, Final Award (Sept. 3, 2001), 9 ICSID Rep. 66 (2006); World Trade & Arb. Mat'ls, *supra* note 34.

36. Van Harten, *supra* note 24, at 166 (citation omitted).

involved the same issues.[37] Although, in *Lauders*, the tribunal denied recovery, in *CME*, it awarded the investor nearly $500 million.[38]

Broadening the inquiry further, Van Harten suggests that "the burden of incoherence is borne most by those countries that lack the legal and administrative capacity effectively to fight off, or deter, investor claims."[39] According to August Reinisch, "[w]hat is far more serious for the acceptance of investment arbitration in general is a potential loss of confidence stemming from incomprehensible, unpredictable, and/or contradictory decisions and awards."[40] He notes that, in recent times, the manifestations of the jurisprudential incoherence touch the very sensitive balance between the state's sovereign regulatory right and private investment protection, as exemplified by environmental cases such as *Methanex*.[41] Some others, however, suggest that there already is sufficient coherence that sustains the regime,[42] whereas others are hopeful that jurisprudential coherence and predictability will come through time.[43]

37. *See* Reinisch, *supra* note 17, at 907 (mentioning the similarities of the Lauders and CME cases).

38. *Id.* at 907–08.

39. Van Harten, *supra* note 24, at 167.

40. Reinisch, *supra* note 17, at 904.

41. *Id.* at 903 (citing Methanex Corp. v. United States, Final Award on Jurisdiction and Merits (NAFTA Arb. Trib. 2005)). There are many investment arbitration cases involving the issue of indirect expropriation. For a recent analysis and additional citations, see Suzy H. Nikiema, IISD Best Practices Indirect Expropriation (2012), http://www.iisd.org/pdf/2012/best_practice_indirect_expropriation.pdf. For an older NAFTA-focused analysis of the issue, see Vicki Been & Joel C. Beauvais, *The Global Fifth Amendment? NAFTA's Investment Protections and the Misguided Quest for an International "Regulatory Takings" Doctrine*, 78 N.Y.U. L. Rev. 30 (2003).

42. Most notably, in his 2010 article, Professor Salacuse, employing regime theory, suggests that there is "a surprisingly high degree of uniformity and consistency." Jeswald W. Salacuse, *The Emerging Global Regime for Investment*, 51 Harv. Int'l L.J. 427, 467 (2010). He attributes this to the similarity in the substantive rules contained in the nearly 3,000 BITs, and to decision-making by "the epistemic community" of similarly situated mainly Western arbitrators who produce the bulk of the jurisprudence. *Id.* at 465.

43. *See* Brower & Schill, *supra* note 27, at 473–74 ("While some of these problems, in particular unpredictability and incoherence in investor-state dispute settlement, are considerable and in need of serious attention, arguably a solution will come with the passage of time. Increasing dispute-settlement procedures and doctrinal efforts promise to prove that concepts relating to investors' rights, such as fair and equitable treatment and indirect expropriation, are not as vague and indeterminate as some argue. They increasingly will provide yardsticks for the judicial settlement of disputes that have proven to be workable not only in several international fora—such as the Iran-US Claims Tribunal or the various claims commissions established at the beginning of the twentieth century to solve investment-related disputes—but also in domestic courts that entertain disputes concerning the relationship between property protection and competing private and public interests. Thus, the passage of time—bringing with it a continuous stream of investment jurisprudence, a refinement of state practice and treaty making, and growing doctrinal analysis—may help create a better understanding of the content and scope of the central principles of investment protection and result in the creation of a *jurisprudence constante*.") (footnotes omitted).

The second concern pertains to the integrity of the decision-makers. Although it is, at times, "[p]hrased in terms of illegitimacy, this critique becomes an assertion of corruption."[44] Caron notes that because outright corruption among arbitrators is rare, the legitimacy concern relating to corruption in essence touches the "identity, equality, independence and impartiality of arbitrators."[45] Although he identifies the problems and states them very well, he does not belabor the issue further, except critiquing the proposal to create a permanent panel of arbitrators as impracticable and unattractive to the parties who would want to nominate their own arbitrators.[46]

The third concern is the denial of the representation of the public interest—in other words, the state, which is the respondent in investment arbitration, may not necessarily represent the interests of the communities that may be affected by the outcome of the arbitration.[47] Professor Caron puts this in its proper context by saying "[e]levating the community past the state respondent creates a number of obvious political tensions"[48] and suggests that civil society involvement through amicus filings might be a good solution.[49]

The fourth concern is more fundamental and one that concerns the curtailing of state public interest, especially in regulatory takings cases. This concern goes to the heart of what Van Harten explains as the accountability problems of "The Businessman's Court" sitting in judgment of sovereign decisions.[50] Professor Caron suggests that the convergence of interests around this issue, as exemplified by China's increasing outward investment and changing attitudes, might help resolve the problem in the long term.[51] Although that is true in some respects when China is taken in isolation, the fundamental question is enduring.

Apart from the macro level systemic concerns, there are concerns at the micro level involving each arbitration; they largely include mundane challenges that any kind of adjudicatory system faces, such as efficacy, cost, competence, poor reasoning, and ethics.[52] There is no shortage of suggestions as to how to make improvements in these areas.[53]

44. Caron, *supra* note 24, at 518.

45. *Id.*

46. *Id.* at 519. A very interesting point Professor Caron notes from experience is how "parties at present will go to great lengths to avoid ICSID making the appointment of the chair from its roster." *Id.*

47. *Id.* at 520.

48. *Id.*

49. *Id.*

50. Van Harten, *supra* note 24, at 152–84.

51. Caron, *supra* note 24, at 521 ("The old dichotomy has ceased to exist for some and we now find ourselves in a much more nuanced situation. In other terms, we could say that there once were upstream states and downstream states. But now there is only a lake where there is a convergence of interest of the states bordering the lake.").

52. *Id.* at 522–23.

53. *See, e.g.*, Reinisch, *supra* note 17, at 908–16 (proposing means of quality assurance, appellate mechanism and de facto precedence).

1. Empirical Studies

ICSID does make vital information about most cases, including the names of arbitrators and counselors, available on its website.[54] However, there is a dearth of comprehensive and systematic empirical analysis of these cases. With that note, this section proceeds to review the limited available studies in association with the ICSID database.

As of March 28, 2012, the ICSID database shows that 233 cases have been concluded and 142 cases are pending.[55] Whereas 70 percent of the arbitrators have come from Western Europe and North America, only 2 percent of all arbitrators have come from Sub-Saharan Africa.[56] In terms of the host states, whereas only 1 percent of cases involved Western European states, 16 percent of all cases involved Sub-Saharan African states.[57] ICSID data further shows that whereas 85 percent of all cases involved an investor from a developed country as the claimant and a developing country as the respondent, only 10 percent of all cases involved an investor from a developing country as the claimant and a developing country as the respondent.[58] Quite interestingly, one of the two empirical studies of the ICSID database conducted recently suggests that arbitrators from developing countries arbitrate cases mainly between an investor from a developing country and a developing state.[59] Most significant, 95 percent of all arbitrators so far have been men—described as "members of an exclusive and lucrative club, whose members are sometimes compared to a club of mainly European, gray-haired and well-connected men."[60] No sophisticated empirical studies are needed to prove the glaring diversity deficit, but what do the studies conclude?

The Convention's requirements of arbitrator qualifications are generic: good moral character, impartiality, and technical competence.[61] This rule cannot explain the disproportionately Western appointments. Explanation may lie in history, location, and affiliation. No attempt is made to provide a comprehensive explanation here; however, it is important to note that such appointments necessitate the hiring of counsel with a similar background that makes them acceptable to the arbitrators. Apparently for that reason, developing host states hire European and American law

54. *Cases*, ICSID, https://icsid.worldbank.org/apps/ICSIDWEB/cases/Pages/AdvancedSearch.aspx (last visited Mar. 30, 2016).

55. *Id.* As of March 30, 2016, the ICSID database shows that 357 cases have been concluded and 211 cases are pending. *Id.*

56. *Id.*

57. *Id.*

58. *Id.* For the World Bank's and OECD's classification of "developing" and "developed" nations, see Susan D. Franck, *Development and Outcomes of Investment Treaty Arbitration*, 50 HARV. INT'L L.J. 435, 446–47 (2009) [hereinafter Franck Study].

59. Waibel & Wu Study, *supra* note 14, at 27.

60. *Id.* at 18.

61. ICSID Convention, *supra* note 1, art. 14(1).

firms disproportionately.[62] The fees for leading arbitration specialists sometimes exceed $1,000 per hour, which does not include additional fees for their associates at several hundred dollars an hour.[63] By contrast, most developed countries mostly rely on in-house counsel in ICSID cases.[64]

A couple of focused, smaller empirical studies have tested the impact of certain personal characteristics of arbitrators on case outcome. The first such study was conducted by Professor Susan Franck of Washington and Lee Law School. She describes her findings in her article "Development and Outcomes of Investment Treaty Arbitration."[65] The second empirical study was conducted by Professors Michael Waibel of Lauterpacht Center at Cambridge and Yanhui Wu of USC Marshall School of Business. It is titled "Are Arbitrators Political?"[66] Although they do not focus on the exact same set of variables, the two studies arrive at inconsistent findings to the extent they converge on the topics. Such inconsistencies might suggest the inevitable shortcomings of quantitative and even qualitative measurements of outcome to assess the nature or quality of justice in these kinds of cases; however, a combination of quantitative studies and a careful qualitative examination of selected cases might shed some light on the reality of ICSID arbitral justice. Therefore, the following sections focus on the above cited quantitative studies, followed by a careful review of selected cases involving African states for context.

2. A Closer Look at the Empirical Studies

It is fair to say that the ICSID database has been ripe for empirical analysis for some time now. Although more comprehensive analysis is almost certainly forthcoming, the inquiry here will be limited to the two relatively recent studies mentioned above.

Professor Susan Franck's study empirically tested three hypotheses:

> First, what kind of interaction effect might exist between the development status of the government respondent and the development status of the presiding arbitrator that could influence the outcome? Second, how does the respondent's development status affect outcome, if at all? Third, how does the presiding arbitrator's development status affect outcome, if at all? In other words, is

62. *See* Waibel & Wu Study, *supra* note 14, at 27–28. ("[A]rbitrators from developing countries are significantly underrepresented. The proximate cause goes deeper: most host countries hire European and US law firms and legal counsel to defend against ICSID claims.") (footnote omitted).

63. *Id.* at 14 n.35 (citing SCHREUER, *supra* note 1, art. 60, ¶. 8).

64. *See id.* at 21 ("For example, the United States, Mexico, Canada and Argentina, which account for twenty percent of respondent states in our dataset, routinely handle all aspects of investment disputes in-house. Outside attorneys are only used on occasion to supplement in-house legal capabilities.").

65. Franck Study, *supra* note 58.

66. Waibel & Wu Study, *supra* note 14.

> there a main effect for either respondent state's development status or presiding arbitrator's development status?[67]

What the Franck study labels "development status" is apparently the development status of the country that hosts the investment that generated the controversy, and the development status of the country of the presiding arbitrator's nationality.[68] The study relied on two sources for the determination of development status: OECD membership and World Bank's income-based classification (high, upper-middle, lower-middle, and low income).[69]

The study found that "there was no significant pattern of relationship between the World Bank status of the presiding arbitrator, the World Bank status of the respondent state, and the winner of an investment treaty arbitration."[70] It further found that for the selected sample of awards, "the number of winners and losers were statistically equivalent."[71]

To arrive at this conclusion, the Franck study analyzed 49 cases presided over by 49 arbitrators rendering 47 awards. A closer look at the numbers suggests that 36 of the 49 arbitrators came from high income or OECD countries. The representation of upper-middle, lower-middle, and low-income countries was 8-5-0 respectively.[72] Because there were zero presiding arbitrators from low-income countries, the study collapsed the numbers corresponding to the upper-middle and lower-middle countries (i.e., eight plus five) and ran the equation against the 36.[73] That is how it found statistical equivalency and concluded that "[t]he consistency in these results offers a powerful narrative that there is procedural integrity in investment arbitration."[74]

Before observations about these findings are offered, it important to look at one additional and interesting finding, which is that "presiding arbitrators from the developing world made larger awards against developing countries and smaller awards against developed countries."[75] This being the only source of bias the study found, it suggests that "[e]ven at this stage, it is worth considering what should be done to address the potential bias of arbitrators from the developing world in favor of the developed world."[76] In trying to explain the possible source of bias, the study speculates that "[it] may be that arbitrators from the developing world (particularly

67. Franck Study, *supra* note 58, at 454 (footnotes omitted).

68. *Id.* at n.111 and accompanying text.

69. *Id.* at 455–56.

70. *Id.* at 462.

71. *Id.* at 460.

72. *Id.* at 459 tbl.2.

73. *Id.* at 459–60.

74. *Id.* at 464.

75. *Id.* at 478.

76. *Id.*

those seeking repeat appointments) believe that rulings in favor of the developed world are the price of admission to the 'club.'"[77]

Several observations could be made about this study. First, it looks at the least controversial issue. There is little concern, if any, that arbitrators might be biased for or against a state based on its level of development. If the United States enacts environmental laws that render Canadian investment in California unprofitable, the development stage of the potential presiding arbitrator's country might be the last thing that the selection process would look at as the ideological leanings and previous track record are more important than whether he or she is from Australia or Indonesia. It is clear that a person's ideological leanings could be influenced by that person's upbringing, education, exposure, personal interest, and a whole host of other factors, which might include place of birth or perhaps, more important, place of residence. Nationality, however, is simply a poor indicator of political, ideological, or any other kind of bias. Second, the numbers do not seem to be well balanced for a valid quantitative measurement when the study is forced to collapse categories to help the analysis. One notable fact is that there were no presiding arbitrators from low-income countries in the dataset although low-income countries routinely arbitrate cases before ICSID. That is one of the fundamental deficits that the study fails to adequately address. Third, the study concludes that to the extent there is bias or even lack of integrity, it implicates arbitrators from developing countries who seem to impose more substantial penalties in the form of an award against developing countries possibly motivated by their desire to be more acceptable to the "club." Although the finding itself seems interesting, the attributed motive almost contradicts the main finding, that is, lack of development-based bias. A question might be asked, if the "club" is not entirely biased, why would arbitrators from developing countries think that they would gain more acceptance by imposing more significant awards against developing countries—unless, of course, they are misjudging their colleagues' perceptions, which the study does not suggest. Finally, the study omits the most serious and more credible allegation of bias, namely, ideological bias in favor of private investors (read multinational corporations) no matter where they make their investment. This question is often framed as "investor-bias" or "host-country-bias."[78] Nobody could credibly allege that such bias is decisively associated with the development status of the arbitrator's country of nationality. Significantly, however, Professor Franck's previous[79] and subsequent studies more or less replicate the same results.[80]

77. *Id.* at 479.

78. The Franck Study expressly excludes this inquiry. *See id.* at 479 n.16 and accompanying text ("This research does not evaluate differences in whether investors come from the developed or developing world because approximately 10% of investors were from the developing world.").

79. In her 2007 study, finding no pro-investor bias, Professor Franck concludes that "[r]ecognizing the limitations, the initial descriptive quantitative data from public awards suggest investment treaty arbitration appears to be functioning relatively well. There is, nevertheless, room for improvement." Susan D. Franck, *Empirically Evaluating Claims about Investment Treaty Arbitration*, 86 N.C. L. Rev. 1, 83 (2007).

80. Her 2011 study that compared the ICSID case outcome with other investment arbitrations also finds no bias on the basis of the development status (expressly noting Latin America). Susan D.

Drawing on the rich social science literature that substantially assesses the impact of personal characteristics—such as political ideology and collegiate politics—on case outcomes in domestic court litigation,[81] Waibel and Wu test different hypotheses relative to ICSID case outcome, focusing on decisions on jurisdiction and host state liability. Relevant for the purposes of this article are the following hypotheses: (1) "Arbitrators who are pro-investor will tend to vote in favor of affirming jurisdiction and liability of host states. Conversely, arbitrators who are pro-state are more likely to favor the host state;"[82] (2):

> Arbitrators who judge the actions of host countries that belong to the same legal family will tend to assert jurisdiction less often and hold the host state

Franck, *The ICSID Effect? Considering Potential Variations in Arbitration Awards*, 51 VA. J. INT'L L. 825, 913 (2011).

81. Among the sources they rely on are: RICHARD A. POSNER, OVERCOMING LAW (1995) (criticizing originalism in favor of a mixture of liberalism, pragmatism, and economics); GLENDON A. SCHUBERT, QUANTITATIVE ANALYSIS OF JUDICIAL BEHAVIOR (1959) (exploring bloc voting among Supreme Court justices, the justices' incentives to vote in such blocs, and the consistency of the justices' stances on recurring topics); Orley Ashenfelter, Theodore Eisenberg & Stewart J. Schwab, *Politics and the Judiciary: The Influence of Judicial Background on Case Outcomes*, 24 J. LEGAL STUD. 257, 281 (1995) ("In the mass of cases that are filed . . . the law—not the judge—dominates the outcomes."); Michael A. Bailey & Forrest Maltzman, *Does Legal Doctrine Matter? Unpacking Law and Policy Preferences on the U.S. Supreme Court*, 102 AM. J. POL. SCI., 369 (2008) (determining that law can play an important role in a judge's opinion, as demonstrated by statistical analyses into stare decisis, deference to Congress, and protection of speech); William N. Eskridge, *Overriding Supreme Court Statutory Interpretation Decisions*, 101 YALE L.J. 331, 334 (1991) (asserting that Congress is most likely to override the Supreme Court's statutory decisions when the Court is ideologically fragmented, "relies on the text's plain meaning and ignores legislative signals, and/or rejects positions taken by federal, state, or local governments"); Sheldon Goldman, *Voting Behavior on the United States Court of Appeals, 1961–1964*, 60 AM. POL. SCI. REV. 374, 379 (1966) (detailing the voting behavior of judges and how their political leanings may play a part); Daniel E. Ho & Erica L. Ross, *Did Liberal Justices Invent the Standing Doctrine? An Empirical Study of the Evolution of Standing, 1921–2006*, 62 STAN. L. REV. (2010) (contending that liberal justices created the standing doctrine so that administrative agencies would not be subject to judicial review); Stuart S. Nagel, *Political Party Affiliation and Judges' Decisions*, 55 AM. POL. SCI. REV. 843, 844 (1961) (revealing data comparing judges' decisions and political party lines); C. Neal Tate, *Personal Attribute Models of the Voting Behavior of U.S. Supreme Court Justices: Liberalism in Civil Liberties and Economics Decisions, 1946–1978*, 75 AM. POL. SCI. REV. 355, 366 (1981) (identifying personal attributes among judges, such as appointing president, past legal experience, and prestige of pre-law education, and concluding that their "influence . . . is transmitted directly and powerfully to judicial voting behavior"); Timothy B. Tomasi & Jess A. Velona, *All the President's Men? A Study of Ronald Reagan's Appointments to the U.S. Courts of Appeals*, 87 COLUM. L. REV. 766, 767 (1987) (assessing the conservatism of Reagan-appointed judges and finding that "Reagan judges are not significantly more conservative than their Republican colleagues"). Most notably, they cite DAVID W. RHODE & HAROLD J. SPAETH, SUPREME COURT DECISION MAKING 72 (1976) (noting that "judges base their decisions solely upon personal policy preferences"); JEFFREY A. SEGAL & HAROLD J. SPAETH, THE SUPREME COURT AND THE ATTITUDINAL MODEL 64, 86 (1993) ("[T]he Supreme Court decides disputes before it in light of the facts of the case vis-à-vis precedent, the plain meaning of the Constitution and statutes, the intent of the framers, and a balancing of societal versus constitutional interests.").

82. Waibel & Wu Study, *supra* note 14, at 21.

> liable on fewer occasions. Conversely, when arbitrators judge the actions of a host country belonging to a different legal family, they will be more likely to affirm jurisdiction and hold the host state liable;[83]

and (3) "Arbitrators from developing countries are less likely to hold the host country liable because they are more familiar with the economic and social conditions in developing countries and host countries[,] the more likely source of future arbitral appointments."[84]

The first hypothesis is almost a restatement of the obvious: a decision-maker's ideological leanings impact his decisions. Property rights are a subject of serious ideology controversy. As discussed at length above, the ideological divide is enduring. Although the study used proxies as indicators of the ideological leanings of the arbitrators,[85] the finding is not surprising because it is clear that the parties spend significant amounts of time and resources in selecting arbitrators who are likely to be ideologically sympathetic to their side.

The second proposition is also not surprising because of the inherent human inclination to understand and appreciate the familiar. The third proposition, likewise, is not surprising for the same reasons, that is, familiarity and understanding of the circumstances.

The above-noted studies share the same characteristics; however, they all avoid the most fundamental question of the impact of the diversity deficit on outcome. Stated differently, what is the overall price of the cultural barrier that the Africans face when appearing before tribunals composed largely of Western arbitrators represented by counsel and firms who must necessarily share the judges' cultural backgrounds? It might be impossible to empirically measure the cost or explicate the barrier, but the remainder of this chapter attempts to assess by looking at the available data and reviewing selected cases how African states have fared in the last half-century. Before that is provided, however, it is important to look at the historical background to understand why Africa signed on to this project and how that might affect its continued use of ICSID with its new partners—a framework arguably designed for a different purpose.

B. A HISTORICAL PERSPECTIVE

Prior to the adoption of the text of the Convention, the World Bank conducted extensive consultations with various stakeholders from Africa to South America. Fortunately, ICSID has made summaries of the records available in multiple volumes under the title *History of the Convention*.[86] This section relies on these volumes

83. *Id.* at 22–23.

84. *Id.* at 23.

85. *Id.* at 22. The proxy is not a perfect one—they use frequency of appointment by one party or the other as an indication of the political leanings as pro-investor or pro-state. *Id.* at 34–40.

86. History of ICSID, *supra* note 5.

for the discussion of the raison d'être as understood by the African and Latin American countries and the dilemmas they faced.

1. The Doctrinal Debate

A fundamental doctrinal dilemma underpins the law of international investment.[87] Its cogent articulation may be traced back to the famous 1938 exchange of letters between U.S. secretary of state Cordell Hull and the Mexican foreign ministry, prompted by Mexico's seizure of agrarian property belonging to American citizens. These exchanges are highly instructive—Hull wrote:

> The taking of property without compensation is not expropriation. It is confiscation. . . . . We cannot question the right of a foreign government to treat its own nationals in this fashion if it so desires. This is a matter of domestic concern. But we cannot admit that a foreign government may take the property of American nationals in disregard of the rule of compensation under international law. Nor can we admit that any government unilaterally and through its municipal legislation can, as in this instant case, nullify this universally accepted principle of international law, based as it is on reason, equity and justice. . . . . The right of prompt and just compensation for expropriated property is a part of this [international legal] structure.[88]

The response of the Mexican Minster of Foreign Affairs was equally fascinating:

> My Government maintains . . . [that] there does not exist in international law any principle universally accepted by countries, nor by the writers of treatises on this subject, that would render obligatory the giving of adequate compensation for expropriations of a general and impersonal character. Nevertheless, Mexico admits, in obedience to her own laws, that she is indeed under obligation to indemnify in an adequate manner; but the doctrine which she maintains on the subject, which is based on the most authoritative opinions of writers of treatises on international law, is that the time and manner of such payment must be determined by her own laws.[89]

This classic adaptation of what is popularly known as the Calvo doctrine undoubtedly provided the philosophical impetus for the initial unanimous rejection of the

87. The Law of International Investment refers to a set of procedural and substantive rules that generally govern the relationship between the foreign investor, the state of the investor's nationality, and the host state. THE OXFORD HANDBOOK OF INTERNATIONAL INVESTMENT LAW 6 (Peter Muchlinski, Frederico Ortino & Christoph Schreuer eds., 2008).

88. Letter from Cordell Hull, U.S. Secretary of State, to Francisco Castillo Nájera, Mex. Ambassador to the U.S. (July 21, 1938), *as reprinted in* ANDREAS F. LOWENFELD, INTERNATIONAL ECONOMIC LAW 476 (2d ed. 2008).

89. Letter from Mex. Minister of Foreign Affairs to U.S. Ambassador at Mexico City (Aug. 3, 1938), *as reprinted in* LOWENFELD, *supra* note 88, at 477.

idea of a World Bank-affiliated supranational arbitral body by the South American countries.[90] When the ICSID proposal was presented at the annual meeting of the Bank in Tokyo in 1964, all South American states voted no, prompting the Latin press to famously tout "El No de Tokyo."[91] A World Bank-affiliated commentator aptly characterized it as the "Calvoesque rejection of foreign intervention."[92]

The Bank's exchanges with the South American jurists during one of the legal consultative meetings in June 1964 provide valuable insight as to where they stood on the philosophical question and, in fact, offer good contrast with the African jurists' position discussed below. The discussion was led by the then-World Bank general counsel Aron Broches, who later became the first secretary general of ICSID, subsequently serving in that capacity for 13 years.[93]

On the afternoon of Monday, February 3, 1964, Broches opened the first session of the consultative meeting in Santiago, Chile. The first reaction he received was the following seemingly supportive statement by the representative of the Chilean government identified in the report as Brunner:

> [T]he draft convention touched on novel problems and concepts in the field of international law in giving individuals direct access to States before international tribunals. The most enlightened jurists had long denied that only States could be subjects of international law . . . . Direct access of individuals to an international jurisdiction which was found in the Statute of the Central American Court of Justice and had been acquiring increasing importance in the European Economic Community was being projected upon the world plane through the initiative of the International Bank.[94]

As the day progressed, stronger opinions were expressed. Ribeiro of Brazil made the following classic Calvoesquian statement: "[D]espite the optional character of the draft Convention, foreign investors would be granted a legally privileged position, in violation of the principle of full equality before the law."[95] Similarly, Escobar of Bolivia said:

> [T]he sovereignty of States could not be subordinated to the authority of an international institution without being seriously impaired . . . those

90. Lowenfeld, *supra* note 88, at 540.

91. *Id.* at 540.

92. Paul C. Szasz, *The Investment Disputes Convention and Latin America*, 11 Va. J. Int'l L. 256, 259 (1971). Although there are other related reasons for the Latin American countries' rejection of the idea, it is clear that the dominant reason was one derived from the Calvo doctrine: "that the Convention, which of course can be used only in relation to an alien investor, offends against the rule that foreigners must be treated equally with citizens." *Id.* at 261 (citing José R. Chiriboga, *International Arbitration*, 4 Int'l L. 801, 804 (1970)).

93. *Aron Broches Retires as Vice President and General Counsel*, The World Bank, http://go.worldbank.org/JDT8LQZ890 (last visited Mar. 30, 2016).

94. History of ICSID, *supra* note 5, at 305. Note that this statement is a summary contained in the report. It is not an exact transcription of the delegate's statements.

95. *Id.* at 306.

> responsible for preparing the draft had failed to appreciate its adverse effects. Thus the Bank itself seemed to be displaying a lack of confidence in the institutions of the countries wishing to attract foreign capital.[96]

Having made that statement, he finally urged the Bank to abandon the idea altogether.[97]

Another salient issue that the South American experts raised was the proposed affiliation of the Centre with the World Bank and, related to that, its location at the headquarters of the Bank in Washington, DC. Some experts suggested that it be allowed to function in the country where the dispute arose.[98] Responding to these types of concerns, the chair said that if the affiliation of the Centre with the Bank were agreed upon, its location would be of secondary importance, and "should be decided on grounds of practicability."[99]

Despite Broches's able chairmanship and great efforts to convince, the negative sentiment dominated the entire consultative process, explaining the nearly universal rejection of the idea by the South American states.

Commentators later criticized the rejection. According to Paul C. Szasz, for example, "[T]he Centre, as an international institution in which all Contracting States participate equally, must not be considered as a foreign power of the type against which the Latin Americans had for generations girded themselves."[100] In an effort to encourage the South American countries to accept the Convention, the same commentator warned that they were in competition with "capital-hungry and more flexible States."[101] Although there is no reference to specific countries, it is clear that the reference was made to African countries, which overwhelmingly accepted the Convention with enthusiasm from the very beginning. What then explains such a radically different approach by two capital-receiving continents with relatively similar colonial experience? Did they have differing philosophical understandings? Where did Africa stand on the Hull-Calvo debate?

The reason for the different approach taken by African toward the Convention may be illustrated by the African philosophy regarding land ownership. Former International Court of Justice president Judge T.O. Elias expresses the dominant customary African conception of the ownership of land as: "I conceive that land belongs to a vast family of which many are dead, few are living, and countless members are unborn."[102] He notes that these conceptions are largely shared across many

96. *Id.* at 308.

97. *Id.*

98. *Id.* at 312–13 (statement of Mr. Salazar, representative of Ecuador).

99. *Id.* at 313 (statement of Mr. Broches, the Chairman).

100. Szasz, *supra* note 92, at 259.

101. *Id.* at 265.

102. T. Olawale Elias, The Nature of African Customary Law 162 (1956) (quoting a statement made by a Nigerian chief to the West African Lands Committee in 1912).

African societies.[103] Although the expression suggests some form of communalism, individual possessory rights are recognized. Such rights were almost indistinguishable from the concept of fee simple absolute under common law, except, unlike the Crown in England, the African customary chiefs never had a claim of ownership of all land and never considered all inhabitants their tenants.[104] The chief "enjoys only an administrative right of supervisory oversight of the land for the benefit of the whole community."[105] Judge Elias characterizes the African customary land tenure system as "primitive communism" and describes the rights and responsibilities of the individual and the group.[106] Professor Lesley Obiora's account of the conditions of alienability of property is instructive. She writes: "Members of a family, irrespective of sex, were entitled to occupancy and user rights subject to good behavior. While rights accruing via citizenship could not be ceded any more than citizenship on which they rested, persons could transfer their interest in land that they improved."[107] More important, however:

> [T]here was a practical restraint on alienation insofar as the transferee had to be someone acceptable to the local community because the spatial proximity and the conditions of production meant that the transferee invariably associated with and was incorporated into the community. In this sense, political affiliation modified particular rights based on creative preemption.[108]

It is clear, however, that the land and property ownership regime under African customary law—although replete with inconsistencies across the various societies—had solid and sophisticated philosophical foundations and were less solicitous of more rights for outsiders.[109]

As fate would have it, however, with the advent of colonialism, the philosophical foundations of the African notions of property and the modes and hierarchy of its allocation were "distort[ed]" and "disoriented."[110] It is evident that "[c]olonial officials assumed that land must have an owner exercising a full range of rights parallel

103. *Id.* at n.1 and accompanying text.

104. *Id.* at 164.

105. *Id.* at 164–65.

106. *Id.* at 83–92.

107. L. Amede Obiora, *Remapping the Domain of Property in Africa*, 12 U. Fla. J.L. & Pub. Pol'y 57, 60–61 (2000) (citing Elizabeth Colson, *The Colonial Period and Land Rights*, *in* Colonialism in Africa 1870–1960: 3 Profiles of Change: African Societies And Colonial Rule 197, 200 (Peter Duigan, L.H. Gann & Victor Turner eds., 1971); Elias, *supra* note 102, at 167).

108. Obiora, *supra* note 107, at 60.

109. Readings in African Law 356, 356–90 (Eugene Cotran & N.N. Rubin eds., 1970).

110. René David & John E.C. Brierley, Major Legal Systems of the World Today: An Introduction to the Comparative Study of Law, 562 (3d ed. 1985). Although Professors David and Brierley say this in the broader context of the impact of colonial legal systems on African customary law, it is clear that the fate of the law of property was the same.

to those covered by the European concept of proprietary ownership."[111] As Professor Obiora further notes, "[t]he development of new forms of property and technologies of production, the possibilities of individual acquisition, the acculturation of different values, reworked patterns of consumption and the like, redefined the socio-economic terrain."[112] Upon independence, most African countries sought refuge in the communist ideologies of the Soviet Union (USSR), and latterly, the People's Republic of China (PRC).[113] These ideologies have an unwavering stance on ownership of property. Marxism, the essential philosophical foundation, holds that private ownership of property enables the "exploitation of man by man."[114] It makes no distinction between citizens and aliens. If the philosophical foundations of the time were seemingly more aligned with the Calvo doctrine, what then allured the African states into instantly accepting ICSID? Examination of the history might shed some light.

2. Why Was ICSID Accepted?

The historical record clearly indicates that the only reason, for example, that the African states accepted ICSID is because they thought that they had to do so in order to attract private foreign investment to develop their ailing postcolonial economies.[115] Consider the summary of recorded proceedings of the African legal consultative meeting that took place in Addis Ababa between December 16 and 20 in 1963.[116] This meeting was also chaired by World Bank general counsel Broches.[117] It focused on at least four aspects of the proposal: (1) purpose and justification, (2) jurisdiction, (3) affiliation and location, and (4) panels.[118] Each is discussed briefly as follows:

A. Purpose and Justification

The historical record is unambiguous on this point. It suggests that the participating African legal experts overwhelmingly believed that a reputable international

111. Obiora, *supra* note 107, at 62.

112. *Id.* at 66.

113. Beverly I. Moran, *Homogenized Law: Can the United States Learn from African Mistakes?*, 25 Fordham Int'l L.J. 361, 367 (2001) (citing Michael Hodd, The Economies of Africa 34–35 (1991)). For a fuller discussion of Africa's relationship with the USSR and PRC, see Soviet and Chinese Aid to African Nations (Warren Weinstein & Thomas H. Henriksen eds., 1980). For a detailed description of China's involvement with the African nations, see Alan Hutchinson, China's African Revolution (1975).

114. Karl Marx & Friedrich Engels, The Communist Manifesto 172 (1948).

115. *See* History of ICSID, *supra* note 5, at 236 (summarizing a statement by the Executive Secretary of the Economic Commission for Africa calling for a legal regime to promote private foreign investment).

116. *Id.* at 236–98.

117. *Id.* at 236.

118. *See infra* notes 119–42 and accompanying text (providing a detailed summary of the delegates' discussion of these four areas).

dispute settlement mechanism would alleviate Africa's problem of attracting foreign investment. For example, the executive secretary of the Economic Commission for Africa, in a statement he made at the beginning of the meeting, said that:

> [P]rivate capital was not moving in sufficient volume to areas in need of capital, one of the most serious impediments to its flow [was] the fear of investors that their investment would be exposed to political risks such as outright expropriation. . . . The Bank had therefore been led to wonder whether, in view of its reputation for integrity and its position of impartiality, it could not help in removing that obstacle to private investment.[119]

The representatives of almost all of the 29 states present in that meeting echoed that sentiment while raising some concerns about the jurisdiction, affiliation, location, and composition of panels.[120] The record interestingly shows that one of the vocal supporters of the initiative was Judge T.O. Elias, who was then a young representative of the Nigerian government, many years before he ascended to the presidency of the International Court of Justice.[121]

b. Jurisdiction (Powers and Functions of the Centre)

Objections were raised on the most fundamental question of standing of a private investor to proceed against a sovereign state in an arbitral forum.[122] Questions were also raised in connection with the complexities of dual nationality, that is, whether a person including a juridical person having the nationality of the host state as well as another contracting state may avail herself/itself of the benefits of the Convention.[123] A more serious objection to the jurisdiction of the Centre came from the representatives of Cameroon and Tunisia, who said that if a state expropriates property of a foreign investor in the public interest, "the only question that could be submitted to the Centre [should be the] adequacy of [the] compensation."[124] Related to this, the representative from Cameroon asked, "where the parties had undertaken to have recourse to arbitration without specifying the law to be applied . . . would the tribunal be competent to decide upon the legality of such a sovereign act, and if so, by reference to which system of law?"[125] Although these objections mirror the objections

119. History of ICSID, *supra* note 5, at 240.

120. *Id.* at 243–98.

121. *Id.* at 244 ("In the opinion of his Government the document represented an attempt not only to restore the confidence of the investor but also to codify certain principles of customary law and to engage in the progressive development of international law, and he warmly recommended it.").

122. *Id.* at 256 ("[T]he effect of Article II, Section 1 would be to place nationals on a par with States. That represented a departure from customary international law and was a step which should not be taken lightly.").

123. *Id.* at 256–57.

124. *Id.* at 259.

125. *Id.* at 267.

of the South American bloc, they were not raised so vigorously and widely enough as to result in the majority's rejection of the idea.[126]

c. Affiliation and Location

Although the idea that the Centre's affiliation with the Bank would give it appropriate prestige has not been disputed, concerns were raised with respect to the role of the president of the Bank as the chair of the Administrative Council and the location of the Centre at the headquarters of the Bank in Washington, DC. For example, one representative noted, "while the connection of the Center with the Bank would give the Center added prestige, the intention was nonetheless to create an independent body. It might therefore be desirable to indicate at the outset . . . that the seat of the Center could be transferred to another location."[127] Similarly, another delegate questioned the appropriateness of the appointment of the president of the Bank as the chair of the Administrative Council. He noted in particular that "certain countries might not wish to include an arbitration clause in the possible arrangements owing to the preponderant role of the Chairman in the functioning of the Center," and inquired "whether it would not be possible to transfer some of the functions at present vested in the Chairman to some other person or body."[128] The Bank's response to this inquiry was that "the draft Convention had been drawn upon the assumption that the link with the International Bank was considered beneficial and that the President of the Bank was recognized to be a suitable person for the functions vested in him."[129]

As far as the place of the proceedings was concerned, at least two views were expressed: leaving the designation of the place to the Administrative Council or leaving the choice to the parties, with the understanding that the arbitral tribunal would pick the location if the parties failed to agree, similar to most commercial arbitral rules.[130] The final text provided that the "proceeding shall be held at the seat of the Centre."[131] Exceptions included the Permanent Court of Arbitration (PCA) at The Hague, any other facilities with which the Centre had made arrangements, and other places "approved by the Commission or Tribunal after consultation with the Secretary-General."[132]

d. Panels/Arbitrators

The discussion on the panels and selection of arbitrators focused on at least two major points: qualifications and diversity of nationality. The African experts

126. *See supra* Section B(1) (discussing the objections of South American countries to ICSID).

127. History of ICSID, *supra* note 5, at 248 (statement of the representative of United Arab Republic, Mr. Moustafa).

128. *Id.* (statement of the representative of Sierra Leone, Mr. Macaulay).

129. *Id.* (statement of Mr. Broches, General Counsel of the Bank, Chair of the meeting).

130. *Id.* at 278 (statements of Mr. Elias of Nigeria and Mr. Macaulay of Sierra Leone).

131. ICSID Convention, *supra* note 1, art. 62.

132. *Id.* art. 63.

repeatedly emphasized the need for appointing persons with appropriate expertise in the field of international arbitration. For example, the representative of Dahomey (now the Republic of Benin) urged that the Administrative Council should make sure that the arbitrators it appoints are "technically competent."[133] Similarly, T.O. Elias of Nigeria suggested that:

> [I]f the parties to a dispute were to be given the freedom to appoint to a tribunal or commission persons from outside the Panels, that freedom should be qualified by a requirement that the persons so appointed should not be of a quality inferior to those designated to the Panels [by the President of the Bank].[134]

Once the idea of the constitution of a panel of experts from which arbitrators would be drawn for each case, either by appointment or party choice, had been agreed to, a heated discussion ensued on the question of disqualification of arbitrators. The draft provided that arbitrators appointed by the chairman (World Bank president) may only be challenged based on facts that have occurred subsequent to the appointment, whereas party-selected arbitrators may be challenged and disqualified on the basis of "any fact antecedent or subsequent to their appointment."[135] Because of the vigorous resistance to the idea of giving the chairman's appointees a privileged position with respect to challenge and disqualification, the chair of the meeting took note and said that he would seek further opinion in subsequent deliberation with various stakeholders.[136] The final version did indeed abandon such privileged treatment.[137]

The importance of prohibiting arbitrators with the nationality of the disputing parties also raised a controversy. The most appealing opposition to the idea came from Moustafa of Egypt (then called the United Arab Republic). He noted in particular that: "*An arbitrator of the same nationality as the party to the dispute was more likely to understand the issues involved and to be in a better position to offer the necessary explanations; he might even make an unfavorable award more acceptable.*"[138] He seriously questioned the exact reason that nationality could exclude an otherwise qualified arbitrator. The record shows that the chair did not answer this question satisfactorily but simply said that he personally favored the exclusion approach.[139]

133. History of ICSID, *supra* note 5, at 245.

134. *Id.* at 265.

135. *Id.* at 276 (statements of Mr. Macaulay, representative of Sierra Leone) ("[I]f, for example, an arbitrator appointed by the Chairman were challenged on grounds that he had a personal interest in the matter in dispute, the Chairman would be entitled to say that he had known of that interest but had not considered it a valid objection to his appointment, and his decision would be unchallengeable. It is not a matter of questioning the Chairman's integrity but his judgment.").

136. *Id.* (statement of Mr. Broches, chair of the meeting).

137. ICSID Convention, *supra* note 1, arts. 56–58.

138. History of ICSID, *supra* note 5, at 266 (emphasis added).

139. *Id.*

The final text also disregarded the idea of the cultural competence of the arbitrators. It indeed maintained the idea that arbitrators appointed by the chair when the parties fail to agree, "shall not be nationals of the Contracting State party to the dispute or of the Contracting State whose national is a party to the dispute."[140] Although the merits of this approach might be debatable, the final text's entire omission of the cultural competence of arbitrators is worth noting. As a prelude to the discussions that follow, it is important to take note of the exact arbitrator qualifications that the Convention provides in Article 14:

> (1) Persons designated to serve on the Panels shall be persons of high moral character and recognized competence in the fields of law, commerce, industry or finance, who may be relied upon to exercise independent judgment. Competence in the field of law shall be of particular importance in the case of persons on the Panel of Arbitrators.
> (2) The Chairman, in designating persons to serve on the Panels, shall in addition pay due regard to the importance of assuring representation on the Panels of the principal legal systems of the world and of the main forms of economic activity.[141]

It is important to note that the required qualifications are limited to good moral character, technical competence, and impartiality.[142] It is also worth noting that the requirements of diversity in subsection (2) are limited to legal systems and economic activity.

C. QUANTITATIVE INDICATORS

As of this writing,[143] the ICSID database contains sixty-four completed cases involving at least one African state as the respondent. The data is broken down as follows:

1. Arbitrator Nationality

Of the 64 completed cases, 61 provide arbitrator nationality. The data shows that the pool of arbitrators in these cases consisted primarily of Europeans. Of the cases analyzed, 59 percent of the arbitrators of initial case submissions were European. Europeans were appointed presidents of tribunals of initial case submissions in 43 of the 61 cases, which is roughly 70 percent of the cases. In the cases where annulment proceedings commenced, 24 European arbitrators were on panels of ad hoc

140. ICSID Convention, *supra* note 1, art. 38.

141. *Id.* art. 14.

142. *Id.*

143. The statistical analysis included in this section is entirely based on data available on the ICSID website. *Cases*, ICSID, https://icsid.worldbank.org/apps/icsidweb/cases/Pages/AdvancedSearch.aspx (last visited Mar. 30, 2016).

committees for the annulment proceedings. Europeans were appointed presidents of ad hoc committees in 10 of the 14 annulment proceedings, roughly 70 percent of the proceedings.

North America was the second most represented region. North American arbitrators made up 14 percent of the panels of initial case submissions. North Americans were appointed presidents of four tribunals of initial case submissions, which is roughly 6 percent of the cases. Four North American arbitrators were on panels of the ad hoc committees for annulment proceedings and three North Americans were appointed president of ad hoc committees, which is roughly 21 percent of the committees.

African representation on panels was close behind that of North America, with African arbitrators making up 12 percent of the panels of initial case submissions. Africans were appointed presidents of two tribunals of initial case submissions, which is roughly 3 percent of the cases. Eight African arbitrators were on panels of ad hoc committees for annulment proceedings.

Arbitrators from South America made up 5 percent of the panels of initial case submissions. South Americans were appointed presidents of six tribunals, roughly 10 percent. Three South American arbitrators were on panels of ad hoc committees for annulment proceedings.

Arbitrators from the Australia region made up 3 percent of the panels of initial case submissions. Arbitrators from the Australia region headed two tribunals, one as president and one as sole arbitrator (CDC Group v. Republic of Seychelles (ARB/02/14)).[144] Two arbitrators from the Australia region were on panels of ad hoc committees for annulment proceedings.

Arbitrators from Asia and the Middle East made up 3 percent of the panels of initial case submissions. An arbitrator from the Asia/Middle East region was appointed president of one tribunal. Three arbitrators from Asia and the Middle East were on panels of ad hoc committees for annulment proceedings and one was appointed president of the ad hoc committee. The following chart in Figure 1 demonstrates these statistics.[145]

2. Counsel Nationality

The nationality of counsel representing the African states in these proceedings is provided in 32 of 64 cases. Although in 16 percent and 22 percent of these cases, the respondent states were represented by exclusively African and exclusively European counsel respectively, in the great majority of cases—that is, 62 percent of them—the African states were represented by counselors composed of different nationalities including the specific African respondent state, European, American, and Australian.

144. For a breakdown of the arbitrators in this case, see *List of Concluded Cases, supra* note 4; CDC Group plc v. Republic of Seychelles, ICSID Case No. ARB/02/14 (2003), https://icsid.worldbank.org/apps/ICSIDWEB/cases/Pages/casedetail.aspx?CaseNo=ARB/02/14&tab=PRO.

145. The figures in this chapter were prepared by the author, and previously appeared in Won Kidane, *The China-Africa Factor in the Contemporary ICSID Legitimacy Debate*, 35 U. Pa. J. Int'l L. 559 (2014).

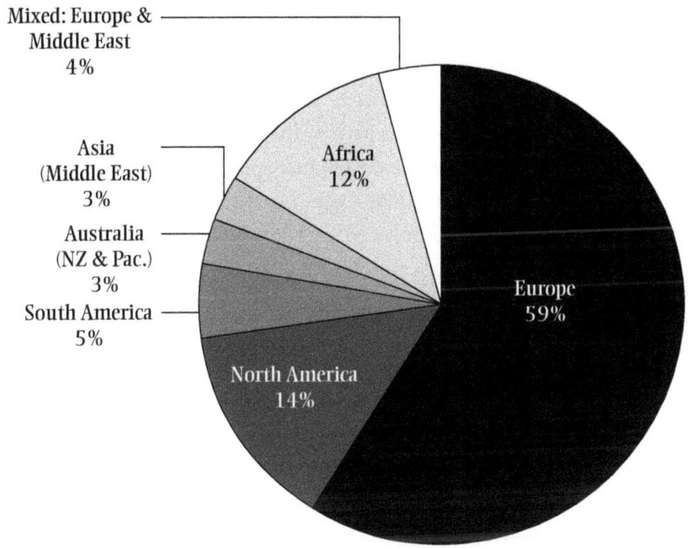

Sample size: = concluded cases from ICSID website with available information on arbitrator nationality; 61 of 64 cases

Figure 1 Arbitrator Nationality: Initial Arbitration Submissions.
Won Kidane, *The China-Africa Factor in the Contemporary ICSID Legitimacy Debate,* 35 U. Pa. J. Int'l L. 559 (2014).

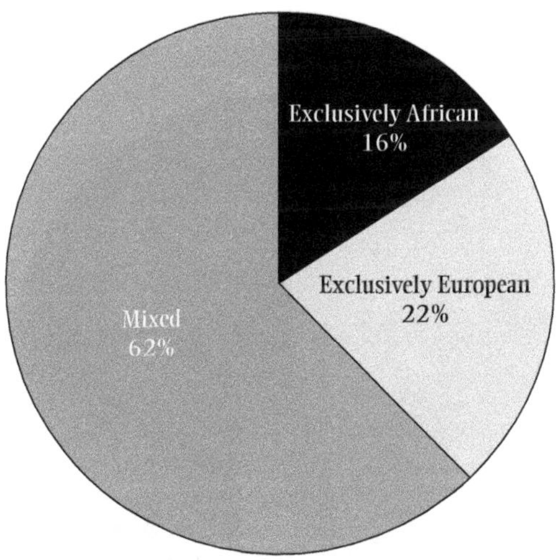

Sample size = concluded cases from ICSID with available information on attorney nationality; 32 of 64 cases

Figure 2 Respondent State Attorney Nationality: Initial Case Submissions.
Won Kidane, *The China-Africa Factor in the Contemporary ICSID Legitimacy Debate,* 35 U. Pa. J. Int'l L. 559 (2014).

3. Claimant Nationality

In 42 of the 64 cases, the publicly available data provides the nationality of the claimants. The majority of the claimants were from Europe, that is, 55 percent with an additional 10 percent representing a joint venture of European and North American investors. In an additional 19 percent of the cases, European investors collaborated with African investors, and in 7 percent of the cases North American investors collaborated with African investors. Only 5 percent and 2 percent of the cases involved exclusively Asian and African investors, respectively.

4. Location

The location of the arbitration (meaning the location of the actual hearing) is indicated in 38 of the 64 cases. In 85 percent of the initial case submissions, hearings took place in Europe exclusively with an additional 13 percent of the initial case submissions holding hearings in Europe along with another location. North America was the hearing location for 2 percent of the initial case submissions. No case was heard in Africa.

The data is thus unambiguous: African states routinely arbitrate cases with private investors almost exclusively in Washington, DC, Paris, or London before three Western arbitrators and represented by Western law firms. They obviously spend a lot of money. What is the nature of the justice that they buy in Washington, Paris, or London?

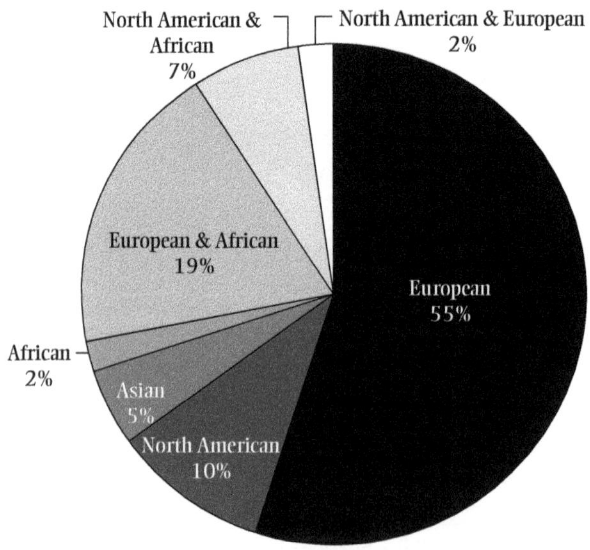

Sample size: = concluded cases from ICSID website with available information on claimant nationality; 42 of 64 cases

Figure 3 Claimant Nationality: Initial Case Submissions.
Won Kidane, *The China-Africa Factor in the Contemporary ICSID Legitimacy Debate*, 35 U. Pa. J. Int'l L. 559 (2014).

5. Outcome on Jurisdiction

Outcome on jurisdictional challenges is indicated in 37 of the 64 cases. A basis for jurisdiction was found in 74 percent of the cases, whereas 13 percent of the cases found no basis for jurisdiction. Mixed outcomes on jurisdiction occurred in 13 percent of the cases.

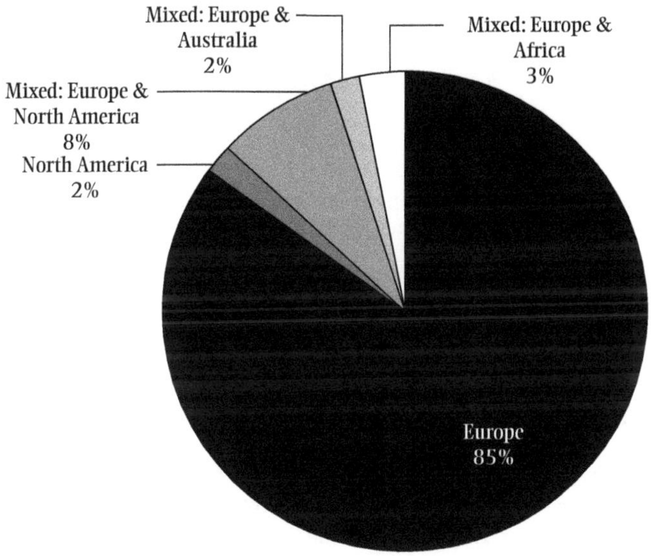

Sample size: = the 38 of 64 concluded cases from ICSID website with available information on hearing location

Figure 4 Location of Hearings.
Won Kidane, *The China-Africa Factor in the Contemporary ICSID Legitimacy Debate*, 35 U. Pa. J. Int'l L. 559 (2014).

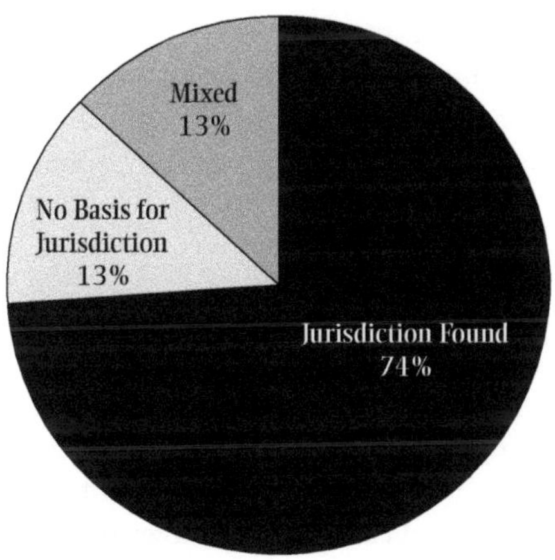

Figure 5 Outcome on Jurisdiction.
Won Kidane, *The China-Africa Factor in the Contemporary ICSID Legitimacy Debate*, 35 U. Pa. J. Int'l L. 559 (2014).

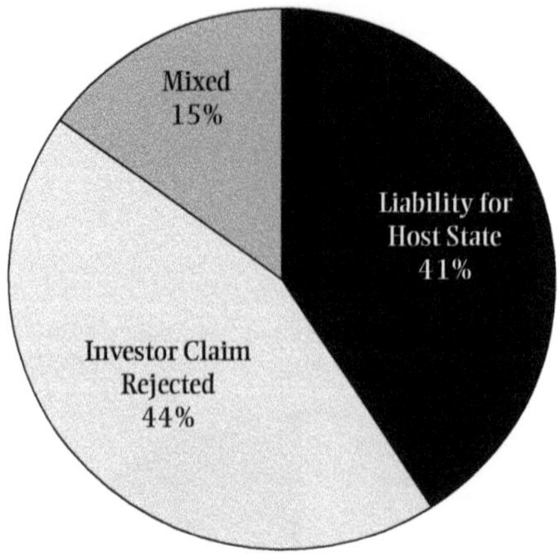

Sample size: = concluded cases from the ICSID website with available information on the merits; 34 of 64 cases

Figure 6 Outcome on the Merits.
Won Kidane, *The China-Africa Factor in the Contemporary ICSID Legitimacy Debate*, 35 U. Pa. J. Int'l L. 559 (2014).

6. Outcome on the Merits

Outcome on the merits of the case is indicated in 34 of the 64 cases. In 44 percent of the cases, investor claims were rejected, whereas 41 percent of the cases found the respondent state liable. Another 15 percent of the cases had a mixed outcome. As shown in the following chart in Figure 6, the outcome on the merits is fairly balanced.

7. Allocation of Cost

Cost allocation is indicated in 34 of the 64 cases. In all but seven cases, the cost was split, that is, each party was required to cover its own expenses and pay half of the costs of the tribunal. In six of the remaining seven cases, the respondent state was required to pay all or some parts of the claimant's costs. In one case the parties were required to pay their own expenses, but the respondent state was required to pay the tribunal's costs, but that was included in the split category in the chart in Figure 7 on the next page. The investor-claimant was required to pay the respondent state's costs in only one case.

D. THE VIRTUES OF ARISTOCRATIC JUSTICE

The study described above shows that in the last half-century, African states defended investment claims in Europe and the United States, and prevailed on the merits in about half of the cases. The data also shows that ICSID tribunals found jurisdiction in the overwhelming majority of cases. It also shows that no matter who prevailed, the tribunals allocated costs evenly in the great majority of cases and awarded costs to the respondent state in only one case. This obviously paints a more complicated picture and invites deeper inquiry; the following sections make such attempt.

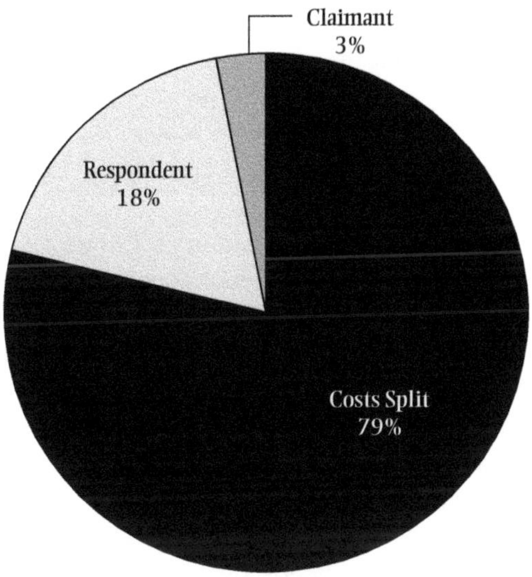

Sample size: = concluded cases from ICSID website with available information on cost allocation; 34 of 64 cases

Figure 7 Cost Allocation.
Won Kidane, *The China-Africa Factor in the Contemporary ICSID Legitimacy Debate*, 35 U. Pa. J. Int'l L. 559 (2014).

1. Who Are the "Virtuous" Men?

In their groundbreaking work, *Dealing in Virtue*, Professors Yves Dezalay and Bryant Garth equate virtue with "symbolic capital":

> Only a very select and elite group of individuals is able to serve as international arbitrators. They are purportedly selected for their "virtue"—judgment, neutrality, expertise—yet rewarded as if they are participants in international deal making. In more sociological terms, the *symbolic capital* acquired through a career of public service or scholarship is translated into a substantial cash value in international arbitration.[146]

They state that this "symbolic capital" can be arbitrarily acquired,[147] and go on to make a historical comparison:

> The careers of these noble individuals recall accounts of the medieval church. The son of a nobleman could become a bishop of the church simply because of family background and social prominence. Others would shave their heads, take vows of celibacy, devote everything to the church, and yet have no chance to rise to a position of eminence, such as bishop. Their hard work would help

146. Yves Dezalay & Bryant G. Garth, Dealing in Virtue: International Commercial Arbitration and the Construction of a Transnational Legal Order 8 (1996).

147. *Id.* at 18.

> maintain the institutional structure that made the position of bishop attractive to the son of a nobleman, but they lacked the social platform to gain the top position.[148]

So how is this related to a career in arbitration? Dezalay and Garth continue to write:

> There is similar phenomenon in arbitration. Without a suitable platform, defined now as more than social class (which is nevertheless useful), the arbitration devotee can never get selected as an arbitrator. There are individuals who, for example, teach at low-prestige schools, work in unknown law firms, or produce scholarship that is deemed to be too marginal, who cannot gain access to this world no matter how much they write, attend conferences, or in general profess the faith. Others need not even profess the faith or write about arbitration to enter the field more or less at the top.[149]

So, who are these noble men? A generic description of their qualifications may read something like "academic standing, scholarly publication, particular kinds of practical experience, training in alternative dispute resolution, connections to business, connections to political power, particular language skills, [and] proficiency in technical aspects of arbitration practice."[150] More important, "the weight of different agents depends on their symbolic capital, i.e., on the recognition, institutionalized or not, that they receive from a group."[151]

Consider the "five-million-pound man," Swiss arbitrator Pierre Lalive.[152] The media report exaggerated the fee he charged in the *Westland* case. It was not quite five-million pounds, but rather 4,697,258 British pounds.[153] Lalive's judgment may or may not be worth that much, similar to many professional services that consumers purchase on the marketplace,[154] but Dezalay and Garth use his career path to exemplify what it takes to join the aristocratic club: together with his renowned older brother, Lalive is a partner

148. *Id.* at 23.

149. *Id.*

150. *Id.* at 19.

151. *Id.* at 18 (quoting Pierre Bourdieu & Loic J.D. Wacquant, An Invitation to Reflexive Sociology 119 (1992)) (emphasis omitted).

152. *Id.* at 19 n.3 (citing Jeremy Edwards, *The Five-Million Pound Man*, Legal Business, Nov. 1994, at 46–49). Lalive obtained such a large fee from the *Westland Helicopters Ltd. v. Arab Organisations for Industrialisation* case involving hundreds of millions. For a discussion of this case, see Justice Colman, *Westland Helicopters Ltd v. Arab Organisations for Industrialisation,* 10 Arab L.Q. 115–43 (1995).

153. *Id.*

154. Note the similarity of this with the recent debate on Wall Street executive compensation. *See* Frank Ahrens, *Isn't That Rich? The Bonus Controversy of 2009*, Wash. Post, http://www.washingtonpost.com/wp-srv/special/opinions/outlook-bonus/ (last visited Mar. 30, 2016) (compiling opinions of politicians and chief executives on the fairness of Wall Street bonuses).

at the Lalive Law firm in Geneva; has written many books and articles; possessed an academic appointment in Geneva; taught at Columbia, Cambridge, the University of Brussels, and the Hague Academy of International Law; and served as president of the ICC's Institute of Business Law and Practice, a member of the London Court of International Arbitration, and president of the Swiss Arbitration Association.[155]

Although the arbitration field is still dominated by persons of this caliber, today's career path is probably more like Jan Paulsson's, whom Dezalay and Garth say is "the closest equivalent in his generation to Pierre Lalive of the older generation."[156] Consider Paulsson's ticket to prominence: multicultural upbringing, excellent academic credentials, early practice exposure to international arbitration, sustained scholarly production, a great platform as a partner at one of the world's most prominent international arbitration firms, and a professor at an American law school.[157] Indeed, to use Professor Salacuse's characterization, these experts are members of an "epistemic community" with the ability to influence policy and shape jurisprudence.[158]

2. Why Do the Africans Appoint the Virtuous Men?

Simply stated, these men are evidently appointed because of their "virtue." Africa is certainly under no obligation to appoint them as arbitrators or counsel. Consider this true statement:

> Overall, who the arbitrator is in terms of expertise and prior experience is the most important single factor in both the decisional and the consensus processes. *Who* he or she is determines the availability of both substantive and fact finding norms, conditions the procedural and role norms that are held, and raises or lowers the degree of influence in interaction with other arbitrators. [159]

155. Dezalay & Garth, *supra* note 146, at 20.

156. *Id.* at 24.

157. *Id.* For Paulsson's current biography, see also *Prof. Jan Paulsson, Honorary President*, Int'l Council Com. Arb. [ICCA], http://www.arbitration-icca.org/about/governing-board/honorary-presidents/Jan_Paulsson.html (last visited Mar. 30, 2016); *and Jan Paulsson, Biography*, Arb. Acad., http://www.arbitrationacademy.org/?page_id=3038 (last visited Mar. 30, 2016).

158. Salacuse, *supra* note 42, at 465–67 (noting that "[s]ince the movement to negotiate investment treaties began, the epistemic community of international lawyers, scholars, jurists, and arbitrators has, through their advising, writing, advocacy, and judicial, and arbitral decisions, shaped the regime of international investment," and noting further that to the extent there is coherence in the regime, it could be attributed to the similarity in the backgrounds of the members of the epistemic community who are mainly Western). Salacuse cites to the ICSID database, which shows 43 percent of arbitrators appointed so far being from only five countries, the United States (120), France (106), Britain (94), Canada (75), and Switzerland (70). *Id.* at 467 n.191 and accompanying text. Salacuse concludes that "arbitrators are very much a part of an international epistemic community with similar training and, in many cases, comparable background." *Id.* at 467.

159. Dezalay & Garth, *supra* note 146, at 8 n.6 (citing Sola Mentschikoff & Ernest A. Haggard, *Decision Making and Decision Consensus in Commercial Arbitration*, *in* Law, Justice, and the

This is often expressed—similar to the well-known real estate maxim—as "arbitrator, arbitrator, arbitrator."[160]

Why do they nominate Queen's Counsel, Sir Ian Brownlie,[161] if the opposing party picks Queen's Counsel Sir Elihu Lauterpacht?[162] If the judge is Lalive, why does the respondent African state choose to hire Paulsson as counsel? If the system is manned by virtuous men of this stature, what options do the Africans have? What sustains the imbalance is simply put as a race to the top. There is no doubt that these learned men bring prestige and produce high quality jurisprudence, but does it necessarily mean that their appointment improves the quality of the justice that the African states receive? Or are the Africans perpetually defending themselves using everything in their arsenal? What is the nature of the justice that emerges out of this process?[163] The case studies provided in the next section will help shed some light.

Individual in Society: Psychological and Legal Issues 295, 307 (June Louin Tapp & Felice J. Levine eds., 1977)).

160. William W. Park, *Arbitrator Integrity, in* The Backlash against Investment Arbitration, *supra* note 24, at 189, 191 n.4.

161. Sir Ian Brownlie is one of the most recognizable names in the area of international law. Before his death in Cairo at age 77, for over a period of 25 years, he appeared before the International Court of Justice in more than 40 contentious cases. Philippe Sands, *Sir Ian Brownlie Obituary*, The Guardian (Jan. 11, 2010, 1:02 PM), http://www.theguardian.com/theguardian/2010/jan/11/sir-ian-brownlie-obituary. He had "a formidable reputation for integrity and independence." *Id.* His book, *Principles of Public International Law*, now in its eighth edition, is one of the most widely used treatises in the world. It has been translated into several languages including Chinese, Japanese, and Russian. "Almost every international lawyer and judge has referred to this classic text." *Id.*

162. Sir Lauterpacht is a prominent jurist with extensive experience as an advocate, adviser, arbitrator, and judge in many different forums involving such areas of the law as natural resources law, investment matters, expropriation, territorial and boundary problems, maritime delimitation, fisheries, and environmental issues. High profile International Court of Justice cases in which he was involved include the *Nottebohm* case, the *North Sea Continental Shelf* cases, the *Barcelona Traction* case, the *Nuclear Tests* cases, *Pakistan v. India Aerial Incident* case, *El Salvador v. Honduras, Kasikili* case, *Qatar v. Bahrain, Malaysia/Indonesia* (Sipadan and Ligitan) case, and the *Avena* case (Mexico v. United States). Arbitral tribunal cases include: Chile/Argentina boundary disputes, the Egypt/Israel Taba arbitration, the Iran-U.S. Claims Tribunal, ICSID, etc. He was adviser on international law to the British Central Policy Review Staff, 1972–1974 and 1978–1980. He also served as an ad hoc judge of the ICJ in the *Bosnia v. Yugoslavia* case (1993–2001), a member and president of the World Bank Administrative Tribunal, chairman of the Asian Development Bank Administrative Tribunal, chairman of the East African Common Market Tribunal, 1972–1975, a Presiding Commissioner of the UN Compensation Commission, an arbitrator in various World Bank (ICSID) tribunals and president of the Eritrea/Ethiopia Boundary Commission. His academic achievements are also equally impressive. For Sir Lauterpacht's full biography, see Lesley Dingle & Daniel Bates, *Professor Elihu Lauterpacht*, Squire L. Libr., U. Cambridge, http://www.squire.law.cam.ac.uk/eminent-scholars-archive/professor-sir-elihu-lauterpacht (last visited Apr. 1, 2016).

163. *See* Dezalay & Garth, *supra* note 146, at 9 ("The operation of the market in the selection of arbitrators therefore provides a key to understanding the justice that emerges from the decisions of arbitrators.").

A. Case Studies

Consider the following three statements on the state of a particular aspect of the law of international investment:

> *There are few if any issues in international law today on which opinion seems to be so divided as the limitations on a state's power to expropriate the property of aliens.*[164]
>
> —*Supreme Court of the United States, 1964*

> *[A]s a matter of general international law, a non-discriminatory regulation for a public purpose, which is enacted in accordance with due process and, which affects, inter alios [sic], a foreign investor or investment is not deemed expropriatory and compensable unless specific commitments had been given by the regulating government to the then putative foreign investor contemplating investment that the government would refrain from such regulation.*[165]
>
> —*NAFTA Tribunal, 2005*

> *"[T]he obligation . . . not to nationalize . . . without fair compensation' . . . [constitutes] one of the generally recognized principles of international law."*[166] *[Hence, full fair market value is appropriate compensation.]*[167]
>
> —*ICSID Tribunal, 1980*

The arbitral process is riddled with complications flowing from legal uncertainty and fact-finding problems inherent in the law, notwithstanding the presence of competent counsel and arbitrators. For African states, this problem is compounded by the serious cultural barriers they face in not only commanding an audience before the virtuous men, but also in communicating with their own counsel. In order to contextualize these problems and assess the nature of justice received by the African states, three case studies are provided below. The purpose of this discussion is to illustrate typical factual and legal issues that arise and their resolution. Case samples were selected for demonstrative purposes only.

Before the selected cases are discussed, it is important to outline the basic framework for the constitution of arbitral tribunals under ICSID. At the most rudimentary level, the legal framework for the constitution of an ICSID tribunal is set forth under Articles 37 through 40 of the ICSID Convention.[168] The party who wants to initiate an arbitration must first submit a request to the secretary general of the

164. Banco Nacional de Cuba v. Sabbatino, 376 U.S. 398, 428 (1964).

165. Methanex Corp. v. United States, Final Award of the Tribunal on Jurisdiction and Merits, 44 I.L.M. 1345, 1456 pt. IV, ch. D, ¶ 7 (NAFTA Ch. 11 Arb. Trib. 2005), http://www.state.gov/documents/organization/51052.pdf.

166. S.A.R.L. Benvenuti & Bonfant v. People's Republic of Congo, ICSID Case No. ARB/77/2, Award, ¶¶ 4.63–4.64 (Aug. 8, 1980), 1 ICSID Rep. 330 (1993) (quoting Defense Memorial, People's Republic of Congo, at 5).

167. *Id.* ¶¶ 4.73–4.79. This statement is my summation on this section.

168. ICSID Convention, *supra* note 1, arts. 37–40.

Centre. If the request is not "manifestly" outside the jurisdiction of ICSID,[169] the secretary general registers the case, notifies the respondent, and facilitates the constitution of the tribunal as soon as possible.[170] The parties appoint either a sole or an uneven number of arbitrators.[171] If a party or the parties fail to appoint an arbitrator or arbitrators, the Convention gives the chairman of the Administrative Council,[172] who is the president of the World Bank,[173] the authority to make the necessary appointments.[174] Ordinarily, the arbitrators are appointed from the Panel of Arbitrators.[175] The Panel is composed of arbitrators nominated by contracting states and those nominated by the chair of the Administrative Council. The Convention gives contracting states the opportunity to nominate up to four arbitrators and the chair to nominate 10 arbitrators. The Convention allows the contracting states to nominate persons who are not their nationals, but requires the chair to appoint persons of different nationalities.[176] Although the disputing parties have the right to make appointments outside of the Panel, the chair's choice is limited to the Panel when he exercises his default appointment authority under Article 38.[177]

With this background on the constitution of ICSID tribunals, the following case studies identify the identity of the arbitrators and parties and their counsel, the place

169. *See id.* art. 36 ("(1) Any Contracting State or any national of a Contracting State wishing to institute arbitration proceedings shall address a request to the effect in writing to the Secretary-General who shall send a copy of the request to the other party. (2) The request shall contain information concerning the issues in dispute, the identity of the parties and their consent to arbitration in accordance with the rules of procedure for the institution of conciliation and arbitration proceedings. (3) The Secretary-General shall register the request unless he finds, on the basis of the information contained in the request, that the dispute is manifestly outside the jurisdiction of the Centre. He shall forthwith notify the parties of registration or refusal to register.").

170. *Id.* art. 37(1).

171. *Id.* art. 37(2). For a detailed description of these provisions, see SCHREUER, *supra* note 1, at 475–89.

172. The Administrative Council is composed of one representative of each contracting state. ICSID Convention, *supra* note 1, art. 4(1).

173. *Id.* art. 5 ("The President of the Bank shall be *ex officio* Chairman of the Administrative Council . . . .").

174. *Id.* art. 38 ("If the Tribunal shall not have been constituted within 90 days after notice of registration of the request has been dispatched by the Secretary-General . . . or such other period as the parties may agree, the Chairman shall, at the request of either party and after consultation with both parties as far as possible, appoint the arbitrator or arbitrators not yet appointed."). For a detailed description of these provisions, see SCHREUER, *supra* note 1, at 490–97. He notes that "Art. 38 is the most important Article designed to safeguard the principle of non-frustration in the constitution of the tribunal." *Id.* at 490.

175. *Id.* art. 40(1).

176. *Id.* art. 13(2). For a discussion of these provisions, see SCHREUER, *supra* note 1, at 45–47.

177. *Id.* art. 40(1–2). For a detailed discussion of these provisions and bibliography, see SCHREUER, *supra* note 1, at 507–15.

of arbitration, the factual and legal issues addressed, the outcome of the merits, and the allocation of cost, followed by a brief commentary on the nature of justice that emerges out of these cases.

CASE STUDY NO. 1: BIWATER GAUFF (TANZANIA) LIMITED (CLAIMANT) V. UNITED REPUBLIC OF TANZANIA (RESPONDENT)[178]

This case, in many ways, is a quintessential investment arbitration involving an African state. The arbitral tribunal was composed of Gary Born, a national of the United States, appointed by the claimant; Toby Landau, a national of the United Kingdom, appointed by the respondent; and Bernard Hanotiau, a national of Belgium, appointed as president of the tribunal by the party-selected arbitrators.[179] The award was rendered on July 24, 2008, and contains a 242-page majority opinion and a 10-page dissenting and concurring opinion by Born. The claimant, Biwater Gauff (Tanzania) Ltd. (BGT), was represented by counsel from the London office of Allen & Overy LLP, including Judith Gill, Matthew Gearing, Hannah Ambrose, Michelle de Kluyver, Autumn Ellis, and Andrew Pullen.[180] The respondent state, Tanzania, was represented by a team of lawyers from Freshfields—consisting of Jan Paulsson, D. Brian King, Jonathan J. Gass, Marijn Heemskerk—along with attorneys from Tanzanian Attorney-General's Chambers, including Julius Mallaba, and the Tanzanian law firm of Mkono & Co.[181] The proceeding took place at both the World Bank's office in Paris[182] and Freshfields' office in London.[183]

In 2003, the World Bank, the European Investment Bank, and the African Development Bank awarded the Republic of Tanzania US $140,000,000 for the purpose of repairing, upgrading, and extending the water supply and sewer infrastructure of its capital city, Dar es Salaam.[184] As the tribunal put it, "[a]s a condition of the funding, the Republic was obliged to appoint a private operator to manage and operate the water and sewerage system, and to carry out some of the works associated with the Project."[185] A lengthy bid process resulted in the selection of

178. Biwater Gauff (Tanz.) Ltd. v. United Republic of Tanzania, ICSID Case No. ARB/05/22, Award (July 24, 2008), https://icsid.worldbank.org/apps/ICSIDWEB/cases/Pages/casedetail.aspx?CaseNo=ARB/05/22.

179. *Id.* ¶¶ 25–27.

180. *Id.* ¶ 1.

181. *Id.* ¶ 2.

182. *Id.* ¶ 31.

183. *Id.* ¶ 85.

184. *Id.* ¶ 3.

185. *Id.*

the claimant, Biwater, a joint venture of a UK corporation and a German corporation, with 80-20 shares respectively.[186] Because the foreign company was required to involve a local Tanzanian company, it selected STM, and they jointly incorporated "City Water" with Biwater as the majority shareholder and STM as the minority shareholder.[187] City Water signed three contracts—collectively called the Project Contract—with the Dar es Salaam Water and Sewerage Authority (DAWASA): the Water and Sewerage Lease Contract, the Supply and Installation of Plant and Equipment Contract, and the Contract for the Procurement of Goods.[188] The Republic—as represented by DAWASA, a parastatal corporation established under Tanzanian law—is listed as a party solely in the Lease Contract, whereas the other two contracts list City Water and DAWASA as parties.[189] Under the Lease Contract—the main subject of the dispute—City Water assumed the responsibilities from DAWASA to manage the water and sewerage operations, and also undertook the responsibility of designing and expanding the system while collecting revenue from customers for an initial period of 10 years.[190] A complex mix of circumstances with roots in the initial bidding process led to a serious failure of the enterprise.[191] The dispute essentially pertained to the allocation of blame for the failure. According to the tribunal, almost every aspect of the business relationship was disputed; however, one thing was unusually clear—that the alleged expropriation or actions taken by the government caused no economic damage to the investor because the enterprise was not profitable from the very beginning.[192] In fact, it was allegedly an "opportunistic" bid that sought to renegotiate the terms after the contract had been awarded.[193]

The tribunal found that the cumulative effect of the Tanzanian government's measures amounted to indirect expropriation, although no economic damage was caused.[194] The factual findings of the tribunal include that the bid was poorly prepared; the project encountered problems almost as soon as it began; it immediately became clear that the enterprise would not work absent a renegotiation; renegotiations failed; and the contract was terminated by DAWASA.[195]

In the process of terminating the contract, the Republic did certain things that rubbed the arbitrators the wrong way. The responsible minister gave a press

186. *Id.* ¶ 4.

187. *Id.* ¶ 5.

188. *Id.* ¶ 6.

189. *Id.* ¶¶ 7–8.

190. *Id.* ¶ 9.

191. *Id.* ¶¶ 14–15.

192. *Id.* ¶ 767.

193. *Id.* ¶ 384.

194. *Id.* ¶¶ 461, 485.

195. *Id.* ¶ 486.

statement about the termination of the contract (apparently he was running for prime minster), the government withdrew some value-added tax exemptions that they had promised, occupied City Water's facilities and took over management, and finally arrested and deported the staff to Britain.[196] On the basis of this, the tribunal finally found that although it agrees "with the Republic's position that the termination of the Lease Contract at this time was inevitable, and was going to materialise within . . . weeks . . . these circumstances cannot avoid the conclusion that an expropriation of BGT's contractual and property rights took place."[197] The tribunal put the theoretical justification as follows:

> [W]hilst accepting that the effects of a certain severity must be shown to qualify an act as expropriatory, there is nothing to require that such effects be economic in nature. A distinction must be drawn between (a) interference with rights and (b) economic loss. A substantial interference with rights may well occur without actually causing any economic damage which can be quantified in terms of due compensation.[198]

Hence, "the absence of economic loss or damage is primarily a matter of causation and quantum—rather than a necessary ingredient in the cause of action of expropriation itself."[199] Because none of the Republic's actions caused any economic damages to the investor, the tribunal's remedy was declaratory in nature.[200] However, the finding of non-compensable fault on the part of the Republic allowed the tribunal to allocate the cost of the proceeding equally and allow the parties cover their own expenses.[201]

Several observations could be made here. The tribunal had no difficulty in determining material facts. It quickly became clear that the project was a failed enterprise from its inception. The Republic had at least two reasons to involve the investor; it was required by the World Bank—which provided the funding—and it believed that the investor would have the resources and the expertise to carry out the project. When it did not work, the Republic took dramatic measures that an ordinary contracting party would not take, including detaining and deporting company executives. Although this caused no ascertainable economic damage to the investment, the tribunal held that it was "the straw that [broke] the camel's back."[202] Ill-advised

196. *Id.* ¶¶ 497–518.

197. *Id.* ¶ 518.

198. *Id.* ¶ 464.

199. *Id.* ¶ 465. To be sure, as the Tribunal put it, "the 'fair market value' of City Water at the date of the expropriation, 1 June 2005, was nil." *Id.* ¶ 797.

200. *Id.* ¶ 807.

201. *Id.* ¶¶ 812–13.

202. *Id.* ¶ 456 (quoting Siemens v. Argentine Republic, ICSID Case No. ARB/02/8, Award, ¶ 263 (Feb. 6, 2007)).

as they might have been, it is not inconceivable that a differently constituted arbitral tribunal might alternatively view the actions as detached sovereign actions, which may be remedied through diplomatic means. The tribunal did indeed sit in judgment on the acceptable levels of government misconduct in absolute terms. These findings are not surprising at all if the identity of the government in question and the nationalities of the mistreated officials played a role in the decision-making process. More important, the finding of an actionable fault on the part of the Republic offered a legal basis for the allocation of cost.

Apart from its own unwise—perhaps politically motivated—behavior, the African state came out of the arbitration a total loser in many ways. When it took the money from the World Bank, it was required to hire a foreign investor. It picked one that was not up to the task for various reasons. The enterprise failed, nearly jeopardizing the water supply of its capital city. It then submitted to international arbitration and selected a learned arbitrator who was apparently offended by the government's erratic behavior. As a result, it ended up paying a large amount of money for basically winning the case. If signing the BITs and submitting to international arbitration was supposed to attract investors, it is difficult to see how this could help the Tanzanian Republic attract more investors. In any case, although the award is supported by detailed analysis and highly sophisticated reasoning, the value of such sophistication to the respondent state is a question worth asking.

CASE STUDY NO. 2: HELNAN INTERNATIONAL HOTELS A/S V. THE ARAB REPUBLIC OF EGYPT (ICSID CASE NO. 05/19)[203]

The tribunal was composed of Yves Derains, a citizen of France, as chairman; Professor Rudolf Dolzer, a citizen of Germany, appointed by the respondent; and Michael Lee, a citizen of Britain, appointed by the claimant.[204] The claimant is Helnan International Hotels, a Danish company. It was represented by several attorneys from the London office of Baker Botts. The respondent, the Arab Republic of Egypt ("Egypt"), was represented by Professor Jan Paulsson of Freshfields and several Egyptian counsels including Dr. Mohamed Abdel Raouf.[205] The arbitration was conducted in Paris.[206]

On September 8, 1986, Helnan entered into a management contract with the Egyptian Organization for Tourism (EGOTH) to manage the Cairo Shepheard Hotel, which EGOTH owned.[207] Although the initial contract was for a period of 26 years, a subsequent amendment permitted EGOTH to sell the hotel and granted

203. Helnan Int'l Hotels A/S v. Arab Republic of Egypt, ICSID Case No. ARB/05/19, Award, (July 3, 2008), https://icsid.worldbank.org/apps/ICSIDWEB/cases/Pages/casedetail.aspx?CaseNo=ARB/05/19.

204. *Id.* ¶ 1.

205. *Id.* ¶ 2.

206. *Id.* ¶¶ 14, 45.

207. *Id.* ¶ 3.

Helnan the option of continuing to manage or terminate the management contract in exchange for adequate compensation.[208]

In 2003, the Ministry of Tourism downgraded the Shepheard from a five-star to a four-star hotel because of unsatisfactory inspection results.[209] The downgrade prompted EGOTH to seek the termination of the management contract on grounds of impossibility of performance because the management contract required Helnan to run the hotel as a five-star.[210] An arbitral tribunal constituted for that purpose in Cairo did exactly that—while awarding Helnan 12.5 million Egyptian pounds for the settlement of debts that it owed in connection with the performance of the management contract.[211] EGOTH paid Helnan the 12.5 million Egyptian pounds, and the Egyptian courts then enforced the award by evicting Helnan and allowing EGOTH to take over.[212]

Based on the BIT between Egypt and Denmark signed in 1999, Helnan initiated this ICSID arbitration. Helnan alleged that EGOTH improperly conspired with the Egyptian Ministry of Tourism to solicit the downgrading of the hotel so that it could sell the hotel unencumbered by the management contract.[213] These measures, Helnan argued, amounted to expropriation and violated many provisions of the BIT, including non-discrimination, as well as fair and equitable treatment.[214] Helnan also made several factual allegations and adduced evidence to prove the allegations.

Perhaps the most important question for the tribunal was whether the downgrade was improperly solicited so that Egypt could privatize the hotel unencumbered by the management contract.[215] Helnan made at least three factual allegations that it said would prove a conspiracy: (1) on June 14, 2003, the Ministry of Tourism conducted an inspection and issued a harsh report; (2) without giving Helnan enough time to cure the problems, the Ministry conducted another inspection on September 4, 2003, filed its report the same day,[216] and three days later, on September 7, 2003, the Ministry downgraded the hotel from five-star to four-star;[217] (3) just 25 days later, EGOTH initiated an arbitration proceeding in Cairo for the termination of the contract—suggesting prior knowledge of the downgrade.[218] These facts

208. *Id.*

209. *Id.* ¶ 5.

210. *Id.* ¶ 6.

211. *Id.* ¶ 7

212. *Id.* ¶¶ 7–8.

213. *Id.* ¶¶ 58–63.

214. *Id.* ¶¶ 50–53.

215. *Id.* ¶¶ 132–137.

216. *Id.* ¶ 58.

217. *Id.* ¶ 134.

218. *Id.* ¶ 35.

collectively show the existence of a collusion to eject Helnan. These facts prove indirect expropriation.[219]

To prove the conspiracy, Helnan called its own witness and presented circumstantial evidence regarding the timing of the inspections and the subsequent decision to downgrade.[220] It also relied on testimony of an Egyptian witness elicited through cross-examination.[221] The tribunal found the hastiness of the two inspections and the immediate decision to downgrade suspicious, but the tribunal's finding of collusion seems to critically rely on the testimony of EGOTH's in-house counsel, who said that her department knew about the downgrade approximately 60 days prior to the commencement of the arbitral proceeding.[222]

The in-house counsel's testimony was so important to the outcome of the decision that the tribunal reproduced it in part. The excerpt of the cross-examination reads:

> Q. When did you first learn of the downgrade of the Shepheard Hotel?
> A. Before initiating the procedures for the arbitration by a very, very short time. Approximately 60 days before.
> Q. I'm sorry, you learned of the downgrade 60 days before initiating the arbitration?
> A. Approximately, yes.[223]

During redirect, the in-house counsel, Dorreya Refaat, retracted the testimony, saying that she was mistaken in her estimate, but the tribunal did not believe her, noting her retraction "was far from . . . convincing."[224] It then held that "the Arbitral tribunal is satisfied that EGOTH and various Egyptian authorities, including the ministry of Tourism, played a significant role in the implementation of a plan aiming at terminating the Management contract."[225] Finally, however, the tribunal held that Helnan failed to prove that the Egyptian state did indeed adopt these measures to get rid of Helnan in order to privatize the hotel.[226] The only evidence that Helnan submitted to this effect was an affidavit by Bahi Nasr, the former chair of the Egyptian Hotels Company, the predecessor of EGOTH.[227] Nasr stated that the former undersecretary of the Ministry of Tourism told him there was an order to downgrade the Shepheard hotel and terminate the management contract so that it could be

219. *Id.* ¶¶ 135–36.

220. *Id.* ¶¶ 64–79.

221. *Id.* ¶¶ 58–64.

222. *Id.* ¶ 154.

223. *Id.*

224. *Id.* ¶ 155.

225. *Id.* ¶ 156.

226. *Id.* ¶ 157.

227. *Id.* ¶ 158.

privatized.[228] However, when Nasr appeared before the tribunal to offer testimony, he claimed he could not recall the particular conversation, but suspected that might have been the plan. Unimpressed with the testimony, the tribunal totally discounted the statement.[229]

Some very interesting observations can be made about the tribunal's handling of the proceedings. First, it appears that the tribunal discounted all oral testimonies offered by Egyptian witnesses on both sides, instead relying exclusively on circumstantial evidence and inferences. It is difficult to determine if a cultural miscommunication between an all-male European tribunal and one female and one male Egyptian witness who testified under cross-examination administered by experienced, mostly European or American counsel in Paris, played any role at all in the decision. But it is a fair question to ask. Second, having convinced itself that a conspiracy existed using mainly circumstantial evidence, the tribunal shied away from attributing that conspiracy to the state. Finally, the tribunal allocated cost equally, as is often done when the investor loses.[230] It required each party to cover its own expenses and share the costs of the proceedings.[231] Some finding of fault on the part of the state is often perceived to be necessary to such allocation of costs.[232] Although the tribunal noted that it allocated costs this way because of the claimant's win on jurisdiction and admissibility,[233] it is more likely that the tribunal's finding of the conspiracy was the basis for the equal allocation of cost. This is because winning on jurisdiction and inadmissibility is inconsequential if the merits are lost, because this only allows a party to present a claim. Ultimately, however, it is clear that the state is the loser in many ways because it had to defend a claim and pay the expenses. It is unnecessary to ask the question of how an all-African tribunal might rule in this case because such a tribunal had already ruled on the related claim of termination in the Cairo arbitration.[234] It is quite notable that the European company Helnan actually appointed an Egyptian arbitrator, Dr. Abdel Wahab, in the Cairo arbitration, although it later accused him of bias in favor of EGOTH.[235] Again, the tribunal's analysis was highly sophisticated, but at the end of the day, the value of such sophistication and the fairness of the results might be questioned.

228. *Id.*

229. *Id.*

230. *See supra* Section C(7) (discussing data related to the allocation of costs among parties in ICSID arbitrations).

231. Helnan Int'l Hotels, *supra* note 203, ¶¶ 171–74.

232. *See supra* Sections C(6) and C(7) (analyzing and depicting data related to outcomes on the merits and allocation of costs).

233. Helnan Int'l Hotels, *supra* note 203, ¶ 173.

234. *Id.* ¶¶ 150, 162.

235. *Id.* ¶ 164.

CASE STUDY NO. 3: GUSTAV F W HAMESTER GMBH & CO KG V. REPUBLIC OF GHANA (ICSID CASE NO. ARB/07/24)[236]

The claimant in this case is Hamester, a German company. The respondent is the Republic of Ghana. The claim was based on a Germany-Ghana BIT.[237] The arbitrators in this case were Professor Brigitte Stern, a French national and president of the tribunal; Dr. Bernardo M. Cremades, a Spanish national appointed by the claimant; and Toby Landau Q.C., a British national appointed by the respondent.[238] Both parties were represented by attorneys based in London, and the proceedings took place in London as well.[239]

The facts of this case are complex. For purposes of this analysis, it is sufficient to state that Hamester signed a joint venture agreement (JVA) with a Ghanaian public enterprise called Cocobod.[240] The principal function of Cocobod is to buy cocoa beans from farmers for marketing and export, and the purpose of the joint venture with Hamester was to upgrade and modernize an old cocoa processing factory and share the profits in a mutually agreed proportion.[241] Hamester and Cocobod (as a minority shareholder) incorporated a company called Wamco for this purpose.[242] After the upgrading work was completed, they agreed that the entirety of the output would be sold to Hamester, but they did not fix the price in writing at that time.[243] A few years later, Wamco became indebted to Cocobod for failing to pay for deliveries that it had taken.[244] Although the parties did not dispute that fact, Hamester denied that it was responsible for the debt, blaming it on failure to agree on price.[245] Subsequently, the two sides made several attempts to agree on pricing, and eventually signed a price agreement. However, Hamester later alleged that it signed this agreement under duress.[246] In a related development, shortly after signing the price agreement, Cocobod failed to supply the required quantity of cocoa beans, blaming its failure on smuggling activities and outbreak of disease.[247] Hamester considered

236. Gustav F W Hamester GmbH & Co KG v. Republic of Ghana, ICSID Case No. ARB/07/24, Award (June 18, 2010), http://www.italaw.com/sites/default/files/case-documents/ita0396.pdf.

237. *Id.* ¶ 1.

238. *Id.* ¶ 8.

239. *Id.* ¶¶ 4–5, 9.

240. *Id.* ¶ 22.

241. *Id.*

242. *Id.* ¶¶ 23–25.

243. *Id.* ¶¶ 29–33.

244. *Id.* ¶ 33.

245. *Id.*

246. *Id.* ¶ 33–41.

247. *Id.* ¶ 42.

Cocobod's failure to supply the cocoa as a breach of their contract.[248] After many efforts to renegotiate the price, Hamester abandoned the JVC (joint venture company) and its managing director left Ghana.[249]

The parties disputed all of the facts including: whether the price agreement was made under duress, whether the failure to supply the required amount of cocoa constituted a breach of contract, and who owed Cocobod money, Hamester or the joint company Wamco.[250] The parties also disputed the circumstances that led to the managing director's departure; although the managing director alleged that he feared for his own and his family's safety, Ghana suspected fraud and opened a police investigation.[251] Related to the departure of the manager, Cocobod's General Manager of Operations, who was also a minority shareholder of Wamco, ordered the suspension of exports altogether.[252] The sequence of the events, as well as the responsibility for each action, was disputed.[253]

Hamester alleged that Cocobod's actions collectively breached Ghana's treaty obligations, including the principles of fair and equitable treatment and non-discrimination amounting to expropriation.[254] The respondent claimed that Hamester was a fraudulent partner from the very beginning, and that Hamester failed to make a bona fide investment.[255] It further alleged that Hamester and its managing director defrauded Wamco throughout the JVC.[256] Alternatively, even if Wamco was responsible for any breach of contract, the breach was not attributable to Ghana and did not rise to the level of breach of treaty obligation.[257] Without the need to determine each disputed fact, the tribunal, after a lengthy legal analysis, decided that none of the alleged acts of breach were attributable to Ghana.[258] It held, in particular, that a breach of contract does not ordinarily rise to a breach of treaty obligation.[259] However, the tribunal allocated the cost of the proceedings equally and required each party to cover its own expenses.[260]

Because this case rested largely on the legal question of attribution, the factual inquiries were not remarkably detailed. Most notably, however, Ghana had to go

248. *Id.* ¶ 43.

249. *Id.* ¶¶ 44–67.

250. *Id.* ¶¶ 205–211, 257–262, 269–276.

251. *Id.* ¶¶ 55–57.

252. *Id.* ¶¶ 53, 269.

253. *Id.* ¶¶ 269–300.

254. *Id.* ¶¶ 68–79.

255. *Id.* ¶ 80–81.

256. *Id.* ¶ 81.

257. *Id.* ¶¶ 84-85.

258. *Id.* ¶¶ 171–312.

259. *Id.* ¶¶ 313–350.

260. *Id.* ¶¶ 359–361.

through the process of defending itself against the German company for a failed business dealing. If every possible form of breach of contract is framed in the context of breach of a treaty obligation, the number of claims that a state would have to defend against could be staggering. Significantly, in this case, the tribunal appears to be sensitive to that possibility. It is probably not unreasonable to expect more consistency in determining these kinds of legal questions as compared to findings of facts, which tend to be more culturally engrained because, at their core, they beg the uncomfortable question of who is better understood or more credible. It is interesting to observe that most, if not all, of the respondent's witnesses seem to be Ghanaians, whereas the expert witness was European.[261] It is difficult to anticipate the possible outcome of this case had the facts been important. But it is fair to assume it would have been much more difficult for the Ghanaians to prove their allegations, including bad faith ab initio and sustained fraud on the part of the European business partner, before an all-European tribunal.

E. CONCLUSION

Both commercial and investment arbitrations suffer from the same problem of stranger justice. Although that is ironically what justifies their very existence, it is also their principal weakness. Unfortunately, it is not a subject that is frankly discussed. This chapter has demonstrated the nature of justice that emerges out of ICSID arbitration involving developing countries of Africa. It is evident that the complicating effects of culture is far greater than what could be captured in a few selected cases. The following several chapters will advance the discussion of the complicating effects of culture in actual international arbitral proceedings.

261. *Id.* ¶ 19 (listing the fact witnesses for Ghana as: Mr. Kwame Sapong, Dr. Sammy Ohene, Mr. Flix Auaye, Mr. Isaac Osei, and Mr. Reinhold Mueller. The expert witness was Mr. John Ellison.).

PART TWO

Deconstructing the Mythology of Specialized Knowledge in International Arbitration

International arbitration is a platform—or a framework as Professor Caron calls it—that is used to resolve the world's diverse commercial and investment disputes. The cases arise out of legal instruments that bind parties as varied as between *Philip Morris v. Uruguay*, and *Salini v. Ethiopia*. There is no rational reason why the most qualified three arbitrators for both cases should be the same three persons. The existing system of commercial and investment arbitration certainly considers service on one a qualification for the other. It is the school of thought that considers international arbitration as a discipline or a trade that one learns through repetition although no two cases typically involve the same laws, cultures, or processes. Such perception comes from the need to learn the front-end and back-end procedural complications that sometimes plague international arbitration. However, resolving such procedural complications, although it requires a specialized knowledge of the procedural aspects of international arbitration, is not the main work that arbitrators are hired to do. Like any adjudicative legal process, in most cases, their main job is to determine facts and apply law. Their qualifications must pertain to their main job. A set of procedural matters that come up in international arbitration are relatively easy to learn, but learning the laws of numerous countries with different legal traditions and developing the cultural competence to determine facts that arise out of diverse societies is not easy, convenient, or even necessary, because there are always people who know the local laws, facts, and customs better.

At the most fundamental level, international arbitration is a legal process for the determination of fact and application of law. The most important qualifications are familiarity with the applicable law and the ability to understand the facts, which in turn requires cultural competence. An arbitrator who is most familiar with the cultural background of witnesses from Uruguay and communicates with them with ease does not necessarily have the same level of cultural competence to communicate and understand witnesses from Ethiopia. The ideal arbitrator is one who knows the applicable law and understands the cultural origin of the facts. This second part provides a detailed discussion of fact-finding and cultural diversity in international arbitration, and is followed by a cultural critique of the elitist approach to selecting decision-makers. These chapters collectively show the nature of the process and deconstruct the mythology of specialized knowledge. Before that, however, it is important to review the epistemology of fact-finding in the various legal traditions to appreciate the challenges of their interaction in international arbitration.

8

Diversity in the Epistemology of Judicial Fact-Finding in the Major Legal Traditions of the World

Indicators for Conduct in International Arbitration

The greatest diversity in legal traditions comes not from substantive prescriptions, but from procedures and the epistemology of finding facts. Facts are probably more culturally sensitive than law—to the extent the two could be readily separated.[1] In any legal proceedings, decision-makers determine facts and apply law. Each legal system has its own epistemology of finding facts. Although many systems within the same family structurally appear similar, the similarity is often superficial, especially when it comes to the determination of facts. A French judge who is trained in the civil law legal tradition would probably have difficulty believing a witness who confuses "yellow" with "orange" or calls both colors by the same name "yellow." A Cameroonian judge, trained in the same tradition, would probably have no difficulty believing the witness as she would know exactly why the witness appears confused about the colors because—as described in the introductory chapter—in many communities in Africa a range of colors are assigned the same name. A Cameroonian judge would not find that difficult to understand.

Every time this writer gives a lecture on issues of culture and brings up the example about the witness who called the color "orange", "yellow" as described in the introduction of this book, the room is often filled with a great sense of disbelief with the exception of two instances. One lecture was given to a group of African scholars at Albany Law School. Several of those in the audience said, "we know exactly what you are talking about." The second instance was at Wits University in Johannesburg, South Africa, where one of the participants, a Cameroonian lawyer

1. For a somewhat contrary suggestion, see, e.g., Bernhard F. Meyer, *Structuring a Bargaining Process*, *in* Inside the Black Box: How Arbitral Tribunals Operate and Reach Their Decisions, ASA Special Series No. 42, 59, 61 (Bernhard Berger & Michael E. Schneider eds., 2014) ("Facts remain facts, whether they are considered under Greek, German, or Swiss law.").

trained in Geneva, among other places, said, "you're talking about the confusion between orange and yellow; these are fairly similar colors, but in my community, we only have three colors: Black, White, and Red." He was wearing blue jeans that day. One of the other participants asked him, "What color jeans are you wearing today?" He said, "that would be black." Another asked, "What color shirt are you wearing today?" He said, "That would be white." The shirt was gray. The conversation ended happily with great laughter.

Every judicial system proceeds based on the assumption that the decision-maker could make an informed decision about the facts. Making an informed decision requires a basic understanding of the nature and credibility of the evidence. Determining credibility is inherently difficult in any system, but it is worse when the decision-maker lacks the most basic cultural perspective. As Professor Lawrence Rosen puts it, "where by design or by circumstance, the 'facts' escape whatever form of legal process is applied, cultural assumptions . . . step in to fill the gap."[2] What mechanisms do the various legal traditions put in place to ensure the appropriate determination of fact? How do they differ? What basic assumptions underpin each? The assessment of these issues is important in understanding how these mechanisms are transplanted into the arbitral arena, and how they interact to produce certain results.

This chapter provides a brief discussion of the rules and procedures of finding facts in the major legal traditions of the world to show the diversity of basic assumptions and methodologies, including ethical and professional expectations. "Our own way of doing things seems so natural to us that often it is only comparison with another way that establishes there is something to be explained."[3] This chapter is designed to provide a background for the discussion of the sources of cultural miscommunications that often arise when arbitrators, counsel, and party litigants from different legal cultures interact in international arbitral proceedings. It outlines the procedures of finding facts and cultural assumptions in the common law, civil law, Chinese, and Islamic legal traditions. A disclaimer is perhaps in order here: almost any generalized statement made about one or the other legal tradition or culture could be disputed, even proven true or false at the same time; however, despite convergences and transplants, some fundamental differences do indeed exist. The following sections highlight the basic features of some of these traditions.

A. FACT-FINDING IN THE COMMON LAW LEGAL TRADITION

Before the epistemologies of judicial fact-finding in the common law legal tradition are discussed, it is important for context to take a brief look at the historical background and fundamentals of the adjudicative system. In their classic comparative law work, René David and John E.C. Brierley note that the history of the common law, at least up until the eighteenth century, is essentially the history

2. Lawrence Rosen, Law as Culture: An Invitation 94 (1941).

3. Mary Ann Glendon, Paolo G. Carozza & Colin B. Picker, Comparative legal Traditions 7 (3d ed. 2007).

of the law of England.[4] The origins of the English common law are often traced to the 1066 Norman Conquest of England.[5] Rooted in the centralized administration of William, Conqueror at Hastings, English common law "grew in rugged exclusiveness, disdaining fellowship with the more polished learning of the civilians."[6]

The common law, which is essentially a system of writs,[7] is characterized as "a law of procedure; whatever substantive law existed was hidden by it, 'secreted in its interstices.'"[8] Traditionally, to bring a legal action, the plaintiff had to identify the right writ and bring it before a jury which "enjoyed a monopoly on . . . substantive decision making."[9] When there was no applicable writ available, there was no action or remedy.[10] Because the actual decision-making on the facts and the applicable law was left to the jury, the judge's responsibility was essentially jurisdictional, that is, to determine whether the said action fit the chosen writ.[11]

As Professor Glenn neatly describes, the jury was originally supposed to know everything about the case, including the facts and the law, which was essentially a local matter.[12] Thus, the duty of the parties' advocates was essentially to argue whether the outcome they sought from the jury was authorized and required by the applicable writ.[13] As the judicial system evolved, even to the point "when witnesses eventually came to be necessary, the lawyers continued to plead to issue, and now brought forth the facts they needed" to prevail under the writ:[14]

> The judge had no responsibility of finding "objective" fact; nor did the lawyers. There was no external law stating with precision the facts to which it applied. Since the members of the jury had day jobs, and were usually illiterate, the

4. René David & John E.C. Brierley, Major Legal Systems in the World Today 307 (1985).

5. *See* Glendon et al., *supra* note 3, at 153.

6. *Id.* at 153–54 (quoting Frederick Pollock & Frederic William Maitland, The History of English Law before the time of Edward I, at 47 (2d ed. 1898, *reissued in* 1968)). For the history of this development, see *id.* at 153–69.

7. A writ is basically an instruction from the Crown to an officer, usually the sheriff, to investigate a legal dispute. *See* H. Patrick Glenn, Legal Traditions of the World: Sustainable Diversity in Law 242 (4th ed. 2010). According to Professor Glenn, by the middle of the thirteenth century, there were about 50 writs, and that number grew by only 25 in the six centuries that followed. *Id.* at 242.

8. *Id.*

9. *Id.*

10. *Id.* This notion is usually stated as "where there is no writ there is no right." Glendon et al., *supra* note 3, at 158.

11. *See* Glenn, *supra* note 7, at 242.

12. *Id.* at 242–43.

13. *Id.* at 242.

14. *Id.*

> argument and proof had to be made orally, in what came to be known as a trial (as in the old trial by ordeal . . . .).[15]

In particular, Glenn goes on describing the judge's role in these terms:

> The trial is a dramatic event in which the judge plays a commanding, but distant, role, as befitting a source of law. Freed from the burden of finding fact, advised on law and fact by the barristers . . . the judge could concentrate on the general contours of the writs [and] the general contours of the law. Judicial rulings by a very small number of royal judges working out of Westminster on circuit eventually came to define the ambit of the writs . . . .[16]

Writs gradually developed into substantive common law,[17] but they originally "reflected, above all, an agrarian, non-commercial, even chthonic society."[18] Being deeply indigenous and complex, the common law enjoyed an appreciable degree of "impermeability" or even "immunity" from outside influence, particularly the civil law.[19] Although it has undergone fundamental changes over the centuries, it is still "the same ship."[20]

15. *Id.* at 242–43.

16. *Id.* at 243 (footnotes omitted) ("The writs were fundamental, however, since they determined when you could get to the jury, and they became the best available indicators of a secreted, substantive, common law.").

17. *Id.* at 243. The most common writs included: writs of ejectment, writs of debts and covenants, writs for trespass, assault or battery, etc. *Id.* at 244. The historical context that necessitated the development of the common law is interesting. According to Glenn, "[t]he Normans incorporated the local jury into the working of their new, modern, royal courts" because they did not want to appear to be imposing their own laws on the locals, who were defeated militarily but had to be governed by law. Glenn further asks, "How could you get rid of all the local, informal traditions, nesting here and there in the countryside? And with what?" He goes on to answer his own questions: "The process of insinuating a common law into a vigorous, and not very friendly, society, was a major undertaking, to be pursued on many fronts." *Id.* at 247.

18. *Id.* at 245.

19. *Id.* Professor Glenn suggests that the claim of immunity is perhaps exaggerated, as there have been notable influences and counter-influences of the systems. *Id.*

20. *See id.* at 253–69. The jury is at the center of the adversarial trial. The jury has been described by Pope Innocent III as "a peculiarly English institution." *See* LORD DEVLIN, TRIAL BY JURY 4 (1966), *in* GLENDON ET AL., *supra* note 3, at 520–21. Its origin is very interesting; historically, it had nothing to do with the administration of justice. The Normans brought the concept with them to England as a means of collecting information from the local people. GLENDON ET AL., *supra*, at 520–22. A juror was a man who would take an oath and provide information to the king for administrative purposes. He had to be a member of the community, and had to possess some knowledge about the day-to day-life of the people. If the king was needed to rule on an issue, he would typically rely on the sworn statement of jurors. The jury only came to be associated with the administration of justice as a later development. *Id.*

The most common Norman method of resolving disputes was a "trial by battle," which determined who the "better man" was, or who deserved the legal victory.[21] Trial by ordeal was another common method.[22] Even after the jury was put to use for purposes of the administration of justice, it was in the context of bringing more witnesses to attest in favor of one or the other party.[23] At some point, one who could produce 12 jurors to testify on his behalf was considered a winner. Thus, the aim of both parties was to produce more jurors than the adversary.[24]

It was during the reign of King Henry II that the jury system was devised as a tool for the administration of justice.[25] The use by circuit courts of juries made perfect sense as the judges were outsiders and the jurors were informed commoners.[26] The jury was eventually transformed from a body of informant men to a body of men that would hear information from others and make a decision based on that information.[27]

The adversarial trial is divided into the pretrial phase and the trial phase, where discovered evidence is presented, which was in part necessitated by the need to accommodate the schedules of 12 jurors, the disputing parties, and the judge.[28] This division has continued to be the hallmark of the common law legal tradition, including in the United Sates.[29] In other words, the drama of adversarial advocacy, originally designed to educate, persuade, and influence illiterate jurors,[30] has continued to dominate modern adversarial trials, even when a jury is not involved.[31]

21. *Id.*

22. *Id.*

23. *Id.*

24. *Id.*

25. *Id.*

26. *Id.*

27. *Id.* Historically, all civil cases in England were tried by jury until the year 1854, at which point the use of the jury began to decline. *See* Ward v. James [1966] 1 Q.B. 273 (AC) (Eng.), *reprinted in* Glendon et al., *supra* note 3 at 525. In 1933 the British parliament enacted the Administration of Justice Act, limiting the use of a civil jury to limited actions as a matter of right and giving the judge the discretion whether to involve a jury in all other cases. The excepted cases were fraud, libel, slander, malicious prosecution, false imprisonment, seduction, or breach of promise to marriage. *Id.* The result was dramatic—the Act effectively killed the civil jury in England. Glendon et al., *supra,* at 532. By the time *Ward v. James* was decided in 1966, only 2 percent of civil cases were tried by jury. *Ward* considered issues relating to the exercise of discretion by the judge to involve or not to involve the jury. *See generally* Ward v. James, *in* Glendon et al., *supra,* at 524–30. *Ward* is considered the principal case that effectively marked the end of the civil jury system in England. *See* Glendon et al., *supra,* at 532.

28. *See* Ugo A. Mattei, Teemu Ruskola & Antonio Gidi, Schlesinger's Comparative Law: Cases-Text-Materials 761 (7th ed. 2009).

29. *See* Geoffrey C. Hazard, Jr., *Discovery and the Role of the Judge in Civil Law Jurisdictions,* 73 Notre Dame L. Rev. 1017, 1018, 1020 (1998).

30. *See* Glenn, *supra* note 7, at 244.

31. *See* Hazard, *supra* note 29, at 1019–20.

Although the system of an adversarial trial, as Chief Justice Burger said, is "a child of the common law, the [American] legal profession has developed in ways that do not parallel England's."[32] For example, England has long abandoned the use of the jury in most civil cases, though America still maintains the option.[33] Pretrial discovery is now uniquely American,[34] and the training, licensure, and discipline of American lawyers are also significantly different from those of their English counterparts.[35]

As far as criminal justice is concerned, in England before the sixteenth century, a person accused of a criminal offense did not have the right to representation if accused of a felony, had no access to the government's evidence, and did not have the right to present his own evidence.[36] Moreover, he would remain detained throughout the entire trial process.[37] Although the rights of the accused have improved dramatically since then—particularly since the mid-nineteenth century—"the process nevertheless retains elements of the earlier trial—that notion that it is a form of combat."[38]

Be that as it may, "[A]ll the common law systems begin with a concept of the adversary system, which defines the roles of the judge and the parties' advocates."[39] Although the role of the judge remains that of judging between competing presentations of evidence, facts, and law, the role of the party litigants is to provide such presentation:[40]

> The judge is not responsible for there being an adequate development of the evidence during trial and *a fortiori* is not responsible for there being adequate pretrial discovery of evidence. Nor is the judge responsible for getting at "the truth." The judge simply chooses between the contentions of law and the versions of facts laid before him by the parties.[41]

32. *See* Warren E. Burger, *The Special Skills of Advocacy: Are Specialized Training and Certification of Advocates Essential to Our System of Justice?*, 42 FORDHAM L. REV. 227 (1973). According to the chief justice, the "turbulent diversity" makes "it impossible to transplant the English system . . . ." *See id.* The basic features of the adversarial model remain similar.

33. *See id.* at 228.

34. *See* Hazard, *supra* note 29, at 1018.

35. *See* Burger, *supra* note 32, at 227–30. This citation does not endorse the chief justice's suggestion that English barristers are better trained, better disciplined and generally better equipped than American lawyers who receive the training differently; the citation is for the difference in the training.

36. *See* GLENDON ET AL., *supra* note 3, at 251–52.

37. *Id.*

38. *Id.*

39. *See* Hazard, *supra* note 29, at 1019 (footnotes omitted).

40. *Id.*

41. *Id.*

The objective of all systems of adjudication is presumably to find out the truth and arrive at a just result.[42] Different systems attempt to accomplish this objective through different means. Consider the adversarial posture in the common law system. The lawyers on each side are supposed to be active, responsive, imaginative, and partisan advocates, whereas the judge is required to be passive, reflective, and neutral.[43] Asked if zealous advocacy by President Nixon's counsels would "involve [the] country in confusion," Dean Monroe Freedman, a renowned legal scholar in the field of legal ethics, said that the adversarial system envisions the same kind of advocacy on both sides.[44] As support for his argument, he quoted Lord Brougham's statement given in 1812 in the Trial of Queen Caroline:

> [A]n advocate, in the discharge of his duty, knows but one person in all the world, and that person is his client. To save that client by all means and expedients, and at all hazards and costs to other persons, and, among them, to himself, is his first and only duty; and in performing this duty he must not regard the alarm, the torments, the destruction which he may bring upon others. Separating the duty of a patriot from that of an advocate, he must go on reckless of consequences, though it should be his unhappy fate to involve his country in confusion.[45]

Almost amused by these statements, Human Rights First Founder, former Columbia Law professor, and pioneer of the federal sentencing guidelines, Judge Marvin Frankel,[46] surmised that "[n]either the sentiment nor even the words sound archaic after a century and half."[47]

Perhaps no writing has so effectively captured the shortcomings of the adversarial system as Judge Frankel's University of Pennsylvania Law Review article. Displaying his renowned unique and beautiful writing, Judge Frankel's message is best presented by generous resort to his own words. In response to Dean Freedman's statement about Nixon's attorneys above, he noted that:

> This is a topic on which our profession has practiced some self-deception. We proclaim to each other and to the world that the clash of adversaries is a

42. This notion and the controversies surrounding it are elaborated further at the end of this section.

43. *See* Marvin E. Frankel, *The Search for Truth: An Umpireal View*, 123 U. Pa. L. Rev. 1031, 1033 (1975) (citing David W. Peck, The Complement of Court and Counsel 9 (1954) (13th Annual Benjamin N. Cardozo Lecture)).

44. *Id.* at 1036 & n.14 (citing Monroe Freedman, *The President's Advocate and the Public Trust*, N.Y.U. L.J. 1, 1, Col. 1 & 2 (1974)).

45. The story and the quotation are provided in *id.* at 1036 (citing 2 Trial of Queen Caroline 8 (J. Nightingale ed., 1821)).

46. It is believed that the Sentencing Guidelines substantially deviated from his original proposals.

47. *See* Frankel, *supra* note 43, at 1036.

> powerful means for hammering out the truth. Sometimes, less guardedly, we say it is "best calculated to getting out all the facts . . . ."[48]

Having acknowledged that the adversarial technique might be useful in ironing out the truth within certain limits, he goes on to state that:

> Despite our untested statements of self-congratulation, we know that others searching after facts—in history, geography, medicine, whatever—do not emulate our adversary system. We know that most countries of the world seek justice by different routes. We know that many of the rules and devices of adversary litigation as we conduct it are not geared for, but are often aptly suited to defeat, the development of the truth.
>
> We are unlikely ever to know how effectively the adversary technique would work toward truth if that were the objective of the contestants."[49]

The respective role of the contestants is what concerns him the most: "Employed by interested parties, the process often achieves truth only as a convenience, a byproduct, or an accidental approximation. The business of the advocate, simply stated, is to win if possible without violating the law."[50] Judge Frankel summarizes his above analysis with a remarkable conclusion: "[The role of the attorney] is not the search for truth as such. To put that thought more exactly, *the truth and victory are mutually incompatible for some considerable percentage of the attorneys trying cases at any given time.*[51]

Judge Frankel goes on to describe the reason the system incentivizes victory at the expense of the truth or just result: "The devices are too familiar to warrant more than a fleeting reminder. To begin with, we leave most of the investigatory work to paid partisans, which is scarcely a guarantee of thorough and detached exploration. Our courts wait passively for what the parties will present, almost never knowing—often not suspecting—what the parties have chosen not to present."[52]

There is also the problem of the rules of professional responsibility:

> The ethical standards governing counsel command loyalty and zeal for the client, but no positive obligation at all to the truth. Counsel must not knowingly break the law or commit or countenance fraud. Within these unconfining limits, advocates freely employ time-honored tricks and stratagems to block or distort the truth. The litigator's devices have utility in testing dishonest witnesses, ferreting out falsehoods, and thus exposing the truth.[53]

48. *Id.* at 1036–37 (quoting Peck, *supra* note 43, at 9).

49. *Id.*

50. *Id.* at 1037.

51. *Id.* (emphasis added).

52. *Id.* at 1038.

53. *Id.* at 1038.

But again, "to a considerable degree these devices are like other potent weapons, equally lethal for heroes and villains. *It is worth stressing, therefore, that the gladiator using the weapons in the courtroom is not primarily crusading after truth, but seeking to win*. If this is banal, it is also overlooked too much . . . ."[54]

If the parties' attorneys are warring gladiators, what are the rules of engagement? Circuit Judge Jerome Frank answers this question in his very successful book, *Courts on Trial*,[55] which devotes some focus to lessons that trial lawyers learn on how to handle witnesses. Permeating this topic is the repeated fact that the attorney's quest is not for the truth, but for success. First, lawyers choose witnesses very carefully, not entirely based on what they know and what they can say, but on how they will do, or what they will say and how convincingly they will say it, in court.[56] Second, if witnesses appear to have deficiencies in their storytelling, the lawyer works closely with them to make sure that they overcome those deficiencies and present the best demeanor before the court. Third, the lawyer will do the exact opposite to the opposing witnesses; they will try every trick known to man to annoy and discredit an otherwise credible witness.[57] One lesson for lawyers advises them to try to discredit an honest and credible witness "by making him appear more hostile than he really is. You may make him exaggerate or unsay something and say it again."[58] Another lesson reads:

> An intimidating manner in putting questions may so coerce or disconcert the witness that his answers do not represent his actual knowledge on the subject. So also, questions which in form or subject cause embarrassment, shame or anger in the witness may unfairly lead him to such demeanor or utterances that the impression produced by his statements does not do justice to its real testimonial value.[59]

54. *Id.* at 1039 (emphasis added).

55. Jerome Frank, Courts on Trial: Myth and Reality in American Justice 82–86 (First Princeton Paperback ed. 1973).

56. *Id.* at 80.

57. *Id.* at 82–86.

58. *Id.* at 82.

59. *Id.* at 82–83. Judge Frank quotes Anthony Trollope's dramatic commentary on the nature of this form of adversarial advocacy. The quote is reproduced below, as it is very instructive:

> One would naturally imagine that an undisturbed thread of clear evidence would be best obtained from a man whose position was made easy and whose mind was not harassed; but this is not the fact; to turn a witness to good account he must be badgered this way and that till he nearly mad; he must be made a laughing-stock for the court; his very truth must be turned into falsehoods, so that he may be falsely shamed; he must be accused of all manners of villainy, threatened with all manners of punishment; he must be made to feel that he has no friend near him, the world is all against him; he must be confounded till he forget his right hand from his left, till his mind be turned into chaos, and his heart into water; and then let him give evidence. What will fall from his lips when this wretched collapse must be of special

These and so many other trial and cross-examination techniques are purposefully designed to mislead the trial judge or jury. Judge Frank concludes:

> In short, the lawyer aims at victory, at winning in the fight, not at aiding the court to discover the facts. He does not want the trial court to reach a sound educated guess, if it is likely to be contrary to his client's interest. Our present trial method is thus *the equivalent of throwing pepper in the eyes of a surgeon when he is performing an operation.*[60]

If litigators, described by Judge Frankel as fighters and as gladiators who care only about winning and not crusading after the truth, are to engage entirely in devious and cunning advocacy, how may the only other party in the courtroom, that is, the judge, make sure that the truth is revealed and justice is done? Again, Judge Frankel's analysis of the judge's role in the adversarial system is extremely instructive:

> The fact is that our system does not allow much room for effective or just intervention by the trial judge in the adversary fight about the facts. The judge views the case from a peak of Olympian ignorance. His intrusions will in too many cases result from partial or skewed insights. He may expose the secrets one side chooses to keep while never becoming aware of the other's. He runs a good chance of pursuing inspirations that better informed counsel have considered, explored, and abandoned after fuller study.[61]

It is interesting to note that, in this kind of system, the judge's interventions could even have negative repercussions. This is so, according to Judge Frankel, because

> [h]e risks at a minimum the supplying of more confusion than guidance by his sporadic intrusions. The ignorance and unpreparedness of the judge are intended axioms of the system. The "facts" are to be found and asserted by

> value, for the best talents of practiced forensic heroes are daily used to bring it about; and no member of the Human Society interferes to protect the wretch. Some sorts of torture are as it were tacitly allowed even among humane people. Eels are skinned alive, and witnesses are scarified, and no one's blood curdles at the sight, no soft heart is sickened at the cruelty.

Id. At the end of this quote, Professor Frank notes that, because of this kind of terror of cross-examination, the retention of a counsel who knows how to do this well could even force a settlement. *Id.*

60. *Id.* at 85 (emphasis added). Even those who consider the adversarial system to have more merits than demerits in helping the system arrive at a just result highlight the harmfulness of the usual advice to witnesses and their treatment in court. *See generally, e.g.*, Stephen McG. Bundy & Einer Richard Elhauge, *Do Lawyers Improve the Adversarial System? A General Theory of Litigation Advice and Its Regulation*, 79 Calif. L. Rev. 313 (1991) (testing different theories on the subject and generally concluding that lawyer advice to clients helps the court arrive at the right decision, but recognizes the fact that advice to testifying witnesses generally has a negative impact on the finding of the truth).

61. *See* Frankel, *supra* note 43, at 1042.

> the contestants. The judge is not to have investigated or explored the evidence before trial. No one is to have done it for him . . . . The judicial counterpart in civil law countries, with the file of the investigating magistrate before him, is a deeply "alien" conception . . . . Without an investigative file, the American trial judge is a blind and blundering intruder, acting in spasms as sudden flashes of seeming light may lead or mislead him at odd times. The ignorant and unprepared judge is the properly bland figurehead in the adversary scheme of things.[62]

Judge Frankel then concludes: "In a system that so values winning and deplores losing, where lawyers are trained to fight for, not to judge, their clients, where we learn as advocates not to 'know' inconvenient things, moral elegance is not to be expected. *The morals of the arena and the morals of the marketplace . . . tend powerfully to shape our conduct*."[63]

Of course, at the center of this discussion is a more fundamental doctrinal dilemma as to the role of the judiciary. A story recounted by Judge Charles Wyzanski about an interesting encounter between Judge Learned Hand and Justice Oliver Wendell Holmes Jr. neatly summarizes the basic doctrinal problem. According to Judge Wyzanski, when Learned Hand was still a district court judge, he went to Washington, DC, to visit Justice Holmes.[64] Among the cases that Justice Holmes was to review were supposedly several decided at the trial level by Judge Hand.[65] At the end of the visit, Justice Holmes gave Judge Hand a ride in his carriage on his way to the Supreme Court building.[66] As Judge Hand stepped out of the carriage, he waved goodbye to Justice Holmes and said: "*Do justice, Sir*." In response, "Holmes beckoned to him and said, 'Sonny, come back here. You don't understand

62. *Id.* He goes on describing the unbalanced system:

> [B]ecause the parties and counsel control the gathering and presentation of evidence, we have made no fixed, routine, expected place for the judge's contributions . . . As a result, [the trial judge's] interruptions are just that—interruptions: occasional, unexpected, sporadic, unprogrammed, and unduly dramatic because they are dissonant and out of character.

Id.

63. *Id.* at 1051 (emphasis added). This passive role of the judge in the adversarial system has been expressed in many other ways. For example, Justice Oliver Wendell Holmes Jr. has been quoted as saying:

> [T]he judge's function [is] interstitial; molecular, not molar. Or to put it in more dramatic terms, the judge was like the Greek chorus in Greek tragedy, not a principal actor but an interpreter of the actors. His grace was the grace of forbearance and sympathetic understanding; not his share of the action and passion of his time except in after dinner speeches.

See Charles E. Wyzanski, Jr., *Equal Justice through Law*, 47 Tul. L. Rev. 951, 954–55 (1973).

64. Wyzanski, *supra* note 63, at 955.

65. *Id.*

66. *Id.*

my job. *It is to apply the law*.'"[67] This anecdote is an excellent demonstration of the conflicting schools of thought on the role of the judiciary, commonly known as the conflict between interpretive judges and activist judges.[68] This fundamental debate manifests itself at the micro level in the courtrooms, and in the attitudes of judges, arbitrators, and counsel.

Coming back to the epistemology of determining facts in the common law legal tradition, at the center of the jury fact-finding idea, at least in part, is a basic assumption that one must be judged by representatives of her community, that is, the idea of the "representative cross-sectional jury."[69] This idea has never been without competing ideologies, namely, the "blue-ribbon juries," composed of "key men of recognized intelligence and probity."[70] In the United States, as of 1967, about 60 percent of federal courts allowed the selection of jurors from among the "key men."[71] In 1968, by passing the Jury Selection and Service Act, Congress abolished the system of "key men," and declared the policy of the United States as "all litigants in Federal courts entitled to trial by jury shall have the right to grand and petit juries selected at random from a fair cross section of the community."[72] About a decade later, in *Taylor v. Louisiana*, the U.S. Supreme Court extended this notion to the state courts.[73]

Americans now have a constitutional right to a particular kind of fact-finder: one drawn out of the cross-section of the community, which includes for a white defendant to have African Americans in the jury pool,[74] and for a male defendant to have females in the jury pool in proportionate quantity.[75] In *Taylor*, the Supreme Court held in particular that:

> We accept the fair-cross-section requirement as fundamental to the jury trial guaranteed by the Sixth Amendment and are convinced that the requirement has solid foundation. *The purpose of a jury is to guard against the exercise of arbitrary power—to make available the commonsense judgment of the community as a hedge against the overzealous or mistaken prosecutor and in preference to the*

67. *Id.*

68. *See id.*

69. Jeffrey Abramson, We, the Jury: The Jury System and the Ideal of Democracy 99 (BasicBooks, 1994) (citing Smith v. Texas, 311 U.S. 128, 130 (1940)).

70. *Id.*

71. *Id.*

72. *Id.* at 99–100 (citing Jury Selection and Service Act, 28 U.S.C. §§ 1861–1869).

73. *Id.* at 100 (citing Taylor v. Louisiana, 419 U.S. 522, 528 (1975)).

74. *See, e.g.*, Peters v. Kiff, 407 U.S. 493, 503 (1972) ("When any large and identifiable segment of the community is excluded from jury service, the effect is to remove from the jury room qualities of human nature and varieties of human experience, the range of which is unknown and perhaps unknowable. It is not necessary to assume that the excluded group will consistently vote as a class in order to conclude, as we do, that its exclusion deprives the jury of a perspective on human events that may have unsuspected importance in any case that may be presented.")

75. *Taylor*, 419 U.S. at 522.

professional or perhaps over-conditioned or biased response of a judge. This prophylactic vehicle is not provided if the jury pool is made up of only special segments of the populace or if large, distinctive groups are excluded from the pool. Restricting jury service to only special groups or excluding identifiable segments playing major roles in the community cannot be squared with the constitutional concept of jury trial. 'Trial by jury presupposes a jury drawn from a pool broadly representative of the community as well as impartial in a specific case . . . [T]he broad representative character of the jury should be maintained, partly as assurance of a diffused impartiality . . . .[76]

The Court added the rationale by saying:

> The truth is that the two sexes are not fungible; a community made up exclusively of one is different from a community composed of both; the subtle interplay of influence one on the other is among the imponderables. To insulate the courtroom from either may not in a given case make an iota of difference. Yet a flavor, a distinct quality is lost if either sex is excluded. The exclusion of one may indeed make the jury less representative of the community than would be true if an economic or racial group were excluded.[77]

There are at least two rationales, according to the Supreme Court: first, diversity improves the deliberations in many subtle ways, and second, the inclusion makes the jury more representative of the community. These objectives are not without controversy. For example, in *We, the Jury,* Professor Abramson accepts the first rationale, but rejects the notion that the jury must be a proportionate representative of the community because that would be tantamount to "abandoning the ideal of color-blind justice."[78] He seeks support for this proposition from Justice Stephen Field's 1880 dissenting opinion in *Ex parte Virginia,* which reads:

> The position that the cases where the rights of colored persons are concerned, justice will not be done to them unless they have a mixed jury, is founded upon the notion that in such cases white persons will not be fair and honest jurors. If this proposition be correct, there ought not to be any white person on the jury where the interests of colored persons only are involved. The jury would not be an honest or fair one, of which any of its members should be governed in his judgment by other considerations than the law and the evidence, and that decision would hardly be considered just, which should be reached by a sort of compromise, in which the prejudices of one race were set off against the prejudices of the other.[79]

76. *Id.* at 528 (emphasis added).

77. *Id.* at 532.

78. Abramson, *supra* note 69, at 107.

79. *Id.* at 107 (quoting *Ex parte* Virginia, 100 U.S. 339, 369 (1880) (Field J., dissenting)).

There is, however, no room for doubt in the decades of empirical research that race and other demographic factors influence the decisions of jurors,[80] but Justice Field's statement, of course, misses the point that the two objectives are, in fact, inseparable. Diversity improves the deliberations in more ways than one: it adds perspectives and also fights prejudice in many subtle ways that even Abramson recognizes when he says: "research indicates that 'when jurors of different ethnic groups deliberate together, they are better able to overcome their individual biases.'"[81]

Ensuring representational milieu is not at all a recent notion. The concept of a mixed jury, meaning a jury composed of half of each of the peers of the party litigants, existed in common law since the thirteenth century. As Professor Abramson describes, "[t]ypically, the right to a mixed jury extended to marginal groups that lacked full legal equality in a society and who therefore could not easily be swept into a homogenized concept of trial by one's peers."[82]

Despite the slightly varying characterizations, the representational jury clearly assumed to have at least three fundamental benefits: broader perspective, diminished bias and prejudice as well as greater political acceptability. Each one of these factors is believed to contribute to the accuracy and fairness of the judicial process in both criminal and civil cases to the extent the common law used juries for the determination of fact.

The benefit that is severely understated is the perspective that the "peer" brings into the decision-making process. It needs no elaborate empirical studies to determine that a juror who grew up in the streets of the south side of Chicago would have a better understanding of the dynamics of the neighborhood and hence be very well equipped to determine facts pertaining to events that occur in those streets, because in addition to having a firsthand experience of the day-to-day interactions out of which particular events arise, he is also more likely to be culturally better positioned to understand the witnesses, who are likely to be members of the same community. Thus, apart from the three benefits regularly acknowledged, there is the added benefit of life experience and perspective, which could be summed up as cultural competence. No matter how the challenges of democracy complicate matters,[83] the

80. *See id.* at 104 (citing, among other studies, the detailed discussions in Nancy J. King, *Post-Conviction Review of Jury Discrimination: Measuring the Effects of Juror Decisions*, 92 MICH. L. REV. 63 (1993); JON VAN DYKE, JURY SELECTION PROCEDURES: OUR UNCERTAIN COMMITMENT TO REPRESENTATIVE PANELS (1977); Nancy S. Marder, *Gender Dynamics and Jury Deliberations*, 96 YALE L. J. 593–612 (1987); Shirley S. Abramson, *Justice and Juror*, 20 GA. L. REV. 257–98 (1986).

81. ABRAMSON, *supra* note 69, at 104.

82. *Id.* at 106 (citing among other works, Van Dyke, *supra* note 80, at 10–11 (noting the colonists brought this system to Plymouth colony and used it in disputes between the natives and settlers.); Lewis LaRue, *A Jury of One's Peers*, 33 WASH. & LEE L. REV. 841–76 (1976); MARIANNE CONSTABLE, THE LAW OF THE OTHER: THE MIXED JURY AND CHANGING CONCEPTIONS OF CITIZENSHIP, LAW, AND KNOWLEDGE (1994)).

83. Note, for example, the situation of a Korean immigrant father who was found guilty of murdering his daughter by a jury that did not contain any Asians, many of whom said they found him guilty mainly because he did not show any emotions when the police arrested him from his home, along with his wife. The Asian community subsequently reacted by saying perhaps the jury was

common law legal tradition, at its core, does recognize the importance of cultural competence through the jury system.

The cultural competence of judges is often tested when they sit in judgment of matters involving minority customs. The shortcomings of the judges in this regard are frequently recognized. For example, in the English case of *Balraj v. Balraj*,[84] a UK resident Indian man petitioned to divorce his Indian resident wife on the basis of five years of separation. Although the five-year separation could be grounds for divorce, the showing of grave hardship could be grounds for refusal. In explaining the difficulty that trial court faces in assessing grave hardship that an Indian woman resident in India might face, the English Court of Appeals stated:

> The family at the time they were living together were Hindus and belonged to a particular group, to use a non-technical expression, in the Hindu caste system. The social customs of different groups of Hindus, as appears from the judgment of the President [of the family court] varies (*sic*) enormously. In order to decide, the impact of first, desertion and secondly, judicial divorce upon this particular wife, it became necessary for the court to try to obtain such a grasp first of the objective social circumstances, customs and more relevant to this family's life in India and secondly, to make an assessment of the personal suffering, handicaps and social deprivations that this particular lady had suffered in the past by reason of her husband's disregard of his matrimonial obligations. Having made that assessment, the court had then to attempt to make further assessment of the probable impact of judicial divorce upon this particular lady and her life circumstances and happiness. It really does not need any exaggerated rhetoric to express the appalling difficulty of such a judicial task. A task which can hardly be done with any sure prospect of complete success in a court in England brought up upon the customs and mores of the different communities in England with which the court is familiar. *For a judge to try to achieve the insight necessary to grasp the prospect of this lady in the outskirts of Hydrabad and the prospects of the daughter of the family living with the mother in Hydrabad calls for the exercise of perhaps grater insight than any English judge should be required to exercise.*[85]

Another good example is the story behind the enactment of the United States Federal Indian Child Welfare Act of 1972.[86] In the 1960s and 1970s, movements for the promotion of the interests of indigenous populations in the United States

culturally incompetent because "Korean fathers, even when they are feeling extreme sorrow, they can't cry." Jennifer Lin, Was the Jury Confused by Culture—or Die He Kill His Daughter?" *See id.* at 101 n.* (citing Jennifer Lin, *Was the Jury Confused by Culture—or Did He Kill His Daughter?*, PHILA. INQUIRER, Apr. 28, 1992, at A1).

84. SEBASTIAN POULTER, ENGLISH LAW AND ETHNIC MINORITY CUSTOMS 6 (Butterworth-Heinemann 1986) (citing 11 Fam. Law 110 (1981)).

85. *Id.* at 6 (citing 11 Fam. Law, at 110–11) (emphasis added).

86. Codified under 25 U.S.C §§ 1901–1963 (1978).

identified a serious problem of a disproportionate removal and placement into foster and other forms of care of Native American children.[87] Congress received evidence showing that one of the reasons was the culturally insensitive application of legal standards such as "child neglect" by state court judges. For example, state court judges would consider abandoned a child being raised by anyone other than the nucleus family, such as aunts or uncles.[88] On the basis of evidence submitted to it, Congress, among other things, found:

> (4) that an alarmingly high percentage of Indian families are broken up by the removal, often unwarranted, of their children from them by nontribal public and private agencies and that an alarmingly high percentage of such children are placed in non-Indian foster and adoptive homes and institutions; and (5) that the States, exercising their recognized jurisdiction over Indian child custody proceedings through administrative and judicial bodies, have often failed to recognize the essential tribal relations of Indian people and the cultural and social standards prevailing in Indian communities and families.[89]

Based on this finding, Congress mandated the consideration of the cultural aspects of each case. First it, recognized terms such as "extended family."[90] As to the standard to be used for placement of an Indian child, Congress provided that:

> (d) Social and cultural standards applicable: The standards to be applied in meeting the preference requirements of this section shall be the prevailing social and cultural standards of the Indian community in which the parent or

87. *See* Tonya Gonnella Frichner, *The Indian Child Welfare Act: A National Law Controlling the Welfare of Indigenous Children* 1–2 (2010), http://www.un.org/esa/socdev/unpfii/documents/The%20Indian%20Child%20Welfare%20Act.v3.pdf.

88. *Id.* at 4 ("For instance, state child welfare laws typically use criteria like 'neglect' as a proper basis for removing a child from his family to foster or adoptive care. The standards used by social workers with narrow conceptions of proper child rearing practices were largely biased towards nuclear families and Anglo-American ideals about family structure. So, these state workers would often interpret 'neglect' to include practices widely and traditionally implemented in tribal communities. The result was the large and disproportionate removal of native children from their homes compared to nonnative children. For example, native communities often raise children under extended family systems within which a variety of community members, such as aunts, cousins, and neighbors, bear the responsibility for a child's care. In contrast, within nuclear families, a child's biological parents predominately bear the responsibility of a child's care. In many cases, state workers deemed a child neglected if left with non-parent community members for an extended period of time, because this type of care arrangement is inconsistent with normal parenting within a nuclear family. This type of justification for removing native children from their families reflects a prejudice against extended family child rearing in favor of nuclear families, and a racist view towards native family structures.").

89. 25 U.S.C. § 1901(4) & (5) (1978).

90. 25 U.S.C. § 1903(2) (1978) ("[E]xtended family member" shall be as defined by the law or custom of the Indian child's tribe or, in the absence of such law or custom, shall be a person who has reached the age of eighteen and who is the Indian child's grandparent, aunt or uncle, brother or sister, brother-in-law or sister-in-law, niece or nephew, first or second cousin, or stepparent.).

> extended family resides or with which the parent or extended family members maintain social and cultural ties.[91]

Obviously considering the failure was in both the standards that were applied and the judges who applied them, the cultural understanding and appreciation of the judges to apply the new standards seem a prerequisite for proper application of those legal standards.

International arbitrators are almost always called upon to grasp the cultural complexities of the parties who appear before them and decide cases the way they consider appropriate or fair. They necessarily suffer from some of the cultural problems that the English Court of Appeal noted in the above passage or the state court judges in the United States who adjudicate child custody matters in the Native American communities. In international arbitration, however, it gets more complicated when the co-arbitrators and counsel come from different legal traditions with entirely different mechanisms of fact-finding and procedural rules, as well as varied conceptions of the nature of admissible evidence, weight, and standards of proof. Some of these major systems are discussed in the following sections.

B. FACT-FINDING IN THE CIVIL LAW LEGAL TRADITION

How does the inquisitorial system address some of the same problems discussed above differently? A brief historical survey provides context. The literature classifies the origin of the civil law into two families: Romanic and Germanic.[92] Owing to centuries of interaction, influence, and counterinfluence, the origins have played a steadily diminishing role in explaining the nature and state of the existing systems. Italian scholar Giuseppe Chiovenda once commented that the contemporary Italian procedure can be said to be "neither more Roman nor less Germanic than the existing procedure of Germany."[93] However, a brief discussion of the origins will be useful in understanding the existing peculiarities of the system.

Roman law has a very long history, but Justinian's sixth century *Corpus Juris Civilis* is considered to be the most natural starting point for purposes of contemporary analysis of the civil law legal tradition.[94] The *Corpus Juris Civilis* consists of four parts: the *Code,* which is the collection of Roman legislation; the *Digest,* which is a treatise of the most important writings; the *Novels,* which is imperial legislation

91. 25 U.S.C. 1915(d) (1978).

92. The countries that are believed to be within the Romanic family include France, Italy, Spain, Portugal, Belgium, the Netherlands, most countries in Latin America, Africa, and Asia. The countries within the Germanic family include Austria, Switzerland, and Japan. *See* MATTEI ET AL., *supra* note 28, at 710.

93. *Id.* at 709 (*quoting* Giuseppe Chiovenda, *Roman and Germanic Elements in Continental Civil Procedure, in* ARTHUR ENGELMANN, A HISTORY OF CONTINENTAL CIVIL PROCEDURE 875, 833, 912 (1983)).

94. The history stretches as far back as 450 B.C., that is, the time of the Twelve Tables. *See* GLENDON ET AL., *supra* note 3, at 18–20.

enacted in the years following the compilations of the *Code* and the *Digest*; and finally, the *Institute*, which is an introductory text for students.[95] The *Code* and the *Digest* together are considered to represent an authoritative restatement of Roman law.[96]

Having remained dormant for centuries following the end of Justinian's reign,[97] the *Corpus Juris Civilis* was rediscovered in Italy around the eleventh century.[98] After the rediscovery, the University of Bologna became the center of the study of legal science in Europe.[99] With the benefit of this very far-reaching and intellectually challenging set of ancient legal materials, legal scholarship flourished and numerous legal thinkers emerged, including Sir Thomas Aquinas in the thirteenth century.[100] According to Professor Glendon, thousands of European law students who came to study in Bologna took back home with them not only the laws that they studied, but also the methods of their teaching.[101] In this organic fashion, Roman law quickly spread throughout Europe and beyond.[102] Glendon suggests that its perceived intellectual superiority is among those factors to be credited for its widespread appeal and acceptance.[103]

The French Civil Code of 1804, which is commonly known as "Code Napoleon," is now considered to be the pioneer of the modern civil code, and consequently the most influential.[104] The German Civil Code of 1896 became perhaps the second

95. *Id.* at 20.

96. *Id.*

97. Professor Glenn notes that during this period of about 500 years, which followed the fall of the Roman Empire, various kinds of chthonic laws reasserted themselves across Europe and elsewhere. *See* GLENN, *supra* note 7, at 145.

98. *See* GLENDON ET AL., *supra* note 3, at 24–25. Before that, it had served different rulers through the ages. The Germans used it in ruling what was previously part of the Roman Empire. According to Glendon:

> Crude versions of Roman legal rules had become intermingled in varying degrees with the customary rules of the Germanic invaders to the point where historians speak of the laws during this period as either "Romanized customary laws" or barbarized Roman laws. Thus, though Roman legal science and Classical Roman law disappeared in the welter, diversity and localism of Carbonnier's "customary thicket", Romanist elements survived and served both as a strand of continuity, and latent, potential universalizing factor in what we now think of as the civil law tradition.

Id. at 22.

99. *Id.* at 24–25.

100. *Id.* at 25.

101. *See id.* at 26.

102. *Id.*

103. *Id.* at 25.

104. *Id.* at 34. The French Code was by no means the first of the modern codes, but it was the most successful. Professor René David attributes the successes to two factors: (1) it was the work of an enlightened sovereign, (2) which was powerful enough to influence its acceptance. *See* DAVID &

most influential.[105] Although the French and German Civil Codes grew from the same roots, they took divergent approaches and developed individually.[106] The French Code, drafted by a commission of four prominent jurists within a very short period of time, and with a touch of the ideals of the revolution,[107] was always meant to be flexible, general, and able to be understood by ordinary citizens.[108] The German Civil Code, on the other hand, was a very detailed project that took "legal scientists" 20 years to complete[109]:

> It was constructed and worked out with the degree of technical precision that had never been seen before in any legislation. A special language was developed and employed consistently. Legal concepts were defined and then used in the same way throughout. Sentence construction indicated the location of the burden of proof. Through elaborate cross-references, all parts of the Code supposedly interlocked to form a logically closed system.[110]

Whereas the French Code was adopted at the beginning of the Industrial Revolution, the German Code had the benefit of being adopted at the end of that era.[111] German legal thought, including legal realism, jurisprudence of interests, and sociological schools of thought, came to have far-reaching influence across the world, including in the United States.[112] This brief discussion of the historical origin and evolution of the civil law system is offered not only to show the divergent roots from the common law discussed in the previous section, but also to highlight the reasons behind its intellectual sophistication.

In the twentieth century, the civil code in Europe gradually decreased in importance and relevance, due in part to the emergence of the regulatory and bureaucratic state and the ceding of portions of state sovereignty to supranational governing and judicial bodies established by international treaties.[113] Nonetheless, the fundamental

Brierley, *supra* note 4, at 64–65. The failed prior codes include the Prussian *Allgemeines Landrecht* of 1794, and the Austrian Civil Code of 1811. *See id.* at 65.

105. *See* Glendon et al., *supra* note 3, at 33.

106. *Id.* at 33–34.

107. The Code is predicated on three ideological foundations: private property, freedom of contract, and patriarchal family. *See id.* at 34–35.

108. *Id.* at 62.

109. *Id.* at 41.

110. *Id.* For a good outline of the system and organization of the two codes, see Mattei et al., *supra* note 28, at 404–19.

111. *See* Glendon et al., *supra* note 3, at 42–43.

112. The writings of Holmes and Pound are believed to have that influence. Later on, the works of Karl Llewellyn and other jurists who fled Germany to the United States during the National Socialist period are considered to have significant influence in mainstream American legal thought. *Id.* at 43–44.

113. *See id.* at 54.

notions of the civil legal tradition, and its peculiar characteristics, which are themselves the products of its long history, continue to distinguish it from the common law legal tradition. The fairly common and salient features of the civil system, in particular the distinguishing characteristic of the procedures, are discussed below.

Professor Geoffrey C. Hazard Jr. summarizes the civil law's procedural system in this manner:

> Under the civil law procedural systems, the judge is responsible for deciding a case according to the truth of the matter. The judge decides both fact and law because there is no jury or anything like it. It is assumed that the truth of the matter will be revealed by relevant evidence. Under the civil law, it therefore follows that the judge is responsible for eliciting relevant evidence.[114]

With respect to the role of the party litigants, Hazard provides that the parties are represented by advocates who assist the parties in presenting their case, but that a fundamental difference in the roles of the advocate as between the common law and civil law is that, rather than employing cunning and trickery to skew the presentation of facts and applicability of the law as in the common law, civilian advocates are conceived of as assisting the judge in his or her quest for the truth, the fulfillment of the judicial responsibility.[115]

Conceptually, "the advocates are supposed to provide comment and suggestions to the judge, with a deference which varies from one civil law jurisdiction to another. But at least in theory they have no power of initiative after they have presented the claims and defenses in the pleadings, except with the assent of the judge."[116]

This highlights several important assumptions and functions of the civil law procedure. First, the judge is responsible for deciding all aspects of the case. Second, the judge's only objective and responsibility is to find out the truth of the matter in the case before him. Third, the judge gets no help from a jury in deciding issues of fact or law. Fourth, the judge is responsible for eliciting all relevant evidence from all sources. Fifth, the advocates' responsibility is to assist the judge in collecting and analyzing the evidence. Finally, the advocates can only provide suggestions and comments to the judge, and once the process is set in motion by the submission of the claim or defense, they may not perform any activities without the leave of the court.[117]

Although this succinct summary is fairly representative of the most common elements of the civil law system, it does not fully capture the intricacies within each civil law country and the significant variations that exist among the various civil law countries.

114. *See* Hazard, *supra* note 29, at 1019.

115. *Id.* at 1019–20.

116. *Id.* at 1020.

117. *Id.* at 1020.

The French system is perhaps the closest to the above description. The French New Code of Civil Procedure enacted in the early 1970s is probably the most currently important and relevant.[118] Several of its characteristics have come to be considered fundamental; two are salient to the present discussion. First, although the judge is responsible for the evidence, the parties share that responsibility under the judge's guidance, including the examination of witnesses, the production of documents, and the commissioning of expert witnesses.[119] More interestingly, the court is not limited to the application of the law identified by the parties. It may reclassify a case, apply a different provision of the law to the developed facts, and arrive at a conclusion.[120] This reinforces the view that the judge is the seeker of the truth and the guardian of the law, that is, an honest broker.[121] It must also be noted that the notion of proof by balance of probabilities, or a preponderance of the evidence, is more or less nonexistent. At the risk of over simplification, it is sometimes claimed that in the French system, "a fact is either proven or not."[122] And second, in each case, a file called the dossier is built by the court.[123] The dossier contains the claim, the defense, and all pieces of gathered evidence.[124] Each party must have a copy of this expansive record.[125]

Although principally inquisitorial, the German laws of civil procedure seem to contain more elements of adversarial justice than the French system.[126] The most

118. *See* John Bell, Sophie Boyron & Simon Whittaker, Principles of French Law 86 (2d ed. 2008).

119. *Id.* at 87. Technically, the claimant bears the burden of proof; however, the opposing party is required to help in adducing evidence. *Id.* (citing Civ. (1) 20 Mar. 2005, *Procédures* 2005 no.123 (Fr.)).

120. *See id.* at 87–89. Article 12 of the French Civil Procedure Code states that "[The judge] must give or restore the exact classification to the facts transactions [*actes*] which are the subject of the litigation and not stay with the characterization suggested for them by the parties." *Id.* at 88. Although this seems to be a correct representation of the civil procedure law as it stands today, it is important to note that the whole notion of reclassification of case by the judge without the parties' submission is not entirely without controversy. *Id.* The new Civil Procedure Code provides that, where the parties have agreed to keep their legal classification, that is, if they identify the law and ask the court to be governed by that (some sort of choice of law), the court is required to apply that law alone and not reclassify, unless the case affects inalienable rights. *Id.* at 89.

121. *Id.* at 89. Note, however, that there is a suggestion in the literature that the involvement of the judge may depend on the complexity of the case, with more involvement in more complex cases, and more reliance on the parties' submissions in less complex cases. *See, e.g.*, Catherine Elliott, Catherine Vernon & Eric Jeanpierre, French Legal System 179–80 (2d ed. 2006) (suggesting that in less complex cases, the judge's role is more or less like that of the judge in the adversarial system).

122. *See* Bell et al., *supra* note 118, at 87.

123. *Id.* at 90.

124. *Id.* at 90–91.

125. *Id.* at 90.

126. *See, e.g.*, Howard D. Fisher, The German Legal System & Legal Language 115 (2d ed. 1999). One of the maxims of the German civil procedure is that "it is for the parties to proceedings

important civil procedure law in Germany is the Code of Civil Procedure, more commonly known as the ZPO.[127] There are several reasons the ZPO is more just than other adversarial systems. First, in all civil actions before the district court in Germany, representation by counsel is mandatory.[128] This fact itself suggests the level of expectation for counsel involvement. Stadler neatly summarizes the remarkable aspect of the court's power and the parties' roles:

> The Court has an obligation to prepare the trial. It has the power to demand that the parties elaborate fully on all relevant alleged facts. Within the limits inherent in principle of party presentation, the court will provide some guidance for the pleadings, and to some extent, will even assist a party that failed to present all relevant facts through oversight, inadvertence or mistake.[129]

The same basic principles underpin criminal and administrative procedures in the civil law system. If anything, the procedures in the public law arena demand more active involvement of judges and allow less room for manipulation by counsel. For example, in France, criminal proceedings are characterized by judicial investigation of the crime.[130] The judge *d'instruction* is empowered to collect evidence, including by conducting searches and seizures, interviewing witnesses, and even visiting the crime scene if necessary.[131] The judge is required to look at not only inculpatory evidence, but also exculpatory evidence, because the mission of the judiciary is principally to find out the truth.[132] After the judge completes the investigation with the help of the prosecutor and the defendant, she will issue a final report identifying the nature of the crime and the possible charges that the government may pursue, and submits the dossier to the office of the Procureur de la Republique, who in turn

to introduce facts and applications. The opposite of this principle is the so-called '*Inquisitionsprinizp*' (examination maxim or inquisition principle), which applies, for example, in criminal and administrative proceedings."

127. Introduction to German Law 365 (Mathias Reimann & Joachim Zekoll eds., 2d ed. 2005). This was most recently amended in 2002. *Id.*

128. *Id.* at 367. Indigent plaintiffs and defendants do have a statutory right to counsel. *Id.*

129. *Id.* at 370 (*citing* Zivilprozessordnung [ZPO] [Code of Civil Procedure], § 139).

130. *See* Walter Cairns & Robert McKeon, Introduction to French Law 173 (1995) (citing Code civil [C. civ] arts. 92, 97 (Fr.)). French criminal procedure is governed by the Code of Criminal Procedure of 1808, amended many times since its enactment. *Id.* at 169. The procedure is complex, but the entire criminal prosecution and trial process seems to be divided into six distinct stages: reporting of the offense, preliminary investigation by police and referral for judicial investigation, judicial investigation of the crime by a judge and issuance of a report recommending the institution of a criminal prosecution, the main trial, and enforcement of the outcome. *See id.* at 169–76. For a good overview of this process, see Renée Lettow Lerner, *The Intersection of Two Systems: An American on Trial for an American Murder in the French Cour D'Assisses*, 2001 U. Ill. L. Rev. 791 (2001).

131. *See* Cairns & McKeon, *supra* note 130, at 172–74.

132. *See* Lerner, *supra* note 130, at 802.

forwards it to a panel of three judges who will decide whether prosecution is warranted.[133] "If they decide there is [reason to prosecute], then they issue the formal charge . . . and transfer the case to the appropriate trial court."[134]

During the actual trial, the judge remains the principal actor, in charge of conducting the lines of inquiry and the questions, although the opposing parties are involved by suggesting questions they feel may be appropriate or beneficial to their case. As Professor Renée Lettow Lerner puts it, "there is a direct line of communication between the fact-finders and the witness."[135] In fact, the prosecutor and defense counsel would face disciplinary action, even disbarment, if they were ever to attempt to contact and interview non-party witnesses, as that is the exclusive domain of the judge.[136] According to Professor Lerner, who served as an expert witness in a high profile criminal trial in France, the

> flexible order of the trial allows witness testimony to resemble a discussion. Witnesses can directly respond to the statements of other witnesses, in a sort of dialogue. They are also allowed to speak in their natural voices, initially in narrative form. Neither party has carefully coached them before trial, the parties' direct and cross-examination do not constrain them, and their statements are not interrupted by evidentiary objections. As a result, witnesses are more relaxed and often forthcoming with information.[137]

More interestingly, and again in simplistic terms, the French system does not seem to strictly impose the burden of proof on either of the parties. As such, the fact-finder is asked whether she is fully convinced that the alleged act occurred and that the defendant is the one who caused it.[138] This suggests that, in keeping with the inquisitorial tradition, the parties and the judge collaboratively establish the facts without allocating any particular burden, which is conceptually different from the Anglo-American burden allocation system. To one with an Anglo-American background, it could even be difficult to understand. In any case, the most important aspect of judicial investigation and active judicial involvement throughout the process is, as Lerner puts it, "[a]n indigent defendant is not placed at such a disadvantage, having

133. *See id.* at 801–02.

134. *See id.* at 806. This particular panel is the Chambre de l'instruction. *Id.*

135. *See id.* at 807.

136. *See id.* at 802–03 (citing Code de Procédure Pénale [C. pr. pén] arts. 101–102). She also notes that, as the prosecutor is not technically a member of the bar, disbarment is not exactly the nature of the penalty. *See id.* at 83 n.43 (relying on generally John Leudsdorf, Man in His Original Dignity: Legal Ethics in France (2001)).

137. *See id.* at 853. She further notes that this system allows the defendant to choose to speak in most cases. *Id.*

138. This might seem like the familiar Anglo-American "beyond a reasonable doubt" standard, but Professor Learner suggests that the French version, which reads: "Avez-vous une intime conviction?," is difficult to translate, but it could mean "Are you deeply, thoroughly convinced?" *See id.* at 800–01.

to rely on a poorly funded legal aid system,"[139] including for the gathering and use of exculpatory evidence, as the judicial investigator would do that for him.[140]

Although German criminal procedure appears to be relatively more adversarial than the French system, at least during trial, it is still substantially similar. The German Code of Criminal Procedure of 1879 (StPO) still governs criminal prosecution in Germany.[141] Under the StPO, the criminal prosecution process has three distinct phases: (1) investigation by the state attorney's office, which looks at both inculpatory and exculpatory evidence;[142] (2) the submission of indictment to the appropriate pre-trial court, which determines whether there is sufficient evidence warranting a trial,[143] and if so; (3) the commencing of the actual trial. At trial, in keeping with the inquisitorial tradition, the judge leads the presentation of evidence and questioning, maintaining a prominent and active role.[144] As in the French system, and depending on the nature and severity of the crime, lay judges participate in making the final decision.[145]

Notions of official investigation and party passivity also characterize administrative proceedings in the civil law system. In France, the rules of administrative procedures are contained in the *Code de Justice Administrative*.[146] The administrative law system attempts to balance two competing interests: the government's administrative task and the protection of citizens from excesses and governmental abuse of power. With this balance in mind:

> [J]udges do not rely on the parties to provide them with those arguments on which they can rely in coming to their decision ("decisive argument"): the case is constructed, the facts unearthed, and the line of reasoning developed through the work of the *judge rapporteur* during the stage of the instruction.[147]

Although legal representation is available in most administrative proceedings, according to Bell et al. "The lack of representation is unlikely to be damaging to a

139. *Id.* at 801 (emphasis added).

140. *Id.* at 805–06. The judge's final decision, as well as preliminary rulings throughout the investigation, may be appealed to the next level. The appellate court reviews both questions of law and fact, including new facts as appropriate. *See* CAIRNS & MCKEON, *supra* note 130, at 172–74.

141. Amended several times since its adoption in 1879, the German Criminal Procedure Code (Strafprozessordnung, StPo) is the principal body of law that governs German Criminal Procedure. It is supplemented with the Judicature Act (Gerichsverfassungsgesetz, or GVG). *See* REIMANN & ZEKOLL, *supra* note 127, at 421–22.

142. *See id* at 423 (citing StPO, §§ 158, 160, 162, 163, 167, and 169).

143. *See id.* (citing StPO, §§ 170, 200).

144. *See id.* at 424–25 (citing StPO §§ 58, 213–225, 243, 244, 258, 260).

145. *See id.* at 425.

146. Adopted in May 2000, the *Code de justice administrative* consolidates all the rules that apply in all administrative courts. *See* BELL ET AL., *supra* note 118, at 119 & n.319.

147. *Id.* at 119.

person's chances of success since . . . the case is literally taken over by the court itself from the moment it is introduced."[148]

In addition, administrative proceedings are also characterized by the following stages: (1) the court appoints an officer, called the *rapporteur*, to create a dossier of each case, which contains the challenges, the administrative decision, and all the evidence; (2) all administrative courts are empowered to seek and obtain relevant documents from administrative agencies; (3) the *rapporteur* then produces a note outlining the facts, the evidence, the law, and a draft judgment, and then forwards it to the *Commissaire du gouvernement*, which prepares a legal opinion, (4) that leads to trial.[149] At trial, the *rapporteur* presents the dossier by outlining the parties' arguments. The parties are then invited by the administrative court to comment.[150] The *Commissaire du gouvernement* then reads their conclusions, concluding the public hearing.[151] The judges then consider all the arguments and evidence in private and reach a decision that must address all points of contention.[152] An appeal will lie either to the *Cour Administrative d'Appel* or to the *Conseil d'Etat* depending on the nature of the appeal.[153] The appellate tribunals may consider both questions of fact and law.[154]

As indicated above, the procedure is essentially inquisitorial in the sense that judicial officials are in charge of the investigation of facts and the application of law, with only limited help from the parties. In relation to this, the role of the judicial officer charged with developing the dossier is captured well in the following passage by French jurists J. Mossot and J. Marimbert: "The *rapporteur* may be faced with applications coming from ordinary citizens little versed in rules of law in which the subject-matter or legal basis remains concealed rather than being made clearly explicit."[155] In these cases, the *rapporteur* interprets the application in a constructive way, not confined to the letter of the appeal, but also not contradicting what it says. This effort to reclassify applications is most often made for the benefit of the applicant.[156]

148. *Id.* at 121 (emphasis added).

149. *Id.* at 123–24.

150. *Id.* at 124.

151. *Id.* at 125.

152. *See id.*

153. *See* L. Neville Brown & John S. Bell, French Administrative Law 115 (1993).

154. *Id.* at 115. It is important to note here that the duality of the French court system—the regular courts and the administrative courts—has a long history, and that judicial review of administrative decisions in the context of the Anglo-American system is unknown. The French administrative system is self-contained. For a good discussion of the position of the administrative courts within the French constitutional system of separation of powers, see *id.* at 8–58.

155. *Id.* at 96–97 (*quoting* J. Massot & J. Marimbert, Le Conseil d'Etat 153 (1988)).

156. *Id.* at 96–97.

Although German administrative law appears to be more complicated because of German federalism,[157] administrative proceedings are similarly inquisitorial.[158] An interesting aspect of this is that, even if a party, which may include a government agency, fails to cooperate, the adjudicating authority is authorized and required, within reasonable limits, to ascertain the merits of the case ex officio.[159]

It must be noted that the diversity within each and the lack of familiarity of the subtleties of each system even by the learned authors extensively cited makes a totally accurate description of each system very difficult, but it is also evidence of the profound differences in assumptions that arbitrators who come from different traditions bring to the arbitration room.

C. FACT-FINDING IN THE CHINESE LEGAL TRADITION

Historically, Chinese law has been influenced by centuries of domestic and external conceptions of law and legal institutions.[160] Professor Stanly Lubman writes: "Both my law practice and scholarly activities constantly remind me of the difficulties that Chinese and Westerners have comprehending each other and surrounding the cultural barriers between them. These problems have become even more visible as reform has transformed China."[161]

For millennia, Chinese law has benefited from the Confucius code of orderly behavior (from the Han Dynasty (206 B.C.E.–220 C.E.) until the end of the Qin Dynasty and the formation of the Chinese Republic in 1911).[162]

157. For a discussion of the administrative system, see REIMANN & ZEKOLL, *supra* note 127, at 87–103.

158. *See id.* at 103–04.

159. *See id.* at 105 (*citing* Untersuchungsgrundsatz [VwVfG] [Federal Administrative Act], § 24 (Ger.)).

160. *See* STANLEY B. LUBMAN, BIRD IN A CAGE: LEGAL REFORM IN CHINA AFTER MAO, at xvi (1999). Other English language references on the general topic of Chinese legal culture include: the multivolume JOSEPH NEEDHAM, SCIENCE AND CIVILIZATION IN CHINA (1954); FUNG YU-LAN, A SHORT HISTORY OF CHINESE PHILOSOPHY (Derk Bodde ed., Simon and Schuster 1997); JIANFU CHEN, CHINESE LAW: CONTEXT AND TRANSFORMATION (2008), and others cited throughout this section.

161. LUBMAN, *supra* note 169, at xv–xvi.

162. *See* JAMES M. ZIMMERMAN, CHINA LAW DESKBOOK: A LEGAL GUIDE FOR FOREIGN-INVESTED ENTERPRISES 36–38 (3d ed. 2010). Some of the specific percepts are:

(1) positive law (*fa*) cannot bring about harmony or proper conduct, it only encourages evasion of the law,
(2) in the interest of the harmony of the family, the clan, the community and the state, the duties and obligations of people not their rights must be emphasized,
(3) rulers must practice virtue and lead by example,
(4) social hierarchy is the key to stability and must be respected,
(5) within this hierarchy obedience must be met with benevolence,
(6) good conduct cannot be imposed but must come from within the person,

The culture of avoidance of dispute and the fear of arbitrariness that often accompany the involvement of authority, coupled with the more rooted culture of fear of "losing face," appear to have enduring influence in contemporary Chinese law and society. [163] As James M. Zimmerman counsels, "the concept of face is akin to status, and a person will go to great lengths to avoid 'losing face.'"[164] He further warns that, "[f]oreigners involved in negotiating with the Chinese need to appreciate this concept."[165]

The most contemporary body of law governing the conduct of civil litigation in China is the Civil Procedure Law of the People's Republic of China (CPL).[166] The CPL's degree of emphasis on conciliation is unique, and as such culturally significant.[167] Conciliation has its own chapter. Indeed, it is also mentioned throughout the Code starting from Article 9 as part of the chapter on objectives and general principles; it authorizes courts to offer conciliation at every step of the litigation up to and including during appellate review.[168]

Chinese society clearly prefers conciliatory and less confrontational settlement of disputes although its use in modern times is a subject of curiosity and

(7) everyone must attempt to resolve his own disputes with others an resort harmony,
(8) taking a legal action against another is a sign of weakness in the form of inability to resolve dispute and restore harmony,
(9) rule's involvement in dispute resolution often leads to arbitrary justice, and must be avoided as much as possible.

See John W. Head & Yanping Wang, Law Codes in Dynastic China: A Synopsis of Chinese Legal History in the Thirty Centuries from Zhou to Qing 32–52 (2005).

163. *See* Zimmerman, *supra* note 162, at 39, n.5.

164. *Id.*

165. *Id.*

166. [Civil Procedure Law of the People's Republic of China] (promulgated by Order No. 44 of the President of the People's Republic of China on Apr. 9, 1991, effective), http://www.china.org/cn/english/government/207339.htm [hereinafter Chinese Civil Procedure Law]. This law replaced the 1982 Civil Procedure Law. China has had a civil procedure code since 1910 when Western powers demanded the modernization of the laws in exchange for relinquishing extra territorial jurisdiction. *See* Zimmerman, *supra* note 162, at 1009–10.

167. Under PRC law, conciliation and mediation refer to the same procedure, and as such they are used here interchangeably. *See* Jingzhou Tao, *Arbitration in China, in* International Commercial Arbitration in Asia 40, n.54 (Philip J. McConnaughay & Thomas B. Ginsburg eds., 2d ed. 2006) (noting that the Chinese term "*tiaojie*" could be translated as both conciliation or mediation).

168. Interestingly, the Chinese Civil Procedure Law provides in Article 128: "At the end of the court debate, a judgment shall be made according to law. Where conciliation is possible prior to the rendering of a judgment, conciliation efforts may be made; if conciliation proves to be unsuccessful, a judgment shall be made without delay." More interestingly the Chinese Civil Procedure Law further provides in Article 155: "In dealing with a case on appeal, a people's court of second instance may conduct conciliation. If an agreement is reached through conciliation, a conciliation statement shall be made .... After the conciliation statement has been served, the judgment of the people's court which originally tried the case shall be considered rescinded." Chinese Civil Procedure Law, *supra* note 166, art. 128 & 155.

speculation.[169] China codified informal methods of mediation in 1954.[170] By 1987, the Chinese mediation system grew to become the world's largest, with 6 million certified mediators mediating millions of all sorts of cases ranging from family to tort to labor every year.[171] However, commentators note that "see you in court" is now becoming more common in China.[172]

Another culturally interesting aspect of litigation has been the now-changing tolerance for "advocacy outside the courtroom" by way of conferring with the judge ex parte, a practice that is said to have changed in recent years.[173]

The procedural and evidentiary rules in China are being revised. Pilot programs of the proposed Uniform Provisions of Evidence of the People's Court (Uniform Provisions) seem to be in effect in Beijing and Shenzhen.[174] These rules appear to be inspired by the Federal Rules of Evidence of the United States.[175] It remains to be seen if "the music of the law changes[] when the musical instruments and the players are no longer the same."[176] Such question is important because "[t]he social outcome of implementing a codified law is often determined not by the form and language used in the statute or process that executes law but by the people's attitudes, expectations, and value systems regarding what ought to be restrained and what otherwise ought to be rewarded or compromised."[177]

Until 2002, the production and admissibility of evidence in China was regulated by brief provisions in the CPC. In 2002, the Supreme People's Court issued evidence regulations titled "Some Regulations concerning Evidence in Civil Litigation"[178] These sources of law categorize evidence into various categories; documentary,

169. *See, e.g.*, Stanley B. Lubman, *Dispute Resolution in China after Deng Xiaoping: "Mao and Mediation" Revisited*, 11 COLUM. J. ASIAN L. 229 (1997).

170. *See* Jun Ge, *Mediation, Arbitration and Litigation: Dispute Resolution in the People's Republic of China*, 15 UCLA PAC. BASIN L. J. 122, 123–24 (1996).

171. *Id.* at 123–24.

172. *See* Xiaobing Xu, *Different Mediation Traditions: A Comparison between China and the U.S.*, 16 AM. REV. INT'L ARB. 515, 516 n.5 (2005) (*citing* A GUIDE TO THE SEVERAL RULES ON THE HEARING OF CIVIL CASES INVOLVING PEOPLE'S MEDIATION AGREEMENT AND THE SEVERAL RULES ON THE PEOPLE'S MEDIATION WORK 15 (2002)).

173. *Id.* at 118.

174. *See* John J. Capowski, *China's Evidentiary and Procedural Reform, the Federal Rules of Evidence, and the Harmonization of Civil and Common Law*, 47 TEX. INT'L L. J. 455, 457 n.6 (2012) and accompanying text.

175. *Id.* at 473–490.

176. *Id.* at 497 (quoting Mirjan Damaska, *The Uncertain Fate of Evidentiary Transplant: Anglo-American and Continental Experiments*, 45 AM. J. COMP. L. 839, 839–40 (1997)).

177. *Id.* (quoting XIN REN, TRADITION OF THE LAW AND LAW OF THE TRADITION, STATE, AND SOCIAL CONTROL IN CHINA 7 (1997)).

178. Anthony Poon & Peng Shen, *Civil Litigation*, *in* DISPUTE RESOLUTION IN CHINA 131–32 (Michael J. Moser ed., 2012).

material, audiovisual, testimonial, statement of the parties, expert conclusions, and records of inspections.[179]

The Evidence Regulations establish a hierarchy of evidence according to its probative value. Specific kinds of documents issued by governmental and social organizations are ranked higher than all forms of evidence, and testimonial evidence appears to be given a low ranking.[180]

The PRC does not have rules on pretrial discovery.[181] In fact, a party litigant neither has the right to turn over documents nor the obligation to provide its own documents to the opposing party. Discovery appears to be alien to the Chinese legal system.[182] However, party litigants could ask the court to collect evidence from the parties. The court may also on its own motion collect evidence that it needs.[183] Although, under the Evidence Regulations, the courts could enforce their demand through contempt procedures,[184] the circumstances under which the court may seek evidence from the parties are not unlimited. These circumstances include when the parties present conflicting evidence, or the facts indicate that there might be a possible harm to a state interest or the interest of other individuals and the public, and, of course, there is a catch-all provision that gives the court the discretion to collect evidence that it deems necessary.[185]

Interestingly, the terms "burden" and "standard of proof" do not appear in the CPL. The Civil Evidence Rules contain some provisions on the burden of proof. They require the moving party to adduce evidence in support of its claim or face consequences.[186] But still the role of the court in seeking and obtaining evidence remains paramount.[187]

179. *Id.* at 132.

180. *Id.* at 132–33 ("At the risk of overgeneralization, it can be said that judges have a strong preference for written documents rather than witness statements, because they perceive that witnesses have few compunctions about giving false evidence and it is difficult for them to verify witness statements if the statement is denied by the opposing party.").

181. *Id.* at 138.

182. *Id.*

183. Chinese Civil Procedure Law, *supra* note 166, art. 64.

184. *Id.* arts. 103–104.

185. Poon & Shen, *supra* note 178, at 138.

186. Mo Zhang & Paul J. Zwier, *Burden of Proof: Developments in Modern Chinese Evidence Rules,* 10 Tulsa J. Comp. & Int'l L. 419, 436. (2003) (citing Zuigao Renmin Fayuan [Supreme People's Court], *The Several Rules of Evidence concerning Civil Litigation,* 75 Gazette of the Supreme People's Court of the People's Republic of China 1 (2002), art. 2, http://www.law-lib.com/law/law-iew.asp?id=16829)).

187. *Id.* at 435–36 ("[I]f there is no specific provision in the law or if the burden of proof could not be ascertained under the Civil Evidence Rules, or other judicial interpretation, the people's court may make a determination on the matter of the burden of proof. But it is required that the determination as such be made on the basis of principles of fairness and good faith with a consideration of the party's ability to produce the evidence.").

Under the CPL, at a trial called a "courtroom investigation," the presentation of evidence proceeded in the following manner:

(1) presentation of the statements by the parties;
(2) informing the witnesses of their rights and obligations, giving testimony by the witnesses and reading of the statements of absentee witnesses;
(3) presentation of documentary evidence, material evidence and audio-visual reference material;
(4) reading of the expert conclusions; and
(5) reading of the records of inquests.[188]

The court asks witnesses questions and may allow the parties to ask questions.[189] The word "cross-examination" appears only once in the CPL in connection with all forms of evidence, and thus is not necessarily limited to testimonial evidence.[190] The cross-examination of evidence is conducted within limits and under guidance from the court, which could also join in conducting the examination itself.[191] Indeed, some have suggested that "[t]here is no tradition of zealous advocacy [in China]. To the contrary, aggressive argument, raising of issues and propounding of rights, is viewed as being impolite."[192]

Further, under the CPL, "At the end of the court debate, a judgment shall be made according to law. Where conciliation is possible prior to the rendering of a judgment, conciliation effort may be conducted; if conciliation proves to be unsuccessful, a judgment shall be made without delay."[193] This is probably the most unusual aspect of the Chinese trial system, where conciliation is offered as an option after the trial is completed.

D. FACT-FINDING IN ISLAMIC LEGAL TRADITION

The complexity within the Islamic legal tradition and the diversity that characterizes it hardly allows any form of generalization.[194] However, some fundamental

188. Chinese Civil Procedure Law, *supra* note 166, art. 124.

189. *Id.* art. 125.

190. *Id.* art. 66. ("Evidence shall be presented in the court and cross-examined by the parties, however, evidence that involves state secrets, trade secrets or the private affairs of individuals shall not be presented in an open court session.").

191. *See* Zhang & Zwier, *supra* note 186, at 448–51 (discussing several provisions of the Evidence Rules, mainly articles 47–60).

192. Capowski, *supra* note 174, at 455, 481 (quoting Sam Hanson, *The Chinese Century: An American Judge's Observations of the Chinese Legal System*, 28 WM. MITCHELL L. REV. 243, 245 (2002)).

193. Chinese Civil Procedure Law, *supra* note 166, art. 128.

194. For a thorough treatment of the historical background and substantive prescriptions of some fundamental areas of Islamic law, see RAJ BHALA, UNDERSTANDING ISLAMIC LAW (SHARI'A) (LexisNexis 2011).

processes are worth highlighting to exemplify the cultural issues faced by international arbitration specialists when they interact with arbitrators, practitioners, and parties who come from this tradition.

The origins, sources, and doctrinal foundations and even the meaning of what is called Islamic law (sharia) are complex. As S.G. Vesey-Fitzgerald puts it:

> Law, then, in any sense in which a Western lawyer would recognize the term, is but a part of the whole Islamic system, or rather, it is not even a part but one of several inextricably combined elements thereof. Sharia, the Islamic term which is commonly rendered in English by "law" is, rather, the "Whole Duty of Man" . . . even courtesy and good manners are all part and parcel of the Sharia.[195]

At the most basic level and in its simplified form, there are four recognized classic sources of Islamic law: the Holy Quran, the authoritative Traditions about what the Prophet himself said or did, Analogy, and Consensus of the community.[196] Although, at least in theory, sharia has universal application vis-à-vis all Muslims wherever they reside, in reality there are at least six categories of countries in terms of the applicability of sharia law.[197] Officially Islamic but secular legal systems such as Iraq before 2005; Islamic majority country with secular legal system such as Jordan and Syria; secular country and legal system, such as Turkey; Islam as the basis for law applying to a segment of the population, as in for Palestinians in Israel; Islam as part of a mixed legal system such as in Pakistan; and finally Islam as the sole legal system governing all aspects of life—private and public—as in Saudi Arabia.[198]

Justice Felix Frankfurter once contrasted his court with that of the Islamic law judge, the Kadi (sometimes spelled Cadi or Qadi) by saying: "We do not sit like a Kadi under a tree dispensing justice according to considerations of individual expediency."[199] Professor Rosen comments that "As in so many other instances the image of the exotic has thus come to serve westerners as a standard against which we measure either our supposed advance along the enviable road of civilization or

195. *See id.* at xx (quoting S.G. Vesey-Fitzgerald, *Nature and Source of the Sharia, in* 1 Law in the Middle East 86 (Majid Khadduri & Herbert J. Liebesny eds., The Middle East Institute, 1955)).

196. Lawrence Rosen, The Anthropology of Justice: Law as Culture in Islamic Society 41 (Cambridge University Press 1989). *See also* David & Brierley, *supra* note 4, at 457 ("There are four sources of Muslim Law: The Koran (*Qur'an*), the sacred book of Islam; the *Sunna,* the traditional or model behavior of the prophet, God's messenger; the *ijma* or consensus of scholars of the Muslim community; and the *kiyas* (or *qiyas*), juristic reasoning by analogy.").

197. Bhala, *supra* note 194, at xxix.

198. *Id.* at xxxix–xxx.

199. Rosen, *supra* note 196, at 58. According to Professor Rosen, Justice Frankfurter was echoing what had been said a few years before by Lord Justice Goddard of the English Court of Appeals in a particular case: "The court . . . is really very much put in the position of a Cadi under the palm tree. There is no principle on which he is directed to act. He has to do the best he can in the circumstances, having no rules of law to guide him." *Id.*

our felt loss for that state of nature or social harmony we imagine simpler societies have been able to retain."[200]

Before the colonial disruption of life in the Islamic world, Professor Rosen notes that "the qadi was often seen quite-positively as a model of the ideal magistrate, a man who bespoke the common standards and beliefs of his people with just that air of grace and wisdom, that dignity of attire, manner, and utterance that called forth visions of an Old Testament sage."[201]

Qadi judicature seems to defy classification in terms of the balance between the rule of law and discretion. Traditionally Qadis enjoyed immense discretion in adjudicating cases, but their authority was not unlimited. As Rosen puts it, "Prophetic traditions, judicial analogies, and local practices" defined the contours and "provided a conceptual framework that did not so much govern a host of relationships as fashion the broad terms by which they were conceived."[202]

Qadis are traditionally appointed by political authorities, specifically the sultan, but local approval is often necessary.[203] "[T]he central goal of the qadi is to put people back into a position of negotiating their own ties, within the bounds of the permissible, and that the entire process—of fact-finding and questioning, of using experts and legal presumptions—contributes to the reinforcement of the local in the context of the judicial cognizable."[204]

Even after the advent of colonialism and adoption of European codes, which defined judicial and other forms of hierarchy, qadi justice continued with its own unique form of offering a negotiated settlement. Rosen notes:

> [T]he judge's discretion is at times clearly influenced by a sense of fairness that yields a result contrary to the clear letter of the law. At work, however, are not just the qadi's own values but an underlying concept of harm [the assessment of which is] deeply suffused by those cultural concepts that concern character of human nature, the likely harm that may be done by persons of different backgrounds and character, and a sense of locally acceptable standards that will have been drawn within the ambit of the court's consideration by a process that constantly seeks to limit judicial arbitrariness by pressing issues into the mold of the conventions of the place.[205]

In determining credibility of a witness, Rosen says, allowing for some diversity, Islamic courts tend to rely more on the "person's 'origin'" than what exactly he offers in that particular instance.[206] In other words, his credibility is judged by his position in the society,

200. *Id.*

201. *Id.*

202. *Id.*

203. *Id.*

204. *Id.*

205. *Id.* at 67.

206. *Id.* at 99–100.

his ties to others, and his prior conduct—exactly the types of character evidence that rules of evidence in some Western jurisdictions seek to exclude.[207] "The 'facts' are thus filled in more by the appraisal of the person than observable circumstances, and the experience of human nature and customary social relationships suffuse legal thought to such a degree that they are hardly noticed as sources of the law.[208] What an Arab judge deems indispensable, a British or American judge cautioned to ignore. Unless a party has put his or her character in evidence, Anglo-American law generally precludes its introduction."[209] The treatment of character evidence obviously differs from jurisdiction to jurisdiction, but such level of emphasis on character as the most important source of credibility seems to be one of many unique features of the Islamic courts.[210]

Another interesting anecdote that Rosen notes is the failure of the jury system in Morocco in the late twentieth century. He states, rather convincingly, that it was because of cultural reasons that the Moroccan jurors found it difficult to assess the credibility of witnesses and others who make presentations without having the opportunity to personally engage the witnesses in conversations and assessing them in person.[211] This shows the importance of a one-on-one relationship to assess credibility and ascertain facts.

Professor René David makes a distinction, albeit somewhat generalized, between the psychological makeup of the Muslim judge from the common law as well as the Romanist jurist in that:

> He is accustomed to . . . thinking that law is made up of individual solutions to particular cases, handed down from day to day in relation to the special needs of the moment, rather than of general principles set forth a priori from which the appropriate inference will be drawn for each fresh situation . . . . [The Muslim jurist] will avoid generalization and even definition.[212]

E. CONCLUSION

Different legal traditions have remarkably different epistemologies of determining facts. In international arbitration, a combination of these and even more legal

207. *Id.*

208. *Id.* at 100.

209. *Id.*

210. *Id.* Judges in the continental system do see character evidence as part of their inquisitorial function, but often don't share it with lay jurors who sit with them in certain criminal cases. *Id.*

211. *Id.* at 151 ("These jurors told me that it was not possible, without having such interpersonal contact, for them to determine if the person was telling the truth. And if one watches the ways in which Moroccans assess others, this is perfectly comprehensible: They simply must engage the other in direct discussion if they are to feel they have the information they need for appraising him. In the absence of such a relational mechanism jurors found themselves at a loss to decide many cases, and the whole experiment was abandoned.").

212. David & Brierley, *supra* note 4, at 462 (quoting Louis Milliot, *La pensée juridique de l'Islam*, Revue Internationale de Droit Comparé, 441–48 (1954)).

traditions frequently come together to make sense of legal disputes. The arbitrators, the parties, and their counsel come with differing assumptions of who may provide evidence, who must not; who may present evidence, who must not; who may determine credibility, who must not; and what is considered credible, what is not. The rules of procedure and evidence that are typically used in international arbitration such as the IBA Rules on the Taking of Evidence discussed below, attempt to reconcile the varying assumptions and create a common culture, but they often mask the invisible cultural barriers encountered in many cases. The challenge remains. The following chapters will further deepen the cultural inquiry.

9

Fact-Finding and Cultural Diversity in International Arbitration

The rich corpus of international arbitration literature downplays the role of culture and the impact of cultural miscommunication for the accurate determination of facts. There seems to be a generally held belief that cultural analysis or inquiry complicates an already complicated system rather than simplifying it. This might be a good approach if the status quo were to be acceptable to all. However, the increasing diversity of the users of arbitration services as well as the players are increasingly bringing the status quo under closer scrutiny.

The international arbitration literature mainly focuses on front-end and back-end jurisdictional obstacles pertaining mainly to the uncomfortable sharing of authority between national courts and international arbitral tribunals. Because international arbitration is a framework under which a multiplicity of disputes ranging from Albania to Zambia are settled, the only unifying principles are procedural in nature. No one arbitrator could possibly specialize in the laws and cultures of Albania and Zambia and all other nations in-between.

The core of international arbitration is not defining the jurisdictional parameters. To the extent jurisdictional problems arise, they are invariably occasional and unfortunate complications. One can specialize in those complications, but nonetheless, that remains a specialization in jurisdictional complications. In the great majority of cases where matters progress smoothly, and indeed, after jurisdictional complications are cleared whenever they arise, the fundamental task remains the determination of facts and the application of law. As professor John Crook eloquently formulates:

> Should they pause to reflect, most international lawyers would likely accept the thought that the science and art of deciding legal disputes involves at least three inter-related components. The first two involve determining the relevant law and the relevant facts. There comes stage three—applying the law to the facts.[1]

1. John Crook, *Fact-Finding in the Fog: Determining the Facts of Upheavals and Wars in Inter-State Disputes*, in Catherine A. Rogers & Roger P. Alford, The Future of Investment Arbitration 313, 314 (2009).

The special knowledge that is needed is familiarity with the specific applicable law and the knowledge of the cultural origin of the facts. International arbitral tribunals of all types ranging from state-to-state arbitration to simple commercial arbitration struggle with their fundamental function of determining facts. Obviously "the search for the truth is considered a—if not the—major objective of adjudication."[2]

A. "FACT-FINDING IN THE FOG"

Professor John Crook's book chapter "Fact-Finding in the Fog"[3] is just about the only recent meaningful contribution to the issue of fact-finding in international arbitration. Based on his own experience, he brings to light the profound challenges of determining facts in factually complex cases involving states. Although he believes that the challenges are more pronounced in state-to-state matters concerning facts that occurred in times of war, most of this commentary on the challenges of fact-finding apply to all forms of arbitral fact-finding where the decision-makers are total strangers to the circumstances of the facts.

Most instructively, he begins his inquiry by offering this stern warning: "'[n]othing a court does affects the public perception of its fairness so clearly' as its examination and weighing of the relevant facts."[4] Professor Crook's concern being on the determination of facts arising in wartime circumstances, he begins his essay with the following quote by Carl von Clausewitz: "The great uncertainty of all data in war is a peculiar difficulty, because all action must, to a certain extent, be planned in a mere twilight, which in addition not infrequently—like the effect of a fog or moonshine—gives to things exaggerated dimensions and unnatural appearance."[5]

The unnatural appearance that war brings about is perhaps not unique to actual war circumstances, as Professor Crook would suggest. Disputes involving years of large-scale interactions of any kind tend to obscure facts to make them appear unnatural. As stated above, Professor Crook begins with a very simple but very useful statement:

> Should they pause to reflect, most international lawyers would likely accept the thought that the science and art of deciding legal disputes involves at least three inter-related components. The first two involve determining the relevant law and the relevant facts. Then comes stage three—applying the law to the facts.[6]

2. MICHELLE T. GRANDO, EVIDENCE, PROOF, AND FACT-FINDING IN WTO DISPUTE SETTLEMENT 10 (2009) (citing, among other authorities, E.W. THOMAS, THE JUDICIAL PROCESS: REALISM, PRAGMATISM, PRACTICAL REASONING AND PRINCIPLES 327 (2005)). Grando further writes that "accurate decisions are more likely to be complied with . . . the pursuit of truth—namely, maximization of accuracy in fact-determination or simply 'accuracy'—is one of the main objectives of the process of adjudication." *Id.* at 12.

3. Crook, *supra* note 1, at 313–37.

4. *Id.* at 320 (quoting THOMAS M. FRANCK, FAIRNESS IN INTERNATIONAL LAW AND INSTITUTIONS 335 (1995)).

5. *Id.* at 313 (quoting CARL VON CLAUSEWITZ, ON WAR 138 (1976)).

6. *Id.* at 314.

These are, of course, the main tasks that arbitrators in most types of arbitration are hired to do. When the jurisdictional complications of establishing authority and identifying the law are over, the members of the tribunal must hear evidence and determine facts and apply them to the selected law.

Professor Crook's focus in this work is on inter-state disputes, but before he proceeds to the discussion of that particular issue, he suggests that the tools for the determination of facts available to investor-state tribunals help them make these fact determinations relatively easily and accurately. A commentary on this is provided below, but as to inter-state disputes, he categorically indicates that "the handful of modern international tribunals that has faced factually complex inter-state disputes has not done a particularly persuasive job of fact-finding."[7] This is not a surprising statement but he outlines the reasons very well at least in the context of the fog of war. Having surveyed some examples of cases in which the determinations of facts appeared erroneous, including in the Nicaragua case,[8] Professor Crook adds the following very instructive commentary:

> Adjudicators in inter-state cases also often show a marked preference for basing outcome on legal grounds and undisputed facts whenever possible. The life experiences of the eminent legal personalities selected to decide such cases, and the distinguished scholars who appear as advocates before them, often have centered on the study of law. Their professional forte is not likely to be vigorous and sustained (and often tedious and time consuming) inquiry into thousands of pages of documentary annexes.[9]

Continuing his most helpful commentary, he notes: "The appeal of structuring decisions so as to avoid resolving factual disputes may be particularly strong in cases rooted in activities or technical areas unfamiliar to the fact-finders."[10]

Finally, he counsels:

> Potential government litigants should regard demonstrated ability to deal with complex facts on par with a potential arbitrator's or judge's legal views.

7. *Id.* at 320. He adds his interesting observations: "Foreign ministry legal advisers generally are not fools. In assessing the relative attractions of international litigation for fact-heavy cases, they will carefully assess both the facts and the law. And well-advised legal advisers will do so, well aware of the limitations on fact-finding procedures discussed here." *Id.*

8. *Id.* at 320–23 (citing Military and Paramilitary Activities in and against Nicaragua (Nicar. v. U.S.), Judgment, 1986 I.C.J. Rep. 14 (June 27), and also citing Judge Stephen Schwebel's dissent as detailed in Stephen M. Schwebel, *Three Cases of Fact-Finding by the International Court of Justice*, *in* FACT-FINDING BEFORE INTERNATIONAL TRIBUNALS 14–19 (Richard Lillich ed., 1991)).

9. *Id.* at 325.

10. *Id.* at 326.

> For example, given the elimination of compulsory military service in many countries, modern international advocates, like those before whom they appear, are not likely to have had practical experience with military affairs. Thus, both the advocate and the decision-makers in the cases involving such matters may lack relevant factual context for assessing factual

> Participants in international litigation typically spend hours combing through the legal literature, seeking potential decision-makers' views on issues of substance. Comparable research into their experience and views in dealing with factual issues is also warranted. This assessment may be more difficult because the handling of facts may not be apparent from the face of awards or scholarly writings, but the difficulties should not be overstated. Some arbitral panels' awards, and writings and opinions of some decision-makers, show keen sensitivity to fact-finding.[11]

After properly describing the serious challenges of fact-finding in inter-state disputes, Professor Crook appears to conclude that these challenges are unique to inter-state disputes and even suggests that "investor-state arbitration should provide useful reference points for improved fact-finding in complex inter-state disputes."[12] He does not support this conclusion with any persuasive data or argument about why he thinks the investor-state arbitration process is less prone to factual errors, or even why he thinks that all of the problems that he outlines are not equally applicable to investor-state or even commercial arbitration.

The reality is that most, if not all, of the fact-finding challenges that plague the state-to-state arbitration matters affect investor-state and commercial arbitration as well. Crook makes a few rather convincing points. The first important point is what he describes as the life experiences of the eminent arbitrators and distinguished advocates who appear before them as being on the law rather than on factual matters. He also emphasizes their lack of time to sift through volumes and volumes of factual records. He, however, fails to mention that investment and commercial arbitration processes are not immune from these problems. The second point is what Crook describes as the lack of experience on certain specific technical matters. Investment and commercial arbitrators are also not immune from these problems.

> disputes. They have no personal store of experience to test what may be wholly inconsistent portrayals of complex events advanced by the parties.

Id. (citing Thomas M. Franck, *Fact-Finding in the ICJ, in* Lillich, *supra* note 8, at 22).

11. *Id.* at 329. To illustrates this point, Crook quotes from Judge Roslyn Higgins' opinion in the Oil Platforms cases:

> [T]he Court hardly deals at all with the evidence relating to the alleged use of the platform in the laying of mines. There was a huge amount of evidence presented to the Court. Some of it was direct and some of it indirect. Some of it was from several sources, some mere repetition from a single source. Some sources were partisan, some neutral. Some were reports of participants, others of those removed from the scene. Some were contemporaneous, some not. There is no attempt by the Court to sift or differentiate or otherwise examine this evidence. It merely says that it is "not sufficiently convinced" with it, without any further analysis or explanation.

Id. at 329 (quoting Separate Opinion of Judge Higgins, in Oil Platforms (Iran v. U.S.), Judgment, 2003 I.C.J. Rep. 161, ¶ 38 (Nov. 6)).

12. *Id.* at 337.

Last, he highlights arbitrators' propensity to avoid finding facts and predicating their decisions on the law and undisputed facts, and how that could contribute to factual error. Again, these phenomena also impact investment and commercial arbitrators. Overall, almost every challenge of fact-finding that Professor Crook describes affects all forms of international arbitration. Professor Crook does not address the complicating effects of cultural diversity in the determination of fact, which is the main focus of this book. A deeper inquiry into that follows.

B. CULTURE AS FACT; FACT AS CULTURE

Consider[13] the following statement by a renowned Swiss arbitrator and author Bernhard F. Meyer: "Facts remain facts, whether they are considered under Greek, German or Swiss law."[14] Is that statement true? He said this in the context of a cultural misunderstanding that he confronted as the chair of an arbitral tribunal composed of two Greek law professors and two Greek parties represented by two Greek lawyers. Meyer is Swiss. A few lines down from that statement, he also says: "The good thing in this process was that once I [the chair] made an independent decision as to the facts underlying a given issue, the two co-arbitrators, most of the time, were able to agree with each other as to the legal consequences thereof."[15] Contrary to what he proposes when saying "facts are facts whether Greek or Swiss," the outcome is interesting; the chair makes the findings of fact and the two sides agree on the legal consequences. That is often the case, but the problem is the assumption that the findings of fact are accurate just because the two sides had no choice but to accept the conclusion.

There is no doubt that the Greek lawyers on each side probably understood both the facts and the law better than the chair, but they had agreed to accept the findings of the chair; that was the deal they made when they agreed to the arbitration clause. Ironically, the facts are determined by the most ignorant of all the parties. In other words, the reality is that the parties often know exactly what happened between them but they present their stories in the most misleading manner to the chair in the course of the proceedings to help the chances of success for their respective side.

Indeed, even in judicial proceedings where facts are less culturally indeterminable, as Professor David Chavkin puts it, "[w]hile lawyers cannot knowingly present false testimony, it is often impossible to know exactly what happened in and around an event."[16] He notes, for example, in a divorce case both the husband and wife may tell a lawyer an honest account of the events that led to the divorce.

13. This subtitle of this subsection is an adaptation of LAW AS CULTURE AND CULTURE AS LAW: ESSAYS IN HONOR OF JOHN PHILLIP REID (Hendrik Hartog & William E. Nelson eds., 2000).

14. BERNHARD BERGER & MICHAEL E. SCHNEIDER, INSIDE THE BLACK BOX: HOW ARBITRAL TRIBUNALS OPERATE AND REACH THEIR DECISIONS (ASA SPECIAL SERIES NO. 42), at 61 (Juris 2014).

15. *Id.*

16. DAVID F. CHAVKIN, CLINICAL LEGAL EDUCATION: A TEXTBOOK FOR LAW SCHOOL CLINICAL PROGRAMS 42–43 (LexisNexis, 2002).

Although they could be completely contradictory and cannot be true at the same time, both accounts could also be honestly believed to be true by the affiants. He notes further that "[b]oth stories cannot be completely accurate, but both stories may be honestly told. And the 'truth,' if it could be divided, might be contained in either story or might be contained equally in both."[17] To strengthen his proposition, he cites the famous Japanese classic film *Rashomon* (which is based on two short stories by Ryunosuke Akutagawa, directed by Akira Kurosawa), in which several people seeking to obtain shelter at the crumbling "Rashomon Gate" in Kyoto tell a story about a woman's rape and her husband's murder. Although all of them are talking about the same events, the accounts are considerably divergent. In some cases, those who proclaim that they "don't tell lies" provided second statements that directly contradicted their first.[18] In conclusion, Chavkin's remarks:

> Which of the stories is "true?" Are any of the stories "true?" And, how would we, as the audience for the various stories, make that determination? As critic James Berardinelli has noted, the film reminds us of "the inability for any one man to know the truth, no matter how clearly he thinks he sees things."[19]

The final and most profound conclusion: "Perspective distorts reality and makes the absolute truth unknowable."[20] To emphasize the profound difficulty that fact-finders often encounter, he reproduces a brilliant cartoon representation of a jury deliberation room where the statement reads under the title "The completely honest jury . . . ": "We find the plaintiff's lawyer's half-truths and innuendoes easier to swallow than the defendant's lawyer's half-truth and innuendoes . . . ."[21]

And, of course, culture's exponentially complicating effect cannot be denied. Its very subtle and uneven impact cannot be overstated. Consider this Valentine's Day NPR Report about a scientific research certain university researchers from Stony Brooks conducted. At the risk of sounding random, here is the story: traditionally, Western societies have believed that their conception of romantic love is not shared by other societies, such as the Eastern societies. Certain cultures in India, for example, have discouraged or even prohibited romantic love before marriage. Close relationship research was done on more than 175 societies. The finding, as reported by NPR on Valentine's Day 2014, was "remarkable" because the answer to the research question of "whether every society loves the same way" was yes. The researchers felt as though they needed a caveat though, and they concluded that in the poems and other forms of expressions of love, these other societies

17. *Id.* at 43.

18. *Id.*

19. *Id.*

20. *Id.* (emphasis added).

21. *Id.*

such as China and India emphasize the negative aspects of love, such as broken hearts and perhaps infidelity, etc. Significantly, the researchers were so curious about this issue that they actually conducted a scientific study using MRI brain imaging. They recruited couples who were in love from the United States on the one hand and lovers from China on the other. They administered the brain imagining while asking them to think about their respective lovers. What they found was "astonishing." The parts of the brain responsible for love, infatuation, and some such emotions reacted in exactly the same way. A press release by Stony Brook University concluded that:

> Unlike past research based on questionnaires showing cultural differences, this study found that the patterns of brain responsible were extremely similar for Chinese and Americans. For people intensely in love in both cultures, viewing images of the beloved elicited brain activations in the midbrain dopamine-rich reward/motivation system (a system closely related to drug addiction) including the Ventral Tegmental Area (VTA) and caudate.[22]

It is indeed interesting to see that scientists needed a machine to confirm that different people love the same way. The questions they administered apparently yielded different results. In fact, these results led them to believe that people might love differently, or some may not love at all. This, of course, makes sense when reinforced by old stereotypes. The extent of cultural miscommunication and misunderstanding has no boundaries.

C. INTERPRETATION AND APPLICATION OF LAW AS A CULTURAL PRACTICE

The cultural analysis of law generally is not a new area of curiosity.[23] As Professor Naomi Mezey notes, "Law can be seen as one (albeit very powerful) institutional cultural actor whose agents (legislators, judges, civil servants, citizens) order and reorder meanings."[24] The core idea behind it is that "social practices are not logically separable

22. Press Release, Stony Brook News, SBU Researchers and Colleagues Find That in the Brain, Early-Stage Intense Passionate Love Seems to Be Universal (May 28, 2010), http://commcgi.cc.stonybrook.edu/am2/publish/General_University_News_2/SBU_Researchers_And_Colleagues_Find_That_In_The_Brain_Early-Stage_Intense_Passionate_Love_Seems_To_Be_Universal.shtml.

23. There is a respectable body of literature addressing law, social thoughts, and jurisprudence, which include Cultural Pluralism, Identity Politics, and the Law (Austin Sarat & Thomas R. Kearns eds., 1999); and the same editors' two prior books, namely, Law in the Domain of Culture (Austin Sarat & Thomas R. Kearns eds., 1998) and Law in Everyday Life (Austin Sarat & Thomas R. Kearns eds., 1993); Paul W. Kahn, The Cultural Study of Law: Reconstructing Legal Scholarship (1999); Legal Studies as Cultural Studies: A Reader in (post) Modern Critical Theory (Jerry Leonard ed., 1995); Renato Rosaldo, Culture and Truth: The Remaking of Social Analysis (1993).

24. Naomi Mezey, *Law as Culture*, 13 Yale J.L. & Human. 35, 45 (2001).

from the laws that shape them and that social practices are unintelligible apart from the legal norms that give rise to them."[25] Consider the traffic stop examples she gives much later in the essay. Scientific studies conducted in the early 1990s suggested that although only 5 percent of the drivers on a certain Florida highway were persons of color, they constituted 70 percent of those stopped for traffic violations.[26] This certainly is a cultural phenomenon, but it is enabled or at least tolerated by the law.[27] As an example of culture shaping law, she cites the U.S. Supreme Court's invocation of popular culture in upholding *Miranda v. Arizona*[28] in *Dickerson v. United States*,[29] in which it said the *Miranda*-warning "has become embedded in routine police practice to the point where warnings have become part of our national culture."[30] Then,

> If law is culture, then all interpretations of law are cultural interpretations . . . . This interpretation employs "thick description" to give a complex account of the slippage between the production and the reception of law and legal meanings, of the ways in which specific cultural practices or identities coincide or collide with specific legal rules or conventions, thereby altering the meanings of both.[31]

More usefully for our purposes, she notes that "institutionally legal actors participate in creating culturally specific meanings . . . ."[32]

Consider this statement: "It is out of the most ordinary acts that law is constituted as law."[33] It emphasizes the importance of ordinary day-to-day acts as the underlying sources of the nature of law, which Professor Mezey calls "lived experience."[34] In her review of Patricia Ewick and Susan Silbey's book, *The Common Place of Law: Stories from Everyday Life*, she notes,

> Although it generally appears in its reified form as a seemingly external object, at heart the law is the accumulation of the tiny and intimate acts of people

25. *Id.* at 45 ("Put generally, law shapes individual and group identity, social practices as well as the meaning of cultural symbols, but all of these things (culture in its myriad manifestations) also shape law by changing what is socially desirable, politically feasible, legally legitimate.").

26. *Id.* at 53.

27. *Id. See, e.g.*, Whren v. United States, 517 U.S. 806 (1996) (holding that a stop on the basis of a minor violation is considered reasonable under the Fourth Amendment even if it is pretextual).

28. Miranda v. Arizona, 384 U.S. 436 (1966).

29. Dickerson v. United States, 530 U.S. 428 (2000).

30. *Id.* at 438.

31. Mezey, *supra* note 24, at 58.

32. *Id.*

33. Naomi Mezey, *Out of the Ordinary: Law, Power, Culture, and Commonplace*, 26 L. & So. Inquiry 145, 146 (2001) (reviewing Patricia Ewick & Susan Silbey, The Common Place of Law: Stories from Everyday Life (1998)).

34. *Id.* at 145.

> as they go about their business and try to make sense of the world; in other words, the law is the embodiment of social practices.[35]

Law as a deeply cultural phenomenon is beautifully captured by W.H. Auden's poem, "Law, Like Love," partially reproduced in Mezey's review but fully reproduced in *The Common Place of Law*. It reads:

> Law, say the gardeners, is the sun,
> Law is the one
> All gardeners obey
> To-morrow, yesterday, to-day.
>
> Law is the wisdom of the old,
> The impotent grandfathers feebly scold;
> The grandchildren put out a treble tongue,
> Law is the senses of the young.
>
> Law, says the priest with a priestly look,
> Expounding to an unpriestly people,
> Law is the words in my priestly book,
> Law is my pulpit and my steeple.
>
> Law, says the judge as he looks down his nose,
> Speaking clearly and most severely,
> Law is as I've told you before,
> Law is as you know I suppose,
> Law is but let me explain it once more,
> Law is The Law.
>
> Yet law-abiding scholars write:
> Law is neither wrong nor right,
> Law is only crimes
> Punished by places and by times,
> Law is the clothes men wear
> Anytime, anywhere,
> Law is Good morning and Good night.
>
> Others say, Law is our Fate;
> Others say, Law is our State;
> Others say, others say
> Law is no more,
> Law has gone away.

35. *Id.* at 149–50 (citing W.H. Auden (1966, 154) (suggesting that Auden attributes this view to literature as far back as 1939).

> And always the loud angry crowd,
> Very angry and very loud,
> Law is We,
> And always the soft idiot softly Me.[36]

One of the most important points that emerges from *The Common Place of Law* and Mezey's review is that "law has little meaning once it is divorced from those who find it meaningful."[37]

As Mezey aptly characterizes Ewick and Silbey's work, "legal consciousness" is basically "cultural practice."[38] She elaborates in the following terms: "Legal consciousness as cultural practice attempts to integrate human agency and structural constraint by showing how individual understandings and social interactions aggregate to partly shape institutions (agency) while institutions and larger social structures provide the foundations for the constraints on individual understanding and social interaction."[39] The key here is that legal consciousness emphasizes "the finite and limited range of options available to people in either fashioning their interpretations or choosing their behaviors."[40] In her subsequent writings, she warns that "law tends to reproduce the culture of the dominate group."[41] She does, however, reject any suggestion that "culture becomes visible to law only when law must adjudicate the rights and claims of [] cultural others."[42] That is because, according to her, even in

> merry old England, when one might have spoken non-ironically of an "English people", if one were a woman, a slave, a peasant, working class or non-Christian, if one did not have access to law and power, culture was not invisible, nor was the role that law played in forging one's identities and the boundaries of one's communities.[43]

36. W.H. Auden, *Law, Like Love,* http://www.poemhunter.com/poem/law-like-love/ (last visited Apr. 11, 2016); *see also* W.H. Auden (1939), *reprinted in* Patricia Ewick & Susan S. Silbey, The Common Place of Law: Stories from Everyday Life (1998) (in the first pages of the text))

37. Mezey, *supra* note 33, at 150 n.5. She attributes this to Karl Llewellyn, *Some Realism about Realism—Responding to Dean Pound,* Harv. L. Rev. 44, 1222, 1248–50 (1931). Mezey, *supra.*

38. Mezey, *supra* note 33, at 151.

39. *Id.*

40. *Id.*

41. Naomi Mezey, *Law's Culture and Lived Culture: A Comment on Roger Cotterrell's "The Struggle for Law: Some Dilemmas of Cultural Legality,?,"* 4 Int'l J.L. Context 395, 398 (2008). Her notes indicate that the authors she was reviewing suggested that multiculturalism necessitated the inquiry, but she yet again emphasizes "culture has always been at the heart of law and vice versa and that it matters how we think about the relationship of law and culture." *Id.* at 396.

42. *Id.* at 397.

43. *Id.*

To bring it to the world of international arbitration consider this: "The most serious bias in our world of international arbitration is the one that we are least aware of," says Phillip Capper speaking at an arbitration conference in Zurich in February 2013. Repeating the emphasis he notes:

> The most serious bias confronting this group of people in this room or any discussion of international arbitration is the unspoken, often unrecognized legal culture bias; that we bring our formation into the room with us and do not even realize it is there. I have been horrified especially by my co-English arbitrators who have not realized that the English solution is simply an English solution. They may think it is universal, perfect, objective and to be admired and they are wrong on all counts in some cases. Take, for example, some attitudes to privilege amongst English arbitrators. It is this unspoken, unrealized type of bias which seems to me to be the most significant.[44]

44. Phillip Capper, *Dealing with Bias and Obstruction*, *in* Bernhard Berger & Michael E. Schneider, Inside the Black Box: How Arbitral Tribunals Operate and Reach Their Decisions (ASA Special Series No. 42, at 46 (2014) (emphasis in original).

10

The Typical Process for Selection and Challenge of Arbitrators

The processes and rules on the selection and challenge of arbitrators around the world show some common characteristics. This chapter profiles and critics the most widely adopted Model Law of the United Nations Commission on International Trade Law (UNCITRAL Model Law) and the most widely used institutional rules of the International Court of Arbitration of the International Chamber of Commerce (ICC Rules) as a background to the cultural critic of the prevailing elitist approach in the following chapter.

A. APPOINTMENT AND CHALLENGE

1. Appointment

The UNCITRAL Model Law together with the ICC Rules on appointment and challenge offer a fairly representational overview of the dominant protocol for the appointment and challenge of arbitrators in commercial arbitration.

The core of the UNCITRAL Model Law on appointment is Article 9. It provides:

1. If three arbitrators are to be appointed, each party shall appoint one arbitrator. The two arbitrators thus appointed shall choose the third arbitrator who will act as the presiding arbitrator of the arbitral tribunal.
2. If within 30 days after the receipt of a party's notification of the appointment of an arbitrator the other party has not notified the first party of the arbitrator it has appointed, the first party may request the appointing authority to appoint the second arbitrator.
3. If within 30 days after the appointment of the second arbitrator the two arbitrators have not agreed on the choice of the presiding arbitrator, the presiding arbitrator shall be appointed by the appointing authority in the same way as a sole arbitrator would be appointed under article 8.[1]

1. G.A. Res. 65/22, UNCITRAL Arbitration Rules as revised in 2010, at art. 9 (2010), https://www.uncitral.org/pdf/english/texts/arbitration/arb-rules-revised/arb-rules-revised-2010-e.pdf

The Culture of International Arbitration. Won L. Kidane

It sets forth the most familiar rule on the process of appointment of three arbitrators. The process for the appointment of sole arbitrators is more or less the same. Sub-article 1 of Article 9 anticipates a smooth process, and in many cases it works. It works either because the parties genuinely agree, or mostly because they want to avoid the risk of a forced appointment by the appointing authority. Under the UNCITRAL Model Law, the default power for the designation of the appointing authority is that of the Secretary-General of the Permanent Court of Arbitration at The Hague (PCA).[2]

There is some guidance as to who may be appointed as chair or presiding arbitrator. The two most important considerations are: (1) seeking the opinion of the parties and the potential appointees, and (2) the avoidance of appointing a national of one of the parties.[3]

The ICC Rules on the appointment of arbitrators are similar:

> 4) Where the parties have agreed that the dispute shall be resolved by three arbitrators, each party shall nominate in the Request and the Answer, respectively, one arbitrator for confirmation. If a party fails to nominate an arbitrator, the appointment shall be made by the Court. 5) Where the dispute is to be referred to three arbitrators, the third arbitrator, who will act as president of the arbitral tribunal, shall be appointed by the Court, unless the parties have agreed upon another procedure for such appointment, in which case the nomination will be subject to confirmation pursuant to Article 13. Should such procedure not result in a nomination within 30 days from the confirmation or appointment of the co-arbitrators or any other time limit agreed by the parties or fixed by the Court, the third arbitrator shall be appointed by the Court.[4]

The default appointment authority resides in the ICC Court. Indeed, the Court also has the default authority to appoint both the second and third arbitrators if one of the parties fails to exercise its right of appointment for whatever reason. It is not uncommon

(also on the report of the Sixth Committee, U.N. Doc A/65/465) [hereinafter UNCITRAL Model Law].

2. UNCITRAL Model Law, art. 6 ("2. If all parties have not agreed on the choice of an appointing authority within 30 days after a proposal made in accordance 7 with paragraph 1 has been received by all other parties, any party may request the Secretary-General of the PCA to designate the appointing authority.").

3. UNCITRAL Model Law, art. 6(5)&(7) reads, in relevant part:

> 5. In exercising their functions under these Rules, the appointing authority and the Secretary-General of the PCA may require from any party and the arbitrators the information they deem necessary and they shall give the parties and, where appropriate, the arbitrators, an opportunity to present their views in any manner they consider appropriate. All such communications to and from the appointing authority and the Secretary-General of the PCA shall also be provided by the sender to all other parties.
>
> 7. The appointing authority shall have regard to such considerations as are likely to secure the appointment of an independent and impartial arbitrator and shall take into account the advisability of appointing an arbitrator of a nationality other than the nationalities of the parties.

4. International Chamber of Commerce [ICC] Rules of Arbitration, art. 13(4)&(5) (in force as of Jan. 1, 2012) [hereinafter ICC Rules].

for a reluctant party's fate to be determined by three arbitrators that it has not chosen. This usually happens when the non-appointing party has an objection over the constitution of the tribunal, whether because it never agreed to or contests the existence or the validity of the arbitration agreement. At times, when governments of developing countries are the respondents, they fail to take the process seriously, or because they reject the very idea of being judged by private individuals that they have not selected or agreed to their selection. The source of this problem usually is the agreement and what is read into it. As far as developing countries are involved, most of the contracts they sign are form contracts brought by their foreign economic partners. These form contracts contain boilerplate arbitration clauses that are often overlooked. These boilerplate clauses often select one of the commonly selected European seats and also select one of the most commonly selected institutions, such as the ICC, to administer the case. The institutions also relentlessly promote their services while providing only limited information about who exactly the potential arbitrators would be. Only recently has the ICC decided to even publish the names of the arbitrators in ICC arbitration.[5] Even access to its statistics is limited to fee-paying subscribers.

A combination of institutional service promotion, their rules on default appointment, the economic hierarchy of economic partners, the power of the pen of parties that come from the developed world coupled with a developing country's lack of information, and complicity and even negligence have resulted in the appointment, in every area, of a disproportionate number of arbitrators from the developed world, which in turn contributed to the developing countries' arbitration-phobia; a fear of being misunderstood and presumed guilty.

2. Challenge

Under the UNCITRAL Model Law, an arbitrator may be challenged "if circumstances exist that give rise to justifiable doubts as to the arbitrator's impartiality or independence."[6] The ultimate decisional power rests with the appointing authority, which, in many cases is one selected by the secretary-general of the PCA.[7] A situation whereby

5. *See ICC Court Announces New Policies to Foster Transparency and Ensure Greater Efficiency*, ICC (Jan. 5, 2016), http://www.iccwbo.org/News/Articles/2016/ICC-Court-announces-new-policies-to-foster-transparency-and-ensure-greater-efficiency/ ("The Court will from now on publish on its website the names of the arbitrators sitting in ICC cases, their nationality, as well as whether the appointment was made by the Court or by the parties and which arbitrator is the tribunal chairperson. This new policy will apply to all cases registered as from January 1 2016. This information will be published once the tribunal is constituted and updated in case of changes in the tribunal's composition—without however mentioning the reason for the change. This information will remain on the website once the case is terminated. In order not to compromise expectations of confidentiality that may be important to the parties, the case reference number and the names of the parties and of counsel will not be published. Parties will, by mutual agreement, have the option of opting out of this limited disclosure. They may also request the Court to publish additional information about a particular case.").

6. UNCITRAL Model Law, art. 12(1).

7. UNCITRAL Model Law, art. 13(4) ("If, within 15 days from the date of the notice of challenge, all parties do not agree to the challenge or the challenged arbitrator does not withdraw, the party

the appointing authority is asked to decide on a challenge of its own appointee does sometimes occur. It naturally occurs more frequently in default appointment cases.

Under the ICC Rules, the ICC Court has the power to decide on the challenge of arbitrators whether for reasons of lack of impartiality or independence.[8] The Court has enormous power both for appointment and challenges, but when the appointment power is read in conjunction with the power of deciding a challenge, a situation of challenge of the Court's own appointment arises. Indeed, in cases of default appointments, the Court is often asked to decide a challenge on its own appointees. This was exactly what happened in the *Salini v. Ethiopia* case discussed at length in Chapter 3. The prospect of succeeding in such types of challenges is not promising.

The dominant rules and institutions promote a particular form of arbitration in particular places, and perhaps unintentionally also promote arbitrators from particular places and make the appointment process easy, including default appointments—while at the same time granting the decision-making power on challenge to the very authority that appointed the arbitrators. In effect, the process from beginning to end grants profound power to arbitrators, but makes their challenge and removal difficult. They have the power to decide on their own jurisdiction as a matter of the universally accepted principle of competence-competence. Moreover, some rules even grant tribunals the jurisdiction to decide on the challenge of one or more of the arbitrators. Courts of law defer to the decisions of arbitral tribunals except in very limited circumstances discussed in previous chapters. The entire system is thus predicated on one fundamental assumption: the ability to select arbitrators with the required competence, impartiality, fairness, and integrity. Whenever that assumption fails to hold true, justice miserably suffers.

3. The Conduct of Arbitration

Arbitrators have significant discretion on matters of procedure and evidence,[9] but they have some guidance specially in institutional arbitration cases. The UNCITRAL

making the challenge may elect to pursue it. In that case, within 30 days from the date of the notice of challenge, it shall seek a decision on the challenge by the appointing authority.").

8. ICC Rules, art. 14. The entirety of the provision reads:

> 1) A challenge of an arbitrator, whether for an alleged lack of impartiality or independence, or otherwise, shall be made by the submission to the Secretariat of a written statement specifying the facts and circumstances on which the challenge is based. 2) For a challenge to be admissible, it must be submitted by a party either within 30 days from receipt by that party of the notification of the appointment or confirmation of the arbitrator, or within 30 days from the date when the party making the challenge was informed of the facts and circumstances on which the challenge is based if such date is subsequent to the receipt of such notification. 3) The Court shall decide on the admissibility and, at the same time, if necessary, on the merits of a challenge after the Secretariat has afforded an opportunity for the arbitrator concerned, the other party or parties and any other members of the arbitral tribunal to comment in writing within a suitable period of time. Such comments shall be communicated to the parties and to the arbitrators.

9. *See, e.g.*, UNCITRAL Model Law, art. 17 ("Subject to these Rules, the arbitral tribunal may conduct the arbitration in such manner as it considers appropriate, provided that the parties are treated

Model Law and the ICC Rules, coupled with the International Bar Association Rules on the Taking of Evidence, are representatives of contemporary trend.

A. The UNCITRAL Model Law Rules on Procedure and Evidence

The UNCITRAL Model Law grants broad discretion to the arbitral tribunal to decide on issues of procedure and evidence. It anticipates that the presentation of evidence would be necessary, but it leaves the manner of its presentation to the parties and the discretion of the tribunal.[10] If, however, the tribunal decides to hear witness testimony, the only guidance that the Model Law offers is the following provision: "Witnesses, including expert witnesses, may be heard under the conditions and examined in the manner set by the arbitral tribunal."[11] It is totally deferential to the tribunal.

The composition of the tribunal essentially determines all aspects of the taking of evidence as long as basic due process rules are not violated. Tribunals composed of jurists from various traditions frequently fail to agree on matters of procedure and evidence. This is often exacerbated by the presence of counsel appearing on both sides coming with different notions of the presentation of evidence. Thus culturally diverse tribunals inevitably face the problem of reconciling irreconcilable and strongly held notions of what is appropriate and what is not. It could be on matters as fundamental as whether counsel should prepare witnesses before cross-examination. Whether written witness statements should be admissible or not if the witness fails to appear for cross- examination due to no fault of himself or the party that presented him. Whether the submission of a "without prejudice" settlement agreement should result in the exclusion of the evidence, or even the recusal of the members of the tribunal. Whether a witness who submitted a statement should be allowed to submit her statement orally through the aid of counsel in a form of examination-in-chief before cross examination. Whether opposing counsel should be allowed re-cross, and if so, how about a second rehabilitation? National laws of procedure and evidence would ordinarily have answers to these questions, and the answers are always deeply rooted in legal tradition. Each considers its way of doing things superior. When traditions mix, confusion is often the end result, but it is rarely recognized or acknowledged. Terms of reference drafted by tribunals often give the impression that the parties and tribunal are agreed as to certain common standards, but they can never take the years of training in a particular tradition and

with equality and that at an appropriate stage of the proceedings each party is given a reasonable opportunity of presenting its case. The arbitral tribunal, in exercising its discretion, shall conduct the proceedings so as to avoid unnecessary delay and expense and to provide a fair and efficient process for resolving the parties' dispute.").

10. UNCITRAL Model Law, art. 17(3) ("If at an appropriate stage of the proceedings any party so requests, the arbitral tribunal shall hold hearings for the presentation of evidence by witnesses, including expert witnesses, or for oral argument. In the absence of such a request, the arbitral tribunal shall decide whether to hold such hearings or whether the proceedings shall be conducted on the basis of documents and other materials.").

11. UNCITRAL Model Law, art. 28(2).

culture out of all the participants. The outcome of the case is thus determined not only by the objective strength of the merits, but also largely by the perception of the members of the tribunal about the veracity and propriety of the presentation of evidence as well as the credibility of the presenters, who may be misunderstood because of the tribunal's misapprehension of their culture.

b. ICC Rules on Procedure and Evidence

The ICC Rules on Procedure and Evidence do not offer a particularly useful solution to the complicating effects of cultural diversity in the evaluation and admission of evidence for the purpose of determination of facts and identification and application of law in international arbitration. Article 25 of the Rules provide the following:

> Establishing the Facts of the Case
>
> 1) The arbitral tribunal shall proceed within as short a time as possible to establish the facts of the case by all appropriate means. 2) After studying the written submissions of the parties and all documents relied upon, the arbitral tribunal shall hear the parties together in person if any of them so requests or, failing such a request, it may of its own motion decide to hear them. 3) The arbitral tribunal may decide to hear witnesses, experts appointed by the parties or any other person, in the presence of the parties, or in their absence provided they have been duly summoned. 4) The arbitral tribunal, after having consulted the parties, may appoint one or more experts, define their terms of reference and receive their reports. At the request of a party, the parties shall be given the opportunity to question at a hearing any such expert. 5) At any time during the proceedings, the arbitral tribunal may summon any party to provide additional evidence. 6) The arbitral tribunal may decide the case solely on the documents submitted by the parties unless any of the parties requests a hearing.[12]

The ICC Rules, just like the UNCITRAL Model Law, grant the tribunal enormous discretion to determine the facts by using all means that it deems appropriate. The Rules anticipate that the tribunal would decide whether it would be satisfied to determine the facts solely on the submission of documentary evidence or written evidence, or if it would require hearing witnesses. If, in its discretion, and presumably in consultation of the parties, it decides to hear witnesses, the guidance that it gets from the Rules is limited to the following: "The arbitral tribunal shall be in full charge of the hearings, at which all the parties shall be entitled to be present."[13] Being in full charge means whatever the members of the tribunal deem appropriate. There is nothing that would help them reconcile their differing views on the

12. ICC Rules, art. 25.

13. ICC Rules, art. 26 (3). The entirety of the provision reads:

> Article 26: Hearings
>
> 1) When a hearing is to be held, the arbitral tribunal, giving reasonable notice, shall summon the parties to appear before it on the day and at the place fixed by it. 2) If any of the parties, although duly summoned, fails to appear without valid excuse, the arbitral tribunal shall have

admissibility, presentation, and even weighing of evidence. It is all determined by the balance of power on the tribunal, be it quantitatively or otherwise.

But again, being in full charge, the tribunal will often rely on the terms of reference that it must adopt under Article 23(1)(g) of the ICC Rules.[14] Tribunals usually incorporate a set of rules on the taking of evidence by reference. The most frequently referenced set of rules are the IBA Rules on the Taking of Evidence. The following section takes a brief look at these rules to see if they alleviate the complicating effects of cultural diversity in the international arbitral decision-making process.

4. The IBA Rules on the Taking of Evidence in International Arbitration

At their very core, the IBA Rules of Evidence are designed to "reflect procedures in use in many different legal systems, and they may be particularly useful when the parties come from different legal cultures."[15] They are supposed to be representative of the legal cultures of the users of international arbitration globally, but a look at the key players tells a slightly different story, with virtually no representation[16] outside of the Western cultures on the various committees that created the rules.[17]

> the power to proceed with the hearing. 3) The arbitral tribunal shall be in full charge of the hearings, at which all the parties shall be entitled to be present. Save with the approval of the arbitral tribunal and the parties, persons not involved in the proceedings shall not be admitted. 4) The parties may appear in person or through duly authorized representatives. In addition, they may be assisted by advisers.

14. ICC Rules, art. 23(1)(g) ("particulars of the applicable procedural rules and, if such is the case, reference to the power conferred upon the arbitral tribunal to act as amiable compositeur or to decide ex aequo et bono.").

15. International Bar Association [IBA] Rules on the Taking of Evidence in International Arbitration (adopted by IBA Council May 29, 2010), http://www.ibanet.org/Search/Default.aspx?q=Arbitration%20Evidence [hereinafter IBA Rules of Evidence]. See also the Preamble, *id.* at 4, which reads:

> These IBA Rules on the Taking of Evidence in International Arbitration are intended to provide an efficient, economical and fair process for the taking of evidence in international arbitrations, particularly those between Parties from different legal traditions. They are designed to supplement the legal provisions and the institutional, ad hoc or other rules that apply to the conduct of the arbitration.

16. To be fair, among the key players, there are two Chinese, one Japanese, one from the Middle East, and two from Latin America. To be sure, there is no one from Africa. See IBA Rules of Evidence, at i–v. All of their names are reproduced in the next footnote.

17. See IBA Rules of Evidence, at i–v. Members of the Working Party are David W. Rivkin, Chair, SBL Committee D (Arbitration and ADR), Debevoise & Plimpton LLP, New York, USA; Wolfgang Kühn, Former Chair, SBL Committee D, Heuking Kühn Lüer Wojtek, Düsseldorf, Germany; Giovanni M. Ughi, Chair, Ughi e Nunziante Studio Legale, Milan, Italy; Hans Bagner, Advokatfirman Vinge KB, Stockholm, Sweden; John Beechey, International Chamber of Commerce, Paris, France; Jacques Buhart, Herbert Smith LLP, Paris, France; Peter S. Caldwell, Caldwell Ltd, Hong Kong; Bernardo

Substantively, the rules attempt to come up with solutions to some commonly faced problems of cultural diversity—at least within the Western world. The default position, just like the UNCITRAL Model Law and ICC Rules, is great deference to the tribunal,[18] with a consultation requirement.[19]

The IBA Rules of Evidence address one of the most contentious subjects first, that is, document disclosure or discovery. The IBA Rules certainly err on the side of more production, leaning toward broad American-style discovery.

The core principle is set forth in Article 3(3) of the IBA Rules:

> A Request to Produce shall contain: (a) (i) a description of each requested Document sufficient to identify it, or (ii) a description in sufficient detail (including subject matter) of a narrow and specific requested category of Documents that are reasonably believed to exist; in the case of Documents maintained in electronic form, the requesting Party may, or the Arbitral Tribunal may order that it shall be required to, identify specific files, search terms, individuals or other

M. Cremades, B Cremades y Asociados, Madrid, Spain; Emmanuel Gaillard, Shearman & Sterling LLP, Paris, France; Paul A. Gélinas, Gélinas & Co., Paris, France; Hans van Houtte, Katholieke Universiteit Leuven, Leuven, Belgium; Pierre A. Karrer, Zurich, Switzerland; Jan Paulsson, Freshfields Bruckhaus Deringer LLP, Paris, France; Hilmar Raeschke-Kessler, Rechtsanwalt beim Bundesgerichtshof, Karlsruhe-Ettlingen, Germany; V. V. Veeder, QC, Essex Court Chambers, London, England; O. L. O. de Witt Wijnen, Nauta Dutilh, Rotterdam, Netherlands. Members of the IBA Rules of Evidence Review Subcommittee are: Richard H. Kreindler, Chair, Review Subcommittee, Shearman & Sterling LLP, Frankfurt, Germany; David Arias, Pérez-Llorca, Madrid, Spain; C. Mark Baker, Fulbright & Jaworski LLP, Houston, Texas, USA; Pierre Bienvenu, Co-Chair 2008–2009, Arbitration Committee, Ogilvy Renault LLP, Montréal, Canada; Amy Cohen Kläsener, Review Subcommittee Secretary, Shearman & Sterling LLP, Frankfurt, Germany; Antonias Dimolitsa, Antonias Dimolitsa & Associates, Athens, Greece; Paul Friedland, White & Case LLP, New York, USA; Nicolás Gamboa, Gamboa & Chalela Abogados, Bogotá, Colombia; Judith Gill, QC, Co-Chair 2010–2011, Arbitration Committee, Allen & Overy LLP, London, England; Peter Heckel, Hengeler Mueller Partnerschaft von Rechtsanwälten, Frankfurt, Germany; Stephen Jagusch, Allen & Overy LLP, London, England; Xiang Ji, Fangda Partners, Beijing & Shanghai, China; Kap-You (Kevin) Kim, Bae, Kim & Lee LLC, Seoul, South Korea; Toby T. Landau, QC, Essex Court Chambers, London, England; Alexis Mourre, Castaldi Mourre & Partners, Paris, France; Hilmar Raeschke-Kessler, Rechtsanwalt beim Bundesgerichtshof, Karlsruhe-Ettlingen, Germany; David W. Rivkin, Debevoise & Plimpton LLP, New York, USA; Georg von Segesser, Schellenberg Wittmer, Zurich, Switzerland; Essam Al Tamimi, Al Tamimi & Company, Dubai, UAE; Guido S. Tawil, Co-Chair 2009–2010, Arbitration Committee, M& M Bomchil Abogados, Buenos Aires, Argentina; Hiroyuki Tezuka, Nishimura & Asahi, Tokyo, Japan; Ariel Ye, King & Wood, Beijing, China. Most notably, these members are representatives—in the words of the introductory part of the Rules—from "over 2,300 members from over 90 countries" *Id.* at 1 (About the Arbitration Committee).

18. IBA Rules of Evidence, *supra* note 15, art. 1(5).

> Insofar as the IBA Rules of Evidence and the General Rules are silent on any matter concerning the taking of evidence and the Parties have not agreed otherwise, the Arbitral Tribunal shall conduct the taking of evidence as it deems appropriate, in accordance with the general principles of the IBA Rules of Evidence.

19. *See id.* art. 2.

means of searching for such Documents in an efficient and economical manner; (b) a statement as to how the Documents requested are relevant to the case and material to its outcome; and (c) (i) a statement that the Documents requested are not in the possession, custody or control of the requesting Party or a statement of the reasons why it would be unreasonably burdensome for the requesting Party to produce such Documents, and (ii) a statement of the reasons why the requesting Party assumes the Documents requested are in the possession, custody or control of another Party.[20]

These rules along with the grounds of denial set forth under Article 9[21] resemble the famous Rule 26 of the United States Federal Rules of Civil Procedure. Rule 26 sets the scope of discovery as follows:

(b) DISCOVERY SCOPE AND LIMITS. (1) *Scope in General.* Unless otherwise limited by court order, the scope of discovery is as follows: Parties may obtain discovery regarding any non-privileged matter that is relevant to any party's claim or defense—including the existence, description, nature, custody, condition, and location of any documents or other tangible things and the identity and location of persons who know of any discoverable matter. For good cause, the court may order discovery of any matter relevant to the subject matter involved in the action. Relevant information need not be admissible at the trial if the discovery appears reasonably calculated to lead to the discovery of admissible evidence. All discovery is subject to the limitations imposed by Rule 26(b)(2)(C).[22]

But Rule 26 places an important check on such broad rule of discovery. The relevant provision reads:

(C) *When Required.* On motion or on its own, the court must limit the frequency or extent of discovery otherwise allowed by these rules or by local

20. *Id.* art. 3(3).

21. *Id.* art. 9(2).

The Arbitral Tribunal shall, at the request of a Party or on its own motion, exclude from evidence or production any Document, statement, oral testimony or inspection for any of the following reasons: (a) lack of sufficient relevance to the case or materiality to its outcome; (b) legal impediment or privilege under the legal or ethical rules determined by the Arbitral Tribunal to be applicable; (c) unreasonable burden to produce the requested evidence; (d) loss or destruction of the Document that has been shown with reasonable likelihood to have occurred; (e) grounds of commercial or technical confidentiality that the Arbitral Tribunal determines to be compelling; (f) grounds of special political or institutional sensitivity (including evidence that has been classified as secret by a government or a public international institution) that the Arbitral Tribunal determines to be compelling; or (g) considerations of procedural economy, proportionality, fairness or equality of the Parties that the Arbitral Tribunal determines to be compelling.

22. Fed. R. Civ. P. 26(b)(1).

> rule if it determines that: (i) the discovery sought is unreasonably cumulative or duplicative, or can be obtained from some other source that is more convenient, less burdensome, or less expensive; (ii) the party seeking discovery has had ample opportunity to obtain the information by discovery in the action; or (iii) the burden or expense of the proposed discovery outweighs its likely benefit, considering the needs of the case, the amount in controversy, the parties' resources, the importance of the issues at stake in the action, and the importance of the discovery in resolving the issues.[23]

The administration of these rules and finding the right equilibrium between the desire to obtain all relevant evidence while at the same time being mindful of the fairness and economy of the process requires a significant amount of familiarity and unencumbered judgment on the part of judges and arbitrators. Judges who are trained in the same system and grow up learning the rules and their intricate application would have an easier task of striking the right balance, but arbitrators who come from legal traditions that consider discovery an affront to the system of justice would either be very strict or go further than what even the Federal Rules would consider appropriate. This problem is compounded by the undeniable economic incentive that law firms representing the parties in arbitral proceedings would have in generating a large amount of paperwork, which in turn increases the billable hours. If there is anyone who would consider broad discovery objectionable, it is often the party that is subjected to it. Obviously its use by clever counsel can cause delay and confusion, especially when members of the tribunal err on the side of more production, or are perceived as not being experienced enough with the management of discovery requests.

This author has seen disclosure requests as broad as "all minutes of meetings for six years" granted by a tribunal that did not realize that it ordered the production of tens of thousands of pages of repetitive minutes of meetings in a construction dispute.

The IBA Rules on document production are pro-production and give the tribunal broad power to order production or take adverse inferences.[24] Tribunals that are not well equipped to deal with the intricacies of the administration of such disclosure rules would have difficulty controlling the process and maintaining the right equilibrium. Such a task is further complicated by the cultures of the parties and their counsel who may view the very idea of disclosure as an unwelcome intrusion. The

23. Fed. R. Civ. P. 26(b)(2)(C).

24. IBA Rules of Evidence, Article 9(5) states:

> If a Party fails without satisfactory explanation to produce any Document requested in a Request to Produce to which it has not objected in due time or fails to produce any Document ordered to be produced by the Arbitral Tribunal, the Arbitral Tribunal may infer that such document would be adverse to the interests of that Party.

Article 9(2)(g) further states the broad power of the tribunal to exclude evidence for "considerations of procedural economy, proportionality, fairness or equality of the Parties that the Arbitral Tribunal determines to be compelling."

possibilities of mismanagement and abuse are great. Disclosure of adverse information to the adverse party is a notion that does not come to some party litigants so naturally. It is counterintuitive. Its benefits, if any, have to be learned. The learning process is complicated by the diversity of opinions and backgrounds on most international arbitral tribunals.

The other important topic that the IBA Rules of Evidence deal with pertains to fact and expert witnesses. Leaning toward the common law approach, the Rules permit, albeit in awkward formulation, the preparation of witnesses by counsel.

Leaning more toward the civil law tradition, the IBA Rule on the hearing of witness testimony gives the tribunal "complete control of the Evidentiary Hearing,"[25] but further provides that "[i]t shall not be improper for a Party, its officers, employees, legal advisors or other representatives to interview its witnesses or potential witnesses and to discuss their prospective testimony with them."[26]

It does not exactly permit the coaching of witnesses, but it is a Rule that is fairly tolerant of the practice of witness preparation. It is not difficult to imagine how lawyers who come from traditions that permit and even require the preparation of witnesses would interpret this Rule more broadly than those who come from traditions that discourage or even prohibit pretrial witness consultations or preparations. It is also not very difficult to see how members of a tribunal with different backgrounds would view counsels' conduct in this regard.

The breadth of this permissive Rule is further augmented by the requirement of submission of written witness statements containing "a full and detailed description of the facts, and the sources of the witness's information as to those facts, sufficient to serve as that witness's evidence in the matter in dispute."[27]

Once the written witness statements are submitted, each witness is required to appear and testify before the tribunal. The Rules provide that "the Tribunal may limit or exclude any question to, answer by or appearance of a witness, if it considers such question, answer or appearance to be irrelevant, immaterial, unreasonably burdensome, duplicative or otherwise covered by a reason for objection set forth in Article 9.2"[28]

25. IBA Rules of Evidence, art. 8(2). Contrast this with what Geoffrey Hazard says:

> The[common law] judge is not responsible for there being an adequate development of the evidence during trial and *a fortiori* is not responsible for there being adequate pretrial discovery of evidence. Nor is the judge responsible for getting at "the truth." The judge simply chooses between the contentions of law and the versions of facts laid before him by the parties.

Geoffrey C. Hazard, Jr., *Discovery and the Role of the Judge in Civil Law Jurisdictions*, 73 Notre Dame L. Rev. 1017, 1019 (1998).

26. IBA Rules of Evidence, art. 4(3).

27. *Id.* art. 4(5)(c). The witness must also submit documents that she relies on that are not made a part of the record. *Id.*

28. *Id.* art. 8(2).

The tribunal's broad powers in this regard are further extended by the tribunal's authority to ask question at any time,[29] call witnesses,[30] appoint experts,[31] or order that "the Witness Statement or Expert Report shall serve as that witness's direct testimony."[32] Overall, the Rules grant the tribunal the power to control every aspect of the process, including the power to "determine the admissibility, relevance, materiality and weight of the evidence."[33] More important, any misapplication, disregard, ignorance, or negligence on the part of the tribunal would not have an easy remedy because improper, unwise, or even incorrect procedural orders are often cryptic, subtle, individually arguable, collectively without pattern, misleading, and buried in volumes of pleadings and thousands of pages of hearing transcripts. Picking bad procedural orders from among good ones and packaging them as evidence of denial of due process or other grounds of annulment or nonrecognition or refusal of enforcement is not an easy or economically sound exercise, even when the injustice is evident. Indeed, skilled arbitrators know how to make their awards annulment-proof, even when they lack experience with the chosen law or are unfamiliar with the procedural intricacies of the applicable procedural and evidentiary rules. Consider, for example, a tribunal that refuses to admit evidence at the hearing because some pages of the evidence, which were supposed to have been submitted by the deadline, were not submitted due to counsel's oversight. Consider further that the tribunal retained the power to admit evidence at any time if it deemed necessary. Consider further that the missing pages were necessary to determine the exact amount of damages. Consider further that the parties did not disagree about that. Consider further that the tribunal used some other method to determine damages, ignoring direct evidence in the form of a retender price. The tribunal voted two-to-one to make an award to the party that wanted the missing pages admitted, making it the winning party, but failed to award the damages that it would have been entitled to had those pages been admitted. The wining party suspected that the members of the tribunal might have taken advantage of the unfortunate omission to reduce the damages. It would have made no legal or economic sense to seek to annul or challenge the award in any manner, but there was a level of injustice that resulted from the tribunal's exercise of discretionary power on issues of procedure and evidence and the winning party had no feasible remedy.

B. CONCLUSION

The real estate maxim analogy—arbitrator, arbitrator, arbitrator—does not sufficiently warn users of international arbitration as a means of dispute resolution.

29. *See id.* art. 8(2).

30. *See id.* art. 4(10).

31. *See id.* art. 6.

32. *Id.* art. 8(4).

33. *Id.* art. 9(1).

Arbitrators are judges with limited checks and almost unlimited procedural powers. They are frequently asked to determine facts arising out of cultural interactions that they have never been exposed to, they are asked to apply law that they have never seen before, they sit alongside colleagues who often misunderstand them, they are relentlessly misinformed by counsel and expert witnesses on both sides, and they don't share the same cultural background as the witnesses; how often do they get it right? And who are they? The following chapter looks into some of these questions.

11

The Mythology of Specialized Knowledge

A. JAN PAULSSON'S QUESTION: "WHO'S COMPLAINING?"

One of the very few explicit attempts to address the role of culture in international arbitration is Jan Paulsson's very brief essay in the *Art of Advocacy in International Arbitration.* He titled it: "Cultural Differences in Advocacy in International Arbitration."[1] In this essay Paulsson raises all the right questions and provides all the standard answers. A closer look at each question and answer is helpful. First, Paulsson claims that:

> If you want to observe a real clash of cultures, one might be tempted to say, it is hard to find more sound and fury than what emerges when rival French lawyers appear on both sides, or rival Londoners on both sides, or Cairenes or New Yorkers! For then, it often seems, the combatants leave no prisoners, and urge vehemently that starkly different procedural arrangements be adopted, each camp insisting all the while that what they see is but the normal course of well-ordered events. Their opponents, of course, are the ones attempting to mislead the tribunal with self-serving requests that make a mockery of due process![2]

The reason for this, according to him, is because lawyers adopt their respective clients' cultures.[3] "Here's the real clash, it may seem: the 'justice delayed, justice denied' school v. the 'nothing's settled until it's settled' school."[4] Observe how Paulsson's cultural analysis, like all of his peers' analysis discussed later, is limited to the cultural differences between counsel and arbitrators who come from the common law and the civil law legal traditions. The one piece that is always missing is the culture of the parties, who increasingly come from diverse cultural backgrounds that cannot be fitted into any one of the two Western legal traditions.

1. Jan Paulsson, *Cultural Differences in Advocacy in International Arbitration*, *in* The Art of Advocacy in International Arbitration 15–21 (Doak Bishop & Edward G. Kehoe eds., 2d ed. 2010).

2. *Id.* at 15 (emphasis omitted).

3. *Id.*

4. *Id.*

Continuing the above analysis, Paulsson writes:

> Confirmation of this observation seems to be provided, by the way of contrast, in the polite difference often exhibited when opposing counsel truly come from different cultures, as each side outdoes the other in proffering well-mannered, tentative suggestions, full of solicitous understanding for the other side, as though all feel it incumbent to act as goodwill ambassador attesting to the decency and urbanity of their own legal community.[5]

As the above passage attests, international arbitration has become the new "cultured" forum on which the centuries-old striving for cultural superiority or dominance of the two legal traditions is staged. Bear in mind the reference to "decency and urbanity." It is reminiscent of Professor Mary Ann Glendon's suggestion that it is the civil law's perceived intellectual superiority, among other factors, that led to its widespread appeal and acceptance.[6] There is no indication in international arbitration that such is conceded. If anything the opposite appears to be taking hold, that is, the amalgamation appears to tilt toward the common law but still, as Paulsson indicates, the struggle to impress each other continues.

Then, of course, he asks the most important question:

> Is there then no true clash of cultures in international arbitration? Are there only the different procedural preferences that commend themselves to lawyers in light of tactical objectives—which preferences are, moreover, likely to be attenuated when adjustments are made for the different origins of the participants?[7]

Mind you, by participants, he only means the lawyers on each side.

Answering these questions, he goes on, stating:

> There is certainly something to be said for this startling proposition. Nearly three decades of successive editions of the IBA Rules on the Taking of Evidence in International Commercial Arbitration have led to the emergence of a remarkable series of effective compromises with respect to important issues of due process which had once seemed intractable. Similarly, successive editions of rules of leading arbitral institutions have incorporated refinements that reflect steady convergence.[8]

As further evidence of "harmonious conceptions of the international arbitral process," he cites the adoption of the UNCITRAL Model Law on International Commercial Arbitration in many jurisdictions.[9]

5. *Id.* (emphasis added).

6. See Mary Ann Glendon, Paolo G. Carozza & Colin Picker, Comparative Legal Traditions 25 (3d ed. 2006).

7. Paulsson, *supra* note 1, at 15–16.

8. *Id.* at 16.

9. *Id.*

Paulsson, of course, does not leave it as that: he offers the following commentary:

> Yet to conclude that we can cease to worry about clashes of culture would be premature and exaggerated. In relation to the theme of this book, it would be perilous for the advocate to ignore the potential for misunderstanding, and indeed occasionally mistrust, the still lies under the surface of cosmopolitan good manners. To get a proper sense of the prevalence of such disaffection, one would have to know what parties say internally, behind closed doors, reacting to a disappointing ruling; and what arbitrators whisper to each other in deliberations as they reflect on the behavior of the parties and their counsel.[10]

He goes on stating that "[t]he effect of cultural differences on perceptions of the legitimacy of the international arbitral process as a whole is, of course, a matter of fundamental importance."[11] Furthermore, he counsels that "skilled advocates need be attuned to the culture of the arbitrators they face is self-evident; it is an obvious and essential element of the internationally active advocate's credibility and persuasiveness."[12]

He continues to discuss some of the most commonly raised cultural differences in the epistemology of determining facts between civil law and common law, and closes his discussion with the following interesting paragraph:

> Of course, there is no way to answer these questions with any degree of certainty or finality. We cannot even be sure that we learn all that much from experience. No culture is a mechanical "system"; that variables are infinite; experiments are not reproducible. Even if they were monolithic, cultures evolve. International arbitration involves innumerable constellations of different cultures, as reflected in the assumptions of behavior of all participants. We go to work not knowing exactly what to expect. *This is part of the exhilaration of the métier. Who is complaining?*[13]

So, who is complaining? Paulsson's examples are of the stereotypical French jurist who "view[s] witnesses as unreliable and [is] rather certain that it is pointless to hear their self-serving statements?"[14] And the stereotypical English jurist who "believes that a skilled professional can derive much evidence of value from witnesses by confronting them with facts and propositions that reveal self-serving declarations to be significant indicators of untruth"[15]

10. *Id.* (emphasis added.)

11. *Id.*

12. *Id.*

13. *Id.* at 21 (emphasis added).

14. *Id.*

15. *Id.*

International arbitration is a platform that demands to be understood. The stereotypical French and English jurists and their French and English clients, no matter who is representing which side, probably welcome the "exhilaration" that comes along with the uncertainty that Paulsson talks about, but how about the party and counsel who come from cultural backgrounds entirely strange to both? Would they find it so fun, so exhilarating? Wouldn't they complain for being required to understand a mechanism that they "voluntarily" selected that doesn't feel as though it has the reciprocal obligation to understand them?

So much has been written about the exclusivity of the "club" and its efforts to preserve its "earned" privileges, but no one has even had the audacity to expressly advocate for elitism until Jan Paulsson did so in his acclaimed 2013 Oxford University Press book, *The Idea of Arbitration*.[16] This book is as unapologetic as it is thought-provoking. Probably Paulsson's most interesting contributions so far, it is discussed in some detail in the next section.

1. The Audacity of Elitism

Paulsson's case for elitism is not only incredibly daring as a piece of modern legal literature, but also it is substantively indefensible because it appears to be predicated on a fundamentally flawed assumption that there is always a direct relationship between learning "cosmopolitan good manners" and the criteria that he believes that an arbitrator should meet, that is, integrity and aptitude, both of which he gives specific meaning.[17] It is a surprisingly explicit advocacy for the value of reputation and the privilege that comes along with it. Before it is reproduced and discussed, it is important to see how the thesis develops.

Structurally, Paulsson's thesis on "The Case for Elitist Approach" comes at the end of his chapter on "Ethical Challenges."[18] He begins the chapter with his rather accurate characterization of ethical matters as the "Achilles heel" of arbitration.[19] In his own words: "Confidence in the ethical standards of arbitrators and arbitral institutions is the Alpha and Omega of the legitimacy of the process."[20] He explores this theme in eight subsections. The first addresses what he calls "The Weak Spot." He considers the chief justice of Singapore's (Sundaresh Menon's) expressions of misgivings at a certain arbitration conference about international arbitration when

16. Jan Paulsson, The Idea of Arbitration (Oxford University Press, 2013). His more scholarly undertaking is Denial of Justice in International Law (Cambridge University Press, 2003). He offers a more nuanced account of international arbitral justice in the Denial of Justice book than in his most recent writing. *See, e.g.*, Denial of Justice, at 228–65. He notes in conclusion that "[i]ternational tribunals tend to irritate respondent states—whether they are rich or poor—in individual cases; yet their decisions should be respected in order to achieve the long-term benefits of the rule of law." Denial of Justice, at 265.

17. Paulsson, The Idea of Arbitration, *supra* note 16, at 149.

18. *Id.* at ch. 5.

19. *Id.* at 148.

20. *Id.*

he was the attorney general. Menon's message was clear and categorical: he noted that arbitrators are "in essence business people in search of opportunities."[21] His accusation is not limited to characterizing them as business people but goes as far as saying that the "entrepreneurial arbitrator" may "rule expansively on his own jurisdiction."[22] Paulsson then discusses fitness to serve without attempting to refute this, except saying that despite the lack of meaningful and specific disciplinary regulation of arbitrators, they might be subject to some sanctions, be it from their home bar associations or arbitral institutions.[23]

As indicated above, for Paulsson, the two criteria for fitness to serve as an arbitrator are integrity and aptitude.[24] He says integrity is paramount because "great ability may be corrupted; if so, the process is irredeemably flawed."[25] However, mediocre arbitrators may fall short of perfection, but still perform adequately."[26] Integrity for him entails impartiality and independence—two overlapping notions.[27] Aptitude has an ethical dimension in that "it is dishonest to accept appointment without a solid understanding of the relevant domain . . . ."[28] So, the elite arbitrator that Paulsson approves would have both integrity and aptitude in this context. Whereas, by Paulsson's admission, integrity would include lack of bias, aptitude would include "a solid understanding of the relevant domain."[29]

Consider the following case scenario. Two arbitrators compete for appointment. The criteria are integrity and aptitude. The case involves a Chinese oil company and an African government regarding alleged unlawful termination of a production-sharing agreement. The most important question that the arbitral tribunal needs to determine is whether the Chinese company obtained the contracts through fraudulent misrepresentation of its credentials in the first place. Consider further that there are 10 witnesses: Five witnesses, all African, on the government's side who provide testimony to the effect that they were misled by the representations regarding the Chinese company's technical skills and financial abilities. Five witnesses on the company's side, all Chinese, who testify that it was their understanding that the Africans did indeed understand the circumstances of the company before granting the rights and deny the existence of misrepresentation.

Assume further that it is an ICC arbitration, and the seat of the arbitration is in Geneva. The African government nominates an American jurist and the Chinese

21. *Id.* (emphasis added).

22. *Id.*

23. *Id.*

24. *Id.* at 149.

25. *Id.*

26. *Id.*

27. *Id.*

28. *Id.*

29. *Id.*

company nominates a French jurist. The two fail to agree on a chair. Who should the ICC court appoint as chair? Chances are that by default the chair would be a Swiss national because the seat is in Geneva, and local chapters often get to nominate under these circumstances. Recognizing the fact that the parties voluntarily got themselves into this circumstance, a question may be asked if a Swiss jurist is the best possible choice for this case by measures of integrity and aptitude. As indicated above, integrity, among other things, represents lack of bias, and aptitude represents understanding of the relevant domain. Lack of bias on this or the other side could fairly be assumed although it is impossible to find out whether the Swiss nominee harbors the view that African governments are irrational actors or that Chinese business practices are different. In terms of aptitude, the arbitrator needs to have a good understanding of the domain. The domain is likely to be defined by the area of law to which the dispute generally relates. By that measure, the chair is likely to be someone who had some oil and gas experience, although the actual issue is a rather factual one: whether the Chinese company misrepresented its credentials. But then the actual aptitude that is needed is the ability to understand the parties' relationship and their witnesses, that is, some understanding of how African governments grant concession rights, and how Chinese companies obtain them. Moreover, familiarity with the cultures of the witnesses would be ideal. But the arbitrator is likely to be a person with great academic and practice experience in Europe who has never been to Africa or China. An African or a Chinese jurist would not stand a chance under the circumstances of the case. It is just structurally impossible for them to get appointed.

A commonly raised point is that the parties had complete autonomy, and they chose this system. That is true but this characterization is simplistic because their choice is a function of a whole host of factors, but mainly it is a function of the North's relationship with the South in the last couple of centuries. Some jurists from the North who hold a privileged position because of fortuitous circumstances cannot resist the temptation to genuinely believe that their prominence is a function exclusively of their excellence, and criticize their critics for complaining instead of learning cosmopolitan good manners. The problem is that learning the good manners of Geneva or Paris does not contribute to either the integrity or aptitude that is actually required to resolve specific factual issues raised in the above example. The requirement of cosmopolitan good manners as Paulsson describes is an added but yet unrecognized or at least not talked about burden on the mechanism of dispute settlement. It would be difficult to see how in the above example the Swiss jurist, who is likely to be a member of the elite class, would have any advantages to resolve the parties' dispute, over an African or a Chinese jurist with a comparable level of legal education and experience but not in Geneva or London. The elite is, of course, an economic class that is convinced that it provides better services, and often succeeds in convincing others including users of the services. It portrays law and legal processes as technology, and associates the skills with material advancement or urbanization or even industrialization. It ignores the privileged position obtained merely because of membership in a particular society that has historically enjoyed positions of influence. Technology or not, is it true that the elites produce better result? A result that is fair, just, efficient, and acceptable? More specifically one might ask: Does this kind of aristocratic class understand and respect all users of its services?

As will be discussed further, the privileges of the elite class are structurally perpetuated. The elite class already exists, and it owes its existence to some very pragmatic considerations necessitated by historical realities. The West's advantaged position, and its creation of institutions and articulation of doctrine before anyone else could, in turn created opportunities for those proximate to it. By the time the rest of the world adopted, just like a business venture or a piece of technology, the advantage was essentially lost, but the dependency lingers partly because of the mystification of the process by the privileged class, and not so subtle claim of superiority, which could be convincing to those who view the arbitral process as a scientific process that requires a particular kind of scientific knowledge that exclusively resides in the West.

Continuing his discussion of ethical considerations, Paulsson next addresses the limited benefits of disclosure. The core proposition is that "[o]ver emphasis on mechanical disclosure requirements may exclude the honest and do very little to stifle true mischief."[30] Explaining this proposition further, he writes:

> There comes a point of diminishing returns where excessive formalism serves only to assist an obstreperous party in fomenting delay and difficulty. As a result, scrupulous arbitrators may be removed from office for trivial reasons, while hypocritical rascals do not even have to break their stride.[31]

This is absolutely true, and the key term is "hypocrisy." There is no shortage of hypocrisy and self-congratulation in international arbitration. It is a system that operates under the influence of all the wrong incentives. First, the pecuniary rewards are sizable. Second, there is a limited number of high stake arbitral matters. Third, the gains for the service providers is often directly associated with the size of the matter and its complications. Fourth, expeditious resolution often means less reward for the service providers. Finally, repeat players tend to gain more, hence the incentive to downplay conflict, trade favors etc. All of these make hypocrisy a necessary ingredient of the system.

Paulsson provides good examples of conflicts that the current requirements for disclosure do not capture under the IBA or other rules; these uncaptured conflicts are more dangerous than the captured ones, though they remain undisclosed under the current rules. He describes a very interesting, but real, scenario. A presides over Arbitral Tribunal X where B serves as a party-appointed arbitrator. B presides over Arbitral Tribunal Y where A serves as party-appointed arbitrator. The outcome of Tribunal X is very vital for B's career because the party who appointed him is an influential player in the industry in B's country, and would appreciate it if B could "deliver" a victory. Both A and B disclose all the facts of their appointment and their different roles on each tribunal. What they are not required to disclose, which of

30. *Id.* at 152.

31. *Id.*

course they don't, is the implicit understanding that A's help on the X front will somehow be reciprocated by B on the Y front.[32] No amount of disclosure would capture this, but it is a reality that exists. Although Paulsson does not make the conclusion explicit, it is fair to say that the results of both tribunals are rigged. Sadly though, the tolerance of the system for hypocrisy makes them both stand.

This example has the advantage of being a hypothetical with certain assumptions made, but it is difficult to identify if mischief exists under similar circumstances where two arbitrators serve on two different tribunals or assume different roles on two or multiple tribunals. Because the conflict rules are so permissive, and the possible interactions of the same people in different capacities in multiple proceedings is almost infinite, the opportunity and the economic incentives for a quid pro quo always exists. The system seems to purposefully permit it, and Paulsson's suggestion for the maintenance of the elite class perpetuates it even further.

Consider the following true case in which this author was involved as counsel. Opposing counsel A appoints B to serve on Tribunal X. B gets appointed to serve on Tribunal Y, and somehow agrees with party-appointed arbitrator C to elect A as chair of Tribunal Y. A and B disclose both functions. It gets more interesting. A retains expert witness W for the case before Tribunal X. B retains the same witness W for another case pending before a third Tribunal, Z, in which he serves as counsel. W is expected to testify before Tribunal X led by opposing counsel A. B was challenged on grounds of "reasonable suspicion of impartiality or independence," the standard that applied in that particular case, but the challenge was rejected by Tribunal X. No one would ever know if there had been any improprieties, but it is clear that the opportunity exists. Not only does it exist, but also it is almost impossible to identify and remedy because the involved individuals are skilled in packaging legal arguments and writing seemingly strong arguments. It could also be a totally innocent pursuit of economic opportunities with no deals made, but still it is too dangerous to leave it for individual consciences. To state the obvious, the pursuit of economic opportunities is a formidable force that is capable of dictating less than honest choices where such choices are immune from scrutiny. The system tolerates a high level of hypocrisy. It pretends that most of its members are immune from influence. The advocacy to limit the class of individuals who could serve as arbitrators to an elite one necessarily exacerbates this problem.

With this background, Paulsson's case for the maintenance of an elite class is examined below. His brief proposal is reproduced below in its entirety for ease of reference and complete accuracy. It is important to see the prelude to his proposal in section 5.8 of his book. The prelude makes all the right points but does not support the elitism proposition discussed later. The relevant part reads as follows:

> Above all, however, is respect for arbitrates. In his essay On Liberty, Mill wrote that there is always hope when people are forced to listen to both 'sides', but "truth has no chance but in proportion . . . as every opinion which embodies any fraction of the truth not only finds advocates but is so advocated as to be

32. *Id.*

> listened to." What does it involve, to listen to every fraction of the truth so as to give truth a chance? It is surely to acknowledge the dignity of the arbitrants and to attend to their explanations with an open mind and without prejudice. They are not to be disparaged because they express themselves poorly or because their lawyers are not as brilliant as diamonds or as smooth as silk. Access to justice—the right to one's day in court—is a fundamental feature of life in a civilized society. To hear an arbitrant should involve truly listening to that party. The rejection of claims or defenses should be explained with an honest appeal to rationality, demonstrating to the losing party first that its arguments were seriously considered and secondly that the scales were tipped by weigh of reason, not prejudice or caprice.[33]

He further states:

> Anyone accepting to serve as arbitrator, voluntarily placing himself at the service of the parties, should assume that they come before the tribunal with a serious problem, that each side believes it is correct, and that each side expects the tribunal to give it a serious hearing. Is it then not a breach of promise to bully a party, or rush to judgment on the basis of predilection or impatience? Is not a breach of such promise an ethical issue? Is not laziness an ethical issue?[34]

Following these observations, Paulsson provides the following proposal.

> The Case for an Elitist Approach
>
> Given the large stakes and great sensitivities involved in many arbitrations, there seems to be a good case for supporting the emergence and recognition of an elite corps of arbitrators. Here the notion of an elite is that of a meritocracy in terms of substantive competence, procedural adroitness, and above all absolute impartiality. Such a corps cannot be self-appointed. It would be intolerable if it were a closed shop by any standard (culture, gender, nationality). Nor could this be a small circle of friends; the needs of the international community are certainly commensurate with a corps of several hundred first-rate commercial arbitrators.
>
> Properly understood, this notion turns back complaints about self-perpetuating cliques of arbitrators who appoint and reappoint each other, and rather tends to the conclusion that the establishment of an elite corps is a good thing. The mutual recognition of its members does not reflect the unsavory system of quid pro quo; rather, it will build the confidence of all participants in the process.
>
> It is hard to see why it would be good for the arbitral process if as many people as possible had the opportunity to act as arbitrators. Why should arbitration, which routinely involves high stakes and complex issues of both

33. *Id.* at 170 (emphasis omitted).

34. *Id.*

> substance and procedure, be a suitable playing field for amateurs? After all, few voices are heard to suggest that "as many people as possible" should be given a turn at national Supreme Courts. Given the fact that arbitral tribunals typically decide as first and last instances, it may be even more important that their members be the very best at what they are doing. The archetype arbitrator has stature. Why should we not welcome the emergence of a corps of excellent arbitrators widely perceived as immune to favouritism?[35]

To paraphrase James Madison, if arbitrators were angels, they would have immunity from favoritism. A system of justice cannot be built on a presumption of such immunity when diverse groups vie for significant rewards. Indeed, many of Paulsson's assumptions and propositions warrant further comment. The whole proposal is predicated on the assumption that there is a specific kind of virtue that is acquired through education and experience and maintained through reputation. The proposal almost seems inconsistent with his own discussion of "the arbitrator as archetype."[36] Perhaps the most important point he makes in his discussion of the archetype is the following statement: "We wish to be judged by someone wise and familiar, perhaps an idealized version of ourselves—not someone clever and strange."[37] He adds that "the important idea is conceived of resolving differences away from the eyes of intrusive strangers. The vision of serene closure, without loss of dignity, is at the heart of the idea of arbitration. The modern world can hardly replicate the idealized palaver hut, but the simple aspirations remain even as we build more intricate institutions."[38]

One might then ask how the creation (or rather maintenance) of an elite class helps realize the aspiration of the users of arbitration who wish to be judged by someone wise and familiar, not someone clever and strange. The terms Paulsson likes to use include "second-rate," "no short cuts," "amateur," "stature," "no great supply of a particular kind of people," and finally "elitism is no sin."[39] This offers an excellent window through which one could see the mentality that keeps the club closed even when its members admit that it is perhaps not to the best interest of all users of their services. Isn't that an ethical issue, as Paulsson likes to ask?

Elitism is the antithesis of every democratic principle that most societies cherish. The creation of a relatively small group of an economically privileged class of individuals selected "on the basis of demonstrated merits" is a recipe for influence peddling, not a pathway to a fair and just outcome. What Paulsson describes is in

35. *Id.* at 172–73.

36. *Id.* at 4–6.

37. *Id.* at 5 (emphasis added).

38. *Id.* at 7.

39. *Id.* at 172–73. He is not alone in his use of the term "amateur" in the field. *See, e.g.*, Alan Redfern, *The Changing World of International Arbitration*, *in* PRACTICING VIRTUE: INSIDE INTERNATIONAL ARBITRATION 46–51, 51 (David D. Caron & Stephan W. Schill eds., 2015) ("In reality, the growing use and importance of international arbitration expects and demands increased professionalism, from both lawyers and arbitrators. The days of the amateur players are over.")

fact the existing system. A mix of historical circumstances have created an elite club. Paulsson does not deny that, but justifies it by saying "experience and talent are negatively correlated with patronage and influence-peddling." He cites no evidence to substantiate this proposition, and it seems that the opposite might be true, especially when those who have the experience and talent are small in number and are economically interdependent. There is a natural tendency to preserve privilege by attempting to show that others do not deserve it.

But that is not the key problem here. The problem is whether the wise and the familiar could become a member of the elite group. The second question would be—would one remain wise and familiar after joining the elite group? Isn't there an inherent tendency for confidence that borders on arrogance and self-righteousness that comes along with privilege? Isn't that an ethical issue?

Another problematic aspect of the proposal is the adjudication of the merits of deservingness. Talent, experience, independence, and fairness are the key ingredients. Paulsson does not account for the fact that each one of these attributes could be situation dependent and cannot be found in the same group of individuals for all circumstances at all times. He believes that several hundreds of people could resolve the world's international commercial disputes. That is a clear endorsement of the existing regime. But this is fundamentally flawed for several reasons. First, as argued throughout this book, a good judge is someone who is intimately familiar with the cultures of the disputing parties. Strangers cannot possibly comprehend the full scope of the dispute. A former judge of the Canadian Supreme Court may not necessarily be the right judge for a dispute between Nigerian farmers and Chinese investors. Aside from experience and talent, independence, impartiality, and generally fairness are also situation dependent. A fair judge may decide on the basis of the facts and the law alone, but still her perception and appreciation of the law and the facts is always dictated by her own experience and ideological background. Such dictation may not be fair to those who lose because of ideological leanings. One might argue that this is true in court proceedings as well. However, commercial litigants do not pick the judge. They are judged because they are a part of a broader social contract that does not allow them to pick their own judges, but arbitration does. So, why limit the choice to an elite group?

Another of Paulsson's assumptions is that the substance and procedure of international arbitration are so intricate that they limit the number of qualified individuals. This cannot be further from the truth. As a matter of legal doctrine and procedure, international arbitration has absolutely no peculiar complexity. Competency could quickly be acquired. To be sure, yes, there is some complexity, but it is not legal, it is rather purely sociological: a creation of the existing system of influence peddling. Every international arbitration book, including Paulsson's under review here, discusses the same old concepts of competence-competence, separability, selection and challenge of arbitrators, applicable law, annulment, enforcement, etc. And every conference on international arbitration profiles the same concepts time and again like preaching the gospel. Again, the complexity pertains to the sociology of the appointments: whom to appoint among a limited pool of influential individuals, not because of their wisdom and familiarity, but because of the dynamics of their interaction. That is the only algorithm that is complex. So, it is basically a race to the top on the scale of influence. It has nothing to do with independence or fairness. Men are not angels; a party litigant is not likely to appoint an arbitrator who is likely to be fair to both sides, but one who is likely to be fair to the appointing party. So, fairness as a concept is not static. It is malleable. It is situational. A fair judge could be fair in one case and unfair in another. So, the same group of individuals (a few hundred of them) cannot be trusted to resolve all of the world's commercial disputes by choice.

Perhaps the most problematic aspect of the proposal is the likelihood that it—conceptually and practically—encourages the exclusion of the historical "others." The de facto exclusion is evident, but this might give a stamp of official approval for such exclusion because it offers a seeming doctrinal justification. To be fair, Paulsson says that exclusion on the basis of culture (perhaps implicit in that is race), gender, and nationality is not acceptable. However, if experience and reputation are the attributes that he is looking for, at least a generation has to pass before the pool begins to look representational. Even then, as long as the center of gravity remains in the capitals of the West, the few hundred elite arbitrators that Paulsson wishes to create or rather preserve would only have a few uncomfortable outsiders in their midst.

One of Paulsson's responses to the suggestion that the arbitrator pool should be expanded to be representational is that many cases involve high stakes and that the parties must be careful to select the best jurists. As an example he says that nobody suggests that people should have turns sitting on national Supreme Courts. But his argument does not account for the fundamental difference between arbitration and litigation. Litigants in court proceedings are a remote party to a social contract that subjects them to judgments by judges who are elected or appointed for them. Although they may indirectly contribute to the selection or appointment process in a democratic system, their involvement remains remote nonetheless. In arbitration, however, parties voluntarily and directly choose the persons who will sit in judgment of their case. The ability to be judged by those they have directly selected is one of the perceived benefits of arbitration. So there is no reason they should not demand a representative pool. Accordingly, the analogy to Supreme Courts of nations is fundamentally flawed.

Having read Paulsson's case for an elitist approach, how many "amateur" arbitrators would feel comfortable to sit alongside him, and how many "amateur" counsel (which may include his former students) would feel comfortable appearing before him? Isn't this a recipe for keeping the elite club exclusive? Isn't this an ethical issue? No matter how it is packaged, the very essence of elitism is exclusion. Without exclusion there is no elitism. Elitism might be tolerated in many different areas of life but must not be tolerated in a system of justice. It is the antithesis of all principles of fairness on its face. An elite group of privileged and clever jurists with broad discretion and unchecked powers cannot bring about justice to all. They might do so selectively. That is the definition of injustice. That is the nature of elitism.

The discussion would not be complete without his discussion of cultural issues. Paulsson is one of very few people who likes to talk about culture. He addresses the issue in relatively better depth than he has done before in *The Idea of Arbitration* under the rubric "Clashes of Culture."[40] He begins his discussion with cultural issues facing

40. Paulsson, The Idea of Arbitration, *supra* note 16, at 178.

the users of arbitration services or arbitrants, and their lawyers. For the arbitrants, he makes the interesting observation that "business managers from Scandinavia who operate in the international marketplace are likely to share more assumptions about the objectives of dispute resolution with other business managers from Central America than with the members of the Swedish ski club or home owners association."[41] As to lawyers, "[w]hatever turf wars may have been fought by past generations intent on controlling the process by imposing their exceptionalism modern practitioners have adopted a cosmopolitan approach which converges in a range of shared practices. They assuredly compete, but in the same game."[42] When talking about culture, he also talks about "the culture of claimants" and "the culture of respondents"—as for instance the desire for expedience—assuming, of course, that it is the claimant who always wants expediency, which is by no means always true. In any case, having trivialized cultural differences in international arbitration in such a way, he brutally criticizes those who express concerns in the following very explicit and condescending terms that are rarely found in modern published works of any kind:

> A final possibility deserves full attention, because it relates to a type of resistance which may be categorical and chronic. It arises from the objections of those who perceive themselves to be outsiders, lacking resources—skills, influence, and information—which they suspect are at the disposal of their opponents. This is not a clash of culture, since both sides share the same values and assumptions about decent justice, but rather a failure of confidence. It is a serious problem, but quite a different matter. Clashes of culture would be hardwired and intractable. Failures of confidence, on the other hand, can be redressed by concrete measures of intelligent institutional design allowing transparency, appraisal, and participation—while effectively blocking entrenchment and capture by special interest.[43]

He describes the evolution of participation of outsiders in four stages—the initial stage of defensiveness and defeatism, the stage of pragmatic and incidental engagement, the stage of constructive engagement, and finally the stage of equal status. He rightly begins by saying the first stage coincided with the emergence of the postcolonial world but makes no association between his accusation of "defensiveness and defeatism" and colonialism.[44] Rather he associates it with lack of confidence. He seems to suggest that whatever lack of confidence that he believes existed had nothing to do with what arbitration replaced in the postcolonial period. Former colonial powers, of course, protected their economic interest by force.[45] Paulsson would know that in the postcolonial period, arbitration was the second-best thing.

41. *Id.* at 179.

42. *Id.*

43. *Id.*

44. *Id.* at 181.

45. *See,* e.g., Louis T. Wells, *Preface* to THE EVOLVING INTERNATIONAL INVESTMENT REGIME: EXPECTATIONS, REALITIES, OPTIONS, at xv, xvi (José E. Alvarez & Karl P. Sauvant eds., 2011) ("In the rather distant past, the United States and other rich countries would occasionally

His "we told you so" description is interesting. He blames newly independent states for resisting the idea of being summoned to answer charges of expropriation of Western interests in Western capitals, for attempting to use their own resources, and for demanding to be understood. Here is the critical attitudinal problem: the perception of law as technology. Paulsson is not immune from this thinking. The assumption is that there is a superior way of resolving disputes between two parties no matter where they come from—Geneva or Nairobi. Everyone needs to learn the Geneva way. An African witness who calls yellow and orange by the same name is unlikely to impress Paulsson as the world's most credible, most intelligent witness. Yet, the arbitrant is required to understand and be understood by the arbitrators that she selected (more likely selected for her) without the arbitrators' feeling the reciprocal duty to understand her. That is simply because the arbitrator's way is superior—a clear association between industrialization and justice.

Paulsson continues to ridicule the expressed concerns by saying that the stage of pragmatic and incidental engagement resulted in former colonies winning some cases. First, the pragmatism was a result of having no options because arbitration was literally imposed as a means of doing business with the West—even as a condition of getting project loans. Second, the statistics are misleading because they do not account for cases that should never have been initiated in the first place.[46] Those who work with African states might know how unscrupulous and opportunistic businesses exploit the fear of international arbitration and literally extort concessions.

Fast forwarding to the stage of equal status, apart from the interesting choice of terms, he dismisses Africa entirely by saying not many effective arbitration specialists have emerged in Africa—although Africa has been one of the most active users of arbitration services in the West with more than 20 percent of all ICSID cases coming from Africa. So, his analysis leaves Africa out. At least, arguably, by his own admission, as of yet, Africa has no hope for "equal status" inasmuch as some Asian and Latin American specialists have attained. And, of course, he says, "it seems, the time will come when significant cohorts of eminent non-Western arbitrators will be selected by institutions, or by the joint nomination of arbitrators, to decide cases having no connection with their home countries."[47]

Paulsson sums up his detest for the critics in the following forceful manner: "Dogmatic resistance to the arbitral process remains. There are places where decision-makers stubbornly continue to operate in the zone of primitive rejection, disinclined to make the effort necessary to become more successful and integrated participants, as though continued ineptness preserves an entitlement to complain about the process."[48]

act militarily or insist on state-state arbitrations when their investors claimed mistreatment abroad. Later, the United States would threaten (and occasionally act) to cut off aid, vote against loans by multilateral financial institutions to offending countries, and cancel trade preferences. . . .").

46. *See generally*, Won Kidane, *The China-Africa Factor in the ICSID Legitimacy Debate*, 35 U. Pa. J. Int'l L. 559 (2014).

47. Paulsson, The Idea of Arbitration, *supra* note 16, at 182.

48. *Id.* at 183 (emphasis added).

For him the resistance is all because of ignorance, ineptness, lack of effort, failing to understand the system, unable to speak, failure of confidence, primitiveness, dogmatism—all adjectives that he repeatedly uses throughout his book. For Paulsson, it is all the fault of the outsiders. They are not trying hard enough to win a seat next to him. In fact, they even hire him because they lack the confidence to talk.

His main argument appears to be predicated on the assumption that everyone needs to learn his way not only because they have no choice, but also because it is superior. Both assumptions are flawed. First, there are now more choices. Second, arbitral justice in European capitals is not a superior form of justice.

Consider a scenario where a British Virgin Island company with Chinese owners initiates an ICC arbitration with the agreed seat being in Geneva for an alleged unlawful termination of an oil concession agreement in Africa.

First, the reason they selected ICC arbitration in Geneva could simply be because they copied a dispute settlement clause from some prior contract. It is a real possibility. It could also be a habit. It could also be that both siders considered Geneva as a neutral forum without thinking about the consequences of their selection. But it is often not a conscious choice.

Once Geneva is selected as the seat of the arbitration, it would likely dictate many of the choices that the parties will make. The party initiating the proceeding would consider familiarity with the seat in choosing counsel. Selected counsel's selection or recommendation of an arbitrator would certainly be informed by the designated seat. The respondent also considers all of the factors that the claimant had, and thus in all likelihood, the center of gravity being Geneva, the African and Chinese parties will end up with three Francophone European arbitrators, and European or sometimes American counsel on both sides. They essentially face a clever but stranger justice. No matter what the outcome, no participant is likely to enjoy the experience. That is because: (1) European or American counsel for the African or Chinese side would have enormous difficulty understanding the client's case and objectives because of linguistic and more importantly cultural barriers, and (2) if they understand the client's case at great cost, they still have to make the tribunal understand their client's case. It is not easy for an arbitrator from Zurich, who has never been to Africa, to understand an African woman who walks into the hearing room and bows before him prior to taking her seat. He may ask the lawyer who brought her in: "What do you want me to say now?" One might say: "Well I've been in this business for 30 years but I've not seen that kind of drama." That might be true, and it is because that kind of witness—who might be instrumental in determining the facts—is not frequently flown to Geneva, not because of cost reasons but primarily because her counsel suspects that she is unlikely to create a fantastic impression on the tribunal. But then, the tribunal is said to have been selected by the parties, or at least it is difficult to make the argument that it is imposed. However, any attempt to cast it as a product of pure party autonomy grossly underappreciates the complexities of history that defined the contours of modern transnational life.

The key conclusion here is that the system of modern international arbitration and its apologists claim that they dispense superior justice because they are the sole custodians of the required technical competence and integrity. Those who complain are basically losers. This book argues that stranger justice is an inferior form of justice and lacks justification. What sustains it is an entrenched, vocal, insulting, well-represented, but outdated and parochial economic class enabled by the old economic and power hierarchy. It does not dispense superior justice because it demands to be understood without feeling the reciprocal duty to understand. How often prominent arbitrators admit that their failure to understand a witness who comes from a different cultural background is their shortcoming? Although Paulsson repeatedly talks about how "outsiders" lack the skills and everything else that is needed to succeed, and how they should try to learn his ways, never does he even mention the possibility that perhaps he also has a thing or two to learn from complaining cultural "outsiders." He leaves it as: perhaps someday arbitrators from Asia and Latin America may chair tribunals; as for Africa it is not yet foreseeable.[49]

Stranger justice is pretentious justice because the parties' submissions and arguments are carefully choreographed to appeal to arbitrators who have no understanding of the cultural milieu of at least one of the parties. People who have represented non-Western parties would know this. If learned counsel is told by five witnesses—all members of a bid committee—that they awarded the bid to a company without reading the papers submitted to them because they trusted the CEO of the foreign company who told them orally about his company; would that counsel choose to present these witnesses and have them testify before an all-Western arbitral tribunal? The story could be completely true but presenting these witnesses requires a lot of courage. If, however, the members of the arbitral tribunal are representatives of the communities that the parties come from, they would know exactly what the witnesses are talking about. It is just like a Cameroonian judge would not be dumbfounded if a witness—pointing to an orange shirt says it is red, or an Indian mediator who sees one of the parties nodding when the other speaks and later says he completely disagrees with what was said because he would know that he meant he was listening, not agreeing. These are simple examples but cultural moments of miscommunication are subtle yet profound, and undoubtedly affect outcome because every bit of miscommunication whether verbal or nonverbal goes to credibility, a key ingredient in any endeavor to determine facts.

The expertise in the procedural intricacies of international arbitration that elite arbitrators possess does not give them the key to learning the laws and cultures of hundreds of countries so as to be effective, informed, and conscientious judges of cases that grow out of places ranging from Albania to Zambia. In modern times, the reality is, the expertise that people look for in international arbitrators is of a different kind. It is the ability to influence others. It has little to do with the expertise on the law or the facts. Expertise is just a myth that justifies repeat appointments. It is remarkable to see that some beneficiaries of the myth take the flattery seriously.

2. Culturally Different Facts and Concepts: Applied Legal Philosophy

The applied legal philosophy literature lends some theoretical support to the problem of not being understood that practitioners who represent culturally different

49. *Id.*

clients have known all along. On one extreme end, a radical cultural incommensurability theory holds that no judge can acquire a culturally different concept.[50] Anthony Connolly's book, *Cultural Difference on Trial: The Nature and Limits of Judicial Understanding* is advertised as providing:

> [A] sustained philosophical exploration of the capacity of the modern liberal democratic legal system to understand the thought and practice of those culturally different minorities who come before it as claimants, defendants or witnesses . . . Drawing upon recent developments in the philosophy of mind and language and informed by a sound academic and practical grasp of the works of the legal system itself, this book systematically analyses the nature and limits of a judge's ability to understand culturally different thought and action over a course of a trial.[51]

This 2010 book does all of those things, but that is not why it is quoted here. It is quoted here for its relevance to the present discussion about the cultural deficiencies of the arbitral system and the pretension of its apologists that it does not exist. Culture complicates legal proceedings let alone in international arbitration where total strangers come together for the first time ever, as Connolly's book shows; even in liberal democracies, judges, who are members of the same community, have limits on understanding cultural minorities who live amongst them.

Connolly, who once represented indigenous people in Western Australia, appreciates the shortcomings of the radical incommensurability theory, essentially because the theory ignores the "conceptual identity or similarity of some degree or other between the conceptual schemes of any or all judges and any or all culturally different agents."[52] A shared degree of sameness or shared culture obviously ameliorates the incommensurability but does not eliminate it. Where there are no shared cultures and values, the incommensurability gets worse.[53]

The effect of cultural misunderstanding in legal proceedings is analyzed mainly in the context of indigenous populations in settler societies of Australia, Canada, and the United States. There is enormous social science literature, which makes the plausible argument that "judges—are unable to adequately conceptualize the thought and practice (and associated material artifacts) of the members of different cultures. Such agents do not and cannot possess an adequate concept of culturally different phenomena."[54]

50. *See, e.g.*, Anthony J. Connolly, Cultural Difference on Trial: The Nature and Limits of Judicial Understanding 167 (2010).

51. *Id.* at inside cover.

52. *Id.* at 169.

53. *See generally id.* at 165–81.

54. *Id.* at 1. In making this point Connolly relies on many writing by prominent scholars such as Kado Muir, who wrote "legal institutions do not understand Indigenous societies, [they] do not understand their relationship with their land, their belief systems, their history." *Id.* (citing Kado

Connolly continues writing:

> Because possessing a concept of an element of thought or practice involves possessing some set of the concepts actually informing that thought and practice, what this claim amounts to is that in their relations with culturally different groups, legal agents do not possess and are unable to adequately acquire some—perhaps, even any—of the concepts which inform the thought and practice of the members of those groups. They do not possess and cannot acquire what I will term, "culturally different concepts."[55]

He then says, "Few would argue that if a legal system is fundamentally disabled from performing its recognitional and protective role because of an inherent conceptual incapacity on the part of its agents, then that incapacity should be understood and appropriately responded to."[56] His conclusion after an exacting inquiry is that the radical incommensurability critics are probably exaggerating the problem, but the concerns of culturally different minorities and the issue of misunderstanding must be recognized and carefully addressed.[57]

The international arbitration community does not like to talk about the limits of concept acquisition and the complicating effect of culture for the rendition of a just and fair outcome. It pretends that its members have all the qualifications that all circumstances demand. Arbitrants must make themselves understood. The arbitrators owe them no duty to understand their cultures. How frequently do arbitrators decline appointments for fear of cultural incommensurability? The know-it-all protagonists are quick to deny their privilege, demand to be understood, but do not have the modesty to seek to understand the "cultural others" that they insult as defeatist, primitive, amateur, and lacking confidence.

Richard C. Waites and James E. Lawrence address cultural issues in international arbitration in the context of psychological dynamics.[58] In discussing the importance of narrative, they give an example of a typical international arbitration panel. The

Muir, *Reconciling through Understanding*, 4 AUSTL. INST. ABORIGINAL & TORRES STRAIT ISLANDER STUD., NATIVE TITLE RES. UNIT NEWSL. 3–4 (1999)); *see also id.* (citing Mary Ellen Turpel, *Aboriginal Peoples and the Canadian Charter: Interpretive Monopolies, Cultural Differences*, 6 CAN. HUM. RTS. Y.B. 3, 24 (1990) ("cultural differences are not such that they can be managed within the dominant legal conceptual-framework")); *id.* (citing Penelope Pether, *Principles or Skeletons? Mabo and the Discursive Constitution of the Australian Nation*, 41 L. TEXT CULTURE 115, 118 (1998) ("it is commonplace of accounts of indigenous culture . . . that connection with the land is at its heart, in a way radically incommensurable with the non-indigenous . . . legal consciousness.")).

55. *Id.* at 2.

56. *Id.* at 3.

57. *See id.* at 215.

58. Richard C. Waites & James E. Lawrence, *Psychological Dynamics in International Arbitration Advocacy*, *in* THE ART OF ADVOCACY IN INTERNATIONAL ARBITRATION 69–120 (Doak Bishop & Edward G. Kehoe eds., 2d ed. 2010). Waites is a board-certified trial attorney and social psychologist who has authored several writings on social psychology and courtroom trial and arbitration.

dispute regards a shipping contract between an Indian company and a Chinese company. The arbitration panel is composed of arbitrators from Sweden, the United States, and France.[59] The message is that counsel should try to formulate and advance a narrative that is likely to be appealing to all members of the panel regardless of their cultural background. The selected theme is "doing the right thing," which presumably appeals to all of them.[60] What the authors do not discuss in relationship to this is the more profound cultural difference between the parties and also between each party and the members of the tribunal, as well as possibly counsel on each side and witnesses. It is possible that no less than eight cultures are represented in this arbitration, because if it is a shipping contract witnesses could be from all over the world. But what is likely to affect the outcome of the arbitration is the perception that each one of the panel members would have of the parties, their counsel, and their witnesses. And, of course, their assessment of the veracity of the evidence adduced by each party largely depends on what they think of the presenters of evidence. Waites and Lawrence discuss this later point at great length. Their discussion is predicated on the assumption that "culture shapes human life and the human mind and gives meaning to the events and behaviors by creating an interpretive system."[61]

Emphasizing the importance of credibility in persuasion, they note that at times, "similarity is more important than credibility."[62] They continue to state that "[r]esearch in social psychology has supported the principle that only a credible speaker (someone hard to discount) can cause marked change in an arbitrator's thinking when advocating an idea that is greatly discrepant (different) from the preexisting attitude held by an arbitrator."[63]

At the more technical level, they outline the five steps that lead to the decision-making process in a typical arbitration: (1) form a story of what happened, (2) filter the evidence to find support, (3) compare their own story to the allegations, (4) try to make them fit together, and (5) negotiate with other arbitrators.[64] In terms of culture, the key here is comparing their story with the allegation:

> Each of them has a private story to tell about their successes and failures in life. Each of them has a family history that has helped them who they are. Each of them has a unique life outside the arbitration that influences the way they will view the issues during arbitration.[65]

59. *Id.* at 80.

60. *Id.*

61. *Id.* (citing Jerome Bruner, Acts of Meaning (1990)).

62. *Id.* at 98. To be sure, they also make the important point that similarity and credibility are more associated when making personal choices. With objective facts—such as scientific ones—the lectern pays more attention to expertise than similarity. *Id.*

63. *Id.*

64. *Id.* at 109 (emphasis added).

65. *Id.* at 107.

More importantly they add the following very instructive passage:

> Every arbitrator evaluates what transpires in arbitration on the basis of his or her life experiences, attitudes, and pre-dispositions. Arbitrators obviously do not come to the arbitration with blank minds. Their beliefs, values, attitudes, and morals are well entrenched, and everything that is heard and experienced will be filtered and colored by them.
>
> Research in the field of cognitive psychology has indicated that attitudes take on a role of directing or guiding human behavior in one direction or another, as opposed to motivating particular behavior. Therefore, attitudes may be considered to enter the picture predominately at crucial decision junctures. There are literally thousands of published scientific studies designed to understand the formation, maintenance, and change of attitudes that are available to us as reference tools.
>
> In the context of decision making in arbitration, salient beliefs and attitudes will guide individual arbitrators and the entire arbitration panel to reach a decision which conforms to their beliefs and attitudes about the specific issues present in the case.[66]

What is more interesting is the idea that such factors are at work without being recognized by the arbitrators themselves. They write to this effect:

> As we have seen, the result achieved by recent social science studies have clearly demonstrated that an arbitrator's cognitive life experiences have shaped the arbitrator's emotional processing, personality, persuadability, perceptions of casual attribution, perceptions of damages and reactions to attorneys and witnesses. It is equally clear that individual arbitrators and the arbitration panel as a whole are influenced by emotional or effective processing despite their inability to recognize and articulate it.[67]

In their excellent essay, "The United States Perspective and Practice of Advocacy,"[68] practitioners Doak Bishop and James H. Carter take the discussion to the more practical realm. They note the lessons that could be drawn from U.S. jury psychology. Trial lawyers in the United States sometimes hire companies specializing in jury psychology. The companies have highly specialized professionals with master's and PhD degrees[69] and "use scientific and quasi-scientific techniques to study mock jurors and help parties and lawyers prepare for trial."[70]

66. *Id.* at 110. (emphasis added).

67. *Id.* at 111.

68. Doak Bishop & James H. Carter, *The United States Perspective and Practice of Advocacy, in* The Art of Advocacy in International Arbitration 519–581 (Doak Bishop & Edward G. Kehoe eds., 2d ed. 2010).

69. *Id.* at 530.

70. *Id.*

One of the things that these companies do is conduct mock trials before a demographically similar jury. Sometimes they conduct the trial before several mock juries with varied demographics to gauge possible outcomes. Bishop and Carter finally note that:

> From the thousands of jury studies conducted in recent years, there has developed a literature on jury psychology and what technique may be persuasive. The most important determinate of how a jury decides a case is the juror's own values, attitudes, and beliefs.[71]

Bringing this conclusion to the sphere of international arbitration, they note that "[a] basic concept of persuasion is that the advocate should understand the motivation of the decision-maker and design the case to appeal to his or her values, attitudes and opinions."[72] They continue writing:

> It is little discussed in international arbitration, but certainly understood at some level, that a tripartite panel of arbitrators from different cultures and legal systems may have values that differ to a greater or lesser degree. Without intending any stereotyping, it seems indisputable that a variety of values may be found among arbitrators from different legal systems, such as a United States international lawyer, a British Barrister, a French professor of public international law, a practicing lawyer in South America, a professor of private international law from Africa, an Islamic lawyer trained in Shari'a law, and a Chinese law professor. Arbitrators from professions other than the law—engineers, accountants, and insurance or shipping executives—may bring still other values to the case. Even within each of these descriptions, differing values may certainly be found.[73]

They note that amid this incredible diversity "there are common values," and thus urge arbitrators to keep an open mind and avoid being "chauvinistic about their own systems."[74] Having made all of these very interesting points, they highlight one implicit

71. *Id.* at 532 (emphasis added). The passage that follows counsels:

> Although the creation of a favorable "mood" by a lawyer during witness examination and argument may influence and move a juror to a certain extent, counsel is unlikely in a trial to change the values of the jurors. Instead those values must be taken as the starting point of advocacy, and counsel's case should be designed to show how it implicates the juror's values, compelling a favorable result. "Know your audience" is good advice for any public speaker and critical for trial lawyers in large cases. This helps explain the growth of jury psychology studies.

Id.

72. *Id.* at 535.

73. *Id.* at 536. They define values as "basic, deep-seated beliefs such as religious beliefs," (2) attitudes as "lasting convictions that are more flexible than deeply-felt values," and (3) opinions as "current or temporary impressions." *Id.*

74. *Id.*

value that guides many contemporary international arbitrators, that is: "[a] view that arbitrators should decide cases in a manner that allows international commerce to flow and businesses to prosper (at least reasonably and according to law) is likely an understated, but important, value of most international arbitrators."[75] As much as it is true, this is, of course, where some fear borders ideological bias, which makes it difficult for governments and regulators to win cases even when their actions are "reasonable and according to law"—especially when such governments suffer from other negative stereotypes.

At a more practical level, Bishop and Carter give an example of a strategic choice one of them faced in an arbitral proceeding in which the key witness was an Asian-American whom counsel believed would not make a great impression on the tribunal despite the importance and credibility of what he or she had to say.[76] The strategy was reordering witnesses and calling the key witness after a good expert testimony and the opposing side's witness whose testimony was largely discredited. As the story is told by the authors, the Asian-American witness, whom they call "a problematic witness," makes a better-than-expecting showing."[77] There is almost no doubt that the reason counsel considered the Asian-American witness as "a problematic" witness is not limited to the witness not being "a good oral witness," but likely extends to who the arbitrators were. If two of the arbitrators were Asian-American or Asians (if the Asian-American is a naturalized citizen), perhaps sharing some level of "values and attitudes," and perhaps the perceived "deficiencies," he or she would not have been considered a problematic witness, assuming he or she were truthfully testifying to facts that are known to him or her.

Aristotle's general theory of persuasiveness[78] offers a great insight that explains the kinds of strategic decisions lawyers often make in circumstances similar to what is described above (assuming, of course, the accuracy of the assumptions about the composition of the tribunal, but even if it is not true in this case, chances are that in high- stake international arbitration matters, the tribunal would rarely, if at all, have persons of Asian origin unless perhaps the dispute involves Asian parties, in which case the party-appointed one would occasionally be Asian). Broken down into its most basic elements, the theory holds that there are only three technical means of persuasion. They lie in the character of the speaker, the emotional state of the listener, and in the argument itself.[79]

Key among these is, of course, the credibility of the speaker:

> The persuasion is accomplished by character whenever the speech is held in such a way as to render the speaker worthy of credence. If the speaker appears to be credible, the audience will form the second-order judgment that propositions put

75. *Id.* at 537.

76. *Id.* at 540–41.

77. *Id.* at 540.

78. Aristotle's Rhetoric, Stanford Encyclopedia of Phil., http://plato.stanford.edu/entries/aristotle-rhetoric/ (revised on Feb. 1, 2010).

79. *The Three Means of Persuasion, in id.*

forward by the credible speaker are true or acceptable. This is especially important in cases where there is no exact knowledge but room for doubt."[80]

Of Aristotle's familiar three pillars of persuasion (logos, ethos, and pathos), ethos is most relevant as it encompasses the element of likability, which could largely be gained from similarity.[81] It is often said that that is why politicians mention the remotest connection to a particular state or province when campaigning to gain votes, such as "my grandfather once spent the summer here and he loved it."

B. CONCLUSION

Going back to the main question that this book raises, if cultural proximity is so important in many different ways, why is stranger justice not only justified but also advocated as superior in international arbitration, as in Paulsson's book, *The Idea of Arbitration*?

As the discussions above show, the answer to this question is not easy. The imbalance is a combination of historical coincidences not unrelated to the old world order that privileged some over others, as well as contemporary efforts to maintain such privileges in many subtler and more modern ways. This gets complicated by the tendency to equate material advancement with moral superiority and hence the superiority of the quality of justice. Anthony Hopkins captures this in his article titled "Property Rights and Empire Building" very well: "Simultaneously, material advancement and evangelical revival strengthened the belief of most Europeans in the moral superiority of their own civilization. Westerners equated standards of morality with standard of living . . . ."[82] Richard Roberts and Kristin Mann, in their book, *Law in Colonial Africa*, add that "[t]he new faith of Europeans in the moral and material superiority of their civilization convinced them that exporting their culture would be good for Africans."[83]

At times this notion was enforced through the principle of "extraterritoriality"—a system of law whereby "the citizens and subjects of nations possessing European civilization enjoy in countries of non-European civilization, chiefly in the East, an extensive exemption from the operation of the local law."[84] At some point the United States and at least 19 European countries had secured such privileges for their citizens in China, including the United Kingdom, France, and Russia.[85] The United

80. *Id.*

81. The science appears conclusive about the link likability-similarity-credibility.

82. Anthony G. Hopkins, *Property Rights and Empire Building: Britain's Annexation of Lagos, 1861*, 40 J. Econ. Hist. 777, 788 (1980), *in* Law in Colonial Africa 10 (Richard Roberts & Kristin Mann eds., 1991).

83. *Id.* at 11.

84. James M. Zimmerman, China Law Deskbook: A Legal Guide for Foreign-Invested Enterprises 43 (3d ed., 2010) (quoting 2 John Basset Moore, A Digest of International Law 593 (1906)).

85. *Id.* at 593 (citing Harold Scott Quigley, *Extraterritoriality in China*, 20 Am. J. Int'l L. 46, 51 n.21 (1926)).

States Court for China, for example had jurisdiction over civil as well as criminal matters, and appellate jurisdiction resided in the Ninth Circuit Court of Appeals in San Francisco.[86] Western courts in China numbered in the hundreds, and although the Western powers promised to abandon the system as soon as China "modernized" its laws, they never followed through with their promise until the Japan factor in World War II changed everything.[87]

One of the primary objectives of international arbitration is to avoid local bias. The existence of local bias is not a new phenomenon. Many successful systems of law have been predicated on this assumption for millennia (such as diversity jurisdiction in the United States).[88] Parties in international commerce—apart from the often-raised but unsubstantiated assertion that outsiders may fare better in developed systems than in developing systems—recognize that a neutral forum would be better; however, the fundamental question remains: Does international arbitration provide a neutral forum while at the same time maintaining the technical and cultural ability to determine facts, apply law, and arrive at a fair and balanced outcome? As expressed in so many words above, the reasonable doubt pertains to the cultural competence of tribunals arbitrating cases brought before them by one or two parties who come from totally different cultural backgrounds from the arbitrators. A system of justice that demands to be understood without feeling the reciprocal duty to understand cannot be a fair one.

86. *Id.* at 43 (citing WESTEL WOODBURY WILLOUGHBY, FOREIGN RIGHTS AND INTERESTS IN CHINA 44–51 (1920).

87. *See id.* at 47–50. For a fuller discussion of the phenomenon of extraterritorialism and its justifications as it relates to China, see generally TEEMU RUSKOLA, LEGAL ORIENTALISM: CHINA, THE UNITED STATES, AND MODERN LAW 169–200 (Harvard University Press, 2013).

88. Under Article III of the Constitution of the United States, the two principal sources of jurisdiction of federal courts are diversity (as in parties coming from two or more states for fear that the state courts might be biased against the party outside the state), and cases arising under federal law (for obvious reasons). U.S. CONST. art III.

12

Conversations on the Role of Culture in International Arbitration

A. INTRODUCTION

Moments of cultural miscommunication occur in almost every arbitration room where the arbitrators, the parties, and their counsel come from different cultures and legal traditions in any combination. This is a simple observation of fact; it requires no empirical proof. However, measuring the extent of the complicating effects of cultural miscommunication in any arbitral proceeding is a difficult task. This chapter relies on a collection of anecdotal evidence to provide a useful insight into the obscure cultural world of international arbitration. More specifically, this chapter reports the conversations that the author had with International Court of Justice judges, other international arbitrators, and counsel from various legal traditions who have experienced firsthand the effects of cultural diversity in international legal proceedings.

The conversations took place in person in various countries over a period of three years. The few that have been selected for inclusion in this book were chosen for their representation of various legal traditions and perspectives. Before each meeting, I sent the following letter in advance to each jurist who agreed to meet with me:

> I am a member of the faculty of the Seattle University School of Law. I also serve as counsel in international arbitral proceedings. I specialize in international arbitration. The research question that I am looking at is the effect that cultural miscommunication may have on outcome and cost in international arbitration when the arbitrators, the parties and their witnesses as well as counsel on either side come from different cultural backgrounds regardless of the exact combination. More specifically, I am looking at the question of whether or not cultural miscommunication at any level could arguably affect outcome, and if so, in what way. The research is qualitative research rather than quantitative or statistical. It is basically a collection of anecdotal accounts from experienced judges, arbitrators and counsel from various legal traditions mainly from Common Law, Civil Law, Chinese, Islamic, and mixed legal traditions. The questions are very short and very specific but they invite longer commentary

The Culture of International Arbitration. Won L. Kidane

for those who would like to contribute to the debate in more substantial ways. Your response will be included in my forthcoming book: THE CULTURE OF INTERNATIONAL ARBITRATION (Oxford University Press, 2016.) I offer two possibilities for publication. One possibility is anonymous publication. The other one is identified publication. I believe the contribution would be more powerful if the author is identified but I will leave that choice to you.

The responses do not require any research because the book's principal purpose is to report the impressions of those who experience the problem firsthand. I will begin by sharing my own experience.

[I then related the story of the witness who identified an orange card as being yellow, as set forth in Chapter 1]

With this background, I sat down with several jurists from various backgrounds and legal traditions, and this chapter reports some of the conversations. The interviewees who have chosen to remain anonymous are identified as Jurist No. 1, Jurist No. 2, Jurist No. 3, etc.

B. CONVERSATIONS FILE

1. Conversation with Judge Abdulqawi Yusuf, Vice President of the International Court of Justice

My conversation with Judge Abdulqawi Yusuf,[1] vice president of the International Court of Justice, first took place on February 6, 2016, at the Radisson Blu Hotel in Addis Ababa, Ethiopia. I had been meaning to travel to The Hague to meet with him but we incidentally overlapped in Addis Ababa. Judge Yusuf was gracious enough to spare a couple of hours of his time for this conversation. I had already read some of his writings and speeches on arbitration, particularly his sustained criticism of the system for lack of diversity, and nothing he said during our conversation surprised me.

My first question for Judge Yusuf was what legal system he identified himself with. His answer was fascinating. He said he identified himself with both Somali customary law and the civil law tradition received from Italy during Somalia's colonial encounter. His legal thoughts were further influenced by the common law tradition because of his experience with that system throughout his legal career as an international lawyer, most recently during his tenure on the International Court of Justice (ICJ), many of the members of which come from the common law legal tradition.

Before we got into the details of cultural issues, he offered the following precautionary preamble, that is, that the basis of all decisions of the ICJ is international law, and because international law offers a common language, whatever cultural differences exist among the judges are bridged to a large extent by this commonality. In

1. Judge Yusuf's biographical information is available on the official website of the International Court of Justice at http://www.icj-cij.org/court/index.php?p1=1&p2=2&p3=1&judge=168.

any case, the manifestations of cultural differences are principally procedural, that is, the epistemology of determining facts and applying law.

He began by making one matter very clear: cultural background and experience have a profound effect on one's appreciation and processing of one's environment—and that translates into a particular inclination to believe or disbelieve certain facts. Because the judges of the Court come from different legal traditions, an attempt is always made to come up with common procedural tools to streamline the process and arrive at an acceptable result.

Be that as it may, according to Judge Yusuf, the degree of appreciation of certain facts depends on a number of factors but, to him, the most important ones are ideological leaning and legal tradition. These two factors, he says, inevitably affect the finding of facts and application of law, and hence perhaps the outcome of a case. Judge Yusuf said that he wouldn't be surprised if research found that there was a statistically significant split not only along ideological leanings, which cannot be surprising, but also along legal tradition with respect to decision-making bodies containing members from different legal traditions.

That said, however, he emphasizes that there are many instances where the nature of the evidence or its presentation appears unacceptable to everyone on the Court despite its validity under the legal tradition of wherever it comes from. He gives an example of this: in one particular case, one of the parties presented a written witness statement taken by the police. It was explained to the court that the police spoke with the witness and drew a report based on their conversation with the witness. Although such practice was very common in that country's legal tradition, this affected, for Judge Yusuf, the entire testimony because of the assumption that the involvement of the police might have irredeemably tainted the testimony.

This was an interesting observation because while legal traditions differ on the degree of suspicion they assign to witness statements prepared by lawyers, which may range from total acceptance to respectful disregard, when a written witness statement comes in the form of a police report, it crossed the boundary of acceptability at least for Judge Yusuf, and maybe for other judges.

Linked to this, however, he cautions that it is easy to over-appreciate the effects of ideological leanings and background. In many cases, like any court in the world, he said that ideological divides exist but at times, in his experience, such divides tend to correlate to a certain extent to the level of development of the country of origin of the particular judges in terms of the progressive development of international law. This is not by any means a scientific finding but a simple anecdotal observation of serving on the ICJ for about seven years.

In relation to the Court's conduct of proceedings and the role of counsel, Judge Yusuf made another interesting observation. He said that in most cases, the same core group of lawyers from the major centers such as Washington, Paris, and London tend to dominate but there were instances whereby countries were represented by their own national firms. He cited some examples from recent memory such as in the *Democratic Republic of Congo v. Guinea*,[2] the DRC was represented

2. *See* Ahmadou Sadio Diallo (Republic of Guinea v. Democratic Republic of the Congo), Compensation, Judgment, I.C.J. Reports 2012, p. 324.

by DRC lawyers, and in the *Belgium v. Senegal* case,[3] Senegal was represented by Senegalese lawyers. What he said next was more interesting: he said that he thought that in instances where developing countries used their own counsel, it added some credibility to the position that they were advocating. He also said that his observation appeared to have been shared by some of his colleagues on the Court.

This observation is also quite remarkable for other reasons: First, it challenges the dominant narrative that highly sophisticated and expensive counsel is always better and more credible. Second, it also shows that there is a degree of curiosity among the members of the Court about who is appearing on whose behalf, although it is difficult to determine what the impact of such curiosity might be. But third and perhaps more important, Judge Yusuf's observation offers new evidence to the science of persuasion, which links credibility to likability and likability to likeness. Perhaps the science itself is imperfect—or is it?

Judge Yusuf is a well-known critic of the international arbitral process for its lack of diversity, considering it a basic question of legitimacy. I continued my conversation with Judge Yusuf, meeting him in The Hague again, and also listening most recently to his May 2016 Keynote Speech at the biannual conference of the International Council for Commercial Arbitration (ICCA) in Mauritius in which he summarized the customary origins of arbitration in Africa, the colonial disruption of customary law and the delocalization in the postcolonial period, and the need to bring international arbitration back to Africa. His remarks were summarized in part by the Global Arbitration Review as follows:

> Arbitration under the acacia tree
>
> Yusuf reminded delegates that arbitration is not "alien" but "indigenous" to Africa, as part of customary law in the region. In Somalia, it existed long before the colonial period, based on the consent of the parties and with arbitrators chosen from among the elders of a community.
>
> If the arbitrators and disputing parties came from the same community, an even number of arbitrators would be selected who had to decide the case unanimously, he said. Where the arbitrators were from a different community, an odd number was selected and the case decided by majority.[4]

This emphasizes the central point that this book attempts to make by highlighting the importance of the notion of cultural proximity between the decision-maker and the disputing parties. In the traditional sense, the elected arbitrators were elders of the community, presumably with a deeper understanding of the historical and cultural context of each dispute that they were called upon to resolve. Linking it to the prevalence of the rule of law, Judge Yusuf said that: "This practice survived into the early 1990s when 'chaos reigned' in Somalia. Although the 'state apparatus' had

3. *See* Questions relating to the Obligation to Prosecute or Extradite (Belgium v. Senegal), Judgment, I.C.J. Reports 2012, p. 422.

4. Sebastian Perry, *Time to "Relocalise" Arbitration to Africa, ICCA Told*, GLOBAL ARBITRATION REV. (May 10, 2016).

disappeared, people were still able to 'meet under the acacia tree' to resolve local disputes, thus upholding the rule of law."[5]

This customary means of dispute settlement was largely overridden in most parts of Africa by the advent of colonialism, which fundamentally transformed the relationship that African people had with their own laws and legal institutions. As Judge Yusuf told ICCA, "The colonial legislation 'was a legal transplant which failed to grow on African soil,' and created a 'disconnect' between African societies and arbitration for quite some time in the 20th century . . . African customary arbitration had reflected 'a widespread sense of justice' among communities. Without that sense of justice, the rule of law becomes 'a hollow and lifeless concept that is at odds with the realities and needs of society.'"[6]

The sense of hollowness of arbitral justice that African parties feel in Paris, Geneva, or Washington does not require statistical validation, but what Judge Yusuf does not mention in this particular speech is that the colonial rulers considered African customary law a crude form of justice and as such inadequate for the ordering of African affairs, let alone its role in defining the relationship between the colonized and the colonizer. As stated in some detail in various parts of this book, in the postcolonial period, as the relations between the former colonial powers and their former colonies became "gradually legalized," the perception of the inadequacy of the laws and institutions of the former colonies was exacerbated by the failure of "the transplanted seeds to grow" rendering the domestic judiciaries unacceptable. But then when international arbitration as an alternative means of dispute settlement emerged and was promoted by international financial institutions, aid organizations, model contracts, North-South investment treaties, international arbitral institution, education programs, and textbooks, it created the illusion of a supranational legal order that required particular expertise that only the developed world possessed; the obvious result was outsourcing Africa's system to Europe[7] under the pretext that Africans lacked the legal infrastructure and the expertise to resolve disputes that arise within their own territories. As repeatedly mentioned in this book, the problem lies in the perception that disputes have a technological solution.

In the same speech, Judge Yusuf said that:

> Disputing European parties may regard Switzerland as a neutral venue . . . but for African parties in a dispute with Europeans, Geneva is less likely to be seen as neutral. Another problem is the "continued absence" of African arbitrators from the tribunals that resolve Africa related disputes. . . . It is important for the legitimacy of the arbitral process that Africans make a contribution to "standard setting" and the evolution of governance norms. The lack of representation on tribunals hinders "knowledge transmission" and makes

5. *Id.*

6. *Id.* at 2.

7. *Id.* at 3 ("Yusuf said the main problem holding back the contribution of international arbitration to the rule of law in Africa is the 'delocalisation' of the proceedings. He estimated that more than 95 per cent of arbitrations involving an African party take place outside the continent.")

African states more reluctant to embrace arbitration as a dispute resolution mechanism.[8]

Judge Yusuf expressed the problem with a profound sense of modesty that is becoming of the office he holds, but the reality remains that there is no justification, whether it is the supposed lack of expertise or backwardness of the laws. At the most basic level, what arbitral justice requires is conscientious arbitrators who are familiar with the law of the decision and the cultural context of the facts that gave rise to the dispute. Obviously they also have to have the availability, interest, neutrality, independence, relevant skills, and temperament to resolve disputes involving African parties. An arbitral process, like any legal process, is essentially the determination of fact and the application of law. The argument that Africa lacks the capacity to resolve its own disputes is not a credible assertion. My conversation with Judge Yusuf ended there for now.

2. Conversation with Judge Xue Hanqin, Judge of the International Court of Justice

I had the honor of meeting with Judge Xue Hanqin of the International Court of Justice on May 4, 2016, in her office in the Peace Palace.[9] At the outset, I mentioned that I had the opportunity to attend her talk a few years earlier at the annual meeting of the American Society of International Law (ASIL) in Washington DC, and that some of the questions I wanted to raise with her were inspired by her remarks about the limited pool of counsel who appear before the World Court. After a brief discussion about her lecture and also my previous book on dispute settlement in China-Africa economic relations, Judge Xue pointedly asked me to describe the core argument of the book that we were supposed to talk about. My response led to a lengthy conversation about the role of culture in transnational legal proceedings in general.

I mentioned that the essence of my argument is that the new world of international arbitration must be sensitive to the representational deficit not only for the sake of political legitimacy but also for the purpose of ensuring the accuracy and fairness of the outcome in all cases. I argue that if, at the most basic level, the legal process involves three fundamental steps (i.e., the identification of the applicable rules of law, the finding of facts, and application of the facts to the identified law), the best arbitrator should be someone who is familiar with the applicable law, understands the cultural background of the facts, and has the ability to apply the law to the facts. Applying these simple criteria, there simply is no reason, for example, in disputes involving Chinese investors against African states, all three arbitrators have to always be European, although it is not inconceivable that the application

8. *Id.*

9. Judge Xue's biographical information is available on the official website of the International Court of Justice at: http://www.icj-cij.org/court/index.php?p1=1&p2=2&p3=1&judge=170.

of the above criteria may occasionally lead to the selection of all three European arbitrators.

Judge Xue then asked an important question: she said that "if you are saying that the best arbitrators are those who are familiar with the cultures of the disputing parties, and assuming that your argument about a positive correlation between cultural familiarity and the accuracy of arbitral fact-finding, how about the essential elements of neutrality and independence?" Stated simply, the question hypothesizes that all things being equal, aren't Europeans more neutral and independent than say Chinese or African arbitrators in China-Africa disputes, for example. This is, of course, a reality that must be recognized. Indeed, part of the reason for the disproportionate number of Europeans in arbitral proceedings involving all sorts of parties around the world might be the perceived neutrality and independence. Although I agreed with this assumption, I added the following caveat: arguably, cultural proximity does not necessarily deny a prospective arbitrator of neutrality and independence. Those are virtues that need to be weighed on a case-by-case basis. But all things being equal, would, for example, a tribunal composed of a Chinese, an African, and a European chair produce a more accurate, fair, and politically acceptable result? My suggestion was that the reason this is not already a common combination in practice is not because of doubts about neutrality and independence of Chinese or African arbitrators but because of the mythology that considers international arbitration as a field of study that only Europeans and some North Americans and New Zealanders have specialized in. It is the mindset that considers international arbitration as some type of Eurocentric technology. If the legal process is understood as the simple finding of fact and application of law, there is no reason the same pool of arbitrators is considered the best option in every major dispute everywhere. This approach ignores the fact that international arbitration is a framework under which a wide array of disputes involving different parties around the world are supposed to be resolved. The same group of individuals cannot always be the most qualified in all cases everywhere.

Although Judge Xue seems to have appreciated the concern that I outlined, she counsels that the role culture plays in transnational legal processes—be it in the determination of fact or interpretation and application of law—could at times be over-appreciated. She added a very instructive commentary about her own experience on the World Court. She said that there is no doubt that the various members of the Court sometimes assign varying degrees of credence to certain forms of evidence or arguments, and may even be differently impressed by differing styles of argumentation; be that as it may, however, culture is by no means the only explanation for that. There are so many factors that influence one's opinions, inclinations, and impressions; culture is just one of those factors. Clearly, Judge Xue assigns more of a role to professional background such as legal training and experience on the judiciary or foreign service or the academia. For her, these kinds of professional differences may have a more profound influence on the mindset and preferences of the individual member, and may in turn affect the appreciation of law and fact.

Ultimately, however, as the factors that determine one's overall opinions and inclinations are too many to account for, she remains unsure about the singular role culture as a function of origin or belongingness to a particular national or linguistic community might play. Indeed, it would appear that all these factors cumulatively shape one's culture. But at the end, she emphasized that it is not prudent to deny the role of culture in legal proceedings, whatever meaning is assigned to the term "culture" itself. In fact, interestingly, she mentioned that she suspects that what lurks behind the dispute between Japan and Australia in the *Whaling* case[10] is probably the deferring cultural appreciations of the phenomenon, which is rooted in centuries of tradition acceptable to one side but not to the other.[11] Having given these insightful comments, she ended the conversation with the following cautionary note: "As the saying goes, always remember that we are all prisoners of our own house."

10. Whaling in the Antarctic (Australia v. Japan: New Zealand intervening), Judgment, I.C.J. Reports 2014, p. 226.

11. She elaborated this point in a speech she delivered at the University of Manchester the day after I met her in her office, titled Cultural Element in International Law (Melland Schill Lecture University of Manchester, May 5, 2016). The comment pertaining to the cultural aspect of the *Whaling* case is reproduced with Judge Xue's permission as follows.

> Australia filed an Application against Japan, alleging that Japan's scientific whaling program (JARPA II) had breached its obligations under the International Convention for the Regulation of Whaling ("the Whaling Convention") and its other international obligations for the preservation of marine mammals and the marine environment. Australia claimed that the catches of whales with the special permits issued by Japan under JARPA II were over excessive, revealing that the actual purpose of JARPA II was for commercial whaling rather than scientific research. Japan, for its part, argued that its issuance of special permits to catch whales under JARPA II was in conformity with Article VIII, paragraph 1, of the Whaling Convention. During the process, New Zealand intervened as a non-party under Article 63 of the Statute. Notwithstanding Japan's request for a second round of written pleadings, the Court decided to have just one round. As the case was scientific evidence intensive, experts were appointed by the parties and later were cross-examined during the oral hearings. In its Judgment, the Court found, *inter alia*, that the special permits granted by Japan in connection with JARPA II did not fall within the provisions of Article VIII, paragraph 1, of the Whaling Convention and therefore Japan should revoke the extant special permits in relation to JARPA II, and refrain from granting further permits under the programme concerned.
>
> During the proceedings, Japan did not conceal its sentiment of being culturally prejudiced against by the West with regard to its whaling tradition. Procedurally it was apparently unhappy with the Court's decision not to have a second round of written pleadings and the way in which New Zealand handled its intervention, as it had allegedly coordinated its position with Australia. More than that, compared with the Applicant, the Japanese team looked uneasy about the way in which the cross-examination of experts was conducted.
>
> After the delivery of the Judgment, although Japan stated that it would respect the decision of the Court, it continued the scientific whaling activities by reducing the number of target catches of whales.
>
> On 7 October 2015, a year and half after the delivery of the Court's Judgment in the *Whaling* case, Japan deposited with the Secretary-General of the United Nations in his capacity as depositary, a declaration of its acceptance of the compulsory jurisdiction of the Court under Article 36, paragraph 2, of the Statute, which in effect adds one paragraph to Japan's original declaration, excluding from the Court's jurisdiction, " any dispute arising out of, concerning, or relating to research on, or conservation, management or exploitation of, living resources of the sea." Clearly, this new reservation will prevent any future legal actions in the Court against Japan for whaling activities.

3. Conversation with Judge Julia Sebutinde, Judge of the International Court of Justice

Judge Julia Sebutinde of the International Court of Justice kindly received me in her office in the Peace Palace in the afternoon of May 3, 2016.[12] Judge Sebutinde comes to the Court with extensive judicial experience, including service as judge of the Special Court for Sierra Leone between 2005 and 2012 during which time she heard such high profile cases as *Prosecution v. Charles Taylor*, the former Liberian

In my view, even if Japan's presumed concerns were taken care of, it would not have in any event altered the outcome of the Court's decision. There are, however, some cultural elements which may emerge in other contexts as well.

First of all, whaling is a highly sensitive issue in the environmental field. Japan has long been put on the defensive in the public for its whaling activities. Against that background, Japan was very likely more sensitive to the fairness of procedural decisions of the Court. Although under the Rules of Court, it is up to the Court to decide whether there should be a second round of written pleadings, Japan reacted strongly to the Court's decision not to have a second round. Linguistically it is understandable that Japan might feel more confident with written arguments than oral. A second round would have provided it with another opportunity to strengthen its position. However, Japan, as the respondent State, had the last word during the written phase. It should have taken that into consideration before it raised its request.

Secondly, Japan was displeased with New Zealand's intervention. Even though New Zealand intervened as a non-party under Article 63 of the Statute for the purpose of giving its own interpretation to the Whaling Convention, because of its like-mindedness with the Applicant on whaling, its intervention reinforced Japan's impression that the case was culturally biased.

Moreover, as the case heavily involved scientific evidence, cross-examination of the experts appointed by the parties proved crucial (citing President Peter Tomka stated that "it is a procedure that is particularly useful in cases with major scientific content, or where the factual background is a particularly complex one." Speech by H.E. Judge Peter Tomka, President of the International Court of Justice, to the Sixth Committee of the General Assembly, 2014, UN doc. A/69/PV.33.)

Although technically the examination was conducted by its foreign counsels who are skilful with the procedure, culturally Japan was apparently less familiar with the technique of cross-examination than the Applicant, which may amplify its scepticism towards the judicial process.

Lastly, Japan's decision to exclude future legal actions on whaling from the jurisdiction of the Court not just shows its reservation to the decision of the Court in the *Whaling* case, but also reveals a deep-rooted mentality towards lawsuits that Asian culture generally shares; namely, try to avoid confrontation in the courts. While the English saying goes, if you cannot beat it, join it, Asian culture teaches us that, if you cannot beat it, leave it or avoid it (The Chinese version goes: "惹不起,躲得起; 打不过, 躲得过。*re bu qi, duo de qi; da bu guo, duo de guo.*" In ancient China, there is another proverb saying: "Avoid litigation; for once you resort to law there is nothing but trouble.")

Of course, Japan is not the only country that withdraws its acceptance of the Court's jurisdiction after it loses its case. The *Whaling* case, nevertheless, presents a good example demonstrating a clash of cultural differences in the judicial settlement of international disputes. Missing its cultural element, one would not be able to understand why third-party settlement is not a purely technical process.

12. Judge Sebutinde's biographical information is available on the official website of the International Court of Justice at http://www.icj-cij.org/court/index.php?p1=1&p2=2&p3=1&judge=194.

president. Through decades of national and international judicial service, she has had extensive firsthand experience of the complicating effects of cultural miscommunication in legal proceedings. When I told her that my study focuses on the impact of cultural miscommunication in international arbitration, she immediately thought of her own experience in one particular case as one of the judges of the Special Court for Sierra Leone. She narrated it for me as follows.

The case involved a criminal prosecution of a group of men accused of gang-raping an elderly woman in Sierra Leone during that country's civil war in the 1990s. The victim was brought to court to provide testimony. As Judge Sebutinde described it, the woman was led to the witness stand in the semicircular courtroom built up to the United Nations standard, appearing utterly distraught and disoriented although 10 years had lapsed between the events and the testimony. Once she took the witness stand, she kept her head down, at no point making eye contact throughout her testimony. She didn't even appear to have been oriented about the physical location of the judges, prosecutors, and defense counsel in the courtroom.

Her ordeal began as early as the very first line of questioning about her biographical information, about how many children she had and how old they were. Judge Sebutinde paused and said that "one might expect everyone to have a simple relationship with basic numbers but for this elderly woman it was easier to name her seven children than just say the number seven." When she was asked about how many children, her instinct is to name her children rather than say the number "seven." Numbers are not important to her day-to-day life. Ages of her children, she would not remember. Indeed, her notion of time is different. When asked what year, she would say the year such and such events occurred. When asked about time of the day, she would say when the sun was overhead or at the time the cows were coming home rather than noon or 18:00 hours.

As Judge Sebutinde puts it, "one might find this interesting, even amusing, but for her and her community, that is how she led her entire peaceful life until unspeakable misery found her exposing her culture to stranger judgment." But for Judge Sebutinde, who had served as a high court judge in Uganda for several years before her appointment to the Special Court for Sierra Leone, none of this seemed strange at all. She was deeply familiar with every aspect of this.

What she told me next was more remarkable. As the questioning of the witness progressed and she was asked to describe the most serious violation she had endured, at first, she refused to answer the question altogether. For one thing, her husband was seated in the front row. Her children and grandchildren were also in the audience. When she realized that she had to speak about the violation, which was the main reason she was brought into the courtroom as a witness, after much hesitation and agony, in answering the question about what one of the accused persons did to her, she responded: "He made me his wife." Judge Sebutinde, who had heard of a similar response to express the act of rape in the past, had absolutely no confusion about what the witness meant. In that culture, the term "rape" lacks an equivalent terminology appropriate for formal communication, but even if it had such, in Judge Sebutinde's experience, victims are always reluctant to say it publicly, choosing indirect expressions instead. But when the record development of the formal legal process demands an accurate verbal expression to have a formal legal effect, such lack of verbal expression or confusing legal expression could be fatal to the case.

Indeed, Judge Sebutinde had encountered a similar expression when she was a high court judge in Uganda. Significantly, in that particular case, the accused was a young man; the victim was an elderly woman. The accused chose to remain silent, invoking a constitutional right not to testify against himself. When asked to identify the nature of the violation she faced, the elderly woman used the exact same expression: "he made me is wife." Judge Sebutinde recounted the ridicule that the elderly woman faced, including laughter by the accused in the courtroom. But when the prosecutor asked her to be more specific as required by modern day criminal procedure, pointing to the accused, she said "ask him, ask him what he did to me." However, Judge Sebutinde found the woman's testimony credible on the basis of the totality of the circumstances and convicted the accused of rape. In an interesting clash of cultures, the case took its course in the formal judicial system, and Judge Sebutinde's decision was reversed on appeal, mainly because the witness did not identify the act with sufficient specificity and accuracy. The effects of such legal pluralism is, of course, not unique to Uganda. It is the typical feature of the normative world inhabited by communities across Africa and beyond who struggle to meaningfully reconcile transplanted laws and institutions with their ever-dwindling customary laws and traditions.

I then asked Judge Sebutinde if the customary system of law would have handled this situation better. She gave me a very instructive but nuanced response. She said that there certainly are aspects of the customary system of law that could be viewed positively, including the total understanding of what the elderly woman meant when she said "he made me his wife," as well as perhaps the focus on the means of civil compensation; however, there are other aspects of customary justice that cannot be acceptable, such as forcing a marriage as a means of restoring equilibrium or resolving the violation. At the end, she emphasized that many communities around the world inhabit complicated normative universes, and the solution to the problem of legal pluralism and cultural misunderstanding is not easy to come by.

Coming back to the subject of the International Court of Justice on which she has been serving since she left the Special Court for Sierra Leone in 2012, Judge Sebutinde emphasized the hybrid nature of the rules of procedure and the mutual recognition by members of the court of the occasional difference of emphasis on various techniques. Indeed, for Judge Sebutinde, who comes from the common law legal tradition, to the extent there are differing views on issues of procedure and methods of developing the factual record, they are mainly attributable to the legal tradition background of the judges, which means mainly the difference between common law and civil law rather than the country of origin or some other attribute. An example she offered was the reaction of various members of the court when counsel asks leading questions during direct examination of witnesses. Her observation is that despite the hybrid rules, the administration of which is largely left to the president of the court in each individual case, in instances where counsel engage in such line of questioning, the level of discomfort felt by those who come from the common law tradition is not at all shared by those who come from the civil law tradition. She counsels, however, that the existing differences do not seem to present unmanageable difficulties. With that we ended out conversation.

4. Conversation with Jurist No. 1

At the time I sat down with Jurist No. 1, in 2015, he was serving as the president of an Asian arbitrators association. He is a barrister-at-law, chartered arbitrator, and accredited mediator. He holds degrees from Harvard among other academic institutions. He served as an arbitrator, mediator, and counsel for three decades primarily in the Asia Pacific region. He is fluent in both Chinese and English. He is particularly familiar with the challenges of arbitral or even judicial decision-making where there is linguistic and cultural diversity among the decision-makers, counsel, and parties. This is particularly so because in addition to sitting as an arbitrator and serving as counsel in international arbitral proceedings, he also acts as counsel/barrister in domestic court litigation in mixed systems because of his multi-jurisdictional training and licensing.

Witnessing cultural miscommunication is a day-to-day occurrence for him. When I asked him to share his experience in this regard, particularly if he thinks whether cultural miscommunication is a serious problem in international arbitration to the point where it might affect outcome as well as costs, his answer was “most definitely yes.” He said:

> without even getting too far, just consider the cost of live interpretation and translation of documents from one language to another just because one or more of the arbitrators are not proficient in the language of the transaction, the relevant documents, the parties and the witnesses. It is both the cost of translation and the amount of time that it takes to get through the proceedings. The time that the proceedings take could easily double considering the interpretation of witness testimony and the translation of documents. In an industry where time quite literally translates into money, there is no question about the cost implications. As to impact on the determination of facts, there is no doubt in my mind that it affects outcome in more cases than we are willing to acknowledge. Apart from the unavoidable misinterpretation or mistranslation issues that everybody experiences and could easily appreciate, there are subtler ways.

He then continued to give me examples of the subtler forms of cultural miscommunications that could potentially affect outcome. For him, the challenges of cultural diversity are more profound than simple linguistic miscommunication. He told me about a case that he was arguing that morning right before I met him for coffee to talk about these issues. The case was an insider-trading one. The tribunal was composed of two members from China and one from Britain. One of the key witnesses was the director of the company accused of insider trading. The director, a Chinese national, is not fluent in English although he speaks some English because he had studied in the United States for three years. During his testimony, he pled ignorance of the insider-trading rules of the applicable jurisdiction. Jurist

No. 1 did not claim to know what each member of the tribunal might have thought of the testimony—whether they believed the witness or not—but he strongly believed that the two Chinese judges appeared more inclined to believe him than the English one. Although it seemed an overgeneralization, we continued to talk about it a little bit more. I tended to agree with him for the following reason. The level of development of the place where one is raised and educated without a doubt shapes the mindset, instilling a particular barometer for measuring credibility. From my own experience, the level of know-how and perfection expected of professionals in developed countries is not the same as in developing countries. Judges sitting in judgment of professional conduct in developed countries generally come from the same background as the witnesses with certain expectations. Positions of power in business, law, politics, etc. are occupied by persons of some minimum abilities and training. Again this is in relative terms. So, the level of proficiency and versatility expected of someone occupying a position of leadership in developed countries is ordinarily higher than in developing countries. If the judge's expectation is naturally higher, he or she would be less likely to believe the testimony we mentioned above, that is, a Chinese director of a big company that does business internationally who said he did not know that his conduct might have ran afoul of other country's laws relating to insider trading rules. The point is that the Chinese judges' assessment of the credibility of this witness is more likely to be more accurate than the English judge's who might be inclined to apply a more stringent set of criteria for competence commensurate with his or her own background and expectations. Incidentally, Jurist No. 1 did indeed believe the witness, but he does not think that the English member of the tribunal did so. This is pure speculation but a useful anecdote nonetheless.

The conversation then shifted to the general culture of arbitral institutions and the nature of justice that emerges out of them. Jurist No. 1 brought up the modus operandi of some commodities trade institutions. He was critical of the closed nature of the list of arbitrators, and the financial contribution of companies to such institutions, which he believes could provide the wrong incentives, and also the appointment of arbitrators and chairs by these institutions, which he said impinges upon party autonomy. I agreed with him, even providing an example of my own experience before one of these commodities institutions. In one particular case, a decision on jurisdiction took more than four years. We agreed that the culture of some of these institutions is disconcerting at best. We left it as that for the day.

5. Conversation with Jurist No. 2

Jurist No. 2 is a Singaporean jurist who has practiced international arbitration for more than 20 years. When I spoke with him in 2015 in Hong Kong, he was a partner at a major global law firm. He splits his time between Singapore and Hong Kong. He has acted for numerous Chinese and non-Chinese clients and also served as a sole and party-appointed arbitrator in numerous cases. He has also served as chair of three-member panels. He kindly shared with me his perspectives on the issue of cultural miscommunication in arbitral proceedings.

The first case that came to his mind was a dispute between a Chinese party and a Western party. In that case, he was a sole arbitrator. The proceeding was in English, although he spoke Chinese and counsel on both sides spoke Chinese. The witnesses testified in Chinese through an interpreter. The interesting part of it he said was that he often corrected the interpretation, as did the counsel on the other side. He said, "I don't really know how someone who did not speak Chinese could understand the intricacies of the case on the basis of the interpretation. It was fundamentally flawed. For someone who did not understand the language of the witness, the essence of the testimony could have easily been lost in translation."

In another case he acted as counsel for a Chinese company in a dispute against an American company. He started by saying "you know how the Chinese dislike dispute and like settling disputes amicably?" I said somewhat jokingly, "yes, I have heard that story before." He said "Well, it is true," and continued to tell me of one particular incident that came to his mind. The head of this Chinese company that he was representing went to the United States to try and meet with his counterpart to settle the dispute. When he arrived at the office of the American company, he was told that no one was willing to see him and that the American company wanted to go to arbitration, confident that it would win. When he returned to China, he was visibly upset, feeling insulted. He immediately instructed his counsel to vigorously pursue the arbitration. After the pleadings were exchanged and right before the hearing, the American company approached his counsel seeking a settlement. He said they settled on terms that were very favorable to his Chinese client—so favorable that the boss got a huge reward that year. The key point he was trying to make was the reason that the American company thought that it had the better argument was clearly because the Chinese side never articulated its position very well before the lawyers' exchange of pleadings. Indeed, if the American company had known the reasons the Chinese company acted the way it did, it would not have insisted on going to arbitration, unceremoniously dismissing the idea of a settlement by the senior management of the Chinese company. This to him was clearly a cultural miscommunication that affected the outcome.

The conversation then focused on broader issues of arbitrator selection and appointment and the general culture and politics of it. I asked him what composition he would consider ideal when he represents Chinese parties. He said "in disputes involving a Chinese party and a Western party, if you appoint a Chinese arbitrator, in most likelihood, the two other arbitrators would be Western arbitrators. Because it is difficult to find a Chinese arbitrator who would command significant respect among the very small circle of the world's arbitrators, the safest bet would be to appoint a prominent Western arbitrator who has great understanding and appreciation of Asian culture." That would obviously mean that all members of the tribunal would most likely be Western. I asked if that would pose a cultural miscommunication problem. Replying affirmatively, he puzzled over what might the solution be when the politics of appointment possibly compromises the nature and quality of justice. He then said: "the problem really is linguistic not technical competence. If the language of the proceeding were to be Chinese, you would have no difficulty finding excellent Chinese arbitrators who would get to the bottom of the dispute and write great awards." Perhaps, he added: "the key is in the drafting of the arbitration agreement." We agreed on that point and left it at that.

6. Conversation with Jurist No. 3

My next stop was at the Hong Kong International Arbitration Center (HKIAC) at Three Exchange Square. I had attempted to make contacts with the officials for about a week, but I thought I had succeeded when a friend sent me an email saying that one of the officials was willing to see me the next day. Indeed, my friend had forwarded me an email the official had sent him saying: "I understand your contact Mr. Kidane would like to visit the KKIAC. I would be happy to meet him. Kindly let me know what times suit. Best Regards." After receiving this email, I sent my friend an email asking if 10 am would be suitable for the official. Getting no response because my friend was in the middle of a meeting in Beijing, I headed out to the Center without making an appointment, just like the Chinese business executive that Jurist No. 2 described who went to America thinking that he would see his counterparts and settle the dispute. Recall that he was rebuffed and came back home determined to fight. When I arrived at the Center's office on the 38th floor of Two Exchange Square, the place felt quiet. I was asked to wait until the official was notified about my arrival. I did not make an appointment. I had just followed an email lead. I assumed that official would be from China or Hong Kong. Linked to that, I further assumed that the official would be okay with my showing up without an appointment, especially because of the email that was sent saying the official would be able to meet that day. After about 30 minutes of wait, the receptionist asked me to move from the lobby to a small conference room. I was given hot water. While I was waiting for the official to come, I took out my notebook in preparation for our conversation. I anxiously waited for the arrival. A few minutes later, the official opened the door wide, approached me, and without saying hello, forcefully said, with a distinctively American accent: "I was not expecting you this morning. I am in the middle of something. I cannot meet with you now. Your friend did not say that you would come this morning." No Asian man or woman had ever treated me like that anywhere in the world. Because the only purpose of my visit was to study cultural miscommunication, I thought that was an interesting moment. I said, I am sorry, I came without having an appointment. Perhaps I can come back in the afternoon. The official said "Yes, that would be better. Can you come back at 2:30 pm?" I said, "Yes indeed" and left.

On my way back to my hotel, the first thought that came to my mind was not to return to that place. I said to myself, perhaps I should email my friend and tell him that I won't go back to HKIAC because I felt unwelcome. But then, I said to myself, perhaps I should give this official the benefit of the doubt and go back and talk to her like a professional. I also continued to blame myself for making all the assumptions about the official and the center. Indeed, the first thing I did when I got to my hotel was Google the official's name.

Well, once I established the American connection, as strange as it might sound, I felt a little better, as if culture could be an excuse for unacceptable behavior. Perhaps culture makes behavior more acceptable. It occurred to me that it is probably close to impossible for a person born and raised in the Chinese culture to act that way toward strangers no matter what the circumstances might be. As I was making notes, I decided to go back and engage the official in a conversation. While I waited, I continued to think about whether what I just said is true, that is, whether I had ever encountered openly rough treatment in Asia. The one thing that occurred to me was the taxi drivers in Hong Kong. Others might have experienced this but when the drivers say, no, I don't want to pick you up, they waive their hands in a particular way that most people in the part of the world where I live and come from would interpret as an invidious rejection. The first few times that they did that to me, I assumed that it probably was because they were not used to seeing an African-looking man in the streets, and they probably did not want to give me a ride, but I later saw them do it to other people, and thought it was probably cultural miscommunication between the cab drivers and myself. This reminded me of what the general counsel of the Court of Justice of the Common Market for Eastern and Southern Africa (COMESA) once told me after a colleague and I gave a presentation to the judges of the Court of Justice about cultural miscommunication in arbitral proceedings. He is from Malawi. He said that in one case, he had a witness who was brought from a rural area in Malawi to testify before a court of law about a particular matter. When the woman was asked to take the oath, instead of raising her hand in the regular way that people do in many parts of the world, she kept moving her finger around her neck as if she was saying she would slaughter someone. It is hard to describe this movement in words but it is a movement that most people would interpret as "I'll kill you by slitting your throat." But she used that gesture to mean "I swear in the name of God, who would kill me if I failed to tell the truth."

In any case, I returned to the HKIAC for my afternoon appointment. I realized that I arrived 10 minutes early and returned to the ground floor for fear that my early arrival might upset the official again. I got up there at exactly 2:30. After 10 minutes of waiting, the receptionist escorted me to the same breakout room that I had been in during my unsuccessful visit in the morning. A few minutes later, the official came and said "sorry about this morning" as she pulled the chair across the table from me. I said, "No worries" and added "you seemed upset by my unscheduled visit this morning." The official said, "Not at all, it was not that—it was just a very hectic morning." I followed up by saying "in this part of the world people often assume the burden of not displeasing a stranger, I failed to do my research before coming to see you. I should have. I did not realize that you are American." I don't know if the official understood what exactly I meant but we continued to converse with a measure of awkwardness.

I explained my project and continued asking the usual questions. I said, "I understand that your center makes an appointment when it's so designated. What factors do you take into account?" The official said that the Center would take several factors into account, including the parties' agreement on nationality, experience, particularly the ability to control the proceedings, and for technical matters, industry experience, professional qualifications, etc. Pushing a little bit further, I asked, "Do you ever consider cultural suitability—for example, if all the witnesses are likely to be Chinese, would you consider appointing a Chinese?" The official said, "We look at language sometimes but it is never the principal consideration." Continuing the conversation, I asked one last question, which was about the diversity of the roster of arbitrators. The official said that I could take a look online but that she thought it was fairly diverse. That is exactly what I did after the official kindly gave me a 15-minute tour of the impressive facilities.

The HKIAC keeps two different lists called Panel of Arbitrators and List of Arbitrators.[13] People on the Panel of Arbitrators are those with considerable experience as arbitrators; those on the List of Arbitrators are less experienced. It is the sort of people who would at some point graduate to the other roster. The lists are fairly diverse as the official suggested, but the great majority of those on each list are from the United Kingdom, France, Germany, the United States, Hong Kong, and China. To be fair, I spotted one African. He is from Nigeria.[14]

7. Conversation with Jurist No. 4

Jurist No. 4 is a lawyer with a large international law firm in Hong Kong. He is from the United Kingdom, educated at Oxford, and so he brings perspectives from the English common law legal tradition. Before moving to Hong Kong, he practiced international arbitration with an American law firm in London.

When I met him in early February 2015, in Hong Kong, he had been practicing for a little less than a year there. During that short period of time, he had participated in several arbitral proceedings involving parties, arbitrators, and counsel from many different legal traditions and cultures. I asked him many of my usual questions relating to the impact of cultural miscommunication. One arbitral proceeding that he described seemed like the closest to the best possible combination in many ways. Here is what he told me about this particular proceeding. It was a joint venture dispute between a Chinese state-owned enterprise (SOE) operating in the manufacturing sector, from a city of around one million people in eastern China, and a Chinese investor based in Hong Kong. Jurist No. 4's firm represented the Chinese manufacturer. This client was not familiar with international arbitration or the common law trial/evidentiary process. The lead partner in the case was a Malaysian-Chinese lawyer who was educated and qualified in England. She was aided by Jurist No. 4 and other English-qualified lawyers who are Chinese citizens. His team nominated a Chinese academic who was well traveled and had extensive experience in commercial arbitration. The other side nominated a European jurist of the highest stature. What was notable about this particular arbitrator was his extensive experience in Hong Kong and mainland China. He had spent decades in the region, spoke Chinese fluently, and had published extensively on Chinese law, among other things. The presiding arbitrator was from Singapore and also spoke Chinese. Although the proceeding was in English many relevant documentary pieces of evidence were in Chinese. All of the witnesses were also Chinese. None spoke English and so the witness testimony during the oral hearings was also given in Chinese with consecutive translation.

13. http://www.hkiac.org/en/arbitration/arbitrators.

14. *Id.*

One of the first questions I asked Jurist No. 4 was whether he thought the fact that all members of the tribunal were proficient in Chinese improved the quality of justice that the arbitral tribunal was supposed to dispense. He had considered that the ability of the tribunal to review the original Chinese documents (rather than the English translations), and hear the testimony prior to translation, were useful to clear up ambiguity and correct translation or interpretation errors, but he was unsure about the key question that I asked about whether he thought any of the arbitrators were more or less likely to find any of the Chinese witnesses more or less credible because they shared or didn't share a cultural background with the witnesses—all things being equal, of course. This is, no doubt, difficult to assess, and any answer would not be more than speculation. In any case, Jurist No. 4 thought that experienced international arbitrators were accustomed to hearing evidence from witnesses from a variety of backgrounds, often making adjustments for the difficulty in answering questions through a translator. Less experienced arbitrators might find it more difficult to assess the credibility of the witnesses than experienced ones. Familiarity with cross-examination and the difficulties of giving evidence about events that are long-past are arguably as important as understanding the cultural context of the speaker. However, he concluded by saying that the tribunal's ability to understand the language of the original testimony appeared to allow the tribunal to distinguish between misunderstandings or mistranslations and evasive answers, which was probably helpful. We left it at that.

8. Conversation with Thomas R. Snider

Thomas R. Snider is a Washington, DC-based shareholder of Greenberg Trauring and a Professional Lecturer in Law of the George Washington University Law School.[15] He specializes in international arbitration and transnational litigation. Snider and I have had a very long professional affiliation and friendship over the last 15 years. We were in the same practice group for about four years in Washington in the early 2000s, and we continued to cocounsel and coauthor academic writings over the years. We have continually had conversations about culture in international arbitration. He kindly shared his reflections on the role of culture in international arbitration with me in writing. It is presented as follows.

He began by noting that "the topic of culture in the context of international arbitration is a complex one, and there are many ways to slice it," and went on offering "some brief reflections on how culture shapes or impacts the international arbitral system through the prism of the parties, counsel, and arbitrators" as follows:

> One could say that international arbitration emerged from a distrust or even fear of foreign cultures. A party from Country A and a party from Country B have a dispute. The party from Country A does not want to resolve the dispute in the courts of Country B, while the party from Country B does not want to resolve

15. Thomas R. Snider's biographical information is available at: http://www.gtlaw.com/People/Thomas-R-Snider.

> the dispute in the courts of Country A. As a result, the parties resort to international arbitration to resolve their dispute. While such a scenario is often cast in terms of neutrality, what may really be at play is not necessarily the reality or even the perception that the courts in another country are biased but rather a fear of the unknown. The rules, procedures, language, players, and other features—the culture, one might say—of a foreign court proceeding are different than what a foreign litigant knows and is familiar with, and these unknowns can be fraught with trepidation. Arguably, therefore, it is the fear of a foreign culture and its legal processes that drives many parties towards international arbitration.

Having described the push factor from a slightly different angle that way, Snider puts the pull factor in the following terms: "Most parties would rather resolve their disputes in a system featuring the cardinal virtue of party autonomy, allowing them, at least in theory, to fashion the procedures to some extent in a way that may give the parties some sense of familiarity. This is so even if they are newcomers to the international arbitration process and may be approaching this system for the first time with a dose of skepticism. In other words, party autonomy trumps the uncertainty and perceived vagaries of an entirely foreign system."

To him this is a rather pessimistic view of culture. In offering the optimistic narrative, he says:

> International arbitration is the primary means of resolving cross-border disputes not because of a mistrust of foreign cultures but precisely because we live in an increasingly globalized world that consists of a mosaic of cultures. These cultures interact with one another through trade, investment, and politics in ways that bind the world closer together but, at the same time, inevitably result in disputes. A mechanism for resolving these disputes that adopts the best aspects of various legal traditions, which, in turn, reflect the cultures behind these legal traditions,[16] is, as a general matter, a much sounder approach for the parties than using a mechanism that merely consists of the parochial features of the legal system of just one of the litigants.

He then addresses culture and the role of counsel. Indeed, he argues that "culture animates international arbitration, creates unexpected nuances in the proceedings, often makes the collection of evidence an adventure, and creates complex choice-of-law and related legal issues that fascinate us as lawyers (though perhaps not the public at large)." In terms of its positive impacts, "culture, in many respects, is what draws many of the best and brightest lawyers to this particular practice. International arbitration is constantly presenting new twists and challenges that keep the practice of law interesting because the parties, counsel, and arbitrators are from different countries and, at least in international commercial arbitration, different national

16. Culture unquestionably impacts a country's legal system and traditions. For a fascinating and entertaining discussion of certain deep-rooted cultural features that are reflected both in a country's legal system and in its national sport pastime, see William T. Pizzi, *Soccer, Football and Trial Systems*, 1 Colum. J. Eur. L. 369 (1995).

laws apply." In actual practice, "it, of course, behooves a party to an international arbitration to utilize a multicultural counsel team or at least use lawyers who are attuned to the cultural nuances of a particular case. Teams with lawyers who trained or have experience in both the common and civil law traditions—or, as the case may be, in other systems such as religious law traditions—will be more nimble in their approach and will inevitably have a better understanding of how culture impacts not only the law but the facts as well."

Adding a cautionary note though he says "that is not to say that multicultural counsel teams always work seamlessly. Almost every international arbitration practitioner will have his or her war stories about misunderstandings that arise between lawyers on the same side in the preparation of a case." He then graciously offers a useful anecdote from his own practice. He describes it in the following terms:

> I recall vividly one case in which another American colleague and I were working on an international commercial arbitration with Japanese co-counsel. We had retained a renowned Japanese lawyer to serve as an expert witness on a matter of Japanese law. After receiving the expert's draft report, which was comprehensive and on point, my colleague and I nevertheless had a long list of questions and points of clarification that arose from the report. We sent this list to our Japanese co-counsel and requested a meeting with the expert to discuss the questions.
>
> Our Japanese colleagues were aghast at our request. There was no way, in their minds, that we could possibly pose these questions to the expert. Doing so would suggest that the report had flaws and that we were not pleased with the expert's work product. Posing our questions would, in the minds of our Japanese colleagues, be rude and impolite. Our view, on the other hand, was that we needed to fully understand the expert's views on each aspect of the legal issue the expert addressed in his report.
>
> After significant back-and-forth with our Japanese colleagues, a compromise was reached under which we agreed to pose some—but not all—of the questions to the expert and to be as deferential as possible in posing the questions we would ask. When the meeting with the expert occurred, we prefaced our discussion by emphasizing that the report was in great shape, that we had some follow-up questions, but that these questions should not suggest in any way that we were not satisfied with the report. The expert seemed eager to get on with the meeting, and a stimulating substantive discussion based on our questions ensued. By the time the meeting was over, we had covered *all* the questions we wanted to ask, no one was offended, and everyone left happy. By spending some time with our Japanese co-counsel ahead of time, we were able to explore our questions with the expert in a way that was culturally sensitive to everyone involved and that resulted in a comprehensive discussion.
>
> At the same time, however, I have always pondered whether we were able to explore our entire list of questions precisely because we hailed from a different cultural background. I suspect that the nuances of Japanese culture may have made it effectively impossible for our Japanese colleagues to have discussed the entire set of questions with the expert. My American colleague and I, on the

> other hand, were from a different culture and were not expected to understand and adhere to the local cultural intricacies. As a result, we were given license to have more latitude in our questioning and perhaps to step (inadvertently) on some toes. If we insulted the expert with our questioning a bit—and, to this day, I do *not* think we did—the fact that we were from another culture enabled our Japanese colleagues to go back to the expert (if they thought it was necessary), explain that the boorish Americans did not understand or fully comprehend the proper local etiquette, and offer an apology on our behalf. Again, everyone would be happy.

Switching his commentary from counsel to the arbitrators, he begins by saying that "it is often said that the selection of arbitrators is the most important decision that the parties make in an international arbitral proceeding. A number of factors go into selecting an arbitrator, and cultural considerations will frequently be one of these factors. The specific cultural considerations will vary from case to case, and their relative importance in the case will vary as well." The most important point is that "When a particular cultural issue is important to a case, the challenge is to identify an arbitrator who understands or is at least attuned to that cultural issue without shortchanging other factors that may be important in the case, e.g., the selected arbitrator's knowledge of the applicable substantive law or technical aspects of a case."

By far the most important commentary Snider offers, which is shared by other commentators, pertains to the fear of over-appreciation of culture at the expense of other useful attributes. He says in particular that "overemphasizing a cultural issue at the expense of another issue that could end up dominating the case runs the risk of the selected arbitrator playing a diminished role in the proceedings if that arbitrator does not possess other skills or attributes relevant to the core issues of the case." He, of course, acknowledges that "this phenomenon is not unique to cultural issues—the same can be said, for example, of an engineer who is appointed in a construction case; there is a risk that, if the other two arbitrators are lawyers by training, the engineer will be (probably unintentionally) marginalized."

Ultimately, Snider has no confusion about the role that he assigns to culture. He says in plain terms that "culture is important in almost every case but rarely of paramount importance. Accordingly, culture will often have a role to play in the selection of arbitrators but will seldom drive the selection process exclusively or even predominantly." It appears that he is more concerned about the political legitimacy aspect of it than anything else. His conclusion makes this clear. He notes:

> In the end, one of the best ways to strengthen the international arbitration system—be it international commercial arbitration, investor-state arbitration, or even state-to-state arbitration—is to continue to open the system up to parties, counsel, and arbitrators from different cultures. Doing so will bring fresh ideas, approaches, and techniques to a system that is already an amalgamation of ideas, approaches, and techniques. The international arbitration system continues to evolve, and new players are entering the system at a faster pace

than ever before. We are seeing more diversity in terms of gender, nationality, culture, and other considerations but have a long way to go. The system will continue to evolve towards a more inclusive and diverse array of players and at an accelerating pace, though, as with so many things in life, not without some bumps along the way.

That positive note concludes this chapter.

13

Summary of Conclusions

The community of nations has succeeded in creating functionally superior legal frameworks for the recognition and enforcement of arbitral agreements and arbitral awards across international frontiers, most notably in investment and commerce. For complex historical, political, economic, cultural, and practical reasons, states have chosen to treat arbitral awards, at the global level, better than court judgments, and allowed the flourishing of private justice in transnational economic relations. This book has critically examined the legal frameworks, central theories, and operations of international arbitration through a cultural prism.

Legitimately entrenched by deferential frameworks, ideologically encouraged by advanced economies, politically tolerated by developing countries, empirically justified by academics, commercially promoted by arbitral institutions, and economically rewarded by private interests, international arbitration has developed its own culture: a culture of legal flamboyance. Indeed, it claims that it dispenses superior and innocent justice to multinational and multicultural parties doing business across international boundaries. This book has shown that, deconstructed to its most basic elements, international arbitration's superiority and innocence is no greater than a function of the superiority and innocence of particular arbitrators who sit in judgment of particular cases involving diverse parties from around the world.

In particular, this book has posited that the vacancy created for private actors by the international legal instruments and compliant domestic regimes was quickly filled by able players who gave content and texture to the legal frameworks. In the early years of the maturation of the modern investment and commercial arbitration legal frameworks, the players and their theories were not disagreeable to the dominate economic and political forces of the time because they reflected and essentially preserved the existing hierarchy. As time passed and the older economic and political hierarchy became increasingly complicated as a result of the emergence of new market forces that injected borderless and fresh economic dynamics, the old theoretical justifications came under closer scrutiny. This book is nothing more than a part of that scrutiny.

At the most technical level, the legal frameworks impose severe restrictions on sovereign or democratic control over the decisions of arbitral tribunals sitting in judgment of investment and commercial matters of all types. The deference to

The Culture of International Arbitration. Won L. Kidane

private actors without meaningful checks and balances has nurtured a culture of condescension, as demonstrated in the various chapters of this book. Its excesses were such that even a supranational legal order manned by elite arbitrators has been openly advocated. Such advocacy has not even given rise to a serious outrage within the epistemic community because it is promoted as "elitism of merits," an oxymoron on its own accord. As this book has attempted to show, what the dominant culture considers merit often has little to do with what arbitrators are hired to perform. Arbitrators are judges. They sit in judgment of cases and controversies. In most cases, as Professor John Crook usefully imparts, their work involves three steps: the identification of the applicable law, the determination of fact, and the application of the law to the facts.[1] If that is what they are supposed to do, the criteria for their selection must at a minimum bear a substantial resemblance to such tasks. Key among them are familiarity with the applicable law (including perhaps the rules on its own selection), the cultural competence to understand the facts, and the scholastic aptitude, temperament, and integrity to apply the facts to the law and render a fair judgment. An economically and politically disinterested and genuine application of these criteria cannot invariably lead to the concentration of almost all of the world's leading arbitrators in the developed world of the West for five decades when the parties in fact come from diverse cultures around the world. As one of this author's colleagues frequently likes to ask: "When did this whole notion that total strangers to the applicable law and the parties are the best judges come to be accepted?," an insinuation to the classic legal maxims *iura novit curia* and *da mihi factum, dabo tibi ius* and their replacement with what seems to be unlimited burden of education imposed on the parties in international arbitration.

If material advancement and theoretical sophistry were to be positively and proportionately correlated to the accuracy, innocence, legitimacy, and acceptability of the final outcome, the lack of representation as a democratic shortfall alone could perhaps be tolerated. However, as this book attempted to demonstrate on the basis of reference to numerous scholarly works and social science data, cultural familiarity is essential for the understanding of facts and interpretation and application of law. Indeed, these are observations that are difficult to contest. A group of total strangers would have profound difficult in finding facts and interpreting and applying laws that come from unfamiliar cultures. Even when they can perform the tasks reasonably well, no plausible argument could be made that they could do so better than those who are more familiar with the culture and the law. As such, the justification for exclusivity lies somewhere else than the ability to render superior privatized justice.

Privilege and authority unjustified through relevant merits inevitably provoke curiosity and invite commentary. This book has offered some observations. Two of them are summarized below. First, from a historical vantage point, the theoretical

1. John Crook, *Fact-Finding in the Fog: Determining the Facts of Upheavals and Wars in Inter-State Disputes*, *in* Catherine A. Rogers & Roger P. Alford, The Future of Investment Arbitration 313, 314 (2009). ("Should they pause to reflect, most international lawyers would likely accept the thought that the science and art of deciding legal disputes involves at least three inter-related components. The first two involve determining the relevant law and the relevant facts. Then comes stage three—applying the law to the facts.")

origin and development of contemporary international arbitration, like most principles of law, has its roots in the dominant Western legal traditions. Western laws and institutions have a long history of transplantation into other societies around the world. The rest of the world has always been in a constant state of learning Western law, and the Western world has constantly been teaching the law. For better or worse, the teacher-student relationship did not end along with colonialism. This hierarchical relationship created the illusion of not only the superiority of the mechanics of dispute settlement, but also justified the economic class of elite arbitrators who do not lack the theoretical sophistry to justify their privileged position. The accompanying post–World War II economic hierarchy solidified the understanding that the developing world lacked the technical expertise to resolve its own disputes, just like it lacked the material advancement and the technological know-how to progress its economy. The incrementality of the development of the judiciary and maturation of democratic institutions in many parts of the developing world strengthened this narrative. This in turn raised the important question of the standard of treatment of foreign capital and commerce in developing countries. In short, the protection of Northern capital and assets in the South required legal frameworks operated by Northerners in the North. As a result, disputes involving the South have been effectively outsourced to Northern capitals via a claim of superiority of the arbitrators and the arbitral institutions that administer the cases. A combination of all of these factors sustained the mythology of expertise and cemented the existing status quo ante. Like in every aspect of life, however, as consciousness gradually grew both in the North and in the South, and the world economic order got more complicated and diverse cultures converged, chronic concerns of legitimacy became acute and the mythology of expertise came to be questioned. This book is a part of that acute urgency of legitimacy and a timely question on the mythology.

Second, an entitled and privileged economic class is known in history to develop a level of theoretical sophistry and condescension that societies would eventually come to resent. The elite group of arbitrators is not immune from such arrogance of power. The manifestations are many. A claim of superior knowledge, integrity, and self-righteousness led to unimaginable tolerance for conflicts, secrecy, and lack of ethical standards as well as outright hostility to any kind of question or scrutiny. The legal frameworks have been used by an interested economic class as a structural shield from scrutiny. International arbitration thrived behind closed doors. This book has attempted to show the excesses of unchecked power vis-à-vis cultural others.

At the most fundamental level, one of the principal legal instruments, the New York Convention, was initially promoted as a United Nations project to developing countries. Similarly, the ICSID Convention was also promoted by the World Bank as a part of its investment attraction and development agenda. The UNCITRAL Model Law was in fact initially proposed by the Asia Africa Legal Consultative Committee (AALCC). In all of these cases, developing countries were promised technical assistance to acquire expertise, whatever that meant. It is unlikely that they anticipated for lack of expertise answering charges in Northern capitals before predominantly Northern jurists for more than 50 years after the adoption of these instruments even when their dispute is with Southern economic partners. Once the New York Convention project stopped being a United Nations project and was relegated to interested chambers of commerce, the needs of developing countries were gradually forgotten. ICSID has a similar story. Five decades is not an insufficient time to study five provisions of the New York Convention or the principle of fair and equitable treatment, but the reality is that there was never a genuine appetite to yield decisional authority to developing countries. Not only was the level and kind of the desired competency completely achievable but it was anticipated that it would be achieved within a short period of time. Evidently without irony, the perceived lack of expertise continues to justify exclusion to this day.

It is important to highlight in conclusion, however, that this exclusion from decision-making would not have been possible without the complicity of developing countries themselves. No attempt has been made to provide a detailed analysis of this phenomenon in this book; however, the problem has a surprisingly simple short-term solution and it lies in the arbitration agreement, which is the principal source of arbitrator authority. Many developing countries often copy model clauses contained in form contacts drafted in the developed world and pay inadequate attention to them at the time of relationship formation. The simple solution is to begin looking at the agreement more carefully. To address the cultural problems this book has discussed at length, parties could set forth cultural diversity of arbitrators as one of many criteria. For example, in a contract between a Chinese company and an African state, the arbitration agreement could provide for a Chinese arbitrator, an African arbitrator, and a European, South-American, North-American, or any other neutral chair. There is no limit as to how this could be artfully formulated. If, for example, an African state is involved, it could insist that whoever appoints her, the chair of the tribunal be a national or resident of a member state of the African Union. If all three arbitrators were to be European, Chinese, or African, it is not difficult to imagine the complications that cultural miscommunication between the tribunal and the parties would create, not to mention the question of legitimacy and overall acceptability of the whole process as well as the outcome. Jury psychology literature and social science data suggest that a diverse group not only engages in a more complex analytical exercise because of diversity of perceptions, observations, and opinions but also is more likely to get the facts right.[2] We also know from

2. *See* Doak Bishop & James H. Carter, *The United States Perspective and Practice of Advocacy*, *in* The Art of Advocacy in International Arbitration, 519–81, 532 (Doak Bishop & Edward G. Kehoe eds., 2d ed. 2010) ("From the thousands of jury studies conducted in recent years, there has developed a literature on jury psychology and what technique may be persuasive. The most important determinate of how a jury decides a case is the juror's own values, attitudes, and beliefs." *See also* Jeffrey Abramson, We, the Jury: The Jury System and the Ideal of Democracy 104 (BasicBooks, 1994) ("research indicates that when jurors of different ethnic groups deliberate together, they are better able to overcome their individual biases." (citing, among other studies, the detailed discussions in Nancy J. King, *Post-Conviction Review of Jury Discrimination: Measuring the Effects of Juror Decisions*, 92 Mich. L. Rev. 63 (1993); Jon Van Dyke, Jury Selection Procedures: Our Uncertain Commitment to Representative Panels (1977); Nancy S. Marder, *Gender Dynamics and Jury Deliberations*, 96 Yale L. J. 593–612 (1987); Shirley S. Abramson, *Justice and Juror*, 20 Ga. L. Rev. 257–98 (1986). *See also* Samuel R. Sommers, *On Racial Diversity*

experience that arbitrators educate and influence each other. In this new and more diverse world of international arbitration, exclusion must not be continually given specious theoretical justifications. Diversity must be embraced not only because it adds legitimacy and improves outcome but also because it is a step forward in the right direction of ensuring checks and balances. After all, as James Madison would metaphorically say: if arbitrators were angels, there would be no need for checks and balances.

and Group Decision Making: Identifying Multiple Effects of Racial Composition on Jury Deliberations, 90(4) J. PERSONALITY & SOCIAL PSYCHOLOGY 597–612, 598 (2006) ("Whites demonstrated a more complex thinking when assigned to a diverse group than when assigned to an all-white group."); Peters v. Kiff, 407 U.S. 493, 503 (1972) ("When any large and identifiable segment of the community is excluded from jury service, the effect is to remove from the jury room qualities of human nature and varieties of human experience, the range of which is unknown and perhaps unknowable. It is not necessary to assume that the excluded group will consistently vote as a class in order to conclude, as we do, that its exclusion deprives the jury of a perspective on human events that may have unsuspected importance in any case that may be presented.")

Bibliography

Abramson, Jeffrey, *We, the Jury: The Jury System and the Ideal of Democracy* (New York: BasicBooks, 1994).

Abramson, Shirley S., *Justice and Juror*, 20 *Ga. L. Rev.* 257 (1986).

Ahrens, Frank, *Isn't That Rich? The Bonus Controversy of 2009*, *Wash. Post*, http://www.washingtonpost.com/wp-srv/special/opinions/outlook-bonus/ (last visited Mar. 30, 2016).

Aristotle's Rhetoric, *Stanford Encyclopedia of Phil.*, http://plato.stanford.edu/entries/aristotle-rhetoric/ (revised on Feb. 1, 2010).

Aron Broches Retires as Vice President and General Counsel, *The World Bank*, http://go.worldbank.org/JDT8LQZ890 (last visited Mar. 30, 2016).

Asouzu, Amazu A., *International Commercial Arbitration and African States: Practice, Participation and Institutional Development* (Cambridge: Cambridge University Press, 2001).

Auden, W.H., *Law, Like Love*, http://www.poemhunter.com/poem/law-like-love/ (last visited Apr. 11, 2016), *reprinted in The Common Place of Law: Stories from Everyday Life* (Patricia Ewick & Susan S. Silbey, eds., Chicago: University of Chicago Press, 1998).

Avruch, Kevin, and Peter W. Black, *Conflict Resolution in Intercultural Settings: Problems and Prospects, in Conflict Resolution Theory and Practice: Integration and Application* 131–40 (Dennis J. Sandole & Hugo van der Merwe eds., Manchester, UK: Manchester University Press, 1993), *reprinted in International Conflict Resolution: Consensual ADR Processes* 50 (Jacqueline Nolan-Haley, Harold Abramson, and Pat K. Chew eds., St. Paul, MN: Thomson West, 2005).

Been, Vicki, and Joel C. Beauvais, *The Global Fifth Amendment? NAFTA's Investment Protections and the Misguided Quest for an International "Regulatory Takings" Doctrine*, 78 *N.Y.U. L. Rev.* 30 (2003).

Bell, John, Sophie Boyron, and Simon Whittaker, *Principles of French Law* (2d ed., New York: Oxford University Press, 2008).

Berman, Paul Schiff, *Global Legal Pluralism*, 80 *S. Cal. L. Rev.* 1155 (2007).

Bhala, Raj, *Understanding Islamic Law (Shari'a)* (New Providence, NJ: LexisNexis, 2011).

Bishop. Doak, and James H. Carter, *The United States Perspective and Practice of Advocacy, in The Art of Advocacy in International Arbitration* 519–81 (Doak Bishop and Edward G. Kehoe eds., 2d ed., Huntington, NY: Juris, 2010).

Blackaby, Nigel et al., *Redfern and Hunter on International Arbitration* (5th ed., New York: Oxford University Press, 2009).

Born, Gary, *International Arbitration: Cases and Materials* (New York: Aspen, 2011).

The Culture of International Arbitration. Won L. Kidane

Born, Gary, *International Commercial Arbitration* (2d ed., Alphen aan den Rijn, The Netherlands: Kluwer Law International, 2014).

Boulle, Laurence, and Miryana Nesic, *Mediator Skills and Techniques: Triangle of Influence* (Haywards Heath, UK: Bloomsbury Professional, 2010).

Bradshaw, Brad, *The Science of Persuasion: A Litigator's Guide to Juror Decision-Making* (2d ed., Chicago: A.B.A, 2015).

Briner, Robert, *Philosophy and Objectives of the Convention, in U.N. Enforcing Arbitral Awards under the New York Convention: Experience and Prospects, U.N. Sales No. E. 99. V.* 2 (1999), http://www.newyorkconvention.org/travaux+preparatoires.

Brower, Charles N., and Stephan W. Schill, *Is Arbitration a Threat or a Boon to the Legitimacy of International Investment Law?*, 9 *Chi. J. Int'l L.* 471 (2009).

Brown, L. Neville, and John S. Bell, *French Administrative Law* (4th ed., Oxford: Clarendon Press, 1993).

Bryant, Susan, *The Five Habits: Building Cross-Cultural Competence in Lawyers*, 8 *Clinical L. Rev.* 33 (2001).

Buckley, Neil, and Courtney Weaver, *France and Belgium Freeze Russian State Assets over Yukos Case*, *Fin. Times* (June 18, 2015), http://www.ft.com/cms/s/0/3ab475a6-15da-11e5-a58d-00144feabdc0.html#axzz3tLfF1VF1.

Bundy, Stephen McG., and Einer Richard Elhauge, *Do Lawyers Improve the Adversarial System? A General Theory of Litigation Advice and Its Regulation*, 79 *Calif. L. Rev.* 313 (1991).

Burger, Warren E., *The Special Skills of Advocacy: Are Specialized Training and Certification of Advocates Essential to Our System of Justice?*, 42 *Fordham L. Rev.* 227 (1973).

Cairns, Walter, and Robert McKeon, *Introduction to French Law* (London: Cavendish, 1995).

Capowski, John J., *China's Evidentiary and Procedural Reform, the Federal Rules of Evidence, and the Harmonization of Civil and Common Law*, 47 *Tex. Int'l L.J.* 455 (2012).

Capper, Phillip, *Dealing with Bias and Obstruction, in Inside the Black Box: How Arbitral Tribunals Operate and Reach Their Decisions* 46 (Bernhard Berger & Michael E. Schneider eds., ASA Special Series No. 42, Huntington, NY: Juris, 2014).

Caron, David D., *Investor State Arbitration: Strategic and Tactical Perspectives on Legitimacy*, 32 *Suffolk Transnat'l L. Rev.* 513 (2009).

Caron, David D., and Stephen W. Schill, *Practicing Virtue: Inside International Arbitration* Oxford: Oxford University Press, 2015).

Charlie Chan in Egypt (20th Century Fox, 1935).

Chavkin, David F., *Clinical Legal Education: A Textbook for Law School Clinical Programs* (Newark, NJ: LexisNexis, 2002).

Chen, Jianfu, *Chinese Law: Context and Transformation* (Leiden/Boston: Martinus Nijhoff, 2008).

Chew, Pat K., *The Pervasiveness of Culture*, 54 *J. Legal Educ.* 60 (2004), *in International Conflict Resolution: Consensual ADR Processes* 57 (Jacqueline Nolan-Haley, Harold Abramson, and Pat K. Chew, St. Paul, MN: Thomson West, 2005).

Chicago Journal of International Law, 9 *Chi. J. Int'l L.* (2009).

Chow, Daniel C.K., and Thomas Schoenbaum, *International Business Transactions* (New York: Aspen, 2005).

Code Duello, Fact Index, http://www.fact-index.com/c/co/code_duello.html (last visited Mar. 20, 2016).

Colman, J., *Westland Helicopters Ltd. v. Arab Organisations for Industrialisation*, 10 *Arab L.Q.* 115 (1995).

Connolly, Anthony J., *Cultural Difference on Trial: The Nature and Limits of Judicial Understanding* (New York: Routledge, 2010).

Constable, Marianne, *The Law of the Other: The Mixed Jury and Changing Conceptions of Citizenship, Law, and Knowledge* (Chicago: University of Chicago Press, 1994).

Corporate Europe Observatory, *Chapter 4: Who Guards the Guardians? The Conflicting Interests of Investment Arbitrators* (Nov. 27, 2012), http://corporateeurope.org/trade/2012/11/chapter-4-who-guards-guardians-conflicting-interests-investment-arbitrators.

Cotran, Eugene, and Austin N.E. Amissah, *Preface, in Arbitration in Africa* (Eugene Cotran and Austin N.E. Amissah eds., The Hague: Kluwer Law International, 1996).

Crook, John, *Fact-Finding in the Fog: Determining the Facts of Upheavals and Wars in Inter-State Disputes, in The Future of Investment Arbitration* 313 (Catherine A. Rogers and Roger P. Alford eds., New York: Oxford University Press, 2009).

Darian-Smith, Eve, *Laws and Societies in Global Context: Contemporary Approaches* (New York: Cambridge University Press, 2013).

David, René, and John E.C. Brierley, *Major Legal Systems of the World Today: An Introduction to the Comparative Study of Law* (3d ed., London: Stevens & Sons, 1985).

De Vera, Carlos, *Arbitrating Harmony: "Med-Arb" and the Confluence of Culture and Rule of Law in the Resolution of International Commercial Disputes in China*, 18 *Colum. J. Asian L.* 149 (2004).

Delvolvé, Jean-Louis, Jean Rouche, and Gerald H. Pointon, *French Arbitration Law and Practice* (The Hague: Kluwer Law International, 2003).

DePalma, Anthony, *NAFTA's Powerful Little Secret; Obscure Tribunals Settle Disputes, but Go Too Far, Critics Say, N.Y. Times* (Mar. 11, 2001), http://www.nytimes.com/2001/03/11/business/nafta-s-powerful-little-secret-obscure-tribunals-settle-disputes-but-go-too-far.html?pagewanted=all&src=pm.

Deutscher, Guy, *Does Your Language Shape How You Think? N.Y. Times* (Aug. 26, 2010), http://www.nytimes.com/2010/08/29/magazine/29language-t.html.

Dezalay, Yves, and Bryant Garth, *Dealing in Virtue: International Commercial Arbitration and the Construction of a Transnational Legal Order* (Chicago: University of Chicago Press, 1996).

Dingle, Lesley, and Daniel Bates, *Professor Elihu Lauterpacht, Squire L. Libr., U. Cambridge*, http://www.squire.law.cam.ac.uk/eminent-scholars-archive/professor-sir-elihu-lauterpacht (last visited Apr. 1, 2016).

Downing, Richard W., *The Continuing Power of Cultural Tradition and Socialist Ideology: Cross-Cultural Negotiations Involving Chinese, Korean and American Negotiators*, 1992 *J. Disp. Resol.* 105 (1992).

Draetta, Ugo, *Behind the Scenes in International Arbitration* (Huntington, NY: Juris, 2011).

Dugger, Celia W., *World Bank Neglects African Farming, Study Says, N.Y. Times* (Oct. 15, 2007), http://www.nytimes.com/2007/10/15/world/africa/15worldbank.html.

Eberhardt, Pia et al., *Profiting from Injustice: How Law Firms, Arbitrators, and Financiers Are Fueling an Investment Arbitration Boom* (Helen Burley ed., Brussels: Corporate Europe Observatory and the Transnational Institute, 2012), http://corporateeurope.org/sites/default/files/publications/profiting-from-injustice.pdf.

Elias, T. Olawale, *The Nature of African Customary Law* (Manchester, UK: Manchester University Press, 1956).

Elliott, Catherine, Catherine Vernon, and Eric Jeanpierre, *French Legal System* (2d ed., New York: Longman, 2006).

Essounga, Yvette N., *A Review of the Effect of National Culture on Corporate Culture: An Example of the United States & France*, 9(5) *Rev. Bus. Res.* 70 (2009).

Establishment of the SICC, Singapore International Commercial Court, http://www.sicc.gov.sg/About.aspx?id=21 (last visited Mar. 20, 2016).

Fisher, Daniel, *Arbitration vs. Litigation: It Is Not an Either-Or Proposition, Forbes* (Nov. 8, 2015), http://www.forbes.com/sites/danielfisher/2015/11/08/arbitration-vs-litigation-its-not-an-either-or-proposition/.

Fisher, Howard D., *The German Legal System & Legal Language* (2d ed. London: Cavendish, 1999).

Flader, Dieter, *Comment on Jan Paulsson's Essay: Cultural Differences in Advocacy in International Arbitration, Transnat'l. Disp. Mgmt* 1 (2011), http://www.transnational-dispute-management.com.

Franck, Susan D., *Development and Outcomes of Investment Treaty Arbitration,* 50 *Harv. Int'l L.J.* 435 (2009).

Franck, Susan D., *Empirically Evaluating Claims about Investment Treaty Arbitration,* 86 *N.C. L. Rev.* 1 (2007).

Franck, Susan D., *The ICSID Effect? Considering Potential Variations in Arbitration Awards,* 51 *Va. J. Int'l L.* 825 (2011).

Franck, Susan D., *The Legitimacy Crisis in Investment Treaty Arbitration: Privatizing Public International Law through Inconsistent Decisions,* 73 *Fordham L. Rev.* 1521 (2005).

Franck, Susan D. et al., *The Diversity Challenge: Exploring the "Invisible College" of International Arbitration,* 53 *Colum. J. Transnat'l L.* 429 (2015).

Frank, Jerome, *Courts on Trial: Myth and Reality in American Justice* (Princeton, NJ: Princeton University Press, 1973).

Frankel, Marvin E., *The Search for Truth: An Umpireal View,* 123 *U. Pa. L. Rev.* 1031 (1975).

Frequently Asked Questions on ICC Arbitration, http://www.iccwbo.org/faqs/frequently-asked-questions-on-icc-arbitration/#Q4 (last visited Mar. 16, 2016).

Frichner, Tonya Gonnella, *The Indian Child Welfare Act: A National Law Controlling the Welfare of Indigenous Children* (2010), http://www.un.org/esa/socdev/unpfii/documents/The%20Indian%20Child%20Welfare%20Act.v3.pdf.

Friedman, Lawrence M., *Law and Society: An Introduction* (Englewood Cliffs, NJ: Prentice-Hall, 1977).

From New York (1958) to Geneva (1961)—a Veteran's Diary, in U.N., Enforcing Arbitral Awards under the New York Convention: Experience and Prospects 5–7, U.N. Sales No. E. 99. V. 2 (1999), http://www.newyorkconvention.org/travaux+preparatoires.

Gaillard, Emmanuel, *Legal Theory of International Arbitration* (Leiden/Boston: Martinus Nijhoff, 2010).

Gaillard, Emmanuel, *Sociology of International Arbitration* 31 *Arb. Int'l* 1 (2015).

Galagan, Dmytro, and Patricia Živković, *The Challenge of the Yukos Award: An Award Written by Someone Else—a Violation of the Tribunal's Mandate? Kluwer Arb. Blog* (Feb. 27, 2015), http://kluwerarbitrationblog.com/2015/02/27/the-challenge-of-the-yukos-award-an-award-written-by-someone-else-a-violation-of-the-tribunals-mandate/.

Gary Born, Wilmer Hale, https://www.wilmerhale.com/gary_born/ (last visited Mar. 19, 2016).

Ge, Jun, *Mediation, Arbitration and Litigation: Dispute Resolution in the People's Republic of China,* 15 *UCLA Pac. Basin L.J.* 122 (1996).

Geert Hofstede—Cultural Dimensions, InSync Training & Coaching, http://www.insync-training.nl/artikelen/hofstede_cultural_dimensions.pdf (last visited Feb. 22, 2016).

Ginsberg, Tom, *The Culture of Arbitration,* 36 *Vand. J. Int'l L.* 1335 (2003).

Glendon, Mary Ann, Paolo G. Carozza, and Colin B. Picker, *Comparative Legal Traditions: Text, Materials and Cases on Western Law* (3d ed. St. Paul, MN: Thomson West, 2006).

Glenn, Patrick H., *Legal Traditions of the World: Sustainable Diversity in Law* (4th ed., New York: Oxford University Press, 2010).

Goldhaber, Michael D., *2015 Arbitration Scorecard: Deciding the World's Biggest Disputes, TAL Asian Lawyer* (July 1, 2015), http://www.international.law.com/id=1202731078679/2015-Arbitration-Scorecard-Deciding-the-Worlds-Biggest-Disputes.

Graham, John L., *Culture and Human Resources Management, in The Oxford Handbook of International Business* (Alan M. Rugman & Thomas L. Brewer eds., New York: Oxford University Press, 2001).

Grain and Feed Trade Association (GAFTA), http://www.gafta.com/ (last visited Mar. 11, 2016).

Grando, Michelle T., *Evidence, Proof, and Fact-Finding in WTO Dispute Settlement* (New York: Oxford University Press, 2009).

Harvard International Law Journal, 50 *Harv. Int'l L.J.* (2009), http://www.harvardilj.org/2009/06/issue_50-2.

Hazard, Geoffrey C.Jr., *Discovery and the Role of the Judge in Civil Law Jurisdictions*, 73 *Notre Dame L. Rev.* 1017 (1998).

Head, John W., and Yanping Wang, *Law Codes in Dynastic China: A Synopsis of Chinese Legal History in the Thirty Centuries from Zhou to Qing* (Durham, NC: Carolina Academic Press, 2005).

Hofstede, Geert, *Culture's Consequences: Comparing Values, Behaviors, Institutions, and Organizations across Nations* (2d ed., Thousand Oaks, CA: Sage, 2001).

Hofstede, Geert, Gert Jan Hofstede, and Michael Minkov, *Cultures and Organizations: Software of the Mind* (3d ed., New York: McGraw-Hill, 2010).

Hong Kong International Arbitration Centre (HKIAC), *Panel of Arbitrators and List of Arbitrators*, http://www.hkiac.org/en/arbitration/arbitrators.

Hopkins, Anthony G., *Property Rights and Empire Building: Britain's Annexation of Lagos 1861*, 40 *J. Econ. Hist.* 777 (1980), *in Law in Colonial Africa* 10 (Richard Roberts and Kristin Mann eds., Portsmouth, NH: Heinemann, 1991).

House, Robert J., *Culture, Leadership, and Organizations: The Globe Study of 62 Societies* (Robert J. House, Paul J. Hanges, Mansour Javidan, Peter W. Dorfman, and Vipin Gupta eds., Thousand Oaks, CA: Sage, 2004).

Hutchinson, Alan, *China's African Revolution* (Boulder, CO: Westview Press, 1975).

ICC Arbitration Rules (1998), Lex Mercatoria, http://www.jus.uio.no/lm/icc.arbitration.rules.1998/.

ICC Court Announces New Policies to Foster Transparency and Ensure Greater Efficiency, International Chamber of Commerce (ICC) (Jan. 5, 2016), http://www.iccwbo.org/News/Articles/2016/ICC-Court-announces-new-policies-to-foster-transparency-and-ensure-greater-efficiency/.

ICC Rules of Arbitration (2012), *International Chamber of Commerce (ICC)*, http://www.iccwbo.org/products-and-services/arbitration-and-adr/arbitration/icc-rules-of-arbitration/.

International Bar Association Arb 40 Subcommittee, *The Current State and Future of International Arbitration: Regional Perspectives* (2015), http://www.ibanet.org/LPD/Dispute_Resolution_Section/Arbitration/Publications.aspx.

International Bar Association Rules on the Taking of Evidence in International Arbitration (adopted by IBA Council May 29, 2010), http://www.ibanet.org/Search/Default.aspx?q=Arbitration%20Evidence.

International Centre for Settlement of Investment Disputes, *Cases*, https://icsid.worldbank.org/apps/icsidweb/cases/Pages/AdvancedSearch.aspx (last visited Mar. 30, 2016).

International Centre for Settlement of Investment Disputes, *History of the ICSID Convention, v.* II-1 (1968, reprinted 2009).

International Centre for Settlement of Investment Disputes, *The ICSID Caseload—Statistics* (2012), https://icsid.worldbank.org/apps/icsidweb/resources/pages/icsid-caseload-statistics.aspx.

International Centre for Settlement of Investment Disputes, *The ICSID Caseload—Statistics* (2016-1), https://icsid.worldbank.org/apps/ICSIDWEB/resources/Documents/ICSID%20Web%20Stats%202016-1%20(English)%20final.pdf.

International Investment Agreements (IIA) Databases, United Nations Conference on Trade and Development, http://unctad.org/en/pages/DIAE/International%20Investment%20Agreements%20(IIA)/IIA-Tools.aspx.

Introduction to German Law (Mathias Reimann and Joachim Zekoll eds., 2d ed. The Hague: Kluwer Law International, 2005).

Jan Paulsson, U. Miami School of Law., https://www.threecrownsllp.com/team/jan-paulsson/ (last visited Dec. 11, 2016).

Jan Paulsson—Biography, Arb. Acad., http://www.arbitrationacademy.org/?page_id=3038 (last visited Mar. 30, 2016).

Jan Paulsson—Honorary President, Int'l Council Com. Arb. (ICCA), http://www.arbitration-icca.org/about/governing-board/honorary-presidents/Jan_Paulsson.html (last visited Mar. 30, 2016).

Kidane, Won, *China-Africa Dispute Settlement: The Law, Economics and Culture of Arbitration* (Alphen aan den Rijn, The Netherlands: Kluwer Law International, 2011).

Kidane, Won, *The China-Africa Factor in the Contemporary ICSID Legitimacy Debate*, 35 *U. Pa. J. Int'l L.* 559 (2014).

LaRue, Lewis, *A Jury of One's Peers*, 33 *Wash. & Lee L. Rev.* 841 (1976).

Lauchli, Urs Martin, *Cross-Cultural Negotiations, with a Special Focus on ADR with the Chinese*, 26 *Wm. Mitchell L. Rev.* 1045 (2000).

Law as Culture and Culture as Law: Essays in Honor of John Phillip Reid (Hendrik Hartog and William E. Nelson eds., Madison, WI: Madison House, 2000).

Lawless, Niall, *Cultural Perspectives on China: Resolving Disputes through Mediation*, 4 *Transnat'l Disp. Mgmt.* 2, www.transnational-disputemanagement.com/article.asp?key=1294.

LCIA Arbitration Rules (2014), *London Court of International Arbitration (LCIA)*, http://www.lcia.org/Dispute_Resolution_Services/lcia-arbitration-rules-2014.aspx#Article 30.

Lehman, Susan, *Podcast: Beware the Fine Print, N.Y. Times* (Nov. 11, 2015), http://www.nytimes.com/2015/11/11/insider/podcast-beware-the-fine-print.html?_r=0.

Lerner, Renée Lettow, *The Intersection of Two Systems: An American on Trial for an American Murder in the French Cour D'Assisses*, 2001 *U. Ill. L. Rev.* 791 (2001).

Letter from Cordell Hull, U.S. Secretary of State, to Francisco Castillo Nájera, Mexican Ambassador to the U.S. (July 21, 1938), as reprinted in Andreas F. Lowenfeld, International Economic Law (2d ed., New York: Oxford University Press, 2008).

Letter from Mexican Minister of Foreign Affairs to U.S. Ambassador at Mexico City (*Aug. 3, 1938*), *as reprinted in Andreas F. Lowenfeld, International Economic Law* (2d ed., New York: Oxford University Press, 2008).

Li, Mingsheng, *When in China . . . Foreign Companies Should Devise a Localization Strategy That's Based on a Thorough Understanding of the Complex Chinese Business Culture*, 25(6) *Comm. World* 34 (Nov.–Dec. 2008).

List of Concluded Cases, International Centre for the Settlement of Investment Disputes (ICSID), https://icsid.worldbank.org/apps/ICSIDWEB/cases/pages/concluded-cases.aspx?status=c (last visited Mar. 26, 2016).

List of Contracting States and Other Signatories of the Convention, International Centre for the Settlement of Investment Disputes (ICSID/3) (as of Nov. 17, 2015), https://icsid.worldbank.org/apps/ICSIDWEB/icsiddocs/Documents/List%20of%20Contracting%20States%20and%20Other%20Signatories%20of%20the%20Convention%20-%20Latest.pdf.

List of Contracting States and Other Signatories of the Convention, International Centre for the Settlement of Investment Disputes (ICSID) (as of Nov. 1, 2013), http://icsid.worldbank.org/ICSID/FrontServlet?requestType=ICSIDDocRH&actionVal=ShowDocument&language=English.

Lubman, Stanley B., *Bird in a Cage: Legal Reform in China after Mao* (Stanford, CA: Stanford University Press, 1999).

Lubman, Stanley B., *Dispute Resolution in China after Deng Xiaoping: "Mao and Mediation" Revisited*, 11 *Colum. J. Asian L.* 229 (1997).

Lubman, Stanley B., and Gregory Wajnowski, *International Commercial Dispute Resolution in China: A Practical Assessment*, 4 *Am. Rev. Int'l Arb.* 107 (1993).

Mann, F.A., *The Doctrine of International Jurisdiction Revised after Twenty Years, in Collected Courses of the Hague Academy of International Law, Vol.* 186 (Leiden/Boston: Martinus Nijhoff, 1984).

Marder, Nancy S., *Gender Dynamics and Jury Deliberations*, 96 *Yale L.J.* 593 (1987).

Marx, Karl, and Friedrich Engels, *The Communist Manifesto* (1948).

McConnaughay, Philip J., *Rethinking the Role of Law and Contracts in East-West Commercial Relations*, 41 *Va. J. Int'l L.* 427 (2001).

Menon, Sundaresh, *Singapore Chief Justice, Address at the Chartered Institute of Arbitrators London Centenary Conference* (July 2, 2015), https://www.ciarb.org/docs/default-source/centenarydocs/london/ciarb-centenary-conference-patron-39-s-address-(for-publication).pdf?sfvrsn=0.

Menon, Sundaresh, *Singapore Chief Justice, Keynote Address, Standards in Need of Bearers: Encouraging Reform from within at Chartered Institute of Arbitrators: Singapore Centenary Conference* (Sept. 3, 2015), http://www.ciarb.org.sg/wp-content/uploads/2015/09/Keynote-Speech-Standards-in-need-of-Bearers-Encouraging-Reform-from-.pdf.

Mexico City Declaration on Cultural Policies, World Conference on Cultural Policies, UNESCO (Aug. 6, 1982), http://portal.unesco.org/culture/en/files/12762/11295421661mexico_en.pdf/mexico_en.pdf.

Meyer, Bernhard F., *Structuring a Bargaining Process, in Inside the Black Box: How Arbitral Tribunals Operate and Reach Their Decisions* 59 (Bernhard Berger and Michael E. Schneider eds., ASA Special Series No. 42, Huntington, NY: Juris, 2014).

Mezey, Naomi, *Law as Culture*, 13 *Yale J.L. & Human.* 35 (2001).

Mezey, Naomi, *Law's Culture and Lived Culture: A Comment on Roger Cotterrell's "The Struggle for Law: Some Dilemmas of Cultural Legality,"* 4 *Int'l J.L. Context* 395 (2008).

Mezey, Naomi, *Out of the Ordinary: Law, Power, Culture, and Commonplace*, 26 *L. & So. Inquiry* 145 (2001).

Moran, Beverly I., *Homogenized Law: Can the United States Learn from African Mistakes?*, 25 *Fordham Int'l L.J.* 361 (2001).

Moses, Margaret L., *Privatized "Justice"*, 36 *Loy. U. Chi. L.J.* 535 (2005).

Moses, Margaret L., *The Principles and Practice of International Commercial Arbitration* (2d ed., New York: Cambridge University Press, 2012).

Nafziger, James A.R., and Ruan Jiafang, *Chinese Methods of Resolving International Trade, Investment, and Maritime Disputes*, 23 *Willamette L. Rev.* 619 (1987).

Needham, Joseph, *Science and Civilization in China* (Cambridge: Cambridge University Press, 1954).

Nikiema, Suzy H., *International Institute for Sustainable Development (IISD) Best Practices Indirect Expropriation* (2012), http://www.iisd.org/pdf/2012/best_practice_indirect_expropriation.pdf.

Obiora, L. Amede, *Remapping the Domain of Property in Africa*, 12 *U. Fla. J.L. & Pub. Pol'y* 57 (2000).

Paulsson, Jan, *Cultural Differences in Advocacy in International Arbitration, in The Art of Advocacy in International Arbitration* 15–21 (Doak Bishop and Edward G. Kehoe eds., 2d ed., Huntington, NY : Juris, 2010).

Paulsson, Jan, *Denial of Justice in International Law* (Cambridge: Cambridge University Press, 2005).

Paulsson, Jan, *Denial of Justice in International Law, Lecture given during the 2003 Hersch Lauterpacht Memorial Lectures, Cambridge University* (Nov. 10, 2003).

Paulsson, Jan, *Forward, in Arbitration in Africa: A Practitioner's Guide* (Lise Bosman ed., Alphen aan den Rijn, The Netherlands: Kluwer Law International, 2013).

Paulsson, Jan, *The Idea of Arbitration* (Oxford: Oxford University Press, 2013).

Perry, Sebastian, *Time to "Relocalise" Arbitration to Africa, ICCA Told, Global Arbitration Rev.* (May 10, 2016).

Phillips, Philip G., *A Lawyer's Approach to Commercial Arbitration*, 41 *Yale L.J.* 31 (1934).

Pizzi, William T., *Soccer, Football and Trial Systems*, 1 *Colum. J. Eur. L.* 369 (1995).

Poon, Anthony, and Peng Shen, *Civil Litigation, in Dispute Resolution in China* 131–32 (Michael J. Moser ed., Huntington, NY : Juris Pub, 2012).

Poulter, Sebastian M., *English Law and Ethnic Minority Customs* (London: Butterworth-Heinemann, 1986).

Pound, Roscoe, *The Causes of Popular Dissatisfaction with the Administration of Justice*, 29 *A.B.A. Rep. pt. I* 395 (1906).

Press Release, European Commission, Commission Proposes New Investment Court System for TTIP and Other EU Trade and Investment Negotiations (Sept. 16, 2015), http://europa.eu/rapid/press-release_IP-15-5651_en.htm.

Press Release, International Centre for Settlement of Investment Disputes, Bolivia Submits a Notice under Article 71 of the ICSID Convention (May 16, 2007), https://icsid.worldbank.org/ICSID/StaticFiles/Announcement3.html.

Press Release, International Centre for Settlement of Investment Disputes, Ecuador Submits a Notice under Article 71 of the ICSID Convention (July 9, 2009), https://icsid.worldbank.org/ICSID/StaticFiles/Announcement20.html.

Press Release, Stony Brook News, SBU Researchers and Colleagues Find That in the Brain, Early-Stage Intense Passionate Love Seems to Be Universal (May 28, 2010), http://commcgi.cc.stonybrook.edu/am2/publish/General_University_News_2/SBU_Researchers_And_Colleagues_Find_That_In_The_Brain_Early-Stage_Intense_Passionate_Love_Seems_To_Be_Universal.shtml.

Queen Mary University of London, *International Arbitration Survey: Corporate Choices in International Arbitration—Industry Perspectives* (2013), http://www.pwc.com/gx/en/arbitration-dispute-resolution/assets/pwc-international-arbitration-study.pdf.

Readings in African Law (Eugene Cotran and Neville N. Rubin eds., London: Frank Cass, 1970).

Reinisch, August, *The Future of Investment Arbitration, in International Investment Law for the 21st Century: Essays in Honour of Christoph Schreuer* 894 (Christina Binder, Ursula Kriebaum, August Reinisch, and Stephan Wittich eds., New York: Oxford University Press, 2009).

Rogers, Catherine A., *Ethics in International Arbitration* (New York: Oxford University Press, 2014).

Rogers, Catherine A., *Transparency in International Commercial Arbitration*, 54 *Kan. L. Rev.* 1301 (2006).

Rosen, Lawrence, *Law as Culture: An Invitation* (Princeton, NJ: Princeton University Press, 2006).

Rosen, Lawrence, *The Anthropology of Justice: Law as Culture in Islamic Society* (Cambridge: Cambridge University Press, 1989).

Ross, Alison, *Dealing with Defensiveness: Garth Shares Views Two Decades after Seminal Book, Global Arb. Rev.* (Nov. 18, 2015), http://globalarbitrationreview.com/news/article/34351/dealing-defensiveness-garth-shares-views-two-decades-seminal-book/.

Rudnitsky, Jake, and Anton Doroshev, *Russia Set for Global Asset Fight over Yukos after Seizures, Bloomberg Bus.* (June 18, 2015), http://www.bloomberg.com/news/articles/2015-06-18/russia-braces-for-global-asset-fight-over-yukos-after-seizures-ib2boyg9.

Rush Hour (New Line Cinema, 1998).

Ruskola, Teemu, *Legal Orientalism: China, the United States, and Modern Law* (Cambridge, MA: Harvard University Press, 2013).

Salacuse, Jeswald W., *The Emerging Global Regime for Investment*, 51 *Harv. Int'l L.J.* 427 (2010).

Salacuse, Jeswald W., and Nicholas P. Sullivan, *Do BITs Really Work? An Evaluation of Bilateral Investment Treaties and Their Grand Bargain*, 46 *Harv. Int'l L.J.* 67 (2005).

Sanders, Pieter, *The Making of the Convention, in U.N., Enforcing Arbitral Awards under the New York Convention: Experience and Prospects*, 3–4, *U.N. Sales No. E. 99, V.* 2 (1999), http://www.newyorkconvention.org/travaux+preparatoires.

Sands, Philippe, *Sir Ian Brownlie Obituary, The Guardian* (Jan. 11, 2010), http://www.theguardian.com/theguardian/2010/jan/11/sir-ian-brownlie-obituary.

Sauvant, Karl P., and Lisa E. Sachs, *The Effect of Treaties on Foreign Direct Investment: Bilateral Investment Treaties, Double Taxation Treaties, and Investment Flows* (Oxford: Oxford University Press, 2009).

Schein, Edgar H., *Organizational Culture and Leadership* (4th ed., San Francisco: Jossey-Bass, 2010).

Schreuer, Christoph H., *The ICSID Convention: A Commentary* (2d ed., New York: Cambridge University Press, 2009).

Shalakany, Amr A., *Arbitration and the Third World: A Plea for Reassessing Bias under the Specter of Neoliberalism*, 41 *Harv. Int'l L.J.* 419 (2000).

Silbey, Susan S., *J. Locke, OP. CIT: Invocations of Law on Snowy Streets, in Using Legal Culture* 120–52 (David Nelken ed., London: Wildy, Simmonds & Hill, 2012).

Silver-Greenberg, Jessica, and Michael Corkery, *In Arbitration, a "Privatization of the Justice System," N.Y. Times* (Nov. 1, 2015), http://www.nytimes.com/2015/11/02/business/dealbook/in-arbitration-a-privatization-of-the-justice-system.html?_r=0.

Silverthorne, Colin P., *Organizational Psychology in Cross-Cultural Perspective* (New York: New York University Press, 2005).

Sommers, Samuel R., *On Racial Diversity and Group Decision Making: Identifying Multiple Effects of Racial Composition on Jury Deliberations*, 90(4) *J. Personality & Social Psychology* 597 (2006).

Soviet and Chinese Aid to African Nations (Warren Weinstein and Thomas H. Henriksen eds., New York: Praeger, 1980).

Suffolk Transnational Law Review, 32 *Suffolk Transnat'l L. Rev.* (2009).

Szalai, Imre Stephen, *Outsourcing Justice: The Rise of Modern Arbitration Laws in America* (Durham, NC: Carolina Academic Press, 2013).

Szasz, Paul C., *The Investment Disputes Convention and Latin America*, 11 *Va. J. Int'l L.* 256 (1971).

Tao, Jingzhou, *Arbitration in China, in International Commercial Arbitration in Asia* 40 (Philip McConnaughay and Thomas B. Ginsburg eds., 2d ed., Huntington, NY: Juris, 2006).

Tao, Jingzhou, *Arbitration Law and Practice in China* (3d ed., Alphen aan den Rijn, The Netherlands: Kluwer Law International, 2012).

Taslim O. Elias, 76, is Dead in Nigeria; Headed World Court, N.Y. Times (Aug. 16, 1991), http://www.nytimes.com/1991/08/16/obituaries/taslim-o-elias-76-is-dead-in-nigeria-headed-world-court.html.

The Backlash against Investment Arbitration: Perceptions and Reality (Michael Waibel et al. eds., Austin, TX: Kluwer Law International, 2010).

The Effect of Treaties on Foreign Direct Investment: Bilateral Investment Treaties, Double Taxation Treaties, and Investment Flows (Karl P. Sauvant and Lisa E. Sachs eds, New York: Oxford University Press, 2009).

The Federalist No. 51 (James Madison) (Ian Shapiro ed., New Haven, CT: Yale University Press, 2009).

The Handbook of Organizational Culture and Climate (Neal M. Ashkanasy, Celeste P. M. Wilderom and Mark F. Peterson eds., 2d ed. Thousand Oaks, CA: Sage, 2011).

The Oxford Dictionary of Quotations (Angela Partington ed., 4th ed., New York: Oxford University Press 1992) (1st ed. published in 1941).

The Oxford Handbook of International Investment Law (Peter Muchlinski, Frederico Ortino, and Christoph Schreuer eds., New York: Oxford University Press, 2008).

Trakman, Leon E., *"Legal Traditions" and International Commercial Arbitration*, 17 *Am. Rev. Int'l Arb.* 1, (2006).

UNCITRAL Arbitration Rules ("UNCITRAL Model Law"), G.A. Res. 65/22 (Dec. 6, 2010), https://www.uncitral.org/pdf/english/texts/arbitration/arb-rules-revised/arb-rules-revised-2010-e.pdf.

United Nations Commission on International Trade Law, *Rules on Transparency in Treaty-Based Investor-State Arbitration*, http://www.uncitral.org/uncitral/en/uncitral_texts/arbitration/2014Transparency.html.

United Nations Conference on Trade and Development, *Economic Development in Africa Report 2010: South-South Cooperation: Africa and the New Forms of Development Partnership*, 1, *U.N. Doc.* UNCTAD/ALDC/AFRICA/2010.

United Nations Secretary-General, *Note on Consideration of Other Measures for Increasing the Effectiveness of Arbitration in the Settlement of Private Law Disputes (Item 5 on the*

Agenda) United Nations Conference on International Commercial Arbitration, U.N. Doc. E/CONF.26/6 at 6 (May 1, 1957), http://www.arbitration-icca.org/media/0/12734521657370/4281_001.pdf.

Utter, Robert F., *Dispute Resolution in China*, 62 *Wash. L. Rev.* 283 (1987).

Van Dyke, Jon, *Jury Selection Procedures: Our Uncertain Commitment to Representative Panels* (Cambridge, MA: Ballinger, 1977).

Van Harten, Gus, *Investment Treaty Arbitration and Public Law* (New York: Oxford University Press, 2007).

Von Mehren, Robert, and Nicholas P. Kourides, *International Arbitration between States and Private Parties: The Libyan Nationalization Cases*, 75 *Am. J. Int'l L.* 476 (1981).

Waibel, Michael, and Yanhui Wu, *Are Arbitrators Political?* (Nov. 5, 2011) (unpublished manuscript).

Waites, Richard C., and James E. Lawrence, *Psychological Dynamics in International Arbitration Advocacy, in The Art of Advocacy in International Arbitration* 69–120 (Doak Bishop and Edward G. Kehoe eds., 2d ed., Huntington, NY : Juris, 2010).

Wells, Louis T., *Preface, in The Evolving International Investment Regime: Expectations, Realities, Options* (José E. Alvarez and Karl P. Sauvant eds., New York: Oxford University Press, 2011).

Werner, Jacques, *Making Investment Arbitration More Certain: A Modest Proposal*, 4 *J. World Inv.* 767 (2003).

White & Case LLP & Queen Mary University of London, *International Arbitration Survey: Improvements and Innovations in International Arbitration* (2015), http://www.whitecase.com/publications/insight/2015-international-arbitration-survey-improvements-and-innovations.

Wilderom, Celeste P.M., Ursula Glunk, and Ralf Maslowski, *Organizational Culture as a Predictor of Organizational Performance, in The Handbook of Organizational Culture and Climate* 193–209 (Neal M. Ashkanasy, Celeste P.M. Wilderom, and Mark F. Peterson eds., 2d ed., Thousand Oaks, CA: Sage, 2011).

Wyzanski, Charles E.Jr., *Equal Justice through Law*, 47 *Tul. L. Rev.* 951 (1973).

Xu, Xiaobing, *Different Mediation Traditions: A Comparison between China and the U.S.*, 16 *Am. Rev. Int'l Arb.* 515 (2005).

Yong, Lacey, and Alison Ross, *Africa Must Have More Representation on Tribunals, Says Somali Judge*, 10 *Global Arb. Rev.* 2 (Oct. 15, 2015), http://globalarbitrationreview.com/news/article/34232/tribunals-need-africans-says-somali-judge/.

Yu-lan, Fung, *A Short History of Chinese Philosophy* (Derk Bodde ed., New York: Simon and Schuster, 1997).

Zhang, Mo, and Paul J. Zwier, *Burden of Proof: Developments in Modern Chinese Evidence Rules*, 10 *Tulsa J. Comp. & Int'l L.* 419 (2003).

Zimmerman, James M., *China Law Deskbook: A Legal Guide to Foreign-Invested Enterprises* (3d ed. Chicago: A.B.A., 2010).

Index

The Culture of International Arbitration. Won L. Kidane

Printed in Australia
Ingram Content Group Australia Pty Ltd
AUHW011820191124
403019AU00002B/7